GENERAL GEORGE CROOK
His Autobiography

GENERAL GEORGE CROOK

His Autobiography

EDITED AND ANNOTATED BY

MARTIN F. SCHMITT

FOREWORD BY

JOSEPH C. PORTER

NORMAN AND LONDON
UNIVERSITY OF OKLAHOMA PRESS

Library of Congress Cataloging-in-Publication Data

Crook, George, 1828–1890.
  General George Crook: his autobiography.

  Bibliography: p.
  Includes index.
  1. Crook, George, 1828–1890. 2. Indians of North America — Wars — 1866–
1895. I. Schmitt, Martin Ferdinand. II. Title.
E83.866.C93   1986   973.8'092'4   85-40938
ISBN 0-8061-1982-9 (pbk.)

Contents

Illustrations

Maps

Foreword

by Joseph C. Porter

Major General George Crook was one of the most intriguing and controversial officers of the Indian-fighting Army. Ulysses S. Grant and William T. Sherman both praised Crook as the Army's most skillful Indian fighter, while critics blamed Crook for the disaster that befell George A. Custer and his men at the Battle of the Little Big Horn. Philip Sheridan, once a close friend of Crook, regarded him as "soft" on Indians, while humanitarians often praised his treatment of Native Americans.

Crook was as paradoxical as he is controversial. An aggressive and innovative campaigner, he occasionally waged ruthless punitive expeditions against hostile Indians, attempting to strike their villages and camps in order to destroy food, shelter, and morale. Yet, despite his fierceness on the warpath, he displayed a remarkable sensitivity to their plight. He openly sympathized with their reasons for fighting, and he frequently censured fellow officers for their lack of open-mindedness.

The Lakotas, the Apaches, and the Poncas were three tribes that Crook especially tried to help. It should be remembered that Crook had fought the Lakotas and the Apaches. In the 1870s the Omaha tribe of Nebraska permitted Crook to become one of only two white men to join one of their honored warrior societies.

Crook's relationship with the Oglala Lakotas perhaps best epitomizes his contacts with American Indians. His first acquaintance with them was during the Sioux War of 1876. Crazy Horse said that Crook was more to be "feared by the Sioux than all other white men." In 1881 the Oglala at Pine Ridge gave John G. Bourke open access to their Sun Dance because he was Crook's aide-de-camp. Since Bourke had come from *Wi-ćań-hpi-ya-mni,* or "Three Stars," the Oglala would permit him "to see all" of the Sun Dance. After Crook's death in 1890, the Oglala chief Red Cloud said: "Then General Crook came; he, at least, had never lied to us. His words gave the people hope. He died. Their hope died again. Despair came again."

Crook's success on the warpath and his genuine concern for Indian welfare came from his knowledge of the environment and cultures of Indians. His awareness of tribal societies allowed him to shape his most effective military weapon—the use of Indian auxiliaries against hostile Indian bands. The general most effectively utilized Indian allies in Arizona in the early 1870s and again in the Southwest in the 1880s.

In the Tonto Basin campaign of 1872–73, Crook exploited the fluid social structure of the Western Apaches to enlist Western Apache scouts by the dozen to wage war against hostile Western Apache bands. This tactic brought the war to the remotest sanctuaries of the Apaches. Warriors who had derided the fighting ability of the soldiers were suddenly terrified of being struck by their own warriors. Crook's scheme brought peace to Apacheria by 1873.

Crook's most daring and spectacular use of Indian auxiliaries was the Sierra Madre campaign of 1883. Arguably, this was Crook's finest hour in his Indian-fighting career. Accompanied by nearly 200 Western Apache scouts, fewer than fifty soldiers, a few officers, and numerous packers, Crook crossed the border into Mexico and penetrated the Sierra Madre sanctuaries of the renegade Chiricahua Apaches.

After an initial skirmish with the Chiricahuas, Crook proceeded by sheer bluff and negotiation. Eventually he convinced Geronimo and the other Chiricahua leaders to return peacefully to the reservation in Arizona. His own personal daring and willingness to gamble, his reliance upon the Western Apache scouts, and his precise knowledge of how to negotiate with the Chiricahua headmen all contributed to Crook's triumph.

Crook achieved less success as an Indian fighter on the northern Great Plains. During the Sioux War his largest fight against the Lakota and Northern Cheyennes was the Battle of the Rosebud on June 17, 1876. After a hard-fought struggle against the Indians, Crook claimed victory, but, at best, it was an empty standoff for the Army. The Lakotas and Cheyennes decisively stopped Crook's advance, and his column was immobilized for several critical weeks awaiting reinforcements and supplies. Because of his performance at the Rosebud some critics held Crook partially responsible for the fate of Custer at the Little Big Horn. Yet it is stretching a point to hold Crook accountable for Custer's decisions and deployment of his forces at the Little Big Horn.

Despite the dubious results of the Battle of the Rosebud, Crook's use of Indian auxiliaries again had proved opportune. Shoshoni and Crow warriors had joined Crook to fight their traditional Lakota and Northern Cheyenne enemies, and during the early moments of the Indian attack at the Rosebud the Crows and Shoshonis bore the brunt of the fighting. They were an Indian shield that gave Crook precious time to begin deployment of his men. Later in the battle, the Crows and Shoshonis very effectively counterattacked the enemy. With Crow and Shoshoni assistance Crook managed to salvage an empty, marginal draw, and without them he could have had an unmitigated disaster on his hands.

Crook had an enigmatic personality. Seemingly modest in appearance, he was archly conscious of his public image. He felt genuine sympathy for the Indians, yet he was stern, reticent, even cold to those around him. His long-time aide John G. Bourke once remarked that Crook was brusque and taciturn to the point of severity. Crook was occasionally insensitive to those most devoted to him. It is remarkable how little he mentioned his wife, Mary, in his autobiography. While Bourke served Crook from 1872 until 1886 and went through many campaigns with the general, he received only one brief reference in the general's memoirs.

Although he complained about the efforts of rival officers to secure good press for themselves, Crook was very intent on his own public image. He relied upon the highly literate officers on his staff, such as Bourke, to manage the newspapers on his behalf. This arrangement extended beyond the death of Crook when Bourke published *On the Border with Crook* (1891), which firmly established Crook's place in western American history.

It is obvious that Crook wished to portray his recollection of events for posterity, and before his death he began his *Autobiography*. Crook managed to get his volume as far as June 18, 1876, the day after the Battle of the Rosebud, where it abruptly stops. In 1942, Martin F. Schmitt discovered the manuscript of the *Autobiography* in the library of the Army War College in Washington, D.C. Schmitt began to edit and annotate the original document and to prepare additional chapters about Crook's career after 1876. In 1946 the University of Oklahoma Press issued *General George Crook: His Autobiography*, edited and annotated by Schmitt. The success and significance of Crook's *Autobiography* warranted a new edition, published in 1960.

Major General George Crook, innovative, controversial, and enigmatic, was a pivotal figure in the Indian Wars of the American West. Three Stars richly deserves (and still awaits) a full-length scholarly biography that closely examines his place in the history of the American West. Until that distant day *General George Crook: His Autobiography* remains a valuable and significant historical source about this unorthodox man and his times. This 1986 reissue of *General George Crook: His Autobiography* reconfirms the foresight of Martin F. Schmitt in 1942 and the original decision by the University of Oklahoma Press to publish this book forty years ago.

JOSEPH C. PORTER

Omaha, Nebraska

Preface to Second Edition

THERE IS great pleasure in knowing that the autobiography of General George Crook, rudely phrased though it be, has been well enough received and is in sufficient general demand to require republication. Interest in the book stems from the realization that it is the personal story of one of the giants of the American West. It is a good story, honestly told; its lack of pretense in a subject where embellishment is usual suggests an authenticity too often lacking in clever writing.

Since the first publication of this volume, no new documents of extraordinary significance have come to light that would modify to any important extent General Crook's estimate of the situation. On the contrary, the temper of Crook's opinions retains its resilience, and his testimony concerning the affairs of the military and the Indian remains unimpeached.

A few additional details of the General's career have been called to the editor's attention. A number of persons have claimed —on what basis is not clear—that they knew of the manuscript autobiography and had been designated, either by Crook or by his widow, to publish the work.

More reliably, a series of forty-five letters to or by Crook in the University of Oregon Library provide new information of some interest. We learn that during his residence in Portland, Oregon, in 1869–70 Crook speculated in real estate, unprofitably, as was his habit. The letters add emphasis to the complicated relationship between Mexican and United States troops during the Apache campaign of 1885–86. The difficulty between the two groups seems to have been deep-rooted; letters between Crook and John Pope and from Marion Maus to Crook suggest a condition of mutual suspicion that amounted to hostility. Crook maintained a system of private spies in Mexican territory, indicating how little confidence he placed in official assurances of co-operation.

Finally, the antagonism between Crook and General Nelson A. Miles is emphasized in a series of letters to Lieutenant L. W. V. Kennon, 1889–90. Crook speaks disparagingly of the "Literary Bureau" controlled by Miles, a publicity ring responsible for newspaper stories that cast doubt on the loyalty of Crook's Indian scout system and emphasized Miles's part in the final surrender of the Apaches. Crook believed, and wrote, that Miles was consumed with an ambition that overruled other considerations.

MARTIN F. SCHMITT

Eugene, Oregon

Preface to First Edition

THE AUTOBIOGRAPHY of General George Crook has been an unknown document for fifty years. Not even John G. Bourke, the
General's biographer, seems to have known that it existed. Only a
single printed reference to it occurs. The Reverend Dr. Harsha, in
a memorial service held in Omaha two days after Crook's death in
1890, remarked that the General had jotted down in a rough way
the principal events of his career. "I trust," he added, "that some
fitting pen will be found to prepare that rugged biography for the
perusal of the world."

Some time after the death of Mrs. Crook in 1895 the General's
personal papers came into the possession of Colonel Walter S.
Schuyler, his one-time aide and friend of the family. Here the
papers remained until 1939, when Mrs. Schuyler presented them
to the library of the Army War College in Washington, where
they were pasted into a scrapbook and filed away without further
notice. In 1942 they were rediscovered by the editor, and the
exciting task of reading and annotating was begun.

The Crook autobiography, which was written between 1885
and 1890, covers the period from 1852, when George Crook graduated from West Point, to June 18, 1876, the day after the Battle
of the Rosebud. Here the story breaks off abruptly; the sudden
death of the General in 1890 prevented completion.

This "rugged biography" is here presented as General Crook
wrote it. The flavor of the West is strong in it; certain words and
expressions characterize the writer more than long descriptions.
Changes in grammar or corrections of phrase would have damaged
one of the greatest assets of the original. They have, therefore, not
been made. Even the names of individual Indians have been preserved as Crook wrote them.

Punctuation and some capitalization only have been supplied
and the material divided into chapters to facilitate reading. The

notes are intended to check the General's statements, augment his versions, or supply an occasional deficiency of detail.

The events not included in Crook's own words have been supplied, before and after the autobiographical portion, from a variety of sources. The General was so prominent in the West that few chronicles of the time lack mention of him. In addition, many of his associates in the army kept copious journals of their own—Bourke, Kennon, Roberts, Schuyler, and Kautz. From their point of view they tell much of the Crook story that the General did not live to relate in his own words.

The resources of the National Archives and the Army War College Library were drawn upon heavily to annotate and supplement the basic document. In addition, the libraries of Congress, Huntington, Newberry, Bureau of Ethnology, Dayton public, and the United States Military Academy and the files of the Historical Section, Army War College, yielded much printed and manuscript material. The assistance of these institutions is gratefully acknowledged.

Brigadier General Charles D. Roberts, who knew General Crook personally and whose father served under Crook for many years, opened his father's papers for inspection and offered many personal facts which would have been unobtainable elsewhere. I am deeply grateful to him for his courtesy and kindness.

A great deal of information and guidance was received from Mrs. Suzanne Phinney and Mrs. Lucille Pendell of the War Records Office, National Archives. Major H. A. DeWeerd, *Infantry Journal*, offered valuable suggestions concerning the arrangement of the material. Master Sergeant Robert C. Green of the War College Library supplied the key to many questions from his remarkable knowledge of army history. Mrs. Marion Rinehart, Washington, D. C., and Mrs. Eunice Mohr, Champaign, Illinois, assisted in what is always the most thankless of tasks, manuscript reading. To all these and other helpers, my sincere thanks.

MARTIN F. SCHMITT

Washington, D. C.

Cadet Crook — $115 on account

"Civilization approached the American Indian with a Bible in one hand and a paper treaty in the other, a bludgeon in her sleeve, and a barrel of whisky in her wagon, not to mention the blight that goeth unto the third and fourth generation. The task of the soldier was to punish the Indian when he applied his crude ideas of justice or revenge, and to force him to obey when he could not be cajoled or scared." Such was the conclusion of Major Eben Swift, reviewing the history of West Point in Indian warfare.

It is quite true that the majority of army officers on frontier duty regarded the Indian service simply as police duty. You got your orders and executed them, thankful for any break in the intolerable routine of western army post life. Too often frontier posts were staffed with mediocre material, with men who had shown little aptitude elsewhere or had been derelict in duty. Beyond forcing, cajoling, or scaring the Indian, little could be expected from them.

To the discerning, however, frontier assignments offered a challenge beyond Indian fighting. The Indian was, to a few, not merely a nuisance to be eradicated or an exciting quarry to be run down, but a human being to be understood, studied, and guided.

Many superior officers were granted opportunity to exercise their talents in Indian administration. Sherman, Sheridan, Miles, Terry, Burnside, Pope, Stuart, Howard, Crook, Hood, and Merritt are but a few generals who shavetailed on the frontier.

Of this be-starred group, General George Crook was the acknowledged master. General Sherman named him the greatest Indian fighter and manager the United States Army ever had.

xix

There were two reasons for Crook's superiority. First, he made the frontier his life work and his life hobby, not simply an interval in a career pointed toward Governor's Island or Washington, D. C. Second, he approached the problems of the frontier, the Indians, not only as a "pacifier," a representative of force, but as a humanitarian and an interested student of his job. Despite maxims to the contrary, he burned powder only when it served the longer aim of peace and understanding.

After a lifetime of struggle with both Indians and whites in every state west of the hundredth meridian, Crook, in an address to the West Point graduates of 1884, concluded that "with all his faults, and he has many, the American Indian is not half so black as he has been painted. He is cruel in war, treacherous at times, and not over cleanly. But so were our forefathers. His nature, however, is responsive to a treatment which assures him that it is based upon justice, truth, honesty, and common sense; it is not impossible that with a fair and square system of dealing with him the American Indian would make a better citizen than many who neglect the duties and abuse the privileges of that proud title."

George Crook was born on September 8, 1828, on a farm near Taylorsville, Ohio. The Crook family, even at that time, was an old one in America, the original bearers coming from Scotland late in the seventeenth century. The name is well represented in Revolutionary War records and appears commonly in parish records, deeds, and wills of the day.

George Crook was the ninth of ten children born to Thomas Crook and Elizabeth Matthews. Thomas Crook had been born in Baltimore County, Maryland, in 1788, and served, according to his own sworn record, in a militia company of Baltimore in 1813, thought to be "Capt. Hazelet's company, engaged in the defense of Fort McHenry at the time the British frigate, Belvidere, captured and destroyed the East Town packet near the mouth of the Petapsco." Shortly thereafter he took sick and was discharged. The rolls of the regiment are lost.

Thomas Crook, who was a tanner, married Elizabeth Matthews of Maryland on February 4, 1812. Their first child, Elizabeth, was born February 18, 1813; and in 1814, Thomas, with his family, moved to Ohio and commenced farming. Here nine children were born: Maria, Catherine, Oliver, John, Thomas, Jr., Walter, James, George, and Charles, the last in 1830.

Of the boys, Oliver, James, and Thomas, Jr., were professional men, doctors and dentists; John, a tailor; Walter, a postmaster and politician; and Charles, a farmer. Elizabeth Crook married Dr. Adam Koogler of Ohio; and Oliver Crook, after graduating from the University of New York, was in partnership with Koogler for some time.

Maria Crook married Samuel Sullivan, operator of a trading post along the Miami and Erie Canal, and later justice of the peace. The first of their eight children, Thomas Crook Sullivan, graduated from West Point in 1856 and rose to the rank of brigadier general in the Commissary Department.

Thomas Crook "was a good manager, practical, industrious, and well-informed. He accumulated 340 acres of excellent land, most of which he improved. He was a justice of the peace for many years, and was otherwise prominent in the affairs of the township. In politics he was a Whig, and afterwards a Republican. He died January 11, 1875."

The Crook farm was on the east bank of the Miami River, in Montgomery County, Wayne Township, noted for its fertile farmland. When, in 1827, the Miami and Erie Canal was opened, it ran directly through the farm, greatly increasing its value, which according to the 1850 census, was $13,600.

According to General August V. Kautz, who spent his boyhood in the same region, prosperous Ohio farmers in that early day "lived well, having plenty of meat, wheat, corn, butter, and eggs. Wine was unknown, the Ohio vineyards not having been started into existence. They dressed principally in homespun, Kentucky jeans, and butternut. Broadcloth was rare for the men, and silk was still rarer for the women. Parlors were not in use; most of the families were limited to one living room, and it was only here and there that an economical housewife saved enough rags for a rag carpet. The best room was the sleeping room of the old people, while the girls and boys were stored away in the garret.

"There was little travel in those days. The community was almost dependent on itself, and customs and sentiment were strictly local. The popular energy went into religion, and the social scale was rated accordingly."

Schooling in 1838 was limited. General Kautz recalled that at the age of eleven he had exhausted the learning of the Georgetown educational system. George Crook was somewhat more fortunate in having Dayton close by, but he was not addicted to books and less inclined to higher education than his brothers. One of his classmates, James A. Greer, later commodore, described him to L. W. V. Kennon as "a farmer's boy, slow to learn, but what he did learn was surely his. He was older, somewhat, than his comrades, and was good natured, stolid, and was like a big Newfoundland dog among a lot of puppies. He would never permit injustice, or bullying of smaller boys."

Apparently George Crook was destined to stay on the farm. But fate in the form of Robert P. Schenck, Whig member of the House, intervened. Or so, at least, Schenck told a Washington, D. C., *Chronicle* reporter in 1883, when "his boy, General Crook," was the national hero. "I had looked over the district to find a bright lad to nominate to West Point to fill an existing vacancy. I was unsuccessful. I finally remembered that old 'Squire Crook, a fine old Whig farmer, and a friend of mine, had some boys, and I sent word for him to come to town. He came in, and I enquired if he had a spare boy he'd like to send off to West Point. After studying awhile he said he didn't know but what he had. I suggested that he send him in. He did so.

"The boy was exceedingly non-communicative. He hadn't a stupid look, but was quiet to reticence. He didn't seem to have the slightest interest or anxiety about my proposal. I explained to him the requirements and labors of the military school, and finally asked him, 'Do you think you can conquer all that?' His monosyllabic reply was, 'I'll try.' And so I sent him, and he came through fairly."

Going to the Military Academy meant that George Crook would have to take a little more schooling. He attended classes at the Dayton Academy under Superintendent Milo G. Williams, "instructor in mathematics, natural philosophy, natural sciences, etc." In December, 1847, Williams wrote Schenck that George Crook's "application and improvement satisfies me that he has a mind which will sustain him honorably in the required course at West Point."

In March, 1848, Representative Schenck formally nominated George Crook for appointment as cadet to fill the vacancy from the Third Congressional District of Ohio. The boy was nineteen years old, and his father described him as "health good, body perfect, height five feet eight inches, and a good English scholar." On June 1, 1848, Cadet George W. Crook paid $115 on account to Captain G. W. Cullum, and bought the sparse equipment permitted at West Point. The initial "W" was the whim of a relative who gave his name to the appointee. Crook never had a middle initial or name, and it was dropped when he graduated.

Cadet Crook did not offer a great deal of mental competition to his classmates. In June, 1849, the examinations left him with a rank of fifty in a class of fifty-six. His highest individual rating for that year was in English studies, where he rose to forty-eighth position. His French was most unfortunate; both 1849 and 1850 saw him at the bottom of that class. In the entire four years at the academy he managed to reach the thirty-second rank only once—his fourth year, subject engineering—but by that time the class had dwindled to forty-three cadets. He graduated thirty-eighth in his class, thus becoming the lowest-ranking cadet ever to rise to the rank of major general, United States Army.

Only in conduct was Crook an example to his fellows. He consistently ranked in the upper half of his class in that department, presumably because he was too busy keeping his academic head above water to indulge in the luxury of demerits. Then, too, he was naturally reticent, and the attractions of Benny Havens' were not for him. However, the post order books record that Cadet Crook, along with J. W. Smith, was in arrest in quarters on May 17, 1849, "for offering compositions to their instructors as their own which were not original"; and on September 7 of the same year, Crook was assigned to two extra hours of guard duty for being absent from drill.

The post order and letter books are unusually free from any mention of Cadet Crook, free from both praise and blame. He was never appointed cadet sergeant, or even corporal, but remained quietly, and deservedly, in the ranks. Not once in four years did Superintendent Henry Brewerton find it necessary to grant permission to Cadet Crook to receive articles from home, a pleasure which most cadets enjoyed from time to time.

Of Crook's fellow cadets, only Sheridan mentions him in his memoirs as having been with him at the academy. Crook's remarks in later life indicate that he associated rather intimately with Sheridan, and to a lesser extent with August Kautz, Sylvester Mowry, Thomas L. Casey, and Alexander McCook.

Crook's reticent and unobtrusive character was his hallmark throughout life. "Probably no officer of equal rank in our army," says Bourke, "issued fewer orders or letters of instruction. 'Example,' he said, 'is always the best general order.'" George Crook carried this principle into every battle of his career, and his men knew that "in our hour of danger Crook would be found in the skirmish line, not in the telegraph office."

GENERAL GEORGE CROOK
His Autobiography

I

PACIFIC COAST
SHAVETAIL

1. *My first impressions were not favorable*

My FIRST STATION after graduation in 1852 was Governor's Island. I was assigned as Brevet Second Lieutenant in the Fourth Infantry, then serving on the Pacific Coast. Myself, with three other classmates, John Mullan, A. V. Kautz, and John Nugen sailed from New York per steamer about the fourth of November for San Francisco.

Having never seen anything beyond my own country home previous to going to West Point, all experiences after leaving New York were entirely new to me. The ocean steamer, smell of bilge water, the motion of the ship, and the vastness of the ocean—add to these the deathly sea sickness which overcame me near Sandy Hook—did not prepossess me in favor of that mode of travel. I scarcely left my bunk until we reached the Isthmus. Although I had my life yet before me, and everything was tinted with bright colors, so great was my aging during this sea sickness that I was indifferent to life, and cared but little whether the vessel went to the bottom or not.

Our route across the Isthmus was by the Nicaragua River, which presented many new features to me. The natives, verdure, and climate were all so different from anything I had ever seen before that I was constantly on the alert for something new or unexpected, and I was so wrought up that it was an easy matter for me to believe even in the marvelous.

We were lightered from the ocean steamer on to three small river steamers at the mouth of the San Juan River in the afternoon. We commenced our journey up the river a sufficient time before dark so as to take in the view of our surroundings. The weather

3

was hot and murky, with frequent showers of rain. The banks of the river were one dense, impenetrable jungle of trees, with vines intertwining their branches. Alligators could be seen watching their chances for prey, lizards climbing in the branches of the trees, at least four feet long, flights of parrots screaming at the tops of their voices.

Our steamer was so crowded that there was scarcely standing room for its passengers. When night came on, it was inky dark. It thundered and lightninged and rained hard. At intervals all was hushed save the waters rushing against the overhanging boughs, sounding like the rushing of the many waters. Altogether it presented one of the wildest and most weird scenes I have ever witnessed before or since.

Some time during the night the steamer in advance of ours ran into the branches of an overhanging tree, which carried away their smokestack, killing the captain, and so disabling the boat that it had to be left. In transferring its passengers to the two other boats, an old lady slipped off the gang plank, and was seen no more.

This seemed to me to be the longest night I have ever experienced. Nothing to eat, no place to rest, and I was tired and sleepy. One man, while dozing during the night, fell overboard, put up a terrible yell the moment he struck the water, swam ashore, and clung to an overhanging branch until rescued by a small boat.

We arrived at Castilla Rapids soon after daylight the next morning, and were received by a detachment of native troops, the mangiest lot I ever saw. Their heads were shaved as a rule; many of them had nothing but shirts on. From appearance their muskets must certainly have been unserviceable. They were quartered in a huckel made of cane reeds, and such, that would not seem to furnish much protection.

Castilla Rapids was said to have been caused by buccaneers a century or so ago obstructing the river by tumbling large boulders in its channel so as to elude their pursuers. There were a few natives living at the place, and one kind of a hotel kept by an American who charged California prices for everything. For instance, we paid a dollar per permission to spread our blankets on the floor of a large parlor and bar room combined, without any furniture save glasses, etc.

4

Rather an amusing scene occurred during the night. The floor was one mass of human beings; the space above it was also filled with people swung in hammocks. Our minds had been kept on a strain ever since our entrance into the country by the blood-curdling stories told of the natives attacking and murdering travelers, etc. ,etc. The savage and brutal countenances of these people assisted our credulity. The rapids made much noise, the night was pitch dark, and sometime during the night one of the hammock strings gave way, discharging its contents on some unlucky sleeper below. As if by magic, everything was a perfect pandemonium, persons yelling at the tops of their voices, pistols clicking all around me, and for fear of being shot, I lay low.

Pretty soon, however, the landlord came in with a light, and order was restored. It was amusing to hear the different individuals swear that they had not been afraid. Since then I have learned that the world is full of just such brave people, but fail to discern their bravery until the danger is past.

Next morning the steamer brought in a load of passengers from California, all eager to hear the latest news from the "States." One poor fellow was brought as a corpse, lying on the deck, covered with a blanket. His remains were buried that day by some of his comrades.

In the afternoon we were transferred into two boats above the rapids, the ones that brought the California passengers. These boats were more capacious than the others, and better in every way, That evening we reached St. Carlos situated on the north bank where the river debouches from Lake Nicaragua. The river above the rapids is wider, and the current not so swift as it was below the rapids. The country on either side was higher, and the jungles gave way to a more open country.

The moon was shining brightly, and the sail across the lake that night was perfectly charming. We arrived at Virgin Bay next morning, and at once commenced disembarking from the steamer on to the backs of mules. The passage here to San Juan del Sur on the Pacific Coast, a distance of twelve miles, was the worst I have ever seen. It was one gigantic mudhole, places where mule and rider would almost sink out of sight. The most of us reached the port that evening one mass of mud from head to foot. Some time

BIG ROAD

RED CLOUD

THREE STARS (CROOK) TOOK RED CLOUD'S MEN TO HELP FIGHT CHEYENNES '76 - '77

IRON HAWK

COUNTING COUP

DEPARTMENT OF THE WEST
BEING THE SCENE OF THE
CAMPAIGNS OF GENERAL CROOK

MAKING MEDICINE

RED SHIRT

HUMP

OGALALAS HELP GENERAL McKENZIE WHIP CHEYENNES

SOLDIER KILLED CRAZY HORSE WITH BAYONET '77

CRAZY HORSE'S BAND LEAVES SPOTTED TAIL AGENCY TO GO NORTH '77-'78

CHEYENNE KILLED WHO BOASTED HE WAS BULLET-PROOF

LOW-DOG

Buford

Ft. A. Lincoln

RED R.

LITTLE MISSOURI

MISSOURI R.

CHEYENNE R.
Camp Sheridan
Camp Robinson
Ft. Randall

Ft Sheridan

CHICAGO

...amie
PLATTE R.
Sidney Bks.

OMAHA

Ft. Leavenworth
Ft. Riley

ST. LOUIS

OHIO R.

...t. Lyon

CANADIAN R.
Ft. Reno
Ft. Gibson
ARKANSAS R.

...scom

Ft. Sill

RED R.

MEMPHIS

MISSISSIPPI R.

COLORADO R.

SAN ANTONIO

RIO GRANDE

Ft. Duncan

HE-DOG

STABBER

SPOTTED ELK

during the night Dutch Kautz[1] came truding along, carrying his carpet sack; said the last he saw of his mule was its ears sticking out of the mud. The next day we waded in the sea, clothes and all, to wash off some of the mud.

That evening we set sail for San Francisco; our luggage not having arrived, we had to leave it behind. Although the water of the Pacific Ocean was smooth compared with that of the Atlantic, I was sick all the way. We arrived in San Francisco about December 1.[2]

San Francisco was then a conglomeration of frame buildings, streets deep in sand; wharf facilities were very limited. Where the Occidental Hotel now stands there was mud and marsh which was overflowed by the tides. Everything was excitement and bustle, prices were most exorbitant, common laborers received much higher wages than officers of the Army, although at that time, by special act of Congress, we were allowed extra pay.[3]

Everything was so different from what I had been accustomed to that it was hard to realize I was in the United States. People had flocked there from all parts of the world; all nationalities were represented there. Sentiments and ideas were so liberal and expanded that they were almost beyond bounds. Money was so plentiful amongst citizens that it was but lightly appreciated.

My first station on the Pacific Coast was at Benicia Barracks,[4]

[1] August V. "Dutch" Kautz remained a lifelong friend of Crook, often being stationed in the same or a neighboring department or division in the West. The Kautz' became famous throughout the frontier for their entertainments and musicals, a rare treat at the isolated posts. Martha Summerhayes, *Vanished Arizona*, 261–65.

[2] The "advantages" of the Nicaragua route were advertised, with a detailed map in a guide by Peter F. Stout, entitled *Nicaragua, Past, Present and Future.*

[3] The Army Appropriations Act of 1851 allowed $325,854 for extra pay to officers and enlisted men serving in Oregon and California. Officers received two dollars extra per day, while the pay of enlisted men was doubled. Adjutant General's Office, *General Order No. 32* (1850).

[4] Benicia Barracks was situated about one mile east of Benicia, California. It was first occupied in 1849 as a quartermaster depot for the Division of the Pacific. *General Order No. 6*, Division of the Pacific (1852), named the post "Benicia," after the town, which name was said to be derived from Francesca Benicia, wife of General Vallejo of Sonora.

In 1852 Benicia Barracks was the point of embarkation for most troops intended for Pacific Coast service, and during the Civil War it became a rendezvous for California Volunteers. Occupation of the site for military purposes

where I was assigned to Company "F" 4th Regiment of Infantry, commanded by 2nd Lt. Edmund B. Underwood.

The roads and walks all about the town and barracks were one mud hole. It was nothing unusual to see the tops of boots sticking out of the mud in the streets where they had been left by the wearer in preference to digging them out.

The Headquarters and one company of the 2nd Regiment of Infantry were also at the barracks. The officers, as near as I can now recollect, were Maj. Day, Capt. Frazier, Lts. Steele and Fighting Tom Wright, 2nd Infantry; Scott and Underwood, 4th Infantry.

With the exception of Capt. Frazier and Steele there was not a day passed but what these officers were drunk at least once, and mostly until the wee hours in the morning. I never had seen such gambling and carousing before or since.

My first duty after reporting was as a file closer[5] to the funeral escort of Maj. Miller, 2nd Infantry,[6] who had just died from the effects of strong drink. Major Day, whose head was as white as the driven snow, commanded the escort, and when all of us officers had assembled in the room where the corpse was lying, he said, "Well, fellows, Old Miller is dead and he can't drink, so let us all take a drink." I was never more horrified in my life.

Duty at the post was rendered in so lax a manner that I did not see my company for one week after I joined. When I would suggest going to visit the company, I would be put off by its commander until some other time.[7] In the early spring I was delighted at an order for companies "B" and "F" 4th Infantry to proceed to

has been almost continuous to the present time. Army War College, Historical Section, *Posts, Camps, and Stations File* (hereafter referred to as *Posts, Camps, and Stations File*).

[5] File closers were officers or noncommissioned officers placed in the rear of ranks or on the flanks of their units in columns, and charged with the duty of supervising the men in ranks. Max B. Garber, *A Modern Military Dictionary*, 121.

[6] Albert S. Miller, a classmate of Major Day and veteran of the Seminole and Mexican wars. He was fifty-one years old.

[7] Company F was at a "camp near Benicia," established August 19, 1852, by eight companies of the Fourth Infantry. In November, 1858, the site, near Benicia Barracks, was occupied by several companies of the Sixth Infantry. The permanent post of Benicia was not large enough to accommodate so many men. *Posts, Camps, and Stations File.*

Humboldt Bay under command of Bvt. Lt. Col. R. C. Buchanan, to there establish a post, the site to be selected by our commanding officer.[8]

Just before leaving I was taken with a violent case of erysipelas in both ankles, and was in great dread for fear I would be left behind. One doctor painted the parts affected with creosote and iodine, but they still kept on getting worse. Next morning another doctor came, Dr. Griffin,[9] who filled me up with calomel and jalap, which made me deathly sick until it commenced operating, after which the disease seemed to leave my system entirely. The next day I marched down to the wharf and embarked with my company. The second doctor, who was pretty full, blackguarded me for my impudence in daring to get well without his permission, remarking that he was expecting an interesting case, but that I had spoiled it, etc.

We boarded the old steamer *Goliah*,[10] an old boat, that, in order to increase its capacity, had been cut into and pierced in the center, so that when the center was on top of a wave the two ends would sag, and produce feelings of insecurity and of the unseaworthiness of the vessel. Its accommodations for the officers were not equal to those in the steerage of the vessels nowadays, while the men were huddled together like so many swine, and but little better cared for.

The weather, after getting out to sea, was rainy and disagreeable; the wind was cold and raw. There was not sufficient shelter

---

[8] *General Order No. 2*, Division of the Pacific (January 20, 1853), instructed "Bvt. Lt. Col. R. C. Buchanan . . . with companies B and F, 4th Infantry to proceed to establish a military post at such point on or near Humboldt Bay as in his judgment will best afford protection to that section of the country against Indians. . . . Assistant Surgeon C. P. Deyerle is assigned to duty with the command." The companies left Benicia on January 27, and encamped at Humboldt Bay on January 30. National Archives, *Regimental Returns, Fourth Infantry*, January, 1853.

[9] Assistant Surgeon Deyerle was the man whose prescription failed, and John S. Griffin the successful but disappointed doctor. Division of the Pacific, *Special Order No. 29* (May 15, 1852).

[10] The *Alta California* (Steamer Edition) of February 16, 1853, reports the return of the *Goliah* under Captain J. T. Wright from Humboldt on the fifteenth. The *Goliah* had left San Francisco on January 28 with 120 tons of government stores.

to keep all the soldiers dry, even, and upon one occasion some of them were standing near the cabin door to get out of the rain when Col. Buchanan spied them, and drove them away with the remark that "By the powers," he expected next they would want him to invite them into the cabin to dine with him, etc. It struck me as being particularly heartless and cruel. They were doing no harm to anyone; the government had not furnished them proper transportation, and instead of complaining they were simply trying to shelter themselves from the rain. Many of their number were seasick, too.

The owner of the ship, "Old Bully Wright," was aboard also. He was a man upwards of sixty years of age, and had been brought up to the life of a "sea dog," and had apparently outlived all the pleasures of life. All avenues to his heart had long ago closed up, so that the only comfort left him was his greed for money.

Upon our arrival off the entrance to Humboldt Bay we stood off and on until the tide and the sea were favorable for us to undertake its difficult passage. Finally all signs were favorable, and we labored on the bar, the old ship nearly breaking in two. All on board experienced great relief when we were safely over.

We crossed in the morning, the sun was shining, and everything was lovely. The forest of the immense redwoods which came down close to the bay with the high "Bald Mountain" in their rear some eight or ten miles back presented a beautiful landscape that was very pleasing and grateful to the eye after our disagreeable sea journey. We steamed up and down the bay once or twice in order that Col. Buchanan could select the most eligible site for the new post to be erected.

Our commander seemed particularly elated at his own importance, and his fitness for the duties assigned him, and lost no opportunity to impress on all of us subordinates how far we fell short of what he expected. He seemed to take delight in wounding the feelings of those under him, and succeeded pretty generally in making himself unpopular amongst the citizens as well as the army.

Finally a point near the little town of Bucksport, which was situated opposite the entrance of the bay, was settled upon, and everything was disembarked and moved to a mesa or plateau about half a mile back from the bay, and work commenced. Most of the site was a prairie, but some clearing of underbrush was necessary.

To this end, together with roads to be built, and quarters, etc., everybody kept busy.[11]

The officers present were Col. Buchanan, Assistant Surgeon C. P. Deyerle, 1st Lt. W. H. Scott, 2nd Lt. Edmund B. Underwood, John C. Bonnycastle, and myself, Bvt. 2nd Lt. I was appointed Adjutant, and in this position was thrown constantly in contact with the Commanding Officer. I soon became familiar with his idiosyncrasies, and avoided him whenever it was possible, for from the first I never believed in that mode of discipline which consisted in trying to break down men's self respect and make a mere machine of them instead of appealing to their better feelings and judgment.

Colonel Buchanan's principle was to allow no subordinate to make suggestions unasked, and told me, on one occasion, never to take the suggestions of a non-commissioned officer but go ahead and do my own way, even if I knew I was wrong. It was clear he must have followed this principle, judging from the number of mistakes he made.

I must say that my first impressions of the army were not favorable. Most of the customs and habits that I witnessed were not calculated to impress one's morals or usefulness. Most of the commanding officers were petty tyrants, styled by some Martinets. They lost no opportunities to snub those under them, and prided themselves in saying disagreeable things. Most of them had been in command of small posts so long that their habits and minds had narrowed down to their surroundings, and woe be unto the young officers if his ideas should get above their level and wish to expand. Generally they were the quintessence of selfishness. Everything within their reach was made subservient to their comforts, and should there be more of anything than they wanted, then the rest might have it.

Many of these officers had the most exalted opinions of themselves and of their importance to our government. In several instances others shared these opinions with them. I used to hear the

---

11 Fort Humboldt was situated directly in the rear of the town of Bucksport, about 220 miles north of San Francisco and 18 miles south of Trinidad. After serving as a base for operations against Indians, it was used as a depot, and finally abandoned, per *Special Order No. 243*, Department of California (1866); *Posts, Camps, and Stations File*.

older officers discussing who would be the prominent officers in case of a big war, and those men who had the reputation of being Martinets were the ones selected in most instances.

When our big war did come, it was the fewest of those men who could expand enough to grasp the situation, and the consequence was that as a rule they were failures, and because they had to be superseded they continually railed at the ingratitude of Republics, etc.

Whenever I could, I went hunting, so that I became very familiar with all the country within reaching distance of the post. Back in the mountains, particularly in the Bald Mountains, there was a great abundance, of elk, deer, and blue grouse, with an occasional bear. There were large flats in places on the edges of the bay that were overflowed by the tides, which swarmed with waterfowl, especially ducks. When we first arrived in the bay the ducks would get up in countless numbers upon the approach of our boat. The flapping of their wings would sound like distant thunder. This was such a new feature to me that I could hardly contain myself until I could get ashore. But my inexperience in hunting made it more difficult to take them than I at first supposed.

I here saw my first Indians, as there were several small bands living on different parts of the bay, but they were poor, harmless, scrofuletic, and miserable creatures who lived principally on fish. Many of them were deformed, and the most loathsome looking human beings that I have ever seen.[12] The Bald Mountain Indians, however, were a different set, and were more or less hostile, killed a good many whites, besides committing other depredations.

The whites became so incensed at the outrages committed by these Indians that some thought those in the bay were in collusion with those in the mountains, so one night a lot of citizens assembled and massacred a number of these poor defenseless beings, who thought, doubtless, that their very condition would be their safeguard. Some of the local newspapers lauded this, one of the most fiendish acts that has ever disgraced civilization. I took part in one expedition against the Bald Mountain Indians, but without result.

I, with a detachment of my company, was sent as escort to a

[12] The bay Indians were the Wiyots, which, with the Yuroks, were the Algonquins of California. The more aggressive hills Indians were Athabascans. Alfred L. Kroeber, *Handbook of the Indians of California*, 109–27.

surveying party in charge of a Mr. Washington from Virginia.[13] We went up the coast to the mouth of the Klamath. Our route lay up the beach, to me a very interesting country. While in camp near Port Orford, one of the soldiers brought me some sand with mica in it. I failed to convince him that it was not gold, so next morning when we left camp for our day's march, he packed it with him.

The mountains generally were not far back from the beach. In places, when the tide was in, the breakers washed up against perpendicular cliffs from two to three hundred feet high. So we would have to wait for the tide to run out before passing these. Some fifteen miles before reaching the mouth of the Klamath River, we camped at Gold Bluffs,[14] where the beach for several miles contained gold mixed in small quantities with the sand.

Their mode of working at that time was at each low tide to traverse this beach with some pack mules loaded with panniers, so that when the waves had thrown up a streak of pay sand, it was shoveled into the panniers, and thence packed to the sluice boxes which separated the gold.

I was told that when the beach was first discovered, it was estimated that it contained $40,000,000, but that their methods of catching the gold were then so primitive and slow (they at that time packed the gold-bearing sand to some point at low tide and there mixed it with quicksilver by oxen treading on it) that before much was saved a heavy sea came and washed it all out to sea. Since then certain seas would throw up some pay sand. Then I believed all this statement, but since then I have heard so much ro-

[13] Henry Washington was deputy surveyor of California under John Coffee Hays. The survey was to select the initial point near Humboldt Bay for the base and meridian lines which were to govern the surveys in the northwest section of the state.

Military escort was obtained for "protection against the savages." The party went along the Pacific Coast to the Klamath, then back to the country east of the timbered land in the section known as "Bald Hills."

Back at Humboldt Bay the surrounding country was thoroughly examined, east and south toward Eel River. A prominent peak, named Mount Pierce, "as a compliment to the President," was finally chosen as the initial point. National Archives, *Deputy Surveyor to Surveyor-General of California*, November 8, 1853.

[14] The Gold Bluffs were discovered in 1850. "To them was directed under highly colored accounts by interested parties, the senseless rush of December 1850. . . . The deposits extended nearly from Crescent City to Humboldt Bay." Hubert H. Bancroft, *History of California*, VI, 364–65 s. n.

mance mixed up with all mining operations that I have become a little incredulous about everything that has mine in it.

After remaining a day or so at the mouth of the Klamath River, we retraced our march down the beach, and there the journey was carried into the Bald Mountain country. I remained there until about the last of October, 1853, when I was promoted to full 2nd Lieutenant in "E" Company, then stationed at Fort Jones, near Yreka, California.[15]

2. *The unexpected was constantly happening*

As THE ROGUE RIVER INDIANS were then on the warpath, I was hurried to join my new station. I sailed from Humboldt Bay to San Francisco in a sailing vessel loaded with lumber, and a very tedious passage we had of it, as we were becalmed for several days. From San Francisco I traveled up the Sacramento River as far as Sacramento on a steamboat. This was a very lively city then, almost as much business done here as there was in San Francisco.

I was amused at the rival hotel busses, or rather their drivers, blackguarding each other. I was the only passenger, and one who didn't get me told me I had better have myself wrapped up in straw, or otherwise I would be all rubbed to pieces before reaching my destination from here to Fort Reading, near the upper end of the Sacramento Valley. Here I met Lt. Underwood, who was 1st Lt. of Company "D." Major Wright was in command, Capt. Morris, regular Quartermaster, and Assistant Surgeon John Campbell were there.

I was given a mule here which I rode up to Fort Jones, passing through Shasta City, one of the liveliest places I had ever seen then. It was situated in the midst of a rich placer region where several thousand miners were engaged in mining. From here my route lay up Trinity River, another mining region where hundreds of men

---

[15] Fort Jones was named after Colonel Roger Jones, adjutant general of the army. It was established on October 16, 1852, by Companies A and E, First Dragoons, and evacuated on June 23, 1858, the site being abandoned in 1866. *Posts, Camps, and Stations File.*

were mining. Money was plentiful, and prices for everything were most exorbitant. I reached Fort Jones the latter part of October.

The post was situated on the edge of a beautiful mountain valley called Scott's Valley, with a beautiful river of the same name running through it. Yreka was some eighteen miles distant. The post consisted of a few log huts, built on the two pieces of a passage plan. Two companies were stationed here. The Commandant was Brevet Major "He! He! be God! G. Washington Patten," Captain, 2nd Infantry.

Capt. B. R. Alden, whom I had left as Commandant at West Point, was also here. It seemed he had left his resignation with his wife before leaving the East to join his company. When the report of his having been wounded by the Indians reached Washington, she handed in his resignation, which, much to his disappointment, had been accepted. The notification had just been sent him here.

As he was an officer strongly imbued with the military spirit, and the local notoriety which his being wounded by the Indians gave him was pleasing to him, he was very loath to leave the service. He finally left that section of the country, where there were prospects of more service, with many regrets, although he was partially paralyzed from the effects of his wound. As a matter of fact, he never regained the use of one arm, and partially one side, and in consequence was unable to participate in our great war of the rebellion, but was most of the time off in Europe trying to recover his health. Soon after the close of the war he died.

In addition to the officers above mentioned were Doctor Sorrel, Lt. C——, 2nd Infantry,[1] and Lt. Dryer, 4th Infantry.

It was the unexpected that was constantly happening ever since I left New York. The most marvelous stories were in circulation concerning most everything, particularly about Indians and bear. As I had seen so many things that to me were wonderful, I was prepared to believe many of these stories of bear coming into camp, chewing people, pulling off their blankets when they were asleep, hugging one to death, tremendous size of the grizzlies, the treach-

[1] Lt. C— is Austin W. Colcord, graduate of West Point in 1850. He had just returned from a protracted spell of "absent without leave." He resigned his commission on May 31, 1855. National Archives, *Annual Returns of the Alterations and Casualties Incident to the Fourth Infantry, 1853* (hereafter referred to as *Annual Returns*).

ery and cruelty of the Indians, the many adventures that were constantly occurring, etc. etc. I was constantly on the "que vive" to meet some of these many adventures.

I was assigned to one of the pens that was not yet finished. There were neither latches nor fastening of any kind on my door. One evening I was lying on my bunk, ruminating before lighting my candle. It was pitch dark. I heard the tread of some animal approaching my door, and suddenly the door flew open, and in walked some large animal, judging from the clicking noise his claws made on the floor as he stalked across the room to the fireplace. Shortly afterwards I heard him turn around and approach where I was lying. My first impulse was to save myself by flight. I reasoned that would not do, as he could easily outrun me, especially as all was dark. It then occurred to me that I had seen a large Newfoundland dog around the garrison during the day, but even then, when he came near the bed and I reached out and felt his shaggy coat, I was not fully relieved for the moment, but when I fully realized the situation, he lost no time in getting out of my house.

Shortly after this I came into my room one evening, soon after dark, went up to the mantel piece and struck a match to light my candle. All of a sudden I felt a whirl around my head, and felt the sensation of my scalp leaving my head. I soon discovered it was an owl who had undoubtedly flown in through the open door during my absence, and was probably blinded by the light, and in its fright lit on my head. His needle-like claws produced the pain in my scalp, as my hair was cut close, and there was no protection. I, however, catching him, turned him loose, much to his delight.

Scattered over the country were a few Shasta Indians,[2] generally well disposed, but more frequently forced to take the war path or sink all self respect, by the outrages of the whites perpetrated upon them. The country was over-run by people from all nations in search of the mighty dollar. Greed was almost unre-

[2] The Shasta Indians occupied the Klamath River from a point between Indian and Thompson creeks to a spot a few miles above Fall Creek. They also claimed the areas drained by two tributaries of the Klamath, Scott, and Shasta rivers. The Shastas were a small tribe; a government field census in 1851 yielded 24 towns on the Klamath, 7 on the Scott, and 19 on the Shasta; inhabitants, 2,000. Kroeber, *Handbook of the Indians of California*, 285–304.

strained, and from the nature of our government there was little or no law that these people were bound to respect.

It was of no unfrequent occurrence for an Indian to be shot down in cold blood, or a squaw to be raped by some brute. Such a thing as a white man being punished for outraging an Indian was unheard of. It was the fable of the wolf and lamb every time. The consequence was that there was scarcely ever a time that there was not one or more wars with the Indians somewhere on the Pacific Coast.[3]

There were a good many Indians about Fort Jones and vicinity from whom I soon learned their grievances. It is hard to believe now the wrongs these Indians had to suffer in those days. I doubt now if there is a single one left to tell their tale. The trouble with the army was that the Indians would confide in us as friends, and we had to witness this unjust treatment of them without the power to help them. Then when they were pushed beyond endurance and would go on the war path we had to fight when our sympathies were with the Indians.

Yreka was situated in the midst of a vast placer district. Its population, including those mining in the immediate vicinity, was estimated at 10,000. It resembled a large ants nest. Miner, merchant, gambler, and all seemed busy plying their different avocations, coming and going apparently all the time, scarcely stopping for the night. Idlers were the exception. Prices for everything were most exorbitant. The medium of exchange was coin exclusively, nothing less than twenty-five cents, and but little of that. Everyone carried their lives in their own hands. Scarcely a week passed by without one or more persons being killed.

[3] Second Lieutenant Kautz, at Fort Orford in 1854, wrote an indignant letter to Major E. D. Townsend, adjutant general of the Division of the Pacific, in which he described an attack by thirty miners on some Indians near Coquille River. Sixteen Indians, two of them squaws, were killed, and four wounded. None of the whites was killed.

"From all that we could gather of the circumstances, there does not appear to have been sufficient cause to justify such a hasty attack. . . . I make this statement in order that the Commanding General may not be misled by newspaper statements."

The indorsement attached to the report remarks that this was but one example showing that "actual collision is usually precipitated by the whites, often eventuating in what is called an Indian war." 34 Cong., 3 sess., *House Ex. Doc.* 76, 86–87.

Shortly after my arrival at Fort Jones the 2nd Infantry was ordered east, which left but one company of the 4th Infantry at our post. With the 2nd left one of the curiosities of the army, Bvt. Major, Captain G. W. Patten.[4] He was a man of about 5 feet five inches in height, and of slight build. He had lost all of his left hand except its thumb and forefinger during the Mexican War, which for all the world looked like the claw of a crawfish.

He was pompous, irritable, and flighty, and of all men I have ever met the least calculated for the army. In addition he had a stoppage in his speech which made his conversation very difficult, and himself very ludicrous at times. His chief trouble was in starting a sentence. He would make such terrible grimaces, and precede most every word by "He! He! be Jesus Christ," (or "God"), so that he was familiarly known as "He! He! be God! Patten." As nothing short of seeing and hearing him talk would give an adequate idea of him, I shall not attempt it. He was very funny for a week or ten days, until he commenced repeating, when he became very tiresome.

Soon after my advent Lt. Bonnycastle joined the company as 1st Lieutenant, and about the first of January, 1854, Capt. H. M. Judah[5] joined by promotion. Soon after his arrival a courier one day came in from Yreka with the information that a party of white men had been killed by Indians on the Klamath River, some twenty miles above Cottonwood. We at once left for the scene of the trouble, leaving a detachment under a non-commissioned officer in command of the post.

Our command consisted of Capt. Judah, Lt. Bonnycastle, Doctor Sorrel, and myself, and about twenty soldiers. At Yreka we were joined by a few Volunteers, and at Cottonwood we were

[4] George Waynefleet Patten graduated from the Military Academy in 1830. He had lost most of his left hand in action at Cerro Gordo. Cullum's *Biographical Register* (I, 467) cites him as the "author of numerous poetical effusions." They were published by Patten in *Voices of the Border* (New York, 1867). Philip D. Jordan, "George W. Patten, Poet Laureate of the Army," *Military Affairs*, Vol. IV, No. 3 (Fall, 1940), 162-67.

[5] Henry M. Judah graduated from the Military Academy in 1843. He remained in California from 1853 to 1861. He died at Plattsburg, New York, in 1866, aged forty-five.

joined by a company of Volunteers commanded by a Capt. Gieger, whose brother was amongst the killed.[6]

Capt. Judah was in command of the whole. He organized his command into an advance guard, main body, and rear guard. I was to command the advance guard, Bonnycastle the main body, and the Volunteers were to be the rear guard, while Capt. Judah was to operate from one part of his command to the other. Our army left the ferry about noon, and commenced our march.

The ground was covered with snow. Our line of march was near the banks of the river. It snowed at intervals; at one time the snow seemed to fall in a mass. Although I was near the main body, I could not see them for the snow. We marched until near dark, when we halted to wait for the rear guard, which had not been seen or heard of since we started.

Finally night came on, and no tidings from the rear. We still waited and waited. Finally it became near ten o'clock, when one of the Volunteers volunteered to go back and see what had become of the missing. He had not been gone long when he came back, on foot, tearing through the brush on the opposite side of the creek, very much excited, and wanted torches brought to show him across the creek, when he would tell all.

Finally he got on our side, almost breathless, and speechless, and afoot. All rushed around him, anxious to hear the trouble. As soon as he could speak, he gasped out that the Indians had massacred all the rear guard. He could hear them exulting on their victory. When asked what had become of his animal, he said he could make better time on foot, so had abandoned it.

The command at once started back on the trail. I was sent ahead with three men to keep two hundred yards ahead of the main body. All the weapons I had was a revolver. (I have often thought since I have learned something of Indian warfare, how helpless I was.) I had not proceeded far before I heard a terrible noise ahead. I soon, however, discovered it proceeded from a lot of drunken muleteers headed by a one-eyed sailor, following along our trail. They could give us no definite information about anyone else. They returned with us to our fires.

[6] According to Frances F. Victor, his name was Greiger. She does not mention that his brother was one of the killed. *Early Indian Wars of Oregon,* 322.

About an hour afterwards Capt. Judah with some more strag-lers came into camp. Judah was so drunk that he had to be lifted from his horse. It seemed that the rear guard had gotten some whisky, and were all drunk, and scattered for at least ten miles back. Every few minutes some person or a pack mule would come straggling in of his own accord. About two o'clock in the morn-ing a mule with the Doctor's and my bedding came straggling. Nobody had anything to eat, and it was very cold and disagree-able, so we spread down our blankets on the snow, feet toward the fire. My boots were so frozen that I could not take them off, so had to turn in with them on.

Some time before daylight our blankets took fire, and in trying to put them out some molten rubber ran over my hand, took the skin off, and gave me a very sore hand. The next day we lay in camp, and parties were sent out and brought in the remainder of our packs and rear guard.

Capt. Judah was sick all day with the delirium tremens. I never heard such blasphemy and obscenity in all my life as I did amongst the Volunteers. The Volunteer who stampeded back into our camp swore he would shoot any persons who said they weren't Indians he heard.

The next morning we started on our march, which still lay up the river and near its bank. We soon came to a mountain torrent that empties into the river. Its bank was fringed with trees on either bank. The spray from the water had frozen to a height of fifteen feet. We had to cut an arch through it so we could pass. We found the dead bodies of the white men frozen, and partly eaten by wolves. The Indians were not very far off in a cave which was at the top of a slope of nearly forty-five degrees, and at the foot of a palisade. The entrance was barricaded with rocks and logs so as to prevent its being taken by a charge. The top of the bluffs was about 100 feet above the cave.

The Regulars were posted at the bottom near the foot of the slope, while the Volunteers were on top of the bluffs. Capt. Gieger, attempting to look over the bluff, was instantly killed by an In-dian's bullet through the brain. Capt. Judah, who was considerable of a demigog, was talking of ordering the Regulars to charge the cave. He being on the sick report, Bonnycastle and I would have to lead the charge. Bonnycastle said alright, if he came out of the charge alright, he would prefer charges against Judah. The charge was not ordered, however.

The next morning I was ordered to proceed to Fort Lane[7] in Rogue River Valley and procure a howitzer to shell the Indians. Doctor Sorrel accompanied me. We rode all that day and until about ten o'clock that night before we came to a house where we could stay all night. In crossing the Siskiyou Mountains, the snow was very light, and at times it was midsides to our horses, and the cold was intense. The next afternoon we reached Fort Lane at the lower end of Rogue River Valley. Capt. A. J. Smith was in command, who concluded he would take his company of the 1st Dragoons and go back with us.

When we reached Capt. Judah's command, we found that officer still sick. Capt. Smith took command, and upon investigation, after trying to shell the cave in vain, found that the Indians were only defending themselves when they killed the white men, that some of the miners had organized an expedition to steal some ponies and squaws, and had made the attack. So he had a parley with the Indians, and drew off, much to the dissatisfaction of the Volunteers, who were anxious to have the Regulars charge the Indians' stronghold that they might come in for some spoils.

The remains of Capt. Gieger were taken back to Cottonwood to be interred, and in the whole population of several hundred people a Bible could not be had to use in performing the burial service. Capt. Smith returned to Fort Lane, and our part of the grand farce returned to our places of abode.

Bonnycastle preferred charges against Capt. Judah, but after much begging on Judah's part, Bonnycastle agreed not to push the charges provided Capt. Judah should transfer out of the company. Judah soon left with a view of a transfer, but after remaining away for some months and failing to accomplish the transfer, returned, and soon after Bonnycastle left, so the matter was finally dropped.

[7] Fort Lane in the Rogue River Valley, Oregon, was established on September 28, 1853, by A. J. Smith, captain of Dragoons. It was near Table Rock, scene of the treaty, and eight miles from Jacksonville. The fort was named after Joseph Lane, territorial governor. It was abandoned in September, 1856, and the troops and stores were moved to Fort Jones. Robert C. Clark, "Military History of Oregon, 1849–59," *Oregon Historical Quarterly*, Vol. XXXVI, No. 2 (March, 1935), 14–51; Division of the Pacific, *Special Order No. 81* (1856).

In those days the Commissary Department kept nothing but the soldier's ration, no deductions were allowed, but we had to pay the original cost, with transportation added. The prices in Yreka were simply beyond our thoughts. My pay was $64. per month, and my mess bill exceeded it. So Bonnycastle, Sorrel, and myself clubbed together and sent to San Francisco for ammunition. In this way we were able to get our shot for 66 cents per pound, and other things in proportion. Sorrel made arrangements for the sale of game in Yreka, and I did most of the hunting. At the end of the month the mess was able to declare dividends. For over a year we never had any meat on our table except game.

I was hunting all my leisure time, so I soon became familiar with all the country within reach of the post. I also used to go hunting with the Indians, and in this way learned something of their habits, as well as those of game. I always had a great passion for hunting, and this was my first opportunity of ever indulging it to any extent.

With the exception of an occasional Indian scare that would send the troops out on short expeditions, nothing of particular note happened during the remainder of 1854. In the fall of that year John B. Hood was assigned to duty with the company, and Bvt 2nd Lieutenant Hood and I hunted a great deal together, and became very intimate. We engaged in ranching together. He sold out on leaving in the spring, and made money, while I held on and lost money.

In the spring of 1855 Lt. Williamson of the Engineers was ordered to explore the Cascade Range of mountains with the view of determining the practicability of building a railroad across it. Lt. H. G. Gibson of the Artillery was to command the escort, which was to be composed of artillery and cavalry. Lt. Hood was to command the cavalry, and I was to be the A.A.Q.M. and A.C.S. of the expedition.[8] Attached to the expedition were two gentle-

[8] A.A.Q.M. and A.C.S.—acting assistant quartermaster and acting commissary of subsistence.

The report of this expedition, written by Lieutenant Henry L. Abbot, is found in "Pacific Railroad Surveys . . . 1854–55," VI, 33 Cong., 2 sess., *House Ex. Doc. 91,* 56–111.

In his letter of transmittal, Lieutenant Abbot said: "Of those who accompanied me when detached from the main command, I feel at liberty to speak in less general terms. Lt. Crook, who was the only officer with me, officially

men from Cleveland, Ohio, Doctors Sterling and Newberry, the former to act as medical officer, while the latter was the naturalist. The whole was to assemble at Fort Reading.[9]

We started out about the last day of July, and crossed over the mountains at Lassen's Butte, and struck the lava beds on the southeastern branch of Pit River, and while traveling down it, Lt. P. H. Sheridan[10] joined us from Reading, and relieved Hood, who had been transferred to the 2nd Cavalry. This was the last time I ever saw Hood, who afterwards became celebrated in the Confederate service.

Our route was down this branch of Pit River to its mouth, then up the main stream to a point some distance above the junction of the west branch, from whence we crossed over to Wright and Tule lakes, both of which had no outlets. The latter had quite a stream running into it, called Lost River. Bordering on the south of this lake are the famous lava beds of Modoc history.[11]

On Lost River is a natural bridge of stone extending across the river, or, in fact, there are two close together. One is horizontal,

---

and personally contributed in a high degree to the success and harmony of the expedition."

The party consisted of Lieutenant R. S. Williamson, Lieutenant Henry L. Abbot, principal assistant, Dr. J. S. Newberry, geologist and botanist, Mr. H. C. Fillebrown, assistant engineer, Dr. E. Sterling, physician and naturalist, Mr. C. D. Anderson, computer, and Mr. John Young, draughtsman. There were also eighteen men under the immediate supervision of Mr. Charles Coleman, packmaster.

The party left Fort Reading on July 28 and returned on November 15, 1855.

[9] Fort Reading was established in May, 1852, by *General Order No. 10*, Division of the Pacific, on Cow Creek, a few miles above "Readings" [ford]. It was a policy of the War Department to name its posts after local geographical points, and therefore the fort was somewhat accidentally named for Major P. B. Reading, who is credited with the first discovery of gold in Shasta and Trinity counties in 1848. The fort was evacuated in May, 1857, and the site abandoned in September, 1866. Joseph H. Jackson, *Anybody's Gold*, 437–39; *Posts, Camps, and Stations File.*

[10] Philip H. Sheridan was Crook's classmate, and they had a lot to talk about. Sheridan gives a short account of his part in the expedition in Chapter III of his *Memoirs*. He joined the party on August 4, and his account of the journey sounds much more hazardous than appears from Crook's description.

[11] In the Modoc War of 1872 to 1873, four companies of Regulars were held at bay by seventy Indians entrenched in the natural fortifications of the lava beds.

and two or three feet under water, while the other is straighter, the upper edge is just out of the water, while the lower part of the bridge is one foot under the water. The two bridges were some few feet apart, and about ten or fifteen feet wide. The strange part is that they are situated in the midst of a sage brush plain, with apparently sand and clay formation.

From Tule Lake we traveled up Williamson's Valley, and part the way up Klamath Marsh, trying to skirt its eastern shore, but finding that impractical, we struck west on an Indian trail which led to a place where the marsh above and below converged to a slough not over 75 yards wide, which we forded with but little difficulty. We now crossed over to the Des Chutes River, where we went into camp until Lt. Williamson explored the Cascade Range for a practicable pass.[12]

All streams in this country, as well as most we had passed from Fort Reading, abounded in trout. Game was plentiful in places. We had a hunter along by the name of Hollinsmith[13] who was to supply the outfit with fresh meat. But either from lack of skill or his timidity to leave the command, he killed but one deer that he brought into camp, but he rode ahead of the column just sufficiently far to scare the game out of reach of those who might have killed some.

From this camp I hunted up in the mountains. I upon one occasion took a couple of the soldiers and went up to the summit on a hunt. It was one of the grandest and most picturesque countries I had ever seen. The summit must have been from twenty to forty miles in breadth, covered with lakes and parks scattered amongst a heavy growth of pine and spruce timber. From one prominence I counted eleven of these lakes, some of which were six or seven miles in length, and almost as wide. Around some of the shores there were beautiful meadows of luxuriant grass.

In some lakes were runs of magnificent trout, which could be had in the greatest quantities just for the catching. In one lake I killed two loons (North American Diver) and shot at a beaver. In

[12] September 3, according to Abbot's report (see n. 8).

[13] Abbot's report says nothing of this mighty hunter. The guide and scout employed by Lieutenant Williamson was called "Old Red," his name given as Bartee. Abbot, on page 59 of his report, says he proved a valuable addition to the party.

another, while walking close to its edge, I heard snorting in the tule which bordered the shore for half a dozen yards, sounding like hogs rooting. Finally I discovered them to be otter. I shot one that measured five feet three inches from tip to tip. Half a dozen others swam out into the clear water at the report of my gun, cocking their eyes up at me, seemed quite tame. I could have killed several others, but had no use for them, the one being all I could carry.

While encamped at one of these lakes, imagining that there was no other human being anywhere in that country, who should drop in on me just before dusk but Lt. Sheridan. He was escorting Lt. Williamson on a side survey, and coming across my trail followed it up and stayed all night with me.[14] We had a grand time together, talking over what we had seen, etc. etc. Soon after he left, I killed a magnificent elk and returned to camp, the meat of which was a godsend to all in camp.

From this camp we moved south, and crossed the Cascade Range of mountains on the old emigrant road down the middle fork of the Willamette River, and followed down the valley of the same name to a point opposite the town of Portland, where we turned off to the east and encamped on the bank of the Columbia River opposite to Fort Vancouver.[15] The river was about three-fourths of a mile wide at this point, of clear blue water. The banks

[14] Lieutenant Williamson was exploring the mountains in the vicinity, while Abbot was on a trip to The Dalles. The entry for September 10 in Abbot's report reads: "We found that Lt. Crook had moved the depot camp to Wy-chus creek." On the eleventh Williamson sent to Crook for more provisions, and this is probably where Sheridan walked in.

[15] Fort Vancouver was located on the north bank of the Columbia River, about 120 miles from its mouth. It was built in 1825 as headquarters for the Hudson's Bay Company, replacing Fort George as the chief western post and was named after Captain Vancouver of the British ship, *Discovery*, which reached the Columbia in 1792.

The Hudson's Bay post flourished until 1845, when a declining fur trade and the advent of American settlers brought about the transfer of the British post to Victoria, on Vancouver Island.

On May 13, 1849, Companies L and M, First Artillery, under Captain J. S. Hathaway, reported at Vancouver and established a camp in the rear of the fort, with permission of the Hudson's Bay Company, calling it Columbia Barracks.

In the fall of 1849 the mounted riflemen under Colonel Loring crossed the continent from Leavenworth to Vancouver; the following spring Hathaway was transferred to Astoria, and Loring assumed command.

were fringed with beautiful trees of spruce, maple, ash, oaks, etc.

Opposite our camp, some three quarters of a mile distant from the other shore, was Fort Vancouver, situated on the upper end of a gentle grassy slope running down to the river bank against a dark background of a dense forest of tall spruce. From this point were visible four high peaks capped with snow all the year round. Upon the whole, it was a grand and picturesque sight.

The artillery part of our escort, having been dismissed after finishing the exploration through the Cascade Range, had returned to Fort Reading, so that Lt. Sheridan and myself, with the cavalry, thirteen in number, were all that was left of the escort.

The Willamette Valley was a magnificent body of land, but was unfortunately settled by a population of mostly old pioneers from Missouri, who came to that country before the spirit of progress had commenced in the East, and consequently were a long ways behind the age. They owned the land in large tracts, mostly 640 acres, would not cultivate it, nor let anyone else.

The Columbia River Indians above the Dalles had just broken out, so Lt. Sheridan with the cavalry was ordered to join the expedition against these Indians. Lt. Williamson had left for San Francisco, so Lt. H. L. Abbot,[16] Williamson's assistant, and myself were now the only officers of the expedition left.

We soon afterwards commenced retracing our steps through the Willamette country on our way to Fort Reading. Nothing of note occurred until we had reached the lower end of the Umpqua Valley, which was separated from the Willamette Valley by a low range of mountains. Just before we reached this point, the Rogue River Indians had broken out, and were supposed to be in

The name Columbia Barracks was changed to Fort Vancouver in 1853, and to Vancouver Barracks in 1879.

During the Civil War the post was a gathering place for Oregon volunteers, and in 1865 it was headquarters of the Department of the Columbia. *Posts, Camps, and Stations File.*

[16] Henry L. Abbot, graduate of the Military Academy in 1854, was perhaps the most versatile character in the annals of the United States Topographical Engineers. He lived to be ninety-six years old, and in the course of his long life he delved into and wrote about almost every major phase of the engineering field, from the thickness of guns to the regulation of rivers.

He related his experiences on the survey in "Reminiscences of the Oregon War of 1855," *Journal of the Military Service Institution of the United States,* Vol. XVL, No. 162 (Nov.–Dec., 1909), 436–42.

the range of mountains forming the southern boundary of that valley.[17]

We arrived at a place called the Six Bits House, a wayside inn.[18] We went into camp near it, where later there came a company of southern Oregon Mounted Volunteers raised for the ostensible purpose of operating against the hostile Indians, and camped near us. When they unsaddled they threw their saddles, bridles and spurs on one pile. The next morning when they went to saddle up the ones who came first found the best. A perfect pandemonium ensued. I thought I had heard obscenity and blasphemy before, but this beat anything I had ever heard.

It seemed that the day previous to our arrival here, Capt. A. J. Smith, 1st Dragoons, in command of Regulars and Volunteers, had had a fight with the Indians some miles southwest of where we were, and if the troops did not get the worst of it, it was a drawn battle, and the troops withdrew to the settlements, and left the Indians monarchs of the woods, and no one knew where they were liable to attack next.

The name of the Capt. of the company at Six Bits House above alluded to was Bowie, a Methodist exhorter.[19] He was a short, stout man. He was left-handed, and wore an old artillery sword about one foot and a half or two feet long. He didn't seem to have any control over his men. After exhorting them for a long time to get ready, probably two-thirds had saddled their horses. He succeeded in getting some of them into line.

He drew his little sword with his left hand, and brandished it over his head, and bawled out, " 'Tenshun the company!" Some answered back, "Go to hell!" while others said, "Hold it, Cap, until I go to the rear," only in not such choice language.

"Now," says he, "at the command 'prepare to mount,' catch

---

[17] For Rogue River War, see Appendix, I, pages 303–304.

[18] Wolf Creek Tavern was known in 1855 as Six Bits House, apparently because it cost six bits to stay overnight—two bits each for supper, bed, and breakfast. Robert W. Sawyer, "Abbot Railroad Surveys," *Oregon Historical Quarterly*, Vol. XXXIII, No. 2 (June, 1932), 126.

[19] The name of this exhorter is doubtful. It is most likely Laban Buoy, captain of Company B, Second Regiment of California Mounted Volunteers. The name appears in the muster rolls of Company B as having enlisted October 23 at Eugene City. Buoy resigned March 20, 1856. Harvey Robbins, "Journal of the Rogue River War, 1855," *Oregon Historical Quarterly*, Vol. XXXIV, No. 4 (December, 1933), 345–58.

your horses by the bridle with your left hand, put your foot in the stirrup, and mount." Suiting the action to the word, in attempting to mount, his foot slipped out of the stirrup and his chin struck the pommel of the saddle and his corporosity shook like a bag of jelly. He looked out at some of the men who were on their horses, when he said, "That's right boys, get up thar."

He finally succeeded in getting the majority of his men in line, and he harangued them thusly, drawing his little sword in his left hand, and brandishing it over his head, " 'Tenshun the company! Now boys, the eyes of your country is upon you! The enemy has had a whole day's rest, and we may expect to have a fight at any time and any place," and a lot more stuff that I don't now recollect.

We finally got under way, and a motlier crew has never been seen since old Falstaff's time. They were mounted on horses and mules of all sizes and degrees, some wore plug hats, and others caps; all were mostly armed with the old-fashioned squirrel rifles. The captain rode at the head of his company, while I brought up at the rear.

We had not proceeded far before we came to a thicket where the Indians could ambush us and inflict great damage on us without our injuring them in return. The captain halted the company, and said, " 'Tenshun the company!" drew his sword as before, "Now, boys, look well to your caps. Guns on right shoulder! Keep your eyes well about you! Look behind every stump and every tree! You may be attacked at any moment, and in case of attack be prepared to resist the attackment!" The men would answer back with some obscenity.

I made the remark that if we were attacked, I would rather be in front than in rear, as there I might have some show of getting away from the Indians, but in rear I should certainly be trod to death. The joke was not particularly relished by the cavalier who heard it. No Indians showed themselves, and we passed unmolested.

We had not proceeded far until we met Capt. Smith, who had returned from the Hungry Hill fight with his wounded. There I met old Dutch Kautz for the first time since we parted in 1852 in San Francisco. It seemed he had started out from Fort Orford[20]

[20] Fort Orford was situated at the head of Trichnor Bay, about ten miles above the mouth of Rogue River. It was established on September 14, 1851,

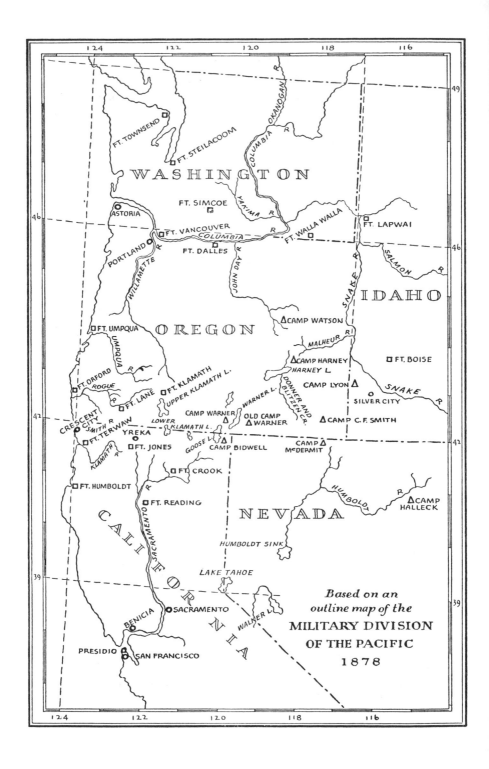

Based on an
outline map of the
**MILITARY DIVISION
OF THE PACIFIC
1878**

to find a road to the Rogue River country. He met some Indians in the woods, and saluted them with compliments of the season, when they answered his salute with a volley at close range. One ball struck him in the chest, and would certainly have killed him but for two books he had in his pocket.[21] The ball struck the corner of one, going through it, but was stopped by the other, knocking him down. The soldiers started to run, saying the Lieutenant was killed, but he jumped up and prevented the stampede. As it was a thick, bushy country he had no trouble in getting away. Kautz came into Fort Lane and reported the whole affair to Capt. Smith, who went out with some Regulars and was joined by some Volunteers.[22]

The next morning our original party left the soldiers, and we continued our journey toward Rogue River Valley. Before getting there, we passed the smoldering ruins of several houses that had been burned by the Indians, most of the inhabitants killed, and in one instance a family had been burned, cattle and hogs had been shot down by the Indians. The chickens were unmolested, but

---

by troops transferred from Astoria. During the Rogue River War, the post was important, being close to the scene of operations, but afterwards there was no need for it, and it was evacuated per order of July 18, 1856. William G. Ledbetter, *Military History of the Oregon Country*, 80; *Posts, Camps, and Stations File*.

21 Victor says he was knocked down by sheer fright, and was the object of much amusement on the part of the Volunteers who heard of it.

22 "On his way to Fort Lane, and within forty-five miles of that place [Lieutenant Kautz] accidentally came upon a hostile band of Indians, who attacked him, and killed two of his men, and wounded another and himself. He made good his retreat to Bates Station, where he arrived the 25th of October.

"Leaving his men there, he proceeded to Fort Lane for re-enforcements. Bvt. Maj. E. H. Fitzgerald, with sixty men of that post was ordered to proceed against the Indians, but on arriving at the ground he found them so safely posted that it would have been useless to make an attack upon them with his command.

"After reporting these circumstances to the commanding officer at Fort Lane, Capt. Andrew J. Smith, the whole of the force at that post, about one hundred and twenty men, and some two hundred and twenty-five Volunteers were got in readiness, and marched against the Indians. They arrived on the grounds on the thirtieth of October, and after fighting the Indians for nearly two days, and finding it impossible to dislodge them gave up the attack. They intended making another effort on the ninth of this month."

This was the Battle of Hungry Hill. Captain Smith lost eleven killed and eighteen wounded. Rodney Glisan, *Journal of Army Life*, 263.

were as wild as quail already; they seemed to realize that something was wrong, and they had no friends.

When we arrived at Jacksonville, Oregon, I learned that Doctor Sorrel had been ordered east, and, anxious to see him before his departure, I rode to Yreka in one day, sixty-five miles, on the same mule I had ridden on the entire expedition. He had left, however, so I did not get to see him. I then went to Fort Reading, and closed up my expeditionary accounts, after which I returned to Fort Jones, remaining there through the winter.

II
ROGUE RIVER
WAR

3. *This was my first Indian*

IN MARCH, 1856, I was ordered in command of Company "E," Capt.
Judah's (better known as "The Forty Thieves"), to proceed to
Fort Lane, near Jacksonville, Oregon, and report to Capt. A. J.
Smith for duty against the hostile Indians.

Not all of the Rogue River Indians were hostile; Old Sam's and
Limpy's bands were friendly. These Indians were ordered to be
removed to the Yamhill reservation, far down in the Willamette
Valley. These Indians were very loath to leave their country and
go to a land they knew nothing of. There was great weeping and
wailing when the time came for them to go. I was to assist in their
removal. Lt. W. B. Hazen was also of the escort.

After we had proceeded to near Imperial Canyon, I was ordered
to return to Fort Lane. Just before I left, one morning as we were
going to start, some white men slipped up in the brush, and shot
one of the Indians in cold blood. I followed their trail for several
miles, but had to give up the pursuit as useless.

Soon after my return to the fort, I was taken sick with acute
rheumatism in the left shoulder and the erysipelas in the left arm.
I don't see how it was possible for me to have suffered more and
lived. So when the expedition left a few days afterwards to operate
against the hostiles, I was unable to accompany it. Lt. N. B.
Sweitzer, 1st Dragoons, was assigned to the command of my company.

Lt. Underwood, who had accompanied the Indians to the
Yamhill reservation, returned three days after I was taken sick. So
much had I fallen off from my suffering that he did not recognize
me. The medical officer at the post was a contract doctor, who

with the commanding officer, was drunk the whole blessed time. My malady did not seem to abate in the least. I took his medicine for some time, until I saw he took no interest in my case, and I lost all confidence in him.

My arm had shrunk away to mere skin and bones, I had lost all use or control of it. An abscess had just been lanced which extended from just above the elbow to the shoulder. The commanding officer came into the room one day, and said, "Look here, old fellow, it won't do to see you die in this way. Let's send to the hospital and get some medical books and read up on your case."

We found one book that said brandy was good to counteract the poison of erysipelas, but it was bad for rheumatism. But on the grounds it was good for one of the diseases, it was prescribed, and as long as it lasted he paid me frequent visits.

Also, a squaw came into my room one day, and wanted to know whom I was going to give my things to when I died, and, knowing what shrewd observers they were, it made me think all the more seriously of my case. So I finally took my own case in hand, and commenced dosing with calomel and jalap, until my system began to show healthy symptoms, when I would several times during the day take a pitcher of cold water and pour it on my shoulder, until the disease gradually left my system altogether.[1]

Strange to say, I have never had scarcely an ache or pain since, with the exception of twice when I was wounded, afterwards erysipelas showed itself. My arm, however, was left weak and lame, and so stiff that I could not get my hand to my head for nearly a year afterwards. I had also used so much morphine that it was some time before I could sleep well without it. I was laid up about one month, but it seemed an age. I was strong and healthy, and my system could throw off any reasonable attack on it.

Sick as I was, I never went to bed except at night. My quarters were next to the commanding officer's, and I was frequently kept awake by their orgies, which sometimes would last all night. One night it was pitch dark when someone rode up, and hollered, "Hello!" The commanding officer rushed out of his house, and

---

[1] Crook had poor luck with doctors in general. The "contract doctor" was a civilian doctor serving temporarily in the military service.

wanted to know what he meant by telling him to "go to hell" in his own house.

It was useless for the poor fellow to disclaim any disrespect, or deny the soft impeachment. The commanding officer yelled out for the Sergeant of the Guard, whereupon the party fled. There was an immense mudhole in the rear of the quarters in the direction of his retreat. I heard something sound like striking soft mud with a clapboard as one of them was thrown from his horse in the mudhole. It turned out afterwards that it was a party of Volunteers who were also drunk and had lost their way.

Shortly after my recovery I was ordered to proceed down Rogue River with a company of 3rd Artillery in command of Lt. Ransom to join Capt. A. J. Smith, to take command of my company. No one knew their exact whereabouts, but I was expected to hunt them up. About this time Capt. Smith had a fight with the hostiles, and came very near losing his entire command. Over two-thirds of my company in command of Lt. Sweitzer were killed and wounded in the fight.[2]

We proceeded down the river under a guide by the name of Mike Bushey.[3] All of us were on foot. The trail was fearfully rough in places, and the hot, broiling sun made the climbing of the steep mountain extremely hard. I made several side scouts with one or two men, looking for signs of the command or of Indians.

While on the top of a high mountain near the mouth of the Illinois River, I was out hunting that afternoon when I came on a fresh trail of Indians. The country was brushy, and the ravines were steep over which the trail led. I followed for some time. It became very fresh, and although I fully realized the danger I was in, I could not resist the temptation.

While following them through a thick, brushy ravine, just the place of all others I didn't want to see them, I saw a black pair of eyes peering at me through the brush. I lost no time in getting up to them, and much to my delight discovered it to be a small party of squaws and children. They said they had become separated

[2] This fight took place on May 27 and 28, 1856. Hubert H. Bancroft, *History of Oregon*, II, 407–409.

[3] Mike was a second lieutenant in the Southern Battalion, Oregon Volunteers in 1855, and a captain by February, 1856. Victor, *Early Indian Wars of Oregon*, 360, 389.

from their people, and that their people had left the country with the soldiers, etc. etc. I took them into camp.

The next morning we marched down a steep mountain to the junction of the Illinois with the Rogue River. We could see no fresh signs, but everything pointed to the fact that both troops and Indians had moved down the river at some time previous, together, which corroborated the statement made by the squaws. From here we retraced our steps back to Fort Lane, where we got the information that the Indians had surrendered and gone with the troops to Port Orford to the Yamhill reservation,[4] where the remainder of them were. The squaws were taken to Fort Lane, and afterwards were sent to join the remainder of their people.

I was promoted 1st Lieutenant March 11, to Company "D" vice Underwood, promoted Captain. My company now being stationed at Fort Jones, I was again stationed there.

During the winter 1856–57, the Indians on Pit River massacred all the white settlers living in Pit River Valley, and destroyed all their property.[5] This valley was situated about 100 miles east of Yreka, with a high range of mountains intervening. As the snow in these mountains was very deep, the news of this massacre did not reach Yreka until some time after it had occurred. Then someone happened to go over on snowshoes.

There was a company of Volunteers raised in Yreka and crossed

[4] The Yamhill, also called the Grande Ronde reservation, was located in a valley on the western border of Yamhill and Polk counties. It comprised about 6,000 acres, and was purchased for $35,000.

The Indians who agreed to move gave up their arms on May 30, and some were taken to the reservation overland, via Fort Lane, while others were marched to Fort Orford, and sent up the coast by steamer.

Lieutenant Sheridan relieved Lieutenant Hazen of command of the reservation, and supervised the building of Fort Yamhill. Philip H. Sheridan, *Personal Memoirs*, 91–93.

[5] The Yreka *Union* published an extra February 7, 1857, reporting "Another Indian Tragedy," "Pit River Massacre," "Two Ferries, and All the Houses on the River Destroyed," "Messrs. H. A. Lockhart, Daniel Bryant, S. R. Rogers,—Boles, and a German named John Probably Killed," "About 30 Head of Cattle Killed."

The two-column story reads that G. S. Whitney and N. D. Fowler started for the ferry from Yreka on January 25. They found the evidences of the Indian depredations, and believed Lockhart was killed shortly after Christmas, 1856. The Lockharts were supposed to have founded Yreka in 1851.

over into that country about the first of March. After operating against these Indians for a month or so, it returned without any results. It was said that they were worsted in a couple of engagements they had with the Indians, but of the truth of this I know nothing.

About the middle of May Capt. Judah, from Fort Jones, started out for the scene of trouble with his company, "E" (Forty Thieves),[6] and my company, "D." Even at that late date the snow was in drifts in places from ten to fifteen feet deep. During the early morning this snow was sufficiently hard to bear up our wagons, but later it would become so soft that the wheels would go down until further progress was arrested by the beds.

After crossing the main divide, our route lay close under Shasta Butte. The melting snow would come down in rivulets during the afternoon, and late at night, but in the mornings all would be dry, and the atmosphere would be more or less frosty.

We proceeded to Lockheart's Ferry, just below the junction of the two forks of Pit River.[7] This ferry was kept by Sam Lockheart. His twin brother, Harry, was one of the unfortunates of the winter before, and as a matter of course, Sam was very bitter, and declared his intentions of killing all the Indians that he saw. He had already killed several, and had the reputation of being a desperate man. He sometime years afterward was killed in Silver City, Idaho.

North of the ferry a couple of miles was a lake formed of large springs, the outlet from which was Fall River, by long ways the larger of the two forks. The water was so clear in these springs that it was difficult to tell where the atmosphere left off and the water commenced. There was notably one spring that must have run 2,000 miner's inches,[8] that was forty-five feet deep, and so clear

---

[6] The soldiers of the regular army were not very popular with many elements of the frontier. The term "forty thieves" might have been the result of a tendency on the part of all professional soldiers to live off the country. No history of the Fourth Infantry offers an explanation of the term, or mentions it, for that matter.

[7] Judah left Fort Jones for the scene of the massacre with sixty-five men, May 18, 1857. National Archives, Commanding Officer, Company E, Fourth Infantry to Adjutant General, Division of the Pacific, May 17, 1857.

[8] A miner's inch is the discharge of water through an orifice one inch square under a head which varies locally. A California miner's inch was .187 gallons per second.

that the smallest trout could be seen at its bottom with ease. This water was ice cold, and full of magnificent trout. I have always had an idea that Rhett or Tule Lake of Modoc fame was the source from which these springs came, as they were situated at the foot, while Rhett Lake was at the head of the lava beds.

Around this lake formed by the springs there was a large area of land covered with tule, or bull rushes. From a prominence just above the ferry we could see a number of Indians weaving about in this tule, their black heads forming a striking contrast with the surrounding green tule. Capt. Judah informed me that he was going to make an attack on the Indians in the tule the next morning, that he expected to lose a number of men, etc. etc. (All of which I have learned to be the merest balderdash.)

The next morning we crossed Fall River, and proceeded to the tules above mentioned. We found the water in the tule from one to two feet deep, covering a hundred acres or more, the upper end of which bordered the lake. I went out into the tule with the men, while Judah remained on the outside. The tule was nearly as high as my head, while some was higher. I traversed that swamp in all directions, but could see neither Indian nor any signs. The nature of the tule and the water precluded leaving any sign.

Sometimes I could see them off at a distance, but by the time I could get there I could see nothing of them. Finally we gave up the search as useless, and returned to camp, to be tantalized by seeing plenty of Indians in the tule. After lying in camp a day or so, Capt. Judah projected an expedition to the east of the river.

I have forgotten to mention that both companies were mounted on mules, with improvised rigging, some with ropes, and others with equally, if not worse, makeshifts to fasten the saddles on the mules, and all did not have cruppers. It was as good as a circus to see us when we left Fort Jones. Many of our men were drunk, including our commander. Many of the mules were wild, and had not been accustomed to being ridden, while the soldiers generally were poor riders. The air was full of soldiers after the command was given to mount, and for the next two days stragglers were still overtaking the command.

Well, we crossed to the ferry, and commenced our journey to some place where we hoped to find the Indians not so wily. We had no guide who knew any more of the country than we did.

Judah with his company took the lead, while I brought up the rear.

After we had traveled for a couple of days without seeing any Indians, we came to the edge of a park with timber on the opposite side. Probably this park was three-quarters of a mile wide. In the center of it was a ridge about as high as our heads, and in the opposite woods and about on a level with this ridge were a couple of old wick-a-ups.[9] There were some crows walking along the ridge opposite these wick-a-ups, so, looking from our standpoint, they were projected about the doors of the wick-a-ups. Judah announced them to be Indians.

He asked his First Sergeant if they were not Indians. His sergeant was a big Irishman by the name of McCarty, who said, "Yes, Captain, I see their children dancing 'firheust' the door."

I saw perfectly plainly what it was, but not being asked, I ventured no suggestions, as he was in the habit of snubbing persons for volunteering suggestions, and there was not the best of terms between us, for I had seen enough of him to realize fully what an unmitigated fraud he was.

So he ordered the charge, taking the lead with his company. The ground was rough, and in places rocky. I could only see what was in front of me, but that was fun enough for one day to see his men tumbling off their mules in the most ludicrous manner. Finally we reached the wick-a-ups, and found them to have been deserted for months, and no sign of any Indians.

It was as good as a circus to look back over the field he crossed to see the men "hors-de-combat," riderless mules running in all directions, men coming, limping, some with their guns, but others carrying their saddles. Capt. Judah had that look of cool impudence which he was such a master of, and I could never make up my mind whether he knew better or not.

We gathered up our demoralized army, and marched back to the ferry. Capt. Judah had just been married the second time, and was anxious to get back to his bride. Soon after getting back to our old camp, he returned to Fort Jones, leaving me with only sixteen men of my company to accomplish what he had failed to

9 The popular name for the bush shelter or mat-covered house of the Paiutes, Apaches, and other tribes of Nevada, Arizona, and adjacent regions. Crook calls almost all Indian houses by that name, probably because of his long association with the Apaches. It is frequently spelled "wickiup."

do with his two companies. He reported upon his return to Fort Jones that there were no Indians in the country, etc. etc.[10]

I fully realized the situation, and knew that there were plenty of Indians, and that my only show was to find where the Indians were, without their knowledge, and to attack them by surprise. I furthermore was satisfied that they watched our movements all the time, and kept out of our way. I also reasoned that seeing Capt. Judah going out of the country with the most of the troops, they would be off their guard.

I had by this time learned enough about Indian craft to have confidence in my being able to hold my own with them, so, shortly after Judah left, I took two soldiers and went off on a scout to see if I couldn't locate some of their camps. I went in a southeasterly direction from the ferry, and on the second day I came on to a small rancheria. Some of the Indians wanted to talk with me, but I would not let them approach me. Telling them I was going to Yreka, of which they seemed to know the name, I was in hopes of throwing them off their guard, and I went back to camp and got all my men.

I left my camp after dark so we would not be seen. I reached the vicinity of the rancheria next day sometime, and lay concealed all that day. Sometime during the night we left camp, intending to surround the Indians just at daylight next morning. The guide, Dick Pugh, and I went ahead to locate the rancheria, while the sergeant was to follow with the company.

By some mistake we became separated, so all that night was spent in hunting each other. The next morning we found each other in the same camp we had left the night previous. So the next night we again moved close to the rancheria, and surrounded

---

[10] On May 27, at the camp on Pit River, Judah instructed Crook as follows: "You are detailed to remain at this camp with twenty-five men of your company for the purpose of protecting travel upon the wagon road between Shasta and Yreka, as well as the ferry at this point.

"You will make occasional scouts between Bear River and Hat Creek station, or such other points as your judgment may dictate, or necessity require, taking care to leave during your absence a small force for the protection of the ferry.

"You will hold yourself bound under this order until countermanded by, or further orders are received from the Headquarters of the Department or myself." National Archives, Commanding Officer, Company E, Fourth Infantry to Commanding Officer, Company D, Fourth Infantry, May 27, 1857.

it by daylight next morning, but all were gone. Just when they had left I could not tell, as a heavy rainstorm had obliterated all sign.

I then sent the company with the guide under a low range of bluffs, while I rode out a little to the left to examine a dim trail I had seen on my recent scout. I had not proceeded far before I saw a squaw track which had just been made. It had doubled on its track, and was on a run, evidently having either seen me or the command. I followed it in hopes of capturing her to get information as to the whereabouts of her people. I soon saw several other tracks all running in the same direction, and also saw a lot of plunder abandoned by them. Directly saw some buck tracks. By this time I could follow them at a gallop.

The chase had now become so exciting that I thought but little of the danger. Soon I saw the Indians running ahead of me. I rode up to a buck, dismounted, and wounded him, and remounted, and killed him with my pistol.

Just then the Indians rose up all about me, and came towards me with frightful yells, letting fly a shower of arrows at me. I had an old muzzle-loading rifle which was now empty, and one barrel of my pistol had snapped. I thought discretion the better part of valor, so I put spurs to my horse, and ran out of the only opening left, about 100 yards, and a big Indian, seemed to me about ten feet high, was running his best to close this up. He had his hair tucked back of his ears, which gave him a particularly ferocious look. His arrows flew all around me with such a velocity that they did not appear over a couple of inches long.

I must have run a couple of miles before I found the command. They being under the bluff had heard nothing. We at once returned to where I had left the Indians, but they had all fled except one old squaw who was lying beside the dead buck I had killed. This was my first Indian.

After a fruitless effort to get some information from the squaw, we followed the tracks of the fleeing Indians until we saw that they had scattered, and were going into some low mountains, when we abandoned pursuit.

We passed over a barren strip of country where a hailstorm had just been. It was so severe that the bark of trees lying down had been beaten off. The ground was covered with pine leaves, and the soft ground was full of holes an inch deep, that I could stick my thumb in where the hail had driven in and melted.

The Indians in this section of the country having been aroused, I thought it useless to stay out any longer, so returned to camp at the ferry, and in a few days took ten men and made a scout to the north of the ferry.

Some miles above the ferry the river cañons for about nine miles, the cañon being very high, and, in fact, it was what is called a box cañon for most of this distance. It afforded good protection to the Indians. The old emigrant road passed near this place, and it was always considered very dangerous, and it was to this place I betook myself in hopes of finding some of the Indians.

We skirted along the right bank of the cañon, which was very deep and precipitous, and very rough, with large blocks of detached rocks lying along the sides where the slope was rough enough to furnish them a resting place. There were but four places where we could get down to the river, even on foot.

All of a sudden, as we turned a sharp bend in the bluff, we saw a camp of Indians down at the water's edge. They saw us at the same time, and commenced scurrying, some running up, and some down, while others swam across the river. I at once dismounted, and, finding a dim trail close by descending down the precipice, I at once commenced its descent with all possible speed, so as to get within shooting distance of them. I saw a buck swimming with his bow and arrows and wolf robe held above his head. I aimed at the edge of the water. At the crack of the rifle he sank, and the robe and weapons floated down the stream.

I at once commenced reloading my old muzzle loader, when the guide at the tops of the bluffs yelled, "Look out for the arrows!" I looked up, and saw the air apparently full of them. Almost simultaneously one hit me in the right hip. When I jerked it out the head remained in my leg, where it remains still.[11] There were a couple of inches of blood on the shaft of the arrow when I pulled it out. The Indians doing the firing were some who had previously swum across, and had secreted themselves in the rocks. They set up a yell when I was hit.

I at once commenced the ascent through a shower of arrows.

11 Crook carried this arrow to the grave with him.

The ascent was so steep that I had to pull myself up by catching hold of bunches of grass, rocks, and such things as I could get hold of. In one bunch of grass I caught hold of two arrows that had been shot at me. The wonder was that I was not hit oftener. By the time I reached the top the perspiration stood out on me in large drops, and I was deathly sick.

As soon as I was able, we returned to our camp at the ferry. I had to ride on horseback and suffered most excruciating pain during the journey. When I reached camp, my groin was all green.

The nearest doctor was at Fort Jones, 120 miles distant, but I was in hopes I could get along without having to send for the doctor, fearing that I would be relieved, as Capt. Judah was inimical to me, and if he found out that I preferred being in the field to Fort Jones, he would certainly order me back, for that was just about his caliber.

I stood it for a couple of days, but my leg got so much worse that I sent Dick Pugh in to Fort Jones after the doctor. When the news of my being wounded reached Fort Jones, much excitement prevailed. The whole command was ordered out, and as usual they got drunk, Judah included, who fell by the wayside, and Lt. Hiram Dryer, and Dr. C. C. Kearney with all the available men came out.[12]

By the time they reached me I was a little better, but the doctor saw nothing to do except let things take their course. The doctor thought the arrow might have been poisoned, as these Indians were noted for using poison in their arrows.[13]

They would poison them in this way: They would catch a rattlesnake, and when they would kill a deer or an antelope, they would take the fresh liver, and let the rattlesnake bite it until it would get full of poison. Then they would run the shafts of the arrows through it. On the shafts were small grooves to hold the poison. Under the most favorable circumstances this poison would retain its strength about one month, but during moist weather it would not last over a few days.

[12] The wound was received June 10, and on June 12 Crook wrote for a doctor, or "someone to extract the flint."

[13] Kroeber describes the same method of poisoning arrows and adds that "the septic effect of such a preparation is likely to have been much greater than the toxic." *Handbook of the Indians of California*, 417.

4. *We charged right in their midst*

I WAS WOUNDED on the tenth of June. So hearty was my system that on the 27th, when the Indians made a raid on some traders and ran off a lot of stock, I managed to mount my horse and follow them. This trail led into the lava beds and west of the lake. Although there were a good many head of cattle, it was difficult to follow their trail in the lava.

This lava had evidently been in a liquid state when it was poured over the country, and in cooling it was forced up in all conceivable shapes. There were fissures in it from ten to fifteen feet across the top that would extend a couple or more miles long. These fissures were so deep that their bottoms could not be seen. A rock thrown down them would almost invariably plunk into water at a depth of from fifty to sixty feet.

No one but an Indian could have driven those cattle through this country, for in addition to the rough character of these rocks, there was a thick undergrowth of brush growing out of the crevices in the rocks where a sufficient amount of earth had collected to support them. While driving by a small, wedge-shaped fissure, a large ox had fallen into it with its feet downward. The Indians had killed it, and disemboweled it through the back, and went on with the balance, evidently intending to come back for the meat later.

Owing to the difficulty of following the trail, and noticing a large mountain, I took a straight course for the mountain, believing that to be their destination. I had not traveled far before we struck a soft piece of ground running nearly in the direction I wanted to go. Finding a trail running through it, I followed it, and had not gone very far before I saw tracks running into it. Judging from the deep impressions their feet made on the soft ground, they were carrying heavy loads.

I at once concluded they had butchered the cattle, and were packing their meat to their camp. Shortly I came to a small pond near the foot of the mountain, where they had encamped the night before. We counted forty-one campfires, with plenty of evidences of their having been eating beef.

Now being well satisfied that their camp was not far off, I returned to my camp. Lt. Dryer and the Doctor were anxious to return to their flesh pots, and I assured them that I would not need their services. So they returned, leaving me again in command. Dryer very kindly left me enough of my company to give me thirty-three men all told, so the next morning I took all my men except one man, whom I left to keep camp, and proceeded to the pond where I had seen the Indian fires.

Upon my arrival there, no Indians had been there since I had left it two days before. I scouted around considerable, but could find no fresh sign. At night I took one man, and went up the side of the mountain, and climbed a tree where I could overlook the lava beds, but could see nothing.

So next morning I packed up, and marched in a northerly direction along the base of the mountain, pretending that I was going to leave the country. After getting in camp I took my gun and prospected for signs up the side of the mountain. I discovered where an Indian had been watching us, so next morning I ascended the mountain in the direction of my previous day's march, but instead of crossing the range when I got to the summit, I turned southward, and marched parallel to my march of yesterday.

We killed two Indians on our march of two days. I killed one, and the soldiers the other, but the mountain was thrusted, so that our march was obstructed from view. We slipped down the side of the mountain, and camped in a ravine not far from the pond and overlooking the lava beds. That evening it rained a little, so that smoke would hang close to camp. I forbade fires till after dark, when they could be made out of sight. Just before dusk I was rewarded by seeing smoke out in the lava beds, about three or four miles distant. The night was dark, and the country ahead of me was so rough that it was useless to try to get close to them before daylight, so all was prepared to leave at daylight the next morning.

In the morning I left two men to guard the mules and camp, and as soon as we could see, we took up our line of march. I led the way. As soon as we got into the lava beds, we had to be guided by direction entirely, as the brush was too thick to see fifty yards ahead, and the whole bed was comparatively level for miles and miles.

The rain the evening before had softened the brush and leaves, so we made comparatively little noise. We started up several fine deer on our way. All of a sudden we came in sight of their outpost, not over fifty yards ahead, in the shape of an Indian who was busy making something, sitting with his head close to his knees. Several men raised their guns to shoot, but I stopped them. We could see the smoke from the rancheria not over one-fourth of a mile distant.

I at once divided my men into three squads, a sergeant and two men to go around to the left, and another sergeant and nine men to go around to the right, to keep out of sight of the Indians, to join and make the attack from the opposite direction from us. I would charge with the remaining ten men, and meet the Indians fleeing away from the attacking party. In the meantime, I detailed one of my men to keep a watch on the sentinel, and to shoot him immediately upon hearing the shots at the rancheria.

After the flanking parties got well under way, the sentinel saw them, and thinking he had not been seen, crawfished off into some brush near at hand. The soldier went up close to him, so as to prevent his escape. Seeing the movements of this soldier satsified the Indian that he was discovered. He came up to the soldier, at the same time giving up his bows and arrows, and commenced explaining what a good Indian he was, that the Indians who were bad and stole the cattle, etc., etc., lived way east.

When he gave himself up, I sent a second soldier to tell the other not to shoot him, but just as he reached him, firing commenced at the rancheria. Not knowing what the second soldier's orders were, he shot the Indian through the head. It so surprised the second soldier that he was sure he was shot.

We then commenced our charge toward the firing. We met the Indians piling out of the rancheria, running from the attack of the other two parties. They were all yelling, women, children, and all. Bucks were imitating wild beast "war whoops," and a worse pandemonium I never saw before or since. We met them face to face, so close that we could see the whites of each other's eyes. The yelling and screeching and all taken together made my hair fairly stand on end.

GENERAL GEORGE CROOK
about 1865

From a photograph by Brady
Courtesy National Archives

GENERAL GEORGE CROOK
about 1865

We killed a great many, and after the main fight was over, we hunted some reserved ground that we knew had Indians hidden. By deploying as skirmishers, and shooting them as they broke cover, we got them. One or two faced us, and made a manly fight, while others would attempt to run. There was but one squaw killed.

The country was rougher than I supposed it could possibly be. The lava in cooling was thrown up in all imaginable shapes, contorted, leaving cores, fissures, and little promontories, looking as if the molten lava had been forced through a sieve and cooled in that shape. In walking over it, some of it would sound like walking over sheets of cast iron, and all was rough as a rasp. Then imagine all this covered over with a thick growth of scrubby juniper pinion, with underbrush. There was one place where a hundred Indians could have hid within three quarters of an acre, and not one of them could have been seen.

Their camp was full of beef, leaving no doubt of their being the guilty parties. Although they left everything in camp, we found nothing of value. After the fight the men searched all around. In the vicinity of the fight they found nothing except women and children. Sometimes they would find three or four in a hole seemingly not large enough to hold one. We took some of them with us to camp, giving them something to eat. Next morning when we left, they were turned loose. To give some idea of the roughness of that lava, some of the men went into the fight with new shoes on, and came out of it barefooted.

This fight occurred on the second of July, 1857.

The men were anxious to have a fight on the Fourth, but we failed to find the subject, although we came near having another fight a few days afterwards as we ran across a buck. In killing him, the reports of our guns alarmed quite a village not far off, who made their escape.

Having alarmed this whole country, we returned to camp. After refitting, we started again on another scout, further to the north and east. We found nothing in the country over which our previous scout was made.

After almost giving up all hope of finding any Indians on this trip, I came across a single Indian track which had just been made. After following it some six or eight miles, it led into a beautiful valley shut in on the north and east by a walled bluff of rocks. By the time it reached the valley, more tracks had joined the one, and, suspecting their camp was not far off, we went into camp at a little spring. I went ahead to a bluff that overlooked the valley, and after watching for some time, I saw some Indians ahead several miles, and from their actions I was satisfied their camp was not far off.

So at midnight that night we got breakfast, packed up, and started for the place where we saw the Indians. Their camp was under a bluff just on the edge of a valley. To fence them in the valley, we went up on the bluffs, so as to get between them and the rough country to the west. We got on the bluff just after day-break, and as we were approaching its edge, an Indian popped up his head, and gave the alarm.

There must have been at least 500 of them, all told. The grass on the valley gave it a straw color, so the contrast of these black Indians scattering over it looked like so many crows, and all of them yelling at the tops of their lungs.

The bluffs were precipitous and rocky, and it took some time for us to get down, by which time the Indians were some distance out in the valley, and scattered in all directions, running at the top of their speed. We were armed with the old Yaeger, or Mississippi rifle, a muzzle loader. The bullet used was the Minnie ball, with a hollow base.[1] I ordered the men to scatter, and each to take his Indian.

I had killed one, when I saw one of the soldiers shooting at an Indian with one of those old-fashioned "Allens pepper boxes,"[2] having discharged his rifle, and keeping his mule between himself and the Indian, with the latter closing in on him. I had just finished

---

[1] The Yaeger [also Yager, Jaeger, Yeger, etc.] was the regulation model 1841 rifle, the first United States Infantry rifle with a percussion lock. It was also known as the Harper's Ferry rifle and the Mississippi rifle, the latter because of its wide use for big-game hunting and Indian shooting in the West.

The Minie bullet was designed with a hollow base in which an iron cup was inserted. The impact of discharge would expand the base of the bullet to fit the grooves in the rifle. Charles W. Sawyer, *Our Rifles,* 140–43.

[2] "Pepper boxes" was a term applied to the multi-barreled hand weapons which preceded Colt's revolver, and were later manufactured by many companies when Colt's patent prevented pistol manufacture. This model was probably produced by the Ethan Allen Company, Worcester, Massachusetts. Charles W. Sawyer, *The Revolver,* 10.

loading my gun when I saw this performance, and saw that the Indian would close in on the soldier in a few moments more unless assistance was given him. So I at once mounted, and put spurs to my horse, and when I had gotten within one hundred yards of them, the Indian, evidently judging that my rifle was loaded, left the soldier, and came at me.

I dismounted and ran ahead, so he would not shoot my horse, to within sixty yards of him. He was half bending and half squatting, with his breast towards me, jumping first to one side, and then to the other, evidently trying to draw my fire, keeping an arrow pointed at me all this time. (This is a position they take when they dodge arrows, which they will do for a small sum.)

He was singing his death song. I took a rest on my knee, and, moving my rifle from one side to the other, following his movements, I got a good aim, when I pulled the trigger, and broke his back. In this condition, while lying on the ground, he shot five arrows into the soldier's mule, three of them going through the saddle and three thicknesses of blankets into the mule before I could kill him with my pistol.

I then loaded and put spurs to my horse, and overtook another Indian who was just making his escape into the foothills to the south, and shot him. It was difficult to tell how many Indians were killed. By the greatest piece of good fortune we had no casualties on our side, although some of our guns were rendered useless by the base of the ball becoming detached and remaining in the gun.

We all rallied at this village, and destroyed what plunder we found. We found large quantities of grasshoppers being dried by them for their winter supply. They caught the grasshoppers by setting fire to the grass, and in that way would burn off their legs.

This fight took place on the twenty-seventh day of July.

Having now gotten all the Indians in this section of the country on the alert, we returned to our camp above the ferry, which I had moved to the west. While on our way back, one day we discovered some Indians in swimming. I drew my mules up in line and dismounted, so that they would not make a noise, and left a couple of men to guard them while the remainder of us started in to surround the Indians, the country being too rough to use our animals. All of a sudden, and without any provocation, a mule we called "Bullhead" set up a bray, so that when we got to the place there was not an Indian to be seen. Mr. Mule for ever after that was in great disfavor with our command.

About this time Capt. J. W. T. Gardiner, 1st Dragoons, arrived on Fall River to establish a post, which he did, and named it after the undersigned.[3]

We had turned up the Indians to the north and east so often that they had become shy. We made some other scouts in their country, but beyond killing an occasional Indian, we could not accomplish anything. Besides, they had stopped their depredations.

I took two men one day and went down the river on its west bank in hopes of locating a camp. I knew there were some not far from us, but the country was rough, and I suspected they were watching us, so it would be useless to go after them with the whole command without first having located their camp so we could move on them after dark.

Our first move was to get on the top of a high, brushy ridge that overlooked quite a valley to the southwest. We watched here for some time when we saw some Indians come trailing in from the direction of the river. We watched them until they had assembled to the number of about one hundred. The squaws commenced gathering grass seed while the bucks stood sentinels.

I left the animals with one of the men, and I took the other and started down the river, keeping to the timber so as to keep out of sight as much as possible. When I came to the trail that the Indians had come on from the river, we jumped from rock to rock so as not to make any sign. We now worked our way toward the river through some soft, ashy hills. We found in there a wash boiler,

[3] *Special Order No. 69,* Headquarters, Military Division of the Pacific (May 28, 1857), reads: "Capt. John W. T. Gardiner, First Dragoons, will take post with his company on Pitt River, California, at or near the mouth of Fall River. Temporary quarters and stables only will be erected at the post."

The post was established on July 1, and occupied until May, 1866, when troops were withdrawn. There was no formally declared reservation, and all claims to the land were relinquished by the Act of February 15, 1881.

Crook does not mention that at this time he had a brush with Captain Judah, who ordered him to return to Fort Jones. Captain Gardiner tried to convince Judah that Crook should stay, but on July 11 Judah wrote a couple of letters, one accusing Gardiner of gross disrespect and the other threatening Crook with court-martial if he did not return at once. Judah's temper cooled off, however, and Crook was permitted to remain. National Archives, Commanding Officer, Company E, Fourth Infantry to Commanding Officer, Company D, Fourth Infantry, July 11, 1857.

photographs, and other things that evidently had belonged to the people who had been massacred the previous winter. We got close to the river, and while listening and looking for the Indians, I fell asleep.

Pretty soon the soldier awakened me and said he heard Indians not far from where we were. I soon discovered that the noise proceeded from some Indians who were in swimming. That satisfied me that their rancheria was not far away. Just below us was a small creek putting in from our side, covered with trees and underbrush. I suspected their camp must be in that brush, but I could not see anything from where we were, but just below this creek, and not fifty yards from it was a little bluff overlooking it.

While it was a risky thing to do, I could not get the desired information unless I got on this bluff. So I went up the creek sufficiently far to prevent discovery, and came on to the point overlooking the creek and river from the rear. I noticed where three fresh squaw tracks had gone back on the bluff, and I was in dread of their returning before getting through with our observations.

After peeping over the bluffs, and getting the desired information, that they were camped on the creek as I had first supposed, we retraced our steps. We had not proceeded far, however, when I saw one of the squaws coming directly towards us. I hid behind a tree, and when she was in a few feet of me I jumped out suddenly in front of her, at the same time pointing my gun at her, and making motions that if she gave the alarm, I would shoot her.

She had a basket with some grass seed in it, and a papoose on her back. She was very much frightened, but not confused. She seemed to realize the situation. She kept motioning that she expected two people to come from the direction she came, and wanted us to hold on. But as I was not looking for any more, and was anxious to get out of that vicinity, I didn't let the grass grow under my feet.

When she saw that her appeals were in vain, and that we turned to go up the river, she sat down, put on her moccasins, and threw her basket away, and was prepared for the journey. I took the lead, and directed the soldier to see that she kept up with me, and did not make her escape. I took a good, brisk gait, she keeping close on my heels all the way. When we passed the trail that led up to and started up to the valley where we had seen the Indians gathering grass seed in the morning, I noticed from the signs that they had returned to the river, and that we, probably, had passed the most dangerous country, and that we had not been discovered.

We continued on until we reached our animals that we had left in the morning with the other man. We mounted, and continued to our camp, arriving there just before dark. I reasoned that there was a chance of our not having been discovered. They might not miss the squaw until it was too dark for them to discover our tracks in searching for her, but they would certainly do so the next morning. Our only show was to surprise the camp, to go down there that night yet so as to be there at daylight the next morning.

We left just after dark, taking a trail over into the valley mentioned before, which we had avoided in the morning to prevent discovery. Where the trail went down into the valley, it was very precipitous and rough. The night came on very dark, a severe thunderstorm overtook us on the mountain. The clouds were inky black, and the darkness was so intense that we could not see our hands before us, except when flashes of lightning lit up the country.

I marched in front, and kept the squaw still ahead of me in order that she, being on foot, could follow the trail. She still carried the papoose on her back. She had plenty of opportunties to escape. Her child would cry occasionally, when she would stop, nurse, and sing to it. Before we reached the vicinity of the rancheria, the storm had passed, and the sky was clear.

When we reached the creek where I saw the Indians in camp the day previous, I saw the Indians had gone. We finally found that their rancheria was across the river and some distance below the mouth of the creek. The river here was nearly one hundred yards wide, and we could tell nothing about its depth. There was but one canoe on our side of the river, and half the bottom was split out of it, so it was useless so far as crossing the men in was concerned. It was then too late to make a raft so as to cross before it got daylight.

The squaw kept urging me, by signs, to hurry up before daylight came for fear the Indians would make their escape. By this time we were opposite where the Indians were, looking at the canoe. By this time the Indians had commenced making fires, and I realized the fact that we could do nothing.

The squaw laid down her papoose, and, taking up her basket

hat which she wore on her head, commenced bailing out the canoe, gradually working her way toward the end farthest from the shore. All of a sudden she dove under the water and disappeared.

It did not seem a minute before all the fires were put out in their camp on the other side. I would not have given her this chance of escape had it not been for the fact that I saw we could accomplish nothing. She had many better opportunities to escape on the march during the night previous. She certainly deserved a crown from her people for the sacrifice she made for them. She left her papoose with us, which could not have been more than three weeks old.

After daylight we managed to stuff grass in the leaky canoe, so that one of the men crossed over in it to the other side of the river and bring over some good canoes that were there. We all crossed over and found that they had left everything in their precipitous flight. We found a good many seines and nets of different descriptions that were well made of some kind of strong thread which did credit to their skill.[4]

We returned to the opposite bank where the papoose was, which by this time was squalling at the top of its lungs. We hung it up on a limb, and I secreted myself with a few of the men, and gave instructions to take the back trail and go over the top of a mountain in plain sight of where we were, so that the Indians would think we had gone out of the country, and come back to camp and get their papoose. But the soldiers, stupid like, halted on top of the mountain in plain view of the whole country.

As soon as I saw this I waited no longer, but followed up, and mounted our horses, and returned to camp, acknowledging ourselves fairly beaten. The Indians had evidently transferred their camp to the opposite bank of the river as a precautionary measure. I never knew whether they had made this change from any suspicion arising from the squaw's absence or not. These Indians were such hard customers that they were naturally suspicious themselves.

I made many other scouts to different parts of this country, so that I became pretty much familiar with it all. But in none of these scouts was I ever again successful in getting any more telling blows on these Indians. We would occasionally come across some

----

[4] Nets were made of two-ply cordage, rolled without tools from the fibers of the *Iris macrosiphon* leaf. Kroeber, *Handbook of the Indians of California*, 85.

straggling Indians, but their main parties must either have scattered, or else they were more vigilant. But one thing was certain: they stopped their depredations.

In the latter part of August or first part of September I made peace with them when they came in and encamped near the post, but having no good interpreter, I was unable to get any particulars from them.

I was particularly struck with their cunning in all their little ways of capturing a livelihood. They dug pits, some of them fifteen feet deep, with sharpened pegs driven in their bottom with the sharp end uppermost, along the game trails. They would carefully remove every part of the excavated earth from within sight, and then so deftly cover over the pit with brush and earth that the unsuspecting game would fall an easy prey. It was from this circumstance that the Indians and the river took their name. I saw one of these pits on the old emigrant road, made evidently to capture emigrant stock.

They managed so that all the country in which they lived was made to pay tribute to them. Game, fish, nuts, roots, grass seed, grasshoppers, crickets, water fowl and their eggs, the larvae of hornets, yellow jackets, etc.

It was amusing to see them locate a yellow jackets nest. These little bees were a nuisance around camp. You could not leave a piece of meat or anything sweet exposed in our camp but what they were into it. So Mr. Indian would get a down from the duck, which was large in bulk, but had no heft to it, and would fasten to its shaft end either a small piece of meat or something sweet. When Mr. Yellow Jacket would seize hold of the coveted treasure and make a bee line for his home, the down would impede his flight so much that Mr. Indian was enabled to keep close enough to find his nest. Then it would be but short work with fire to clean out their nest.

They would also stretch cords across marshy ground, supported by poles driven in the ground at intervals. From these cords they would suspend strings with a slip noose in their ends that would just hang at the edge of the water, so that water fowl feeding along would occasionally get their necks caught in these nooses.

The Indians had gotten quite used to our camp, and seemed to feel perfectly at home, when one morning they were all gone.

They had fled the night previous. I got them back again, but never did know what made them leave.

These Indians were noted all over the Pacific Coast as being amongst the very worst. They had the reputation of being treacherous, warlike, fierce, and wily. They had killed a great many whites at different times. Several expeditions had been made against them, with commands much larger than mine, but this was the first time they were ever subdued. And strange to say, during this entire campaign I did not lose a single man killed, and only had one seriously wounded, Thos. Rourke. He was shot in the lungs, and when the arrow was pulled out, the head remained in his lungs. Although he suffered a great deal with it, when I saw him last, at the outbreak of the war, he was nearly well.

The only way I can account for the few casualties I sustained was from the fact that we invariably charged right in their midst, and confused them, and had them miss me more than once at no greater distance than ten feet, whereas they could hit a man every time at sixty yards when not under excitement.

These arrows in their hands were no insignificant weapons to contend against. At a distance of sixty yards, and even further, they could send an arrow through one's body so that the arrow head would project on the other side, and at this distance they could keep an arrow in the air all the time, whereas we had the old muzzle loading rifle that took so long to reload.

An arrow wound frequently was worse than a gunshot wound, for the latter would as a rule go through the body, whereas the arrow was so constructed that it had one or more short joints together with the head that were fastened together with a little moistened sinew. When it came in contact with the warm blood of your body, it came apart, so that when the arrow was pulled out these other parts were left in your body. Then, in addition, these Indians had the reputation of poisoning their arrows. Capt. A. J. Smith, 1st Dragoons, lost some three men and some horses in an engagement with these Indians some time previous by arrows he supposed were poisoned.

The advent of the muzzle loading gun in the hands of the Indians made them less formidable at close range than they were before, but it was the breech loader that has entirely changed the Indian problem, and has made the Indians of today so formidable.

After making peace with these Indians, it became irksome and monotonous to be lying around camp, so I frequently would take the most of my men out on hunts. We would be gone several days at a time. My favorite place to hunt was at the southeastern foot of Shasta Butte. The melting snows from this mountain sent down the most beautiful rills of ice-cold water which wound around amongst beautiful groves of pine and grassy parks, with large patches of whortle and blue berry bushes here and there, filled with luscious berries.

The scenery was almost fairy-like here. We would pitch our tents and hunt as our fancies would dictate. Game abounded all through this country. Deer and blue grouse were the most plentiful, but there was an occasional elk, bear, or California lion to be seen, with plenty of mountain sheep high up in the mountains.

One day while I was watching a fisher playing up and down a tree squirrel fashion, I saw a band of deer slipping out of a bunch of brush near by. I had my choice, so I shot a nice buck. We would take our surplus game in to the dragoons who were building the post.

About the middle of September I received orders to repair to Fort Jones and straighten up my affairs, when I would proceed to the mouth of the Klamath River, there to establish a temporary post and settle some indifficulties.

I left this country that I had become so identified with in the last few months with many regrets. As we marched through Yreka we were treated as heroes.[5]

---

[5] Company D marched from Fort Jones to Pit River Valley in the month of May, 1857, and was engaged in operating against hostile Indians in the Pit River country in the month of June. In July the company had two engagements with the Pit River Indians, on the second and the twenty-sixth respectively. During August the company operated against hostile Indians in the Pit River country. In September it marched from Fort Crook to Fort Jones, en route for Klamath reservation. In October the company arrived at Klamath reserve and established Fort Ter-Waw. On October 13, 1857, the company had an engagement with the Indians. National Archives, *Annual Returns, Fourth Infantry*, 1857.

5. *I was ordered to organize a navy*

AFTER FINISHING MY BUSINESS at Fort Jones, I took up my line of march down Scotts River to its junction with the Klamath, and followed down that river until we struck the trail leading over to Crescent City. Near the mouth of Scotts River was a big mining camp called Scottsburg. Next to Yreka it was the largest and liveliest place in all that country. Millions of dollars in gold had been taken out of the placer diggings there.

Every few miles down the Klamath, as far as I went, were mining camps of more or less extent. Crescent City was a small place of a few hundred inhabitants, kept alive by being the port for some mining districts in the interior. Its harbor extended clear to China, being simply a little indentation in the coast.

From here our route was by trail, over broken bluffs to the mouth of the Klamath River, and up this river six miles by canoes poled and paddled by the natives. The Indian agency was situated on the right bank of the Klamath River, six miles from its mouth, on a piece of bottom ground well adapted for cultivation, called Wakello.

I at once commenced searching for a suitable location to establish my post, one that would furnish the desired protection, and at the same time have the soldiers sufficiently removed from the agency so as not to cause any friction. I finally selected a beautiful, grassy flat, diagonally across and up the river. There was a small strip of woods running nearly all around the flat immediately on the bank of the river, while a dense forest of redwood furnished the background. This flat must have contained at least one hundred acres. The river was about one quarter of a mile wide, with a strong current, although the tide ran nearly up to it. The name of this flat was Ter-Waw.[1]

[1] On October 21, 1857, Crook wrote to Adjutant General Mackall: "I would most respectfully suggest the post to be named Ter-Waw, from the Indian name of the ground on which it is located." The post was abandoned

As soon as our baggage arrived, we commenced work, erecting our quarters, and in the meantime I was busy learning the Indian situation. I had about ninety men in my company, and, being the only officer with it, had to see personally to everything. I learned that the Indians indigenous to the river were called Al-a-gnas, and there had been a lot of Indians removed to this reservation[2] from the Crescent City region, called Tol-a-nas. Although living so near each other, they were entirely different people and spoke a different language. These Indians were bitterly opposed to staying here, the Al-a-gnas were as bitterly opposed to having them remain, so everything pointed to an outbreak.

I had most positive orders not to fight these Indians unless first attacked by them. I had not been there long before these Indians got up a conspiracy to murder me and destroy the boats that ferried the river, then kill the agent and his employees, sack the place, and then return to their own country. They reasoned that if I was killed the soldiers would be without a head, and they would have nothing to fear from them.

One of the Klamath Indians who heard the conspiracy divulged the secret. By this time I knew enough about Indians to know that unless I took the initiative some of us would be killed. So I made up my mind to surround them at daylight after their plans had become more matured, and their guilt could be definitely fixed on them.

That day some of the conspirators visited my camp, came up to my tent, felt its thickness, then would talk amongst themselves. They were particular in knowing whether I slept by myself. The soldiers' tents were some fifty or sixty yards from mine, all being in the edge of the redwoods. I never let on to them that I knew anything of their plot, nor did I say anything to the soldiers. But I laid my rifle on one side of me, and my shotgun on the other,

---

on June 11, 1861, its usefulness having been served. National Archives, Commanding Officer, Company D, Fourth Infantry to the Adjutant General, Division of the Pacific, October 21, 1857; *Posts, Camps, and Stations File.*

[2] The Klamath reservation was approved by the President on November 16, 1855, and was located on the Klamath River, beginning at the coast of the Pacific and enclosing a strip of territory one mile in width on each side of the river for twenty miles. Alban W. Hoopes, *Indian Affairs and Their Administration,* 59 ff.

with my pistol and bowie knife under my head. I also had a box of brasses belonging to the soldiers' accoutrements in my tent which I set just inside of the front of my tent, so that if they attempted to come in they would wake me up.

I felt so confident that I would be more than a match for them that I hoped they would make the attack. I would be in the dark, while they would be between me and the sky light, which would give me a great advantage. But the next morning the whole thing was precipitated by some Indians making an attack on the agent.

A runner came to me with a note from one of the employees to the effect that the agent had been killed. My men were scattered, more or less, collecting material for building purposes. Many were in the woods. I at once had the "long roll" beaten, and in less than half an hour I was at the agency with all my company except two. We made short work of the disaffected Indians, killing several of them.[3] (The two men left behind were not long behind. They came to the river, and, finding the boats gone, swam it with their accoutrements and arms.)

This put an end to the trouble. Most of the Tol-a-nas ran away, and shortly after the remainder were permitted to go, and all were allowed to remain in their own country.

I now applied myself most assiduously to complete my post. I built the men's quarters first, and got all the post about completed when in the spring of 1858 I was ordered to Vancouver, W. T. to participate in a campaign which was then being inaugurated against

[3] "On the 17th inst. the Indians sent for the agent to come to their houses and see a sick Indian. The agent went, accompanied by one white man. Immediately upon his arrival the Indians made an attack upon them from all sides with knives, and bows and arrows. Fortunately, the two succeeded in keeping them off until the guard came to their rescue, who, after two or three volleys, succeeded in driving the Indians to the brush.

"A dispatch was immediately sent for me, but after my arrival I could only get an occasional shot at them in the brush. The total number of Indians ascertained to be killed is ten, besides a number wounded. Some twenty-six warriors and a number of women and children have since come in, and say they are satisfied to remain. The remainder have gone to Smith River. The number of warriors on Smith River are about 100, and they say they will not come back here alive, and that if I want to fight I will find them on Smith River." National Archives, Commanding Officer, Company D, Fourth Infantry, to Adjutant General, Division of the Pacific, November 24, 1857.

the Indians who defeated Col. Steptoe's command the fall previous.[4]

I was relieved by 1st Lt. J. B. Collins with "B" Company of my regiment, from Humboldt, one of the same companies that I had accompanied in the spring of 1853 to Humboldt Bay, and who had been there ever since, doing nothing, while my company had never been idle.[5]

After reaching Vancouver, we proceeded up the Columbia River as far as The Dalles by boat, and from there we marched across land to the post of Simcoe, some sixty-five miles distant.[6] I have forgotten to mention that Lt. T. E. Turner had joined my company before leaving Fort Ter-Waw, as the post was called; also that I had exchanged the Yaeger guns for the old musket, altered and rifled, and shot the Minie ball, a gun inferior to the Yaeger.[7]

We traveled from Vancouver to Simcoe with Capt. Frazier of the 9th Infantry, who was stationed at the latter place. His regiment was armed with the old Yaeger. I allowed myself to be imposed on by his telling me they could hit the size of a man pretty nearly every time at the distance of 1,000 yards. I took a back seat, and said nothing more. He advised me to exchange my gun for the Yaegers. I told him that I had had the Yaegers, but preferred the present arms. He said our old guns could have been good, etc. etc.

---

[4] In the Battle of Steptoe's Butte, on May 17, 1858, the Indians lost nine killed and forty or fifty wounded, according to their report. The Regulars lost six killed and eleven wounded. This was also called the Battle of Te-hoto-nimme. Secretary of War, *Annual Report*, 1858, 346–48.

[5] Company D left Fort Ter-Waw on June 28, 1858, and arrived at Fort Vancouver, W.T., on July 7. They left Vancouver on July 19, and arrived at Fort Simcoe on August 2, leaving on the tenth for an expedition against the Yakima Indians. They returned to Fort Simcoe on September 25, and returned to Ter-Waw, via Vancouver, on October 16. National Archives, *Annual Returns, Fourth Infantry*, 1858.

[6] Fort Simcoe was established August 8, 1856, in Simcoe Valley on the Yakima reservation, sixty-five miles north of The Dalles. The Yakimas were supposed to have had a fort here as early as 1849 for protection against the Cayuse. The post was used as an Indian agency.

Between Vancouver and Simcoe, Company D stopped at Fort Cascades, and Crook examined and reported on the trails leading from Cascades to the Indian country. *Posts, Camps, and Stations File*.

[7] This was the conversion of the model 1822 musket to a rifle musket. The locks were converted, the barrels grooved, and a rear sight added. Sawyer, *Our Rifles*, 146–47.

When we reached Simcoe, I learned that it was the custom of the old guard to fire at a target, and those who hit the bullseye were let off a tour of guard duty. The next morning after my arrival I very meekly went out to the target to see their men shoot, intending that if they were such superior shots to my men to say nothing about it.

But after seeing them shoot, the next morning I took out with their old guard an equal number of my men. Capt. Frazier was present. Not a man of their guard hit the bullseye, while there was not a man of mine missed it. He at once applied to get guns like mine. I thought it strange that their men should so far beat my men shooting when I had taken such particular pains to instruct them, had taken them out hunting, etc., and generally had such a good sharp edge on them that they thought they could whip all the Indians in the country.

Maj. Bob Garnett, of Rebel fame, who was killed at Cheat River soon after the breaking out of the rebellion, was in command of Simcoe with three companies of his, the 9th Regiment. Capt. Judah had also assembled here with his company of Forty Thieves for duty on the expedition, having marched from Fort Jones to Fort Vancouver. But with his usual ability to escape work he exchanged with one company of the 9th, and remained behind, much to my delight, for I had such contempt for him that his sight was obnoxious to me. He signalled the kindness shown him by Maj. Garnett by being drunk pretty much all the time during our absence.

Our expedition was to punish the Indians who had defeated Col. Steptoe. A band of Indians had murdered a party of prospectors some time during the spring, and it was understood that they were scattered amongst the Yakimas, who were supposed to be friendly, and our expedition was also expected to kill or capture these murderers. The expedition consisted of three companies of the 9th, commanded by Captains Archer, Frazer and Black, and my company of the 4th, the whole commanded by Maj. Garnett.

Our general route lay up the Columbia River. After several days march from Simcoe, it was ascertained that there were some of the murderers in the camp of friendly Indians not far off. So Lt. Jesse K. Allen of Capt. Frazer's company was anxious to go after them. Capt. Frazer, who was detailed to go after them, let

Allen go by himself. He started with a detachment of Frazer's company, to which he belonged, soon after dark, intending to attack the Indians at daylight the next morning. It seemed that in advancing to attack next morning, it was scarcely light yet, when Allen was in front, and, being mistaken by some of his men, was shot by mistake. His death cast a gloom over us all, and was a bad commencement for our expedition.[8] His body was sent back to the post, and we continued our march.

The country passed over was gently rolling, and covered with fine grass, and very fairly watered. We struck the Columbia River a little more than one hundred miles from the post. Game was scarce, except sage hens and a few sharp tailed grouse. There was trout in most of the streams. We made a camp on the Wenatche River.

From here it was ascertained that there were some of the murderers about sixty miles up the river, with a band of Indians who were supposed to be friendly. I was detailed with my company to go in pursuit. So my company was mounted on pack mules with such saddles as could be raked together. We started just before dusk, with a couple of Indians for guides. Just after we got fairly under way, a heavy thunderstorm came up, and the night became pitch dark, so you could not see the man ahead of you. The guides went so fast that it was difficult to keep up with them.

Finally we crossed over a ridge, and came suddenly on the banks of a roaring torrent. The guide bulged in, and we after him. It was the greatest wonder some of the men were not swept off, so strong and deep was the current, with large boulders on the bottom. By this time it had commenced raining. After crossing, we turned up its right bank, and had not gone far before we came to a bluff that made it necessary to leave the river bottom and wind around through the timber and brush to go over it.

The night was so dark and the trail so circuitous, and the men got so tangled that we could not get through it and had to pull back to a little bottom and wait for daylight. In counting noses I

---

[8] Jesse K. Allen graduated from the Military Academy in 1855. Major Garnett reported that Allen's party of fifteen mounted men captured twenty-one bucks, and about fifty women and children. Three men who were recognized as involved in the massacre were shot. Secretary of War, *Annual Report*, 1858, 372.

83651

Camp Warner, Oregon, in 1873

From a photograph by S. J. Morrow, Deadwood
Courtesy National Archives

Horse travois carrying wounded after the battle of Slim Buttes.
The wounded man may be Lieutenant A. H. von Luettwitz,
whose leg was amputated.

found that there were ten men absent. I sent some men back to discharge their guns, so in case they lost their way this would enable them to find us. It rained a little, and was cloudy all night. We lay down, and tied the animals to our legs, but could sleep but little.

Bright and early next morning we started on our journey up this stream. Shortly after daylight we recrossed the stream, and continued up its right bank. The trail lay mostly on bottom covered with a dense forest, a species of redwood; much fallen timber. Our trail was circuitous. For instance, we could come to a fallen tree at right angles to our direction, and would have frequently to go a hundred feet to get over the trunk and return again within ten feet of the place we started.

When you add to this the soft condition of the ground, with frequent bog holes that our animals would almost go out of sight in, and every few yards a yaller jacket's nest, the inmates of which would cause some grand and lofty tumbling amongst the men, you can form some idea of the fun we had that day.

Towards mid-day we commenced getting on higher ground, where the country was more open. About two P.M. we suddenly came upon three animals, saddled, whose riders had evidently fled. Going a short distance further we came up to a young man standing along side of the trail, leaning on his long "Queen Bess" rifle, a perfect picture for a statue. He kept his eyes gazing directly to his front, scarcely noticing us. It was some time before I could get him to talk.

He finally warmed up sufficient to tell us that he was the Chief's son, that the horses we saw belonged to some of the murderers, that they knew we were after them, and that they were going to sell their lives as dearly as possible, that the camp of his father, with whom these Indians were staying, was a few miles ahead, and was on an island in a side stream that was difficult to approach, that these Indians had announced their intentions of ambushing us near the village, etc. etc.

When we got within a couple of miles of their village, as I supposed, I dismounted most of my men, and deployed as skirmishers, going ahead, I leading them in person, so as to prevent surprise. We had traveled some distance in this way when I came to a little open spot, where I halted, having made up my mind just what plan I would pursue.

The young chief was still with us. I reasoned that were we to attack the village, situated as it was, we could not expect to accomplish more than killing a few Indians at best, as we could not surround them. We could not tell who the murderers were, and we would more likely kill our friends than the ones we came after. Besides, the Indians were more numerous than we, and in case they should all turn on us, but few of us would be likely to get out of there alive.

So I took this young chief out to one side, and explained to him what we had come for, the great risk they ran in harboring those men, that in a fight we would have to kill many of our friends, which we were anxious not to do, that they would lose all their stock and many of their families, camp equipage, etc. etc. I suggested that he go to the village and tell his father privately what I had told him, and also to have his father come with him to see me, and in the meantime to disabuse the minds of the murderers that we were there for any hostile intent.

Not long after this the old chief came to see me with his son. So well had the young chief done his work that not long after my camp was filled with their Indians, and amongst them some of the murderers. I had a confidential talk with the old chief and his son. After going over about the same ground as I had with the son earlier, I pointed out to them the benefits which would come to them if they were to have all their Indians come into my camp the next morning to sell berries, etc. etc., when he could point out the murderers to me unobserved, and that I would make arrangements to nab them all without their being known. All of which they consented to do the next morning.

We were encamped on the banks of the Wenatche River—if it could be called a camp, as we had nothing with us except one blanket each behind our saddles, and a couple of days' cooked rations in our haversacks. The stream was swollen until its waters were flush with its banks. The overhanging boughs slushing backwards and forwards in the angry waters sounded like the rushing of many waters. The water looked like it had ashes tossed in it, so full of sediment was it.

On the opposite side of the river, rocky crags rose abruptly over 1,000 feet above us, with shafts and pinnacles shooting still far above these again, all denuded of vegetation from the base of these crags. Some three or four hundred feet above us the detached rocks assumed their natural slope to the water's edge. It had rained often during the day, and now at dusk it commenced a steady pour. The whole scene made an impression not soon to be forgotten.

I laid my blanket by the side of a huge log, spreading my saddle blanket from the top of the log to the ground as a roof. Soon after dark I changed my location to another log, so that in case of treachery they would not know where to find me. My blanket was soaking wet, the ground was sopping wet, and the rain all night made a little puddle about me, but soon I heated up the water, and I slept through till morning without awakening. I never had a sweeter sleep or felt more refreshed in the morning.

The sky had cleared up in the morning, and soon after sun up the Indians came straggling into our camp. About ten A.M. the chief came. By that time our camp was full of them. As fast as the chief would point out one of the murderers, I had a non-commissioned officer and two men to shadow him, so as not to create an apprehension, and when they were all shadowed in this way, at a given signal they were to grab their man. So, at the signal given by me, four men were captured.

The remainder of the Indians, except the chief and his son, suspecting treachery, flew to the bush like so many quail. You could have played checkers on their shirt tails, they stood out so straight. But as soon as the chief explained, they returned, and flocked around these four men and their guard, just the same as white men, out of idle curiosity.

Amongst this crowd was another one of the murderers, who had not been pointed out. He came up to look on. He was also nabbed, and turned out to be the very worst one in the whole business, as he was a medicine man and was one of the ringleaders.

I had them all pinioned, and then told them the object of my mission, and that I intended shooting them before I left. I wanted them to make any final preparations they wished, and reasonable time would be given them, etc. etc. They all acknowledged their guilt, but made the excuse that they were forced or persuaded by others, etc. Except the medicine man, who invoked all kinds of curses against us.

He called his son to him, and gave him what few personal effects he had with him, and made a speech to him in his own tongue, which we did not understand. Just as we left on our return, it was interpreted to us. This son was to go to the village, get his gun, and go down the river in his canoe, and ambush us at each point where the trail neared the river, and kill as many as he could to avenge his death. The other four went through the form of prayers, the burden of which was that the soldiers had come and caught them, and that they were going to kill them.

This whole business was exceedingly distasteful to me, and as my 2nd Lt. Turner rather enjoyed that kind of thing, I detailed him to execute them, which was done in the following manner. The Indians were set down in a line; twenty men were detailed to shoot them. Five of their guns were not loaded, so that no one knew whether his gun was loaded or not.

Soon after the execution was performed, we mounted our already saddled animals, and just as we were starting the medicine man's message to his son was interpreted to us. It is useless to add that no file closers were needed on our return, nor were the yaller jackets nests or the big bog holes any obstacles, either.

We got through the soft bottom with the dense timber some time in the afternoon, and went into camp. That evening one of the minor chiefs overtook us. He said that the son of the medicine man behaved very sensibly about the matter. He said his father was guilty, and that one of the family was enough to die, and he did not propose to lay himself liable. The next day we returned to the command.[9]

This was really the only thing accomplished on the entire trip. After this we prosecuted our march still further up the Columbia until we came to the mouth of the Okanagan River. After going nearly to the British line, we commenced retracing our steps. We found several canoes on the Okanagan River, dug out of pine trees. I was ordered to take twenty men and organize a navy to explore the Columbia River, as on our march up we had frequently

[9] "We arrived at this camp on the 20th, inst., and on the following day I despatched a party of 60 men under Lt. Crook, 4th Infantry, with Lts. McCall and Turner of the same Regiment, to follow up the principal branch of this stream into the mountains, where it was understood some eight or ten hostiles were secreted. On the third day out the party, through the instrumentality of the friendly chief, Skimarwaw and some of his people, succeeded in entrapping five of these men. They were shot in compliance with my orders." Secretary of War, *Annual Report*, 1858, 379.

made detours away from it to avoid impassable localities. The detour was so great that we had to camp away from it one night on "Lake Chelan."

Up to this time I had marched in front with my company every foot of the way, except the side scout up the Wenatche River. I was the only officer in the command who did it. I always contended an infantry officer should march on foot when his men did.

At first we attempted to use the canoes as the Indians did, but after the first day, seeing my men dumped into the water at most every rough place we encountered, I concluded that they lacked the necessary skill to handle these delicate canoes, and that some of them would certainly be drowned before the trip ended. So that night I had two canoes lashed side by side, and in this way we could run all the rapids we encountered without serious difficulty. On several occasions our crafts nearly filled with water, but by having men ready with camp kettles and mess pans to bail out the water, we got along all right, as our boats could not upset as they did when single.

The morning of the day the troops were to camp at Lake Chelan, I left camp with my flotilla at the same time the land forces did. They pretty soon commenced diverging from the river, and we were getting farther and farther away from each other.

I had not gone far, when, turning a sharp bend in the river, we ran into a village of Indians encamped on the flat. They were saucy and ugly-looking. Many of the young braves had their hair roached, half of some of their faces painted white, while the other half were black, frequently with figures made in this paint.

I ran the bows of our canoes on shore, when several stepped up and demanded my canoes as theirs. I showed a bold front, and went forward with my rifle, and threatened to shoot the first Indian who attempted to lay his hands on one of them. Things did not look very salubrious about there, and for fear of trouble, I lost no time in pulling out.

The river today was full of rapids, so that our feet were kept wet by our boats taking water so often. Even between rapids the current was swift, so by two A.M. we were at the point where the command would join us the next day. I selected as a camp a nice clump of willows near the mouth of a little side stream that put into the river at this point. There was also one of the most beautiful land-locked harbors for our fleet to rest in that I ever saw. There was only one small entrance to it, just large enough for one of our craft to enter at a time. I don't think I could have found a better place for defense on the whole river. We were concealed from view in all directions. The trail up and down the river was but a few yards from us, but no one passing on it could see our camp.

Not far from this trail was a rocky point from which a good lookout could be kept. It commanded a view of the trail for a mile or so down the river. After settling the camp, I went up into the rocks to keep a lookout. I had not been there long before I saw a dust coming up the river on the trail. The side creek had deep, sunken banks, covered with willows, so that a person coming up the trail could see nothing on the opposite side until they crossed the creek. I saw the persons making the dust were two Indians riding at the top of their speed. So I arranged my men in the shape of a bag in the low bush on the opposite bank from where they were coming.

Their surprise can be better imagined than told when they ran into this bag, and had the soldiers rise up all around them. They proved to be friendly Indians, but they were so scared, and so gratified to find that we were not going to hurt them that they insisted on my being a big chief, and wanted to present me with two cows. This I respectfully declined, but referred them to Maj. Garnett. He asked me afterwards what I had done to so attach them to me. They insisted so upon his taking the cattle that he finally had to take one to get rid of them.

After this little episode I again took up my watch in the rocks. I had not been there long before I thought I saw a figure across the river resembling an Indian, and at the same time I heard something that resembled a wolf howling. The figure was in a sitting position, and resembled the many rocks in the vicinity, so I thought I was mistaken. After a while I went down to the river and took a bath, and saw nothing.

Toward evening while I was again in my lookout, I saw the same object again across the river. This time I was satisfied it was a squaw. I went to the water's edge, and called out to her what she was doing there, and what she wanted, etc. She indicated her wish to cross over to us. I sent one of our boats over after her. She seemed delighted to get with us. Her story was such a sad one that my heart went out to her.

She said her home was on the lower Columbia River, that she was there among strangers who were not good to her, and she was anxious to return with us to her people. She said she had left the village we ran into above in the morning in company with a lot of other squaws to gather berries, roots, etc. She had dropped out and given them the slip, and came to us, having seen us, and thought we would take her with us. She had a small baby a couple of months old.

I was not altogether free from the suspicion that she might be a spy, so I made her sleep near the fire where I slept, with the soldiers sleeping all around us. During the night I thought I would visit the sentinel who was posted in the brush near by. I hadn't more than gotten out of my blankets with my bare feet before a Mr. Rattlesnake struck his rattles. He was evidently coming to get in bed with me. I called the sentinel who killed him with the butt of his musket.

Toward the afternoon of the next day the command came along, and went into camp a little lower down. I was very glad to welcome them, for I did not like my position there with twenty men with an unknown number of Indians all around us, presumably in vastly superior numbers. From here on down to Priest Rapids,[10] where we left the river to go to Simcoe, I navigated the river with my fleet, much to the envy of the rest who had to trudge along on the dusty trail with the land forces.

There was nothing of particular interest happened on this part of the journey. The scenery was magnificent, and our boats ran down at a great speed without any exertion on our part. We stopped whenever we wanted to, and examined any points of interest. The water was clear enough to see quantities of salmon floating around in the eddy places. The shore and bottom were covered with polished boulders from the size of a hen's egg to that of your head, of a variety of colors. It would make one's head swim

[10] Priest Rapids was named by Alexander Ross' party on its way up from Astoria in 1811, for an Indian in full regalia whom they saw at the lower end of the rapids and took for a "priest."

to look down through the clear water at them when our boats would pass over them so rapidly.

I abandoned my fleet at Priest Rapids with many regrets, as I don't know that ever in my life I enjoyed a trip with such keen zest and pleasure.

Upon our near approach to Simcoe we learned of the death of Mrs. Garnett and child just before our return. We saw but little of him after our return, as his grief kept him to his house mostly. I don't know that I ever served under a commanding officer for whom I had such a high respect. He was strict, but just, and those who did their duty well were certain to be rewarded, while those who failed to do their duty were made to feel it. In this way the hard work was not all put on the willing officer.

From here I was sent in advance in an ambulance. Our team gave out on the way, and we found a band of ponies on the way at a pond. We managed to catch some of them, get the harness on them, and made them pull us through. When I arrived at Fort Vancouver, Col. Newman S. Clarke, commanding the department, and his adjutant general were there, so I was ordered back to Fort Ter-Waw with my company.[11]

We took the steamer at Vancouver, and went around by Victoria to Crescent City, where we disembarked for the mouth of the Klamath. We arrived at Ter-Waw and relieved Lt. Collins, who returned with many regrets, to his post, Fort Humboldt, as this was his first command, and he liked it.

6. *Little secrets of the inner Indian*

Lt. Collins had pushed the building of the quarters fairly, but the garden that we had expected so much from was a failure.

Before leaving for the north, I had acquired some considerable

---

11 Crook requested his transfer back to Ter-Waw on the grounds that he had a company garden there, and wanted to reap the benefits of it before the rainy season set in. National Archives, Commanding Officer, Company D, Fourth Infantry, to Adjutant General, Division of the Pacific, July 29, 1858.

knowledge of the Indian language of these Al-a-gnas, which was now renewed with additional vim, so that I acquired sufficient proficiency in language to be of immense benefit in understanding the Indian character, habits, etc.

It is an easy matter for anyone to see the salient points of Indian character, namely that they are filthy, odoriferous, treacherous, ungrateful, pitiless, cruel, and lazy. But it is the fewest who ever get beyond this, and see his other side, which, I must admit, is small, and almost latent. To do this requires more than mere study and perception. Above all, you must get his confidence, which means more than I can tell here. There are few people who can get an Indian's confidence to the extent that he will tell you all his little "bed rock" secrets, especially those of a sacred character. Until you have all these little secrets of the inner Indian which control his baser part, you need not expect to manipulate him to good actions when his baser passions are aroused.

These Indians were every-day visitors at Ter-Waw. The river made a bend around a flat upon which the post was situated, and as their travel up and down the river was by canoe, all except those absolutely necessary to pole the boat up the swift current would take the path across the flats. In this way we would see all the travelers who came into the country. Klamath River is virtually a cañon from its mouth to a point beyond Yreka.

These Al-a-gnas lived along its banks, on little benches and flats, from the mouth to a point some fifty miles above, when came the Arrannas up the Klamath, and the Hoopas [Hupas] on a branch stream running into the Klamath at that point. Each of these villages was named, and had permanent huts erected out of large puncheon boards split out of the redwood with their crude implements.

Their manner of building was to excavate the earth some three or four feet, set these boards on end, forming in this way the walls of the hut, either in square or rectangle. The boards would batten each other so as to be quite tight. Then the roofs would be made of the same material, in the fashion of the backwoods houses of the pioneers. One side of one of the roofs would project over the other, with a space between the two large enough for the exit of the smoke. The doors were frequently cut in one large upright in the gable end of the house, but more frequently were cut from the adjacent sides of two boards. The shape of the door was either round or oval.

The fire was built on the floor, and in its center. Some of the houses had boulders of a green stone, which by long use were polished smooth and used for chairs.

Their food consisted principally of acorns, fish, grass seed, roots, and occasionally a little venison. Like all Indians who live by their wits, they were expert in taking their game.

Their government was entirely patriarchal; there were no chiefs beyond the heads of families. Their influence would depend on their wealth, which consisted of these large woodpecker scalps with the upper mandible attached, and these would be sewn on a nice piece of buckskin, dressed white. They also valued a long, conical shell found in Queen Charlotte Sound, which they called Ali-cachuck, not unlike the wam-pum of our eastern Indians of early date. Obsidian in large, knife-like shapes was also valuable, but a white deerskin would take all an Indian had. He would sell his own soul for one.

On state occasions this wealth was paraded by being worn around the neck, generally by some member of the family.

In addition to the above articles being hoarded as wealth, they had some sacred significance attached to them that I could never quite understand. For instance, they had a yearly ceremony in putting in a dam in the river at a place called Cappec, for the purpose of catching salmon. It was one of the occasions when all this wealth was paraded. All those who were present at that ceremony would have all their past feuds with each other wiped out.[1]

They were particularly superstitious. They believed firmly in the marvelous. Nothing that occurred, it made no difference how insignificant, but what they had some reason to account for it that was satisfactory to themselves. For instance, if they went out hunting and failed to see game, or if they saw some and failed to kill it, or if it rained while they were out, or if they lost something, and a thousand and one things like that, they would declare that some person had bewitched them, and generally they would tell you the person who did the mischief. I used to try to reason with them

[1] The "Kepel Dam Dance" is described by Kroeber in *Handbook of the Indians of California*, 58–60.

that the deer were not where they hunted, but they would answer that they saw so many deer there before, and they were there now, but someone had turned them into brush or rocks, and nothing could shake their belief.

Most everything in their country had some legend connected with it. Some of them were very interesting and touching. They were very fond of these legends, and would tell you by the hour, if you would listen.

They were firm believers in the devil. When asked if they ever saw the devil they would say no, but they had heard him, and such and such a one had seen him, so that there was no doubt of his existence. They said he had long claws, hooked bill, long tail, and was covered all over with pitch. He could be hidden behind a tree or rock, and when Mr. Indian would be coming along, suspecting nothing, the devil would reach out and take him in, and that would be the last Mr. Indian would ever know.

They had a vague idea of a flood which once drowned everybody except one Indian and a coyote that got back on a high mountain from Fort Ter-Waw a few miles, and that all the Indians sprang from them.

They also have a legend about the coming, years ago, of god and his son, who came from the east. The father, whom they called "Wa-peck-a-maw,"[2] was a very good man. He was continually doing good, while his son was a graceless scamp, who was very wild, and bad after women. Finally his excesses became so great that they could not stand him any longer, so they made up their minds to kill them both. They killed the son, but the father made his escape down the coast. The Indians followed him till he came to a tree, where they could find his trail no longer, and gave up the chase.

The legend goes that he climbed up the tree, and willed the tree to grow over him, and when the Indians arrived they could see nothing of him. When the Indians left, and he saw that he was no longer in any danger, he cast around how to get out of the tree.

Along came a small woodpecker, who agreed to do what he could to relieve him from his dilemma, but as his bill was small, and he could do but little execution, he made only part of his head

[2] Wohpekumeu. Kroeber, *Handbook of the Indians of California*, 73–74.

71

red. Then came the crow, who in those days was rather a pretty bird, partially red and white. The Wa-peck-a-maw tried to strike up a bargain with him, but the crow was too exorbitant in his demands, saying that his bill was large, and could make great execution. He wanted to be made red all over, which terms were objected to. The father would consent to make his head and tail red, but that was indignantly refused, whereupon the Wa-peck-a-maw got angry, and dismissed him with a curse that he and his progeny should be black until the end of time, hence, why the crow is black.

Then along came the large woodpecker, who went to work with a will, regardless of what he was to get, and as he did much execution, his scalp was made red, and that was why his was red, etc. When the Wa-peck-a-maw was released, he disappeared over the sea to the westward, and has never been seen since.

The first white men these Indians saw were some prospectors who came from the east. They immediately thought they were some of Wa-peck-a-maw's people. They at first thought they were painted white. They would rub their fingers on their skin to see if it would rub off. At first they were glad to see the whites and met them with open arms. Afterwards, when the influx of miners overran their country and abused their hospitality by outraging their squaws and shooting them down on the slightest provocation, they became very much incensed and agreed amongst themselves that if they were to kill off all the whites in their country, that would be the last of them, and to this end a good many were killed.

About then the steamers commenced plying up and down the coast, filled with passengers. They watched them for some time at the different ports, Crescent City and some others, and noticed that amongst all these people they never saw the same man twice. So they concluded that the whites were like the sand on the beach, they could not be counted, and so gave up their undertaking as hopeless.

Most of their little legends I have forgotten, and, in fact, I fear I was not a very good listener. They were very much attached to their huts and villages. One told me of her ancestor's hut having once been burned, and the green "Cachon" or chair would not be burned, but took its flight spirally up in the heavens, singing like the "music of the spheres," and was never seen again. It was regarded as an insult to express any doubt as to the truth of these stories.[3]

Andrew Snider,[4] who sutled at the post, and I used to hunt a great deal in the mountains. The trails were frequently so rough that we had to depend entirely upon the Indians to pack our traps in and our game out. It was on these occasions when they would spin their yarns. On one of these hunts we had a big, one-eyed Indian by the name of Sen Cren, who helped paddle our canoe up the river, and then up a mountain torrent high up in the mountains to a small village from where these Indians would help pack us up to the hunting ground.

On the way up the Klamath, Sen Cren told us about his little daughter, how he loved her, and how sorry he was to go away from her, and he felt anxious for fear something might happen to him and he wouldn't get to see his child again, etc. He lost his sheath knife out of our boat, and wanted us to pay for it. We told him that our law was different, that the person contracting to do the service took all such chances at loss. He said their law was different.

When we were going up Blue Creek, the mountain torrent, the mountains on either side were very steep, and consequently quite close to each other. In that country were small birds, "screech owls," that would utter a whistling note. One of these birds piped his little lay on our side of the steep, and was answered by his mate on the other, or else the echo, I forget now which.

Mr. Sen Cren said he knew it was the devil, and no amount of argument would change his mind. He commenced sassing His Satanic Majesty, accusing him of all kinds of mean acts, of carrying off Indians, etc., telling him what a coward he was in attacking unprotected Indians. Why didn't he come down and attack him now that his white friends were with him, armed with guns. He wasn't afraid of all the devils put together. All this was shouted at the top of his voice.

He continued this badinage clear to our landing place, which was below the village. After making our camp, we started off in

[3] In the course of his association with the Indians, Lieutenant Crook assembled at least two vocabularies which are on file at the Smithsonian Institution, Bureau of American Ethnology.

[4] Andrew Snider was post trader at Camp Warner, Oregon, in 1870. He appeared again later in Crook's life as a mine promoter.

73

different directions to hunt until dark, leaving Sen Cren to keep camp. I was the first to return from the hunt, just as it was getting dusk. I slipped up close to the camp unobserved, and hid behind a clump of brush. Sen Cren was standing by the fire, warming himself. I imitated this bird, and he sprang and seized a hand axe we had, and squared himself, telling the devil what a coward he was for refusing to tackle him when his friends were with him, but now, when he saw he was all alone, he was acting out his cowardly nature, but "Come on, I am aready for you." (Showed much more pluck than I thought was in him.)

Just then I threw a rock from my cover. As it neared him he must have sprung ten feet, holding the axe ready for battle. When I showed myself, he experienced great relief. He told me how he thought he was gone, and how so many things had crowded on his mind. The first was that he would never see his little girl again, and how it would distress her, also that no one would know what had become of him. He frankly told me everything, and afterwards when everybody got to making such fun of him, he then declared he knew it was me all the time, etc.

The next morning we went up to the hunting grounds, which was covered with snow. An old bummer joined the party, helping to do the packing on the prospect of getting his belly full of venison. His garb consisted of an old felt hat with all its rim minus except a little bill in front, and an old wool overcoat so rotten that it would scarcely hold together, the original color so faded that it was impossible to tell what it had been.

When night came on, and we were standing around the camp-fire, the old fellow would outdistance Ananias in telling yarns. Many marvelous stories were told in connection with quite a cele-brated Indian hunter amongst them by the name of Marucus, of of whom this old fellow claimed to be a relative. He claimed that Maurcus had killed a white elk once, etc. etc.

Finally, when we turned in, he said he would make medicine so we would have good luck on tomorrow. (It was his making medicine that made Marucus so successful in killing the white elk.) He lay down by the fire and commenced singing his medi-cine song. Later I saw him all of a sudden shoot up in the air, and when he came down to the ground again, he commenced pounding his coat and regretting his luck.

When the excitement cleared away and the damages were assessed, it was discovered that a strip of his coat had burned out from the collar to the tail, and only held together by what was left of the collar. To see him walking around the next morning with the two sides of his cloat flying to the breeze, showing his back, you would suppose he had dropped out of a comical almanac.

When our hunt was over, Snider had some tea left which he gave to this old fellow, who, not knowing what to do with it, seems, put it in his pipe and smoked it. Soon afterwards he hung himself, and the next time we were up there hunting they talked about lynching us for poisoning the old man. The old squaws perched on the tops of their houses, cawing like so many crows, abusing us to everything they could lay their tongues to.

These Indians were very fond of whale blubber. Occasionally one of these monsters would wash ashore, dead. All the Indians far and near would flock to the carcass and gorge themselves on the blubber, and pack off what they could carry. The stench of the animal could be smelled for miles, so it was not desirable to have any Indians near you who had touched the flesh. They couldn't be made to understand that this odor was not pleasant. They would say that ham was just as offensive to their nostrils.

The Indians were also fond of sea lion meat. The distance from bluff to bluff at the mouth of the Klamath River was over one mile. The heavy breakers from the ocean striking the current of the river had thrown up a bank of sand from bluff to bluff. The channel of the river cut its way through this bank of sand and discharged into the ocean with a swift current. Sometimes during a heavy storm this mouth would be closed up, and the river would cut out another channel through this bank, which was from one-fourth to one-half a mile wide, not always in the same place. So the channel had at times been in different places extending from one bluff to another.

Opposite on these two bluffs were villages. The one on the left bank was called Wiltosquaw, the one on the opposite was called Recqua.[5] From their villages the Indians had a commanding view of the beach between the two bluffs. I frequently used to take my

---

[5] Wetlkwali and Rekwoi. Kroeber, *Handbook of the Indians of California*, 9.

rifle and shoot the sea lion when the tide was coming in, so their bodies would be rolled in by the tide. The breakers were also more or less heavy, and as they had to be shot in the head or neck in order to kill them, it required quick work and a good deal of skill to kill them.

The Indians from both villages would keep a lookout, and just as soon as one of these animals made its appearance, they would break from both villages at the top of their speed, men, women, and children. The men armed with a knife from two to four feet long, made out of a saw blade, with the handle about one third of the distance from one of the ends. The blade at this point was narrowed down, so as to form an easy grip for the hand, and this was rounded by wrapping it with the hide of the lion. Both ends of the blade were tapered down to a point, and kept quite sharp.

The squaws carried their baskets strapped to their heads, while the children went to see the fun. The buck would hack and saw away with his knife, and when a piece of meat was detached, he would give it a toss over his head, to be caught by his squaw, who had her eagle eye on him. In the basket it would go. It was a perfect pandemonium, all yelling at the top of their voices, quarreling, jostling, and trying to push each other away from the carcass. After it was all over they would quiet down, and talk and joke over the fun they had had. Some of them would have quite serious gashes on their hands and arms, but seemed to take it all as a good joke. At first I thought they were fighting sure enough, but when I understood it, I enjoyed the joke as much as they did.

To illustrate their customs, laws, etc.—one of the Indians at Recqua had a harpoon given to him by a white man. To this harpoon was attached a long rope for the purpose of capturing sea lion by standing on the edge of the channel of this sand bank. The sea lions would follow the salmon in, and would frequently come near enough to be struck with this harpoon.

One day the owner of this harpoon was going fishing, and suggested to two others that if they would go along and help hold on to the rope, he would share the meat with them. This was all right. The sea was rough, and a sea lion was struck pretty well aft, and being on the top of a breaker at the time, jerked the three into the current and made his escape, harpoon and all.

Two of the Indians managed to get ashore, but the third one

was carried out beyond the breakers. There was a very high sea on, and it was a foregone conclusion that it was impossible to rescue him. Before he was drowned, two Indians had a fight over who should have his knife. The relatives of this man demanded pay for the dead man from the owner of the harpoon, who acknowledged the justice of the law, but declined to pay the price asked, saying that the man was a poor, good-for-nothing fellow, and his commercial value was small, etc. etc. The affair finally culminated in the deceased man's friends killing two of the others, whereupon they retaliated and killed two of the other's friends. Then, after much bickering, they settled the matter.

We frequently used to camp at the mouth of the river, fishing and hunting. We had a company seine that we used to catch salmon and other fish with. Once at the mouth of the river we caught over two ton and a half of porgie at one haul. There was a species of lamprey eel that the Indians caught in quantities that were very fine eating. They had but one entrail that ran through them like a crane's. I have seen the Indians catch in baskets, set something on the same principle as the set net, a canoe very near full of these squirming things.

These Indians, as I before stated, were full of superstitions. One night an Indian came to my house during the small hours, very much excited. He wanted me to hurry up to Sa-aitl, a village a couple of miles from the post. He said that some of the up-river Indians were going to kill them for being witches. I lost no time in getting to the river where he had a canoe waiting for me.

When I reached the village, sure enough there were a lot of excited Indians from up the river who were clamoring for the lives of its inhabitants, declaring that they were witches, etc., that they had bewitched the salmon, and made them run through the mountains instead of up the river where they could catch them, and that their children were hungry, and crying for them. Like all such beliefs, the more unreasonable and absurd they were the more difficult it was to reason them out of them. By arguments and threats I finally prevailed on them to desist. Their whole life seemed to be made up on such small affairs. It was a practical illustration of how nearly all their worry and unhappiness came from their imagination, and not from reality.

In the fall of 1859 I was sent to Rogue River Valley to enquire into some Indian difficulties reported. I had to go from Crescent City to Jacksonville by stage. The first night out from Crescent City we stopped all night at a mining town called "Sailor Diggins."[6] I was taken with most violent pains in my stomach. There seemed to be a ball of fire in it. I ate little or no supper, thinking it was indigestion. I suffered more or less on the whole trip. Upon my return to Ter-Waw the doctor told me it was my liver that was the cause of my trouble. After giving me some strong medicine, as he said, the whole thing disappeared.

Since my return from the expedition under Maj. Garnett in the fall of 1858, until the spring of 1861 when I left for the Presidio where part of the 4th and 9th Infantry were assembled, owing to the breaking out of the rebellion, all this was the first respite I had had from Indians since I entered the service.

I had little or nothing to do after the building of the post was completed, and never in my life enjoyed myself so much. It was the happiest part of my life. I was free from care and responsibility. My rank and position did not interfere with the ambition and excite the jealousies of others who were in a position to make me feel it. I have learned since that what was commendable in me as a Lieutenant is just the reverse since I have become a General Officer. Success in those days was commendated by your superiors, but nowadays it depends on how much your actions interfere with the ambitions and jealousies of your superiors.

In the fall of 1860 I went east by the overland stage from San Francisco to near Jeffersonville, Missouri. Our route lay through Los Angeles, Fort Yuma, Tucson, El Paso, and Fort Smith, Arkansas, and occupied twenty-one days and nights to make the trip. It was the severest ordeal I have ever experienced of this kind. The heat and dust for a great portion of the way was intense. It was impossible to get any refreshing sleep driving all the time. I lost six hats on the trip. I would doze off to sleep, and then would wake up to find my hat gone.

The Indians were bad through Arizona. One station not far from where Fort Bowie stands now had just been taken by Indians. We changed our jaded horses at this station for four wild mules.

---

[6] Sailors' Diggings, at the headwaters of Illinois River, near the present town of Waldo, Oregon, was the scene of rich placer fields about 1852. The discovery was made by a party of sailors, hence the name.

After proceeding some four miles from this station, the mules became frightened, broke loose from the stage, and left us standing on the plain until the driver returned to the station for the horses that had hauled us to the station previously.

While awaiting for the return of our driver, the eastern stage came along. One of its passengers was enquiring in a loud voice if any person from San Francisco was aboard our stage. Upon close inspection I found this individual to be Sylvester Mowry, who was a classmate of mine. I had not seen him since graduation, before he had left the service and had cast his fortunes with Arizona. He thought he was mining. He also had political ambitions as well.[7]

I stopped over at Sherman, Texas, for a few days, having some business there. There was a fair in full progress there. Of all the hard characters assembled there I had never seen in all my life, gamblers, cut throats, thieves of all descriptions seemed to take the lead. There not being sufficient accommodations in the hotel, a traveling companion and myself were put in a bed together in a small outhouse. This small place was filled with beds, and during the night I heard the landlord come in with some guest to show him a bed.

He had no light, but would grope his way from one bed to another, feeling the occupants, and talking aloud to himself. He would go to a bed and say, "Two in this," and next, "Two in this," until he came to a bed with only one in. He would tell the new guest to turn in there. It was the conversation I heard in this dark room that gave me my impression of the people there assembled.

The next day my traveling companion left me for the country, which left me all alone in that hard crowd. I was determined, if possible, not to sleep with any of that bad lot, so I rolled a pair of blankets I had into about the size of a man, and lay them by my side. This had the desired effect, for some time during the night the landlord came around several times and felt my bed, saying there were two in this, etc. So I escaped the disagreeable necessity of having to sleep with these people. I had a malarious attack while

[7] After graduation from the Military Academy, Mowry served on the frontier at San Francisco from 1852 to 1853. He resigned from the army in 1858 and served as representative from the proposed Territory of Arizona from 1857 to 1858. He is the author of the rather scarce *Geography and Resources of Arizona and Sonora* (Washington, 1859). He died in 1871.

here which caused me to take my departure with as little delay as possible.

Our stage journey terminated at a little place called Syracuse, to which point the railroad had just been completed.[8] Just as we arrived at the station, a train of cars came in. I thought I never did see anything so grand and majestic as the locomotive. I had been in California for eight years, and had just spanned the continent on stage, and a very poor and uncomfortable one at that. I from there proceeded to my home near Dayton, Ohio, saw my relatives, and from there went to New York, from where I was ordered out to San Francisco with recruits.

Col. Merchant of one of the artillery regiments was in charge with several junior officers, amongst whom were Louis A. Armistead, Lts. Baker, Reilly, Mills, Kellogg, and myself.

Doctor Shorb and his young wife were also aboard. From San Francisco Doctor Shorb, wife, and I took passage on the steamer *Columbia* for up the coast. The Doctor was going to Fort Umpqua near the mouth of the Umpqua River.[9] We encountered a fearful storm as we neared the mouth of the Umpqua, and in crossing the bar before entering the harbor, a heavy wave struck us aft and combed at least fifteen feet above the deck, pouring down upon it like so much lead, sweeping everything before it. The railing, steering wheel, snubbing posts, lockers, and in fact everything on the deck was swept off, the two men at the wheel included.

The davits from which the boats hung were bent as though they were so much lead. One of the men was afterwards picked up in one of the boats, badly ruptured, while the other poor fellow could be seen in the breakers, struggling for his life. At one time when the ship was in the trough of the sea, the man appeared on the top of the wave above us, and seemed as if he could have jumped down on deck. After that he was lost sight of.

---

[8] In 1860 the Pacific Railway ran west from St. Louis along the Missouri River, terminating at Syracuse, Missouri.

[9] Fort Umpqua was established on July 28, 1856, on the abandoned site of what was once called Umpqua City, on the north bank of Umpqua River, near its mouth. The fort was supposed to discourage any attempt by the Indians to leave the Grande Ronde reservation. One day in the summer of 1862 the paymaster arrived and found everyone of the garrison out hunting. His report of the incident led to the abandonment of the fort. *Posts, Camps, and Stations File;* Writers' Program, Oregon, *Oregon, End of the Trail,* 380.

As soon as the water ran off the deck, the Captain ran with a relieving tackle, and made it fast to the steering apparatus just in time to save the ship from going ashore. We lay by the next day until late in the afternoon to make the necessary repairs and to wait for the sea to run down. The sea remained heavy all the way down to Crescent City, the point I was to land, and the strain on the ship had so wrenched her that she leaked all over. It was raining hard all the time, and the water ran through the deck like a sieve.

The stateroom had several inches of water in there. When the ship would careen the water rushing back and forth had anything but a cheering sound. Sometime during the night a woman in the room next to me had evidently wakened out of a sleep, and, hearing this rushing of the water, and no lights visible, commenced calling the Captain. Getting no response, she called to the mate, and getting no response, commenced praying to be saved. I didn't blame her, for it was calculated to frighten the bravest.

When we neared Crescent City, the sea was so rough that the ship could not venture within a mile of the shore, so we had to lay off until small boats came out to us. It was very difficult to transfer the passengers to the small boats. The woman of the night before was to get off here. She at first declined, but finally, by putting a rope around her waist, she was lowered into a small boat. Even the small boats would occasionally take water, so we were all glad when we reached terra firma.

I was glad to get back to Ter-Waw. I found things about as I had left them.

In the spring of 1861 I proceeded with my company to the Presidio of San Francisco,[10] where I joined several other companies of the 4th and 9th Infantry.

[10] The Presidio of San Francisco was established by the Spaniards in 1776 and occupied by them, and later by the Mexicans, until the United States took possession in 1846. The gold rush greatly increased the importance of this post, because of its proximity to the growing town of San Francisco.

It was officially named Presidio by executive order, November 6, 1850, and Presidio of San Francisco by *General Order No. 3*, in 1938. The reservation now includes Fort Winfield Scott, Letterman General Hospital, and Crissy Field.

The Officers' Club at Presidio was built by the Spaniards in 1776 and enjoys the distinction of being the oldest building in the San Francisco area. War Department, *Military Reservations, California*, 62–69; Augustin G. Rudd, *Histories of Army Posts*, 5.

Shortly after I left, Capt. L. C. Hunt was ordered to Fort Ter-Waw to reap the fruits of my sowing, and, strange to say, it has been ever thus through my life. I have had to do the rough work for others afterwards to get the benefits from it.

In this way I have been the pioneer of all the country on the Pacific Coast, from the British to the Mexican borders.

III
BRIGADIER GENERAL
VOLUNTEERS

7. *The war would be over before we reached New York*

ON THE FIRST DAY OF AUGUST, 1861, I, with ten other officers of the army, left the San Francisco harbor on the Panama steamer for New York to participate in the war. When we reached Acapulco, we heard of the first part of Bull Run up to the time when our troops had been successful. We all felt that the war would be over before we reached New York. But when we arrived in Panama, we heard the sequel, and a bluer set of people could not well have been found.

We also heard that the *Alabama* was cruising about to capture the line of steamers plying between New York and San Francisco, so we felt more or less apprehensive.[1] The pilot that boarded us when we landed in New York informed us of General Lyon's death, and when we landed in New York, everything was very blue.

I was appointed a Captain in the 14th Infantry, and wrote my acceptance from New York City. My acceptance was returned to me with the information that I could remain in my old regiment, and, as my lineal rank would be the same, and as my regiment was in California, it would increase my chances of being allowed to take service in the Volunteers. Then, too, Col. Sacket and R. I. Dodge both advised me to remain in my old regiment.

After remaining in New York a few days, I went over to Washington with a view of getting a leave of absence to go into the Volunteer service. For this purpose I called on General Schenck,

---

[1] He probably means the *Sumter*, for the *Alabama* was not yet a raider at the time. The *Sumter* escaped from the Mississippi River in June of 1861. Raphael Semmes, *The Cruise of the Alabama and the Sumter*, I, 25–29.

to get his assistance. At first he was very cool, making some disparaging remarks about the Regulars, he having had some difficulty with General A. D. McCook and Adjutant-General Thomas. But after while he warmed up, and said he would go with me to the President the next day. The next day we went to see the President, but he was not in, so we started over to the War Department, and met the President on the way.

Gen. Schenck told him our errand, whereupon he told us that at a Cabinet meeting the day previous they had agreed to allow one hundred officers of the Regular Army to take service in the Volunteers. Schenck asked him if he would not give an order to the Adjutant-General. Mr. Lincoln said no, that he never interfered with the running of any branches of the government any more than he would try to mend a watch, for, should he put his foot in it, it would never run again. This gave me a good opportunity to examine his personal appearance. He was the most ungainly man I had ever seen, particularly his legs and feet.

We then went to the Adjutant-General's office. Gen. Thomas was there. When Gen. Schenck told him the object of our visit, he acknowledged the action of the Cabinet the day previous, and volunteered the remark that if he had his way not a single officer of the Regular Army would go into the Volunteer service. Whereupon Schenck told him that thank the Lord he didn't have his own way, and talked very sharp to him. I felt rather alarmed at his talking so to a man of his rank, but I since have learned that he is little more than a clerk, and what influence he has is generally assumed.[2]

I was informed, however, that it would be necessary for the governor of some state to make an application for me. So I at once telegraphed Governor Dennison of Ohio that I was at liberty to accept the Colonelcy of a regiment if he had one to give me. He answered that he would appoint me Colonel of the 43rd Regiment, which was then being organized at Columbus.

[2] Robert Cummings Schenck, who had sent Crook to West Point, had been appointed brigadier general of Volunteers, May 17, 1861. He took part in the first battle of Bull Run.

Never known for his reticence, Schenck usually got what he wanted, in this case Crook's release to the Volunteers. Later in life Schenck practiced law in Washington, and became an authority on draw poker, two closely related skills at that time. He died in 1890.

Upon hearing this, I got an indefinite leave of absence, and at once proceeded to Columbus. I repaired to the state capitol and met the governor, who was just on his way to leave the city. I asked him how near the 43rd was organized. He stated that the Lieutenant-Colonel had been appointed. I stated that I was then ready to take the field, that I knew nothing about raising a regiment, that I had the refusal of a Pennsylvania regiment, but would prefer one from my own state. He at once appointed me Colonel of the 36th Regiment of Infantry, then stationed at Summersville, West Virginia.[3]

The next morning I left for my regiment via the Kanawha River to Gauley Bridge. I found the regiment in rather a demoralized condition. They were mostly from the country, and had been taken from their plows with such clothing as they happened to have on. They were unused to discipline, and were marched from Clarkesburg to Summersville in the heat of summer by Col. Slemmer, a Regular officer, who expected them to know and observe the rules of discipline of the service. He would make no allowances, and was very severe on them, and they thought unnecessarily so. So when they reached Summersville, they were almost in a state of mutiny. Before this they had been very anxious to have a Regular officer for their Colonel, but this treatment had produced a complete revulsion of feeling, so when I arrived and announced myself, I was regarded with much disfavor amongst them.

This was the middle of September, and the summer clothing that the men had brought with them from their plows was worn out, and many of the men were entirely barefooted. I at once set at work in providing for their wants. They were as rare as a piece of beefsteak. Officers as well as men knew nothing of what was

[3] The Thirty-sixth Ohio Volunteer Infantry was organized at Camp Putnam, Marietta, Ohio, in August, 1861. Its first officers were Melvin Clarke, Esq., a prominent lawyer of Marietta, lieutenant colonel, and E. B. Andrews, professor of natural history in Marietta College, major. For the position of colonel it was the strong desire of these officers to have a man of thorough military education. After repeated efforts and many failures, such a man was secured in George Crook of Dayton, then captain in the Fourth Infantry of the Regular Army.

Before Colonel Crook assumed command, six companies marched through several counties of West Virginia to clear the country of large bands of guerrillas. Colonel Crook did not join these companies until they had reached Summerville, in Nicholas County. Whitelaw Reid, *Ohio in the War*, II, 233–34.

expected of them. They thought all they had to do was fight, and thought that drill and discipline were entirely unnecessary, thought it only a waste of time, and that they could fight just as well as they were, etc. etc.

I had repeated talks with the officers, and we would have a mutual understanding. I explained I would not expect too much of them, but on their part they must learn their profession, and those who failed would have to give way to others who would, and that they were not the judges as to whether or not a knowledge of their profession was necessary. I must say that I never saw a more willing set of men in my life.

The regiment represented most all the professions and trades known in the land. We found an abandoned sawmill not far from Summersville. It was reported as worthless, but some of the mechanics took hold of it, and converted it into a first class sawmill. Not only did we saw enough lumber to make the men comfortable, but sufficient was sawed to build a drill house 740 feet long and 33 feet wide, in which I personally superintended daily drills, Sunday excepted, from four to six hours. At night we would have recitations from one to two hours.

Being in the extreme advance, and in the very midst of the "bushwhackers," I had to be very vigilant, and at the same time keep a constant eye on my pickets and outposts who did not properly appreciate the importance of their trust. Never in all my life did I work so hard, mentally and physically, as I did through this winter.

The men, being so entirely unaccustomed to this kind of life, went through a sweating process, as it might be termed. Large numbers were taken down with the typhoid fever. At least a third of them were down at a time, so in this manner all of the soft material that could not stand the hardships of the service were worked off, either by dying, or leaving, sick, and many of them never recovered.

This country was the home of counterfeiters and cut-throats before the war, and it was the headquarters of the bushwhackers. It was well adapted for their operations, for, with the exception of a small clearing here and there for the cabins of the poor people who inhabited it, it was heavily timbered, with thick underbrush, rocky and broken, with dense laurel thickets here and there. The thoroughfares and country roads that traversed this country were like traveling through a box cañon with the forest and underbrush for walls.

It was here that the cowardly bushwhackers would waylay the unsuspecting traveler, and shoot him down with impunity. Their suppression became a military necessity, as they caused us to detach much of our active force for escorts, and even then no one was safe. It was an impossibility for them to be caught after shooting into a body of men, no difference as to its size. The question was how to get rid of them.

Being fresh from the Indian country where I had more or less experience with that kind of warfare, I set to work organizing for the task. I selected some of the most apt officers, and scattered them through the country to learn it and all the people in it, and particularly the bushwhackers, their haunts, etc.

Very soon they commenced catching them, and bringing them in as prisoners. I would forward them to Camp Chase[4] for confinement, by order of Gen. Rosecrans. It was not long before they commenced coming back, fat, saucy, with good clothes, and returned to their old occupations with renewed vigor. As a matter of course, we were all disgusted at having our hard work set at naught, and have them come back in a defiant manner, as much as to say, "Well, what are you going to do about it?"

In a short time no more of these prisoners were brought in. By this time every bushwhacker in the country was known, and when an officer returned from a scout he would report that they had caught so-and-so, but in bringing him in he slipped off a log while crossing a stream and broke his neck, or that he was killed by an accidental discharge of one of the men's guns, and many like reports. But they never brought back any more prisoners.

[4] Camp Chase, near Columbus, Ohio, was organized in the summer of 1861. It was first called Camp Jackson, but soon Chase, in honor of Salmon P. Chase, former governor of Ohio.

The camp was first used as a drill and rendezvous post but later became the quarters of paroled prisoners of war and for the confinement of Rebel prisoners. After the war it was used as a general hospital and as quarters for troops being mustered out.

Camp Chase was discontinued in 1866, and the buildings were turned over to the board of managers for the National Asylum for Disabled Veterans. William H. Knauss, *The Story of Camp Chase.*

Webster, one of the counties adjoining Nicholas, in which Summersville was located, was so bad that we had to burn out the entire county to prevent the people from harboring them. Towards spring about all of them had either been killed or run off within reach of our headquarters. Some of them had taken refuge in Greenbrier County, and would occasionally make a raid on our side of the mountains.

One night these men made a raid on a sutler within a couple of miles of Summersville. That night yet I slipped two companies into two passes that led into Greenbrier County, feeling satisfied that they would try to escape through them. These passes were fifteen to twenty miles distant. I intended the next morning to take some of the companies myself, and hunt over some of the districts of the county, so in case they were lurking there we would drive them through the passes before mentioned.

Bright and early the next morning an old native came up to Headquarters and offered his services as a guide to take us to the country. He thought the guilty parties could be found. As his place corresponded to the place I intended going to, I accepted his services. On our search we saw or heard nothing of them, but they made tracks for Greenbrier County, and in attempting to escape through one of the passes, they received a volley from the company ambushed in a laurel thicket, killing them instantly, there being three of them.[5]

This spread such terror amongst the people that they let them lie there over a month before they buried them. It turned out afterwards that the old fellow who offered his services as guide was the father of one of the bushwhackers, doubtless thinking he was misleading me, little knowing that troops had been sent the night previous to ambush the passes.

This was the last act of the bushwhackers in that section of the country. In fact, I might say that it was the place where this pernicious mode of warfare first originated. The inhabitants said they never had such law and order before, even prior to the war.

In addition to all this work I personally instructed, and audited all the officers' returns and accounts that had to be made out with the view of a proper accountability to the government for all that

[5] U. S. War Department, *The War of the Rebellion*, Ser. I, Vol. V, 496 (hereafter referred to as *The War of the Rebellion*).

was issued them. Some of them demurred at this, saying that officers of other regiments were not required to make out such papers. But they learned all that was required of them.

When at the close of the war I went to Columbus by request to see the regiment mustered out, they then thanked me for what I had done for them. They contrasted their situation with some other regiments who had been waiting for one month at Columbus without being mustered out on account of their papers not having been made out properly. Some of the officers were hiding away from their own men, who were going to whip them on sight. The 36th was mustered out at once, and the utmost good feeling was universal between the officers and men. They then said that they never before fully realized the benefit I did them in compelling them to thoroughly learn their duties.

8. *Our whole army was demoralized*

IN THE SPRING OF 1862 a provisional brigade was formed, composed of the 2nd West Virginia Cavalry, 36th and 44th Regiments of Ohio Infantry. I was to command. We marched to Lewisburg, where we were to act as an advanced post of observation. Shortly afterwards we pushed forward to Jackson River depot to learn the country and something of the enemy's intentions, etc. Beyond driving their few straggling forces out of the country, nothing was done of any advantage to our cause.

We returned, and went into camp on a hill on the west side of Lewisburg, a small village situated in a small hollow. On the east of the village was a hill similar to the one we were on, to the east and south ran the Greenbrier River a couple of miles distant. Pickets were stationed on all the roads leading into town.

At early dawn on the 23rd of May the pickets came rushing in on the eastern road, crossing the Greenbrier River with the information that the enemy in forces was advancing from that direction. Almost simultaneously the enemy appeared on a hill east of the town, and in a very few minutes afterwards they opened on us with their artillery, firing over the town, several of their balls falling into our camp.

Everything was gotten ready at once. The hospital and baggage was sent to the rear, while the two infantry regiments marched into town. As we got to the eastern suburbs, the infantry were formed in line of battle on each side of the main street, and advanced to meet the enemy. It was but a short time before we were engaged at close range with them, our troops meeting a charge of the enemy, which was returned by us at once. The enemy broke and ran, leaving their artillery and a hundred or so prisoners in our hands.

This was the first time my regiment was under fire, and I believe it was the case with the others as well, but old veterans could not have done better, for a more handsome victory was not gained during the war. General Heth was the commander on the opposite side. It was understood that his force was superior to mine, but I had no means of verifying it.[1]

On the battlefield were lots fenced in mostly with boards, so that it was impossible to go mounted. I left my horse, and went on foot in command of my regiment. Whilst near one of these board fences, the enemy's bullets striking against it sounded like hail, and I instinctively held my head to one side so as to prevent the hail from going down my neck. It was in this enclosure I was struck on the foot by a spent ball, which gave me no particular trouble until the battle was over, when my foot became very painful.

The population of the village with but one exception, so far as I know, sympathized with the South, and kept pretty well posted on the enemy's movements and intentions. They knew we were to be attacked, and so certain were they that we would be discomfited that they had breakfast ready for their southern friends. In order that they should not be disappointed, I turned over the prisoners for them to feed.

During the fight, while one of our wounded men was on his

---

[1] "In twenty minutes the Rebels were driven back over the summit of the hill, and utterly routed, with a loss of sixty killed, and left upon the field a hundred and seventy-five prisoners, four pieces of artillery, and three hundred stand of small arms, besides a very large number of wounded, whom they hurriedly carried off the field. The Thirty-Sixth lost seven killed and forty-four wounded, and five captured on picket."

Crook was brevetted major, U. S. Army, May 23, 1862, for "gallant and

way to the hospital, he was murdered by one of the Confederates who had slipped into the town to see some of his friends. The soldiers were much worked up about it, and it was with some difficulty I could restrain them from doing violence to the town under the belief that the dastardly act was committed by some of the inhabitants. The good discipline under which they were finally prevailed.

That night an alarm was given of an attack. I had to mount my horse and investigate the report. I don't know that I ever suffered more than I did on that occasion. Our rear was threatened by a road that led from Union to Meadow Bluffs from where the enemy had made his headquarters. This made it necessary for us to fall back to that point.

My suffering was intense during this move, as all the ambulances were full, so I rode on horseback. As severe as my pain was, I felt that I could not afford to go to bed, as my responsibility was too great to yield to my pain. My system being in splendid condition, I was not long in recovering, although I thought at one time I would have to suffer amputation from inflammation under the "annular belt."

The enemy then took station just across Greenbrier River, on the road leading from Meadow Bluffs to Union, where their headquarters were. We had frequent skirmishes, but none worthy of any consequence. We had a little fight about who should occupy a blackberry patch. We got the blackberries.

I was anxious to learn something of their disposition and strength. The reports of spies, refugees, and such information was very unsatisfactory and uncertain. So I tried sending flags of truce on the direct route, but met with no success. They were prepared for such attempts, giving their pickets most positive instructions not to let any flag of truce to enter their lines under any circumstances.

So the idea occurred to scout around Lewisburg, and as we had left some of our wounded there, it would give a plausible excuse to send that way. Captain (afterwards General) William H. Powell of the 2nd Virginia Cavalry, a very shrewd and determined man, was dispatched on this night. Sure enough, the enemy, not

meritorious services at the battle of Lewisburg, Va." Reid, *Ohio in the War*, II, 235; *The War of the Rebellion*, Ser. I, Vol. XII, 803–808.

expecting any communications in that direction, had given no particular instructions to their pickets. So, by address and assurance Powell was taken into headquarters before the authorities were aware of it.

They stewed and raved, and were inclined to be severe on him, but he claimed the treatment that was due him. He was not responsible for the shortcomings of their pickets, and they realized that he had seen all he desired, so they changed their treatment, but not with good grace. They would not let him return by the short route, but made him come back by the same route he rode in.

Shortly afterwards, I hoped to strike them a severe blow by marching on them by a forced march, but they got out of my way. We had to come back as we went, without having accomplished anything.

We remained here till sometime in August when part of my brigade and the other brigade commanded by Gen. J. D. Cox, who was operating on the other line by Raleigh Court House, were formed into a division known as the Kanawha Division, and then ordered to join the Army of the Potomac, in Washington.

My regiment and part of the 30th Ohio were the only troops of our division who reached Warrenton Junction before Stonewall Jackson cut the railroad,[2] so we were there without our brigades, as we belonged to different brigades. My regiment was 1,100 strong, and was the pride of my heart. I knew every man in it, and had spent so much hard work on it, that I regarded it as one of my own family. I feared that we would be attached to some brigade that would take no interest in it, and feared being sacrificed, so I succeeded in getting detailed as bodyguard to General Pope's headquarters, and in this position went through the second Battle of Bull Run.[3]

Although my position enabled me to see much that even a division commander in a large army could not, I could not get any comprehensive idea of much that was going on. However, I shared the idea of all about me that some disaster was pending. Just before dusk on the evening our army fell back, "Nosey" Ingalls of

[2] "Stonewall" Jackson cut the railroad during his march into position behind Pope's army, August 25.

[3] Crook was then in command of the Third Provisional Brigade and remained in command until August 13, 1862.

Infantry of Crook's command resting near Whitewood Creek in
the Black Hills after the "starvation march" of 1876

Courtesy National Archives

Chato, subchief of the Chiricahuas

the Quartermaster Department came to me, and said, "For God's sake, draw up your men in line and stop the fugitives."[4] He said that our army was badly beaten, and many of the men were falling back in a rout, and, unless stopped, they would not stop short of the Potomac.

I did as he requested, and sure enough we must have caught ten or fifteen thousand men without organizations trying to get to the rear. There were officers who had thrown away their shoulder straps and swords, so as to avoid detection. It was my first introduction to a demoralized army. No one can properly appreciate what a demoralized army means unless they can witness it as I did.

In the front where balls are flying thick and you don't know what moment is to be your last, it is much pleasanter than such a sight. It puts one out of conceit of his own kind to witness such poltroonery as there is there. Here one sees want of manhood in all of its most objectionable features. I thought our whole army was demoralized, and the only consolation I had was that dark was so near at hand, and that might save us.

All seemed commotion and confusion until late at night. The next morning there was a drizzling rain. My camp being on the ridge just behind Centerville, it gave me a good view of the troops on my front. The ten or fifteen thousand stragglers were held by my regiment just in my front, together with a few Confederate prisoners. The stragglers were scattered around in groups, some cooking and smoking, squirming around amongst each other like so many eel. The Confederates kept in a close mass. They were dirty, poorly dressed, and had a hungry look. On the whole they looked like so many laboring men rather than soldiers, for there were many without uniforms. They would occasionally have a set-to with each other, and have fist fights in dead earnest.

General Pope had his headquarters in a large building down in the village, whither I strolled later in the morning. In a large sitting room were assembled several general officers, amongst whom were Pope, Franklin, and several others whose names I have now forgotten. Just then Gen. Sam Sturgis came into the room. He had been ordered up from Alexandria by Gen. Pope for some object or other.

[4] This incident occurred on August 30.

Just as Sturgis entered the room, Gen. Pope looked around and said, "Too late, Sammy, too late." Sturgis said, "Damn it, didn't I tell you that all that was necessary for you to hang yourself was to give you plenty of rope!"

Our troops commenced falling back from here sometime during the day, and towards evening I was ordered to move. It had rained more or less all day, and the roads leading back to Fairfax Court House were wide, macadamized pike, wide enough to admit at least three wagons abreast. This was one mass of slop, kept constantly churning by the many feet and wheels of the retreating army. Just before dusk a brisk fire was opened on our left, and soon afterwards I learned that our troops had a fight at Chantilly and some other place, and that Generals Stevens and Kearny were killed.[5]

Shortly afterwards it became pitch dark, with a heavy rain. All was pandemonium. All were rushing to the rear, apparently regardless of each other. The road was one jam of wagons. Every few moments someone would call out, "Halt! Whose wagon is this!" The reply would almost invariably come back, "General Sigel's headquarters train," "General Sigel's headquarters ordnance train," or "General Sigel's headquarters supply train." Most every wagon or ambulance seemed to belong to General Sigel.

I was told during the evening that Stuart's Cavalry was somewhere in the country.[6] I was in constant dread for fear he would make an attack. I felt that the discharge of just one gun would cause serious disaster. To make matters worse, once or twice during the night I received orders to countermarch. While it was bad enough to go with the stream of this rabble, going against it was next to an impossibility.

It was too dark to see anything, and too dark to see our way to march alongside of the road, so we had to battle and get along the best we could. After awhile along would come another order, directing me again to go to the rear. In this way the whole night was passed.

[5] Isaac Stevens and Philip Kearny were both killed at the battle of Chantilly, part of the Second Manassas, September 1, 1862.

[6] "Jeb" Stuart's cavalry was very much around. A few days before he had made an expedition to the rear of Pope's army, reaching Catlett's station and capturing Pope's official papers and baggage.

The next morning the clouds partially cleared away, and the sun came out towards ten A.M. We halted near Fairfax Court House to get breakfast. We were muddy, bedraggled up to our knees, tired, and sleepy—this is one of the times when one is so glad he is a soldier.

9. It was galling to have to serve under such people

I WAS SHORTLY AFTER THIS relieved from my bodyguard duty, and proceeded to hunt up my brigade, in company with Hugh Ewing, Colonel of the 30th Ohio. As we were passing near Gen. Mc-Dowell's headquarters, he called us in, saying that as we were from Ohio, and he was so misunderstood and was likely to be more so growing out of this recent campaign, he wanted us to understand the whole matter.

He showed us the correspondence between himself and the Secretary of War in relation to the Peninsula campaign. Here he protested against being sent to Shenandoah instead of being allowed to carry out McClellan's original plan of joining him via Hanover Court House. He showed us the communications pro and con—which to my mind made out a very clear case against the War Department.[1]

From here we marched through Washington, where we were joined by the remainder of our division. We marched along with the army going towards Harper's Ferry. We were placed in Burnside's command after McClellan was placed in command of the army. The brigade to which I belonged was composed of the 11th, 28th, and 36th Ohio, Col. Moore in command. While marching through Frederick City [Fredericksburg], our brigade being in advance, Col. Moore with some of his staff got too far in advance of his command, and was captured, which placed me in command of the brigade.

After leaving Frederick City we turned to our left, and entered

[1] This correspondence is found in *The War of the Rebellion*, Ser. I, Vol. XII, Part III.

some fields. The country was rolling. At the far end of the field the ascent was rather steep. This side was surmounted partially by a stone wall, with timber beyond. We knew in a general way that the enemy was somewhere in front, but had no idea of their exact locality.

Just under the crest of this hill our division was drawn up in line of battle, while the enemy was occupying the crest in the edge of the timber, and the stone wall. We lay down as close as we could get to the enemy without exposing ourselves. Some of our men amused themselves by sticking their hats on their ramrods, and raising them high enough to meet the enemy's vision. A dozen bullet holes were made through them.

The two lines of battle were not over fifteen or twenty yards apart, with the advantage being on the other side. Fortunately, we received the order to charge just before they were going to charge us, and by taking the initiative, and by the impetuosity of our charge, their ranks were broken. Their men fled, not to return against us any more that day. A great many of their men were killed. Some of them were bayoneted behind the stone fence. Many more were killed farther down in the woods, near an old well or sunken road.

Farther to our right General Reno was killed that day.[2] Our losses were comparatively light. I cannot help but shedding tears over some of my regiment who were killed, and one pretty boy not over 16 or 17 years of age, a nice mother's boy, who lay mortally wounded, whose pleading face looked so pitiable. I had seen so much of them for the last year, knew them all, and felt as though they were my own family.

This was the battle of South Mountain, fought on the 14th day of September, 1862.[3]

I afterwards learned from my family that the farm where this battle was fought was near to, or the same farm where my mother was born and reared.

[2] Jesse L. Reno, graduate of the Military Academy in 1846, served in the Mexican War and on topographical survey duty. He was major general of Volunteers by July, 1862. He was thirty-nine years old when killed at South Mountain.

[3] Crook's report of the battle appears in *The War of the Rebellion*, Ser. I, Vol. XIX, Part I, 471.

The next day we took up our line of march by the sunken road, where so many of the enemy's dead were still lying, unburied. We passed by a great many troops, and were shown into a sunken cornfield on the left of our army, or at least my brigade was. The enemy was occupying a bluff about one-half of a mile in front of our line, and as soon as I went into the field, they opened on us with spherical case, filled with old, round musket balls. We lay flat on the ground, and could see the shells coming by their burning fuses long before we could hear the report of the gun. The fuses were so timed that they burst overhead, throwing the musket balls in our midst, which amusement they kept up as long as it was light enough to see. Strange to say, we had but very few men hurt by these missiles.

As I stated before, my brigade consisted of the 11th, 28th, and 36th Ohio. The 11th was commanded by Lt. Col. Coleman, the 28th by Lt. Col. Bolinger, and the 36th by Lt. Col. Clarke. As none of our wagons came up, we had to go to bed supperless, nor did we have anything to eat since morning. The next morning my servant went to a house on neutral grounds between the lines of skirmishers. He found that the occupants had fled, but they had left a batch of bread ready to bake, and plenty of nice butter and milk in the cellar. We baked the bread, and returned with such a breakfast that none of us had tasted for many a day.

We could hear firing on our right and front, but knew nothing more. About ten A.M., Capt. Christ on Gen. Cox' staff came to see me, and said, "The General wishes you to take the bridge." I asked him what bridge. He said he didn't know. I asked him where the stream was, but he didn't know. I made some remarks not complimentary to such a way of doing business, but he went off, not caring a cent. Probably he had done the correct thing.

The consequence was that I had to get a good many men killed in acquiring the information which should have been supplied me from division headquarters. I at once sent the 11th Ohio to reconnoiter toward the bluffs from where the shrapnel came the evening before, while I left the 36th near the house, intending, when the position of the bridge was located, to charge it with this regiment and with the 28th Ohio. I went with it to reconnoiter, to our right. I soon saw the situation, and saw that there was a stream running close to the bluff before mentioned, and that the road passed into the bottom of the creek, and thence parallel to the bluff and creek for a couple of hundred yards to the bridge.

I at once ordered a battery of artillery to a commanding position to the right, which commanded and enfiladed the bluffs. In the meantime the 28th found the creek a little further up not over knee deep, with good crossing. As soon as they had crossed, the enemy's position was untenable except with a superior force to the one they had there.

This crossing, together with the enfilading fire of the artillery, caused the enemy to evacuate before I could get back to the 36th. Two Pennsylvania regiments crossed it without loss, and got the credit of taking the bridge. I understood that both their Colonels were made Brigadier Generals for this service.[4] The 11th Regiment pushed near enough to the bluff to lose a large number of men killed and wounded, amongst the former Col. Coleman.

I learned afterwards that Gen. Sturgis with a division was repulsed in trying to take the bridge earlier in the morning, losing some six hundred men, principally against the bluffs where Col. Coleman lost his life. I was expected to accomplish with my brigade what a division had failed to do, and without ever getting the benefit of the knowledge he had gained in his reconnaissance. Such imbecility and incompetency was simply criminal, a great deal of which lasted until the close of the war. It was galling to have to serve under such people. But many of them, by maneuvering in politics and elsewhere, are looked upon by certain people throughout the land as some of our military luminaries.

After the opposite of the creek, Antietam, was occupied, Gen. Cox came over for the first time I had seen him since the South Mountain fight. I was informed that I was to support the Philadelphia Corn Exchange Brigade, who were going to make a charge

---

[4] This was the battle of Antietam. The action of crossing the bridge here described took place on September 17, 1862. Burnside's Bridge was on the left flank of the Union Army below Sharpsburg. Crook managed to cross five companies of the Twenty-eighth Ohio at the ford, and then, under cover of the artillery and sharpshooters, the Fifty-first New York under Colonel Robert B. Potter and the Fifty-first Pennsylvania under Colonel John F. Hartranft crossed the bridge without opposition.

The record does not bear out Crook's remark concerning these colonels' having been promoted by this action. *The War of Rebellion*, Ser. I, Vol. XIX, Part I, 471–72.

to the left of Sharpsburg. I was to use the 11th and 36th, the 28th being detached. I remonstrated that my line would be so attentuated that it would be emasculated, but all to no avail.

While we were lying under the bluffs waiting for the troops to get into position, I strolled up the creek to a wooded knoll that looked over towards the enemy's position at Sharpsburg. I could see from this position. I saw two batteries on a clear field, trained on the road leading to Sharpsburg, evidently intended to open on our troops immediately at the rise of the hill. I reported this to Gen. Cox, who asked Gen. O. B. Willcox to accompany me back and look at the situation. When I had pointed out the batteries, he remarked that they had no men with them, which so disgusted me that I left him and went off.

About two P.M. the Corn Exchange Brigade was in line just on the crest of the bluff, out of sight. They relieved themselves of all encumbrances in the shape of knapsacks, blankets, and a lot of things we people from the West didn't have. Besides, they had on gaudy uniforms, like the Zouave's red pantaloons. Close behind them, also lying in line of battle, was my little attenuated line, plainly dressed, unassuming in actions and appearance, looking more like retainers to those in front than what we really were.

Finally the order for the charge was given, but the moment we raised the crest of the hill and were in full view, we were met with such a hail of musketry bullets, with several batteries dealing death and destruction amongst our ranks, that it would seem nothing could survive it.

After reaching the crest of the hill, we had to pass over quite a stretch of ground before we commenced descending into a hollow lying between the ridge occupied by the enemy and ourselves. The enemy not only had a direct, but a cross fire on us. It was in going down this slope that Col. Clarke, commanding the 36th, was killed by a round shot that came from our left. It struck him sideways, just above the hips, tearing him almost in twain. He died instantly. We were but a short distance apart when it occurred.

By the time we fairly reached the bottom of the hollow, there was not the color of the Corn Exchange left. They had all disappeared somewhere. I noticed comparatively few who were left in the field.

The enemy was occupying a cornfield on this second high

ground. The side of this field towards us had a stone fence, behind which we took shelter. To our right a short distance was Gen. Willcox, aiming a gun in person, all his men gone. He sent out word to us to know why in hell we were not advancing. Just then Col. Scammon came up from my left. He was in temporary command of our division, and sent word back to Willcox that if he would give him written orders, he would march.

The facts were that we were the only troops between the enemy and our transportation, hospitals, etc., just on the other side of the Antietam. Then too, the enemy in this cornfield were as thick as blackbirds, and my few orphans would not have lasted ten minutes had we once gone on their side of the fence. We had our hands so full that we knew but little of what was going on elsewhere, but of course knew that a big battle was going on.

And this was the 17th day of September, 1862.[5]

Under the cover of dark we withdrew to the crest of the bluffs from where we started the charge from earlier in the day. We lay on our arms all night in the midst of the leavings of the Corn Exchange Brigade. We had been unable to get a full supply of clothing out. Most of our men had not seen shelter tents before, so they were thrilled by these luxuries, and as their owners now returned for them, our men were sick.

It was heartrending to hear the wails of the wounded and dying in our front all night. Our men alleviated all this suffering they could, but we had to keep ourselves intact for fear of an attack. Since in the morning when we breakfasted in the sunken cornfield, we had lost the two commanders of the 11th and 36th, besides many others. Also learned that Col. Jones of the 36th Ohio had been wounded, and fell into the hands of the enemy during the day.

We stopped here all the next day in the hot, broiling sun, still all that was between the enemy and our impediments. Toward evening it commenced raining. Just about dusk we were relieved, and sent back not far from the sunken cornfield, to bivouac for the night.

Here our division was reassembled near a small country house occupied by some of the officers. Col. Hugh Ewing became full

---

[5] Crook was brevetted lieutenant colonel, U. S. Army, for his action in Antietam.

of "jig water," and ventilated [sic] himself on Gen. Cox, abusing him for being a coward and imbecile, and declaring he would never obey an order of his again, etc.

Although I was appointed to be a Brigadier General of Volunteers from the 7th of September for the battle of Lewisburg, I did not get it until after this campaign ended.[6]

Soon after we left the Kanawha Valley, the enemy, under Gen. Loring, drove our people out of that country. So I was ordered back to take possession of that country. Soon after we started, Gen. J. E. B. Stuart of Rebel fame made a raid in the rear of our lines. So I was detained at Hancock for a couple of days, hoping I might intercept him. I marched from Clarksburg across the country so as to strike the Kanawha Valley high up, and come on the enemy's flank. But as I neared the valley, they evacuated without any resistance.

After reoccupying that country for awhile, I was ordered with my brigade to re-enforce the Army of the Cumberland, just after the battle of Stone River.[7] We arrived at Nashville about the middle of January, 1863. Soon afterwards I was given a couple of Kentucky regiments besides my own brigade, and went up the Cumberland River in boats to take station at Carthage, Tennessee, to guard that flank and look out for John Morgan's cavalry.[8]

I found that I had been assigned some "mauvaise sauvages," and that I was expected to discipline them. We had no more than landed at Carthage before these men took the town, desecrated the churches by stealing what valuables they had, raided hen houses, etc.

Soon after my arrival there was sent me "Old Jim Spears"[9]

[6] *General Order No. 2*, Headquarters Ninth Army Corps (October 1, 1862) made Crook commander of the Kanawha Division. *The War of the Rebellion*, Ser. I, Vol. LI, Part I, 874.

[7] The Kanawha Division was ordered back to West Virginia on October 6, 1862. From Hancock it traveled the Baltimore and Ohio Railroad to Clarkesburg, leaving the city at the end of October, and reaching Charleston on November 16. Three months later, on January 25, 1863, it embarked on steamers for Nashville.

[8] Crook's position is described in *The War of the Rebellion*, Ser. I, Vol. XXIII, Part II, 110.

[9] James G. Spears was lieutenant colonel of the First Tennessee Infantry. He was dismissed from the service in 1864.

brigade of East Tennessee troops who had been sent away from the Army of the Cumberland to get rid of this element of discord.[10] These were the worst yet, perfectly lawless, and with little or no discipline. Because of my effort to discipline them, they accused me of disloyalty. Gen. Rosecrans, who sent them to me for disciplinary measures, and to rid himself of a troublesome element, had the moral courage to sustain me. My station and duties there were exceedingly unpleasant, and to add to all this, I was affected with serious liver troubles.[11]

I was also assigned to my command Col. Bill Stokes regiment of Cavalry,[12] who had been recruited from the natives in that vicinity. They had many old grievances to reclaim, and were under little or no discipline. I had my hands full, what with looking out for the enemy and restraining the lawlessness of our own people.

In June, when the Army of the Cumberland was preparing to advance beyond Tulahoma, I was ordered to join it with my original brigade and to take part in that movement. My brigade was assigned to the 14th Army Corps, Thomas commanding.[13]

After leaving Tulahoma, a heavy rain set in. The weather had been hot and sultry, and the men had thrown away all their incumbrances that could be dispensed with, even down to their blankets. After marching all day, toward evening of June 26, 1863, I was ordered to relieve Wilder's brigade, who had been fighting all day at Hoover's Gap.[14]

Our troops were lying behind a small elevation, alongside a fence, while the enemy occupied the other side. They kept up a desultory fire all night, the bullets going over our heads. The rain still continued to pour in torrents. The troops had trod up the mud into a thin mush of two or three inches deep. I ordered the

10 See *The War of the Rebellion*, Ser. I, Vol. XXIII, Part II, 179–80.

11 In addition to his troubles here enumerated, Crook wrote to General Garfield: "Contraband women are coming in in such numbers that I cannot afford to feed them. What shall I do with them?" *The War of the Rebellion*, Ser. I, Vol. XXIII, Part II, 366.

12 William B. Stokes was colonel of the Fifth Tennessee Cavalry.

13 George H. Thomas.

14 John T. Wilder was lieutenant colonel of the Seventeenth Indiana Volunteers, who, for their action at Hoover's Gap were called "Wilder's Lightning Brigade."

men to stack arms, and to cook supper if they had any. But they were tired, stacked their arms, and flopped down in the mud and went sound asleep, many of them without blankets.

I had a gum coat, and sat under a tree with the gum coat drawn over my legs and knees so as to keep them dry. The next day it was the same thing, nothing to eat, and the men wet, hungry, and uncomfortable, the bullets of the enemy striking trees all around us. We stayed here all next day and night. The next day we went forward in the general advance. The enemy retreated across the Tennessee River, and our army took up its headquarters at Stevenson, near the banks of the Tennessee.

10. *Impudence and cheek won*

ABOUT THE FIRST OF JULY I was transferred to the command of the 2nd Division of Cavalry, and Gen. Turchin took my brigade, or he exchanged commands. (Gen. Thomas told me afterwards that my old brigade really turned the tide at the battle of Chickamauga.)

During the months of July, August, and the first part of September, I was constantly on the go, making reconnaissances, raids, etc. I went across the Tennessee River, and after seeing the almost impregnable position the enemy had evacuated, I am convinced they did it to draw us across the river, and so reported to Gen. Rosecrans. But he said he had information that the enemy was preparing to retreat. I said nothing more, but my opinions were not changed all the same.

Some time in the early part of September, Gen. Stanley, who was in command of all the cavalry, was ordered to make an advance on the enemy, and in case of his retreat to harass him, fall on his flanks and rear, and cut him to pieces, etc. On our march across Lookout Mountain to Broom Corn [*sic*] Valley we overtook Gen. A. D. McCook's corps, who were destined for the same place. He was halting, resting his men, and we also halted to rest.

The officers were all together when Gen. Staley received a letter from Gen. Rosecrans, accusing him unmercifully of procrastination, unncessary delays, and of want of appreciation of the situation, etc., stating that the enemy was in full retreat, and that instead of his cavalry being on their flanks, destroying them, he had by his delays lost the fruits of all the campaign, etc. Gen. Stanley was taken sick. In fact, he was sick then. He was shortly afterwards compelled to go off duty.[1]

I being next in rank present assumed command of the cavalry corps. When we reached Broom Corn Valley, it was not so certain that the enemy was in full retreat. On the contrary, the belief was quite strong that instead of falling back, he had received reinforcements, and that he was in force at a little place called Lafayette, some 20 miles up the valley.

I was ordered to make a reconnaissance to this place to ascertain the true state of affairs. There were two roads some three or four miles apart that convergd to the point occupied by the enemy. I, with my division, marched on the first road, and ordered Gen. A. D. McCook, who was in command of the First Division of Cavalry, to march on the other road. We were to keep abreast of each other by frequent couriers, etc., so we would arrive at the enemy's forces about the same time, and make the attack simultaneously.

We kept abreast this way for several miles, when I could get no further tidings of the First Division. I sent out a squadron to the other road to investigate. They found a few of the enemy at a well, but had no difficulty in driving them off. About this time my division encountered a similar body of the enemy on the road we were marching on. I gave orders not to fire a shot, but simply to follow them up.

We came to a house about two and one-half miles from the enemy, and after getting all the information off the occupants,

[1] General Rosecrans' letter would have made almost any officer ill:

"I have a message from General Crook asking for turpentine, but whether for horse medicine or bridges does not appear . . . .

"It is a matter of regret to me that your command has done so little in this great movement. If you could do nothing towards Rome nor towards the railroad, you might, at least, have cleared the top of Lookout Mountain to Chattanooga, and established a patrol and vidette line along it.

"But what is worse than this, you had peremptory orders to move, which were reiterated yesterday, expecting you would move this morning. This you do not appear to have done . . . .

"So far your command has been a mere picket guard for our advance." *The War of the Rebellion,* Ser. I, Vol. XXX, Part III, 467–68.

we marched about one mile further, when I ordered a charge. Then the men rushed up to their infantry camp, and scooped up their infantry pickets, mounted behind them on their own horses, and all came out before the enemy was ready. In this way we only had two men hurt and obtained all the information desired. The pickets were some of the Louisiana Tigers, who had just joined with Longstreet's corps.

I at once returned to the place of starting, and found that Gen. A. D. McCook had already started to go back to Chattanooga. I found Gen. A. D. McCook back there with his division, saying that he had met the enemy in force at the mills before Winston, and had retreated. My division had accomplished the desired results, and he was simply showing his behavior in its true light, so I let it go at that. The 7th Division was ordered to Chattanooga, while I was ordered with my division to Brook's Gap, where we remained until the battle of Chickamauga.[2]

On the morning of the 21st of September, I arrived at Crawfish Springs, where I found the 1st Division of Cavalry, which was now commanded by Bob Mitchell, not much of an improvement over Gen. McCook, only he wasn't afraid to fight. He was also in command of the Corps.

When I arrived there about ten A.M. there was a brigade of Jeff Davis' Division, with a battery of artillery lying in a field just in front of and west of a juniper thicket. Gen. Mitchell ordered me to go to the front, and relieve his division, and keep the enemy from crossing Chickamauga Creek. This distance was two and a half miles, and wound around this juniper thicket. I protested against taking any of my artillery with me, but the order was insisted on, so I took two pieces.

When I reached the 1st Division I found it posted in a woods in front of the thicket, which had considerable underbrush. I asked the officer in command where Chickamauga Creek was. He said he'd be damned if he knew. I told him what my orders were, and he said that the woods in his immediate front were full of the enemy. He knew nothing about the creek. As soon as I got in

[2] "From this point we were moved to Dougherty's Gap, which we held until September 19, when we were ordered to the front." Report of General Crook to Major Sinclair, adjutant general, *The War of the Rebellion*, Ser. I, Vol. XXX, Part I, 918.

possession, I had two lines of skirmishers, one dismounted and the other mounted, the former in advance.

I would remain in uncertainty no longer, so I ordered the artillery to open on a certain clump of timber in my front. Both cavalry and infantry came charging out of it like so many hornets, completely enveloping me. I lost a hundred men in about fifteen minutes, and most of them were lost in saving my artillery. I thought certainly I was captured once or twice.

When I got back to where Gen. Mitchell was, I found his cavalry, infantry, and artillery all huddled together in this small field in a helpless condition. Gen. Mitchell came to me and said, "General, you are a military man, I wish you would take charge and straighten things out and make the necessary dispositions."

Some of these troops were not ten yards from the thickets where the enemy could have advanced under cover and have all the advantage of our own troops. There was an open, wooded ridge just back of this field on which I posted the troops, compelling the enemy to cross this field. They did not follow us up as we had expected, but late in the afternoon the enemy commenced advancing, and we fell back.[3]

My division was detailed as rear guard to oppose their advance. Their attack was not persistent, and about dusk desisted altogether. We continued our retreat until morning. The whole country was lit up by burning fences, so we had no difficulty in marching. My fear was that they would attract the enemy's attention, and that

[3] "At this point [Crawfish] I found General Mitchell, who ordered me to take post at once in front of the fords of the Chickamauga and hold that point at all hazards. The only point I could occupy was a thick, rocky woods with heavy underbrush. The enemy was already across the river, occupying a very strong position.

"About eleven o'clock I was attacked by Hinman's division of infantry, a battalion of sharpshooters, and a large body of cavalry. They drove us back steadily, contesting every inch of the ground, about 200 yards, where we held our ground.

"At this time I received an order from Gen. Mitchell to fall back to the hospital, one and one-half miles distant. Our entire force consisted of Col. Long's brigade, about 900 strong. The entire command, both officers and men, behaved very gallantly."

Casualties suffered by the First Ohio, Third Ohio, Fourth Ohio, and Second Kentucky Cavalry, were 9 officers and 127 enlisted men. *The War of the Rebellion*, Ser. I, Vol. XXX, Part I, 918–19.

a flank attack would be made upon us, as we feared that our main army had been badly worsted.

The next morning, just as we reached the point of Lookout Mountain, the enemy was marching to the same point by a converging road, and in a short time more would have cut us off. We exchanged a few shots with them.

I was present when Gen. Mitchell made his verbal report to Gen. Rosecrans and to hear him recount the valorous deeds of his command. How he could have the cheek, after what has passed, surpassed my understanding. It was humiliating to see persons wearing the uniforms of general officers to be so contemptible.[4]

When we reached Chattanooga there was a large rabble without organization which had fled from the battlefield. If the enemy had followed up his victories vigorously, I don't see how it would have been possible for an army to escape disaster. Our back was against the Tennessee River, too deep to ford, with but one pontoon bridge which would have been of little or no value in case of a retreat. Why the enemy did not push their advantage I never could understand. We had made no preparations for a reverse, no defenses were prepared, and our position without them was a weak one. Our troops at once went to work razing houses on the outskirts of town, and commenced throwing up works, which were finished after all danger was over.

Shortly afterwards I was transferred to the opposite side of the river, and ordered to guard all the fords up as far as Knoxville. I protested against being held responsible for a duty that was an impossibility to perform with the number of men at my disposal. The distance was over 50 miles. Parallel to the river and some three miles distant from it was a country road. Every mile or so there were crossroads running from this road to fords on the river. Between these fords were generally thick woods, so that to get from one ford to another rendered it necessary to come around by the main road. It was an impossibility to guard all that distance with

---

[4] In his written report, General Mitchell said: "I must say, in conclusion, that there was never work more opportunely done on the battlefield than the work of the cavalry on the 20th of September at Chickamauga. . . . Brigadier-General Crook, commanding Second Division, deserves the gratitude of the country for the gallant manner in which he discharged his duty throughout the entire advance as well as on the battlefield at Chickamauga." *The War of the Rebellion*, Ser. I, Vol. XXX, Part I, 894.

fifteen hundred men against a victorious enemy with at least 6,000 effective cavalry. But Gen. Rosecrans seemed to be wanting a "scape goat," and he said he would hold me responsible.

I established my headquarters on this main road, and picketed the river as well as it was possible for me to do. I was afraid to post only a few men at a place, for fear they would be captured, and we would be surprised. So I had to put so many men at a place that I had none left for reserve.

Their cavalry could be seen on the other side of the river, and there was a general impression that they were going to cross and make a raid on the rear of our army to destroy communication, transportation, etc.

On the afternoon of the second of October the squadron of cavalry under the command of Capt. Bowman, 4th Regiment of Cavalry Regulars, was guarding one of the fords nearest to where my headquarters were. He reported the enemy making demonstrations on his front as though they were going to cross. He wanted re-enforcements sent him. Demonstrations were also being made at other points at the same time. As I had no re-enforcements to send, I could only instruct them to offer all the resistance possible, and keep me informed of all that transpired. The firing at this ford kept up until evening. Nothing of a definite character was reported.

The next morning, while waiting for reports, a flag of truce was brought in by a couple of Confederates, demanding my surrender. I at once gave orders to pack up everything and pull out on the Chattanooga road, while I entertained the Confederates by questioning them all about themselves.

They were quite communicative, and gave me some important information. At the same time I had dispatched couriers to the different detachments informing them of the situation. Those up the river were to concentrate and offer all resistance possible in case the enemy attempted to go their way, and those down the river were to join me. When all was ready I moved out, taking the "flag of truce" with me, and when I had reached a safe distance, I sent the Confederates with many thanks back to their command. Had I not been informed by them of the near approach of the enemy, my whole headquarters would have been captured.

I at once informed Gen. Rosecrans of the situation, and desired instructions. I was ordered to pursue them with the greatest vigor,

Fort Bowie, Apache Pass, Arizona Territory, in 1886. Crook was quartered in the large frame building at the far corner

GENERAL GEORGE CROOK

FROM A PHOTOGRAPH TAKEN AT OMAHA IN 1886

and was given authority to take all the troops I could get hold of while on this pursuit. By midday the greater part of my command had joined me. We started in pursuit at once, leaving orders for the remainder to follow. We followed them up the Cumberland Mountains. It commenced pouring rain before we had progressed far, and kept it up pretty much all night. We marched until it became too dark to see our hands before us.

When we went into camp in the woods, everybody was tired, hungry, wet, and muddy, and as a matter of course, not in the most amiable frame of mind. Wood was wet, and only after much difficulty was a fire started. It had not more than illuminated the woods, when bang! bang! went a volley of the enemy's bullets, which settled the fire question and supper for that night.

The next morning we resumed our march, following the enemy. Toward evening, as we were descending the mountains, we came up with their rear guard, pushing them as rapidly as circumstances would permit. Just at dusk we encountered their rear division, and kept up the fight until it was too dark to tell friend from foe. At one time we had one of their brigades surrounded, but had to let them go on account of extreme darkness.

On the next morning, the 5th day of October, the sun was shining bright, and the enemy was all gone. We followed after, and when we came to McMinnville, we found the town full of Union soldiers, or at least wearing our uniform. Upon inquiry I learned that a regiment of East Tennessee troops, Infantry, were stationed there, and had surrendered to the enemy without resistance. I was too disgusted to hold any communication with them. I omitted to mention that the enemy had paroled them, not being able to take them with them.

I was informed by parties who had counted the enemy as they passed a given point that they numbered a little over 6,000 men. I had other reasons for believing this to be about correct, from the time it took them to pass given points at different times on the road.

A couple of miles out of McMinnville a force of the enemy was drawn up across the road in a copse of wood that extended on both sides of the road, so that the size of this force could not be judged. Judging from the time they had left the village, I was satisfied that the main body must be much farther in advance of this, and that this was probably a brigade left as a rear guard to detain us, while the main body could march unmolested. Realizing that with my command moving along the road in column it would take me at least an hour to form in line of battle, I concluded to take the chances of its being only a rear guard.

The road was a magnificent, macadamized pike, very wide and straight, the country being gently rolling as far as the eye could see. Colonel Eli Long of the 4th Kentucky Cavalry was in advance. I ordered him to draw sabres and charge the enemy in column of fours along the pike, and not to fire a shot. He was to strike them in the center and continue the charge while the rest of the company would look out for the rest of the enemy.

Fortunately my calculations were correct. It was only a rear guard left to detain us. When Long struck their center, the whole Confederate force broke, and from there to the main body, at least five miles, it was a regular steeplechase. The enemy's loss amounted to about 100, while ours was insignificant.

We compelled their main body to fight, and they pulled out and marched all night. When it got too dark to fight any longer we went into camp and did not resume our march until the next morning. They did not stop in Murfreesboro, as we understood it was their wont, but went on to Duck River before camping.

We camped out of town the next day, much to the relief of our people there, as they feared an attack, and did not know that we had any troops within striking distance of them. They were too weak to make much resistance, and there was a large accumulation of stores there, and their loss would have been of a serious consequence to the troops at Chattanooga.

The next morning we were following them towards Shelbyville, when a citizen who asked what we were looking for said there was a large camp of them just below on Duck River. The main pike ran through Shelbyville, while a country road ran along the left bank of Duck River and joined the pike several miles farther on. The enemy were encamped on this dirt road.

I ordered Minty's brigade to move on the pike to its intersection with dirt road, while I would make the attack with the remainder of the command. The attack was made by a charge which was so sudden and so unexpected that the enemy made but little resistance. Owing to the brushy and swampy nature of the country, we could not reap the full benefit of our victory, as only about so many troops could operate at once. By some mistake Minty's brigade did not move out of camp in the morning, saying he had no orders, etc., so failed to be at the junction of the two roads as directed, and we failed to accomplish the results to which we were entitled.[5]

We still pushed on after reaching the pike until we reached a cedar thicket just short of Farmington, where the enemy had all concentrated. Only a part of them were encamped on Duck River.

The cedar was thick on both sides of the pike, so we could only see what was on the pike. We pushed their skirmish line up to their main body, drawn up in line of battle. Now came the "tug of war." Before, all of our fights were on wooded roads, and were mostly confined to the roads, so we could present as much of a front as they could. But now they were drawn up in line of battle, and I was not only in column yet, but with Minty's brigade absent.

They had two thirds more men than I had, but I was in such a position that I had to fight. I could not retreat. They were not only superior in numbers, but their horses were in much better condition than mine, and should I have attempted retreat they would have cut me all to pieces, especially when they saw the paucity of my force.

So I at once dismounted Wilder's brigade of mounted infantry, and sent them in line to the thicket on the left of the pike, deploying some of the cavalry on the right. I with my staff was just to the right of the pike, and not over 200 yards from a battery of the enemy, posted on the pike, and just hoisting their shells and shrapnel into us. Every few minutes someone near me would be torn into atoms by some of their missiles.

Just then reports from scouts came in that the enemy was turning both flanks. I would have given a great deal for night just then. I thought it was hardly possible to avert disaster. Capt. Stokes of the Chicago Board of Trade Battery had one of his pieces run out on the pike, and sighted the piece himself. The first shot skimmed

---

[5] Crook sent Robert H. G. Minty to the rear for failing to obey orders. In February, 1864, Minty was tried by general court-martial on charge of "disobedience of orders," and "conduct subversive of good order and military discipline." He was honorably acquitted. Crook admitted that he had forgotten to give Minty the orders. Department of the Cumberland, *General Order No. 36 (Fezruary 28, 1864)*; James Larson, *Sergeant Larson, 4th Cavalry*, 206.

just over their battery. The next let down a wheel. The third exploded a caisson. Just then Wilder's brigade made a charge, and, being armed with the Spencer rifle, they poured a terrific and incessant fire on the enemy, giving the impression of a superior force.[6] The whole enemy broke, and did not stop their retreat until they crossed the Tennessee River at Muscle Shoals, over 70 miles distant.[7]

The baggage, wagons, and artillery, and a great many prisoners were left in our hands. I learned afterwards that it was the intention of the enemy to have waited on Duck River until General S. D. Lee and Roddy's commands of cavalry had joined them, when they, with this combined force, were to make a raid through Kentucky. In fact, the flag of truce man told me that they had been promised that this expedition would settle the war. But they had missed in their calculations. They met Lee's cavalry just across the Tennessee River at Muscle Shoals with 5,500 men, and as we were marching back via Huntsville we came near running into Roddy's command of 1,800.

We carried little or no baggage, but subsisted on the country, carrying only our clothing on our backs, much to our discomfort before we got through. One great advantage I had over the enemy on this whole trip was that I knew his force, and he didn't know mine. I was told at army headquarters that Gen. Wheeler's report was captured wherein he said he had fought the whole Army of the Cumberland. This was one of the cases where impudence and cheek won.

About this time Gen. Rosecrans was relieved, and Gen. Thomas placed in command of the Army of the Cumberland. I received orders to remain in the northern part of Alabama and break up a band of cut-throats, bushwhackers, and thieves, and besides to break up an illicit traffic that was being carried on between Nashville and the South. There was a noted character in that country who was the ringleader of these roughs, and who killed Gen. Mc-

[6] The Spencer was a .56 calibre, seven-shot repeating carbine, considered to be the best used in the Civil War. It was patented in 1860 and used extensively by the Union Army. Sawyer, *Our Rifles*, 155–56.

[7] Crook's report of the battle of Farmington, Tennessee, October 7, 1863, is in *The War of the Rebellion*, Ser. I, Vol. XXX, Part II, 684–88.

Cook.[8] I can't just now recall his name, but he was soon captured and his whole outfit scattered to the four winds, a great many being killed.

[8] Robert Latimer McCook died on August 6, 1862, of wounds inflicted on August 5 by guerrillas. He was en route to Dercherd, Tennessee, when his wagon was stopped by Frank P. Gurley and his gang. Gurley's men shot McCook in the stomach, and he died in great agony.

Gurley was afterwards arrested and tried by a military commission. The death sentence was passed, but commuted, and in 1866 Gurley was exchanged as a prisoner of war. *The War of the Rebellion*, Ser. II, Vol. VI, 1029–1033; Vol. VIII, 898.

IV
THE BRAINS OF
THIS ARMY

11. *Men murdered by incompetency*

THE PEOPLE BACK HOME had been petitioning the President to send me back to West Virginia. Grant told me he had passed a wish of the President to have me go back to that country, but another demand had just been sent, and I was informed I would have to go this time. Just then Gen. Grant had been made Lieutenant-General, and said he would like to have me East.

I regretted quitting that army just then, for I stood a good show to have been put in command of all the cavalry of the Army of the Cumberland. I returned to the Kanawha Valley sometime in January 1864, and was assigned to the command of that district.

Shortly afterwards I was ordered to Spottsylvania Court House for consultation with Lt.-Gen. Grant about operations against the Virginia and Tennessee Railroad. It was agreed that I was to make a march against that railroad, destroy the bridge across the New River, and then move along that railroad, destroying it en route until I met Gen. Sigel's force, which was to move via Staunton for the same railroad. Then the combined force was to capture Lynchburg.

General Ord was ordered in on consultation at the same time. We were sent back to Washington by special engine. We arrived in Washington a little after midnight in a pouring rain. Gen. Ord was to pilot us to the Ebbitt House, there being no vehicles to be had, but it seems he got out of the moving end of the car, and kept on until we came to the Potomac River. Then we had to retrace our steps, and reached the Emmitt House at about three o'clock in the morning, wet from head to foot.

I had to leave for the West early in the morning. I returned to Charleston, where my headquarters were, and at once organized for the contemplated campaign. The expedition left the Kanawha Valley about the 1st of May, and marched via Raleigh Court House. Gen. Averell's cavalry was sent to Wytheville to destroy the salt works in that vicinity, if possible.

Nothing of note happened to the main column until we reached Cloyd's Mountain, where we met the enemy under the command of Gen. Jenkins, posted on a bluff, with an open bottom between us and the bluffs, with a stream with a muddy bottom running close under the bluff. The main road passed through this bottom and over the bluffs. The surrounding country was more or less covered with woods and brush.

I at once sent Col. White's brigade under cover to make a flank attack on the enemy's right, while the remainder of the command was held in line of battle, ready to charge the enemy's front the moment Col. White commenced his attack. The charge across the bottom was attended with some loss, but the enemy was completely routed, his loss was several hundred, including Gen. Jenkins, who was killed.

We followed on as rapidly as possible, but they made no further resistance as an organized body. A small force was sent from Wytheville by rail and checked our extreme advance for a few moments, but they too, in turn, gave way, and we took possession of Dublin Depot, close to the bridge, with opposition, both of which we destroyed.[1]

After this we crossed over to Christiansburg, intending to continue along the railroad. But I saw a dispatch from Gen. Lee to the effect that his troops had again been successful in defeating the enemy at the Wilderness. Not having heard a word from Gen. Sigel, and knowing that the safety and success of our enterprise

---

[1] Rutherford B. Hayes, then colonel of the Twenty-third Ohio, wrote his uncle a description of the battle of Cloyd's Mountain: "We charged a Rebel battery entrenched in a wooded hill across an open, level meadow three hundred yards wide and a deep ditch, wetting me to the waist, and carried it without a particle of wavering or even check, losing, however, many officers and men killed and wounded.

"It being the vital point, General Crook charged with us in person. One brigade, from the Army of the Potomac (Pennsylvania Reserves) broke and fled from the field. Altogether, this is our finest experience in the war, and General Crook is the best General we have served under, not excepting Rosecrans." Rutherford B. Hayes, *Diary and Letters*, V, 463–64.

depended on the Army of the Potomac being able to keep the enemy from detaching any part of his command about Richmond and sending them to cut off our retreat, as we were so far away from our base, so I concluded our safety lay in falling back nearer to our base, to a point from which we could at any time join Gen. Sigel's column as per original intentions. So I fell back on Meadow Bluffs.

Heavy rains set in, and the roads were almost impassable. When we reached Greenbrier River, we found a torrent, so that we had to improvise a ferry. We crossed it with much difficulty, taking a couple of days, and our scouts were bringing in reports that the enemy was advancing in force. Soon after we reached Meadow Bluffs we learned of Sigel's repulse, and of his having been super- seded in command by Gen. Hunter.[2] I also received orders to join Gen. Hunter at Staunton. He was to carry out the original plan, and our combined forces would march on Lynchburg.

On our march across from Lewisburg to Staunton we en- countered a small force that annoyed us some by occupying the gaps and passes, but did not detain us. This outfit was known as Mudwall Jackson's[3] command, in contradistinction to Stonewall Jackson. When we reached Staunton we learned of Gen. Hunter's victory over the enemy.[4]

From here the whole force marched towards Lynchburg, via Lexington. We approached the town from the north. Black River ran between us and the village in sunken banks, so that its where- abouts was not visible a short distance away. So I rode to a point to the left of the road to reconnoiter.

It seemed that the cadets from the Virginia Military Institute, together with a few Confederates, had a masked battery in the edge of town which opened on the column as it was approaching, and killed and wounded several men. Gen. Averell was sent by Gen. Hunter to cross the river higher up and to come in rear of the

[2] General Sigel was defeated at the battle of New Market, Virginia, May 15, 1864, and was superseded by David Hunter.

[3] William L. Jackson.

[4] Hunter defeated the Confederates near Piedmont on June 5, 1864, kill- ing and wounding at least 1,500 of the enemy. This opened the way for his junction with Crook at Staunton.

village, which he failed to accomplish, so that the enemy were allowed to make their escape.

They had burned all the bridges across the river, and the banks were so steep, and the river so deep that we had some difficulty in crossing. Up to this time Gen. Averell was Gen. Hunter's chief adviser, but Gen. Hunter commenced losing confidence in the former. Gen. Hunter ordered the burning of the Institute and Gov. Letcher's house. I did all in my power to dissuade him, but all to no purpose.[5]

Gen. Duffie, commanding part of the cavalry, was sent out across the Blue Ridge to reconnoiter and disperse some of the enemy reported there. He did not return in time. We were delayed one or two days in consequence. I learned upon his return that he had been mostly engaged in pilfering, that he had robbed some refugees of some Staunton City bonds, which, after the war, he was trying to dispose of. However, it was this that prevented us from arriving at Lynchburg at least one day earlier.

After leaving here, we still went one day out of a direct route to Lynchburg. I, with my division, arrived within a couple of miles of Lynchburg about midday, but was ordered to remain and wait for the arrival of our other troops before making the attack. After waiting until nearly dark, I had to do all the work as it was, for I got no material assistance from anyone else. I defeated their troops, captured their artillery, and drove their troops off the field. It became too dark to go into the town, so we had to go into camp. Lt. Roberts, ADC, was seriously wounded in this fight.[6]

[5] Both Virginia Military Institute and Governor Letcher's house were burned. However, old Washington College, later Washington and Lee University, was spared.

"Honest John" Letcher was a native of Lexington and governor of Virginia from 1859 to 1864.

[6] Cyrus Swan Roberts was born in Sharon, Connecticut, Aug. 23, 1841.

He enlisted in the Twenty-second New York Volunteers and in June, 1863, was detailed as commissary of musters of the Third Division, Eighth Corps, in West Virginia. In February, 1864, General Crook assumed command of that division.

Lieutenant Roberts served on Crook's staff until the close of the war. He was mustered out in June, 1865, but was at once appointed captain and A.D.C. of Volunteers, and went as aide with General Crook on reconstruction work in North Carolina. He was appointed second lieutenant, Seventeenth Infantry, May 11, 1866, and served with that regiment for thirty-two years.

While in camp, we could hear trains coming into Lynchburg from the opposite direction, bringing in re-enforcements. We could hear the men cheering.[7] Next morning this fact was demonstrated to us by the vast increase of troops in our front. This left us with but one thing to do under the circumstances. So we waited until night, when we withdrew and commenced our retreat on the road we came on.

By the next morning we had put a good many miles between us and the enemy. That night we went into camp at a place called Liberty. The advance came up on us that evening, but beyond a little skirmishing nothing of note occurred. We next moved to Buffalo Gap. That evening the enemy attacked us with considerable vigor. I captured a prisoner who said he belonged to Rodes' Division. He said his division had taken a by-road to come in our flanks, which gave me much alarm.

Gen. Hunter had his headquarters some two and one-half miles in the rear. The lowest of everything fell on me and my division. In advancing on Lynchburg, I was in the advance all the time, and now, in retreat, I was kept in the rear all the time, and had to do all the fighting.

Gen. Hunter had no confidence in the rest of the command, and I shared this opinion with him. Gen. Hunter had gotten so now that he would do nothing without first consulting me, so I had to go back to consult as to what was best to do. We decided that the command, excepting my division, would commence falling back at about three or four o'clock by the shortest route to the Kanawha Valley, and that I would commence falling back soon after dark, leaving our picket fires burning after we left. All this time a brisk fire was going on, which was kept up until dark.

When my division got on the road, the remainder of the com-

While captain, he again served as A.D.C. to General Crook from 1880 to 1886, including the campaigns in Arizona against Geronimo, during which time he acted as field adjutant general. He again joined Crook's staff in 1889 and was with him during the sessions of the Sioux Commission and at Chicago, to the date of the General's death.

Cyrus S. Roberts had three children, two of whom are still living. One is Brigadier General Charles D. Roberts, retired, and the other Laura Pearson, wife of Colonel Tilman Campbell, retired. Charles D. Roberts, *Sketch of the Life of Cyrus Swan Roberts* [MS].

mand had been gone some time. I had not proceeded more than a mile or two before I came upon the command at a halt. I waited awhile, but could find no reason for this halt. I expected any moment to get some word from the front. My greatest fears were that Rodes' Division had either gotten in our front, or had come in on one flank. In either case I felt certain of disaster.

I sent staff officers ahead to learn the cause. About midnight the column commenced moving. Afterwards I learned that the whole trouble was caused by a piece of artillery sticking in the mud. Those in front went off without it, and those in the rear hadn't investigated the trouble, but were mostly asleep. This left a gap of some miles in our column.

This was one of the hardest nights I ever put in. We were worn out by constant marching, and no sleep at nights. It was almost a constant fight since we left Lynchburg. We had little or nothing to eat. One ear of corn was all that I had. I felt the whole responsibility on my shoulders. I had no confidence in those in front. I was so worn out that it was only with the greatest exertions I could keep awake.

The men were dodging out of ranks so they could hide away and go to sleep. I stayed in the rear so as to look out for these things. I knew that the enemy's cavalry would be along early in the morning and gobble up all stragglers. But even the knowledge of that fact had no terrors for the poor, worn-out wretches. I had to be very cross and make myself exceedingly disagreeable, but that all failed to prevent many from falling out.

The troops behind the piece of artillery had closed up on their command during the night, so my division was the only one behind the gap made by the halt. When daylight came, we could not see the command ahead of us. While dragging our weary bodies along, nearly exhausted, unconscious of any danger, all of a sudden we received a volley from an ambuscade from the side of the road. We soon drove them off.

We came up with the command about ten A.M. at the little village of Salem. I complained of my treatment by those in my front, particularly in allowing me to be surprised as we were in the morn-

---

[7] Jubal Early, with Stonewall Jackson's old corps, arrived at Lynchburg with his advance division on June 17.

ing. Hunter cursed Gen. Sullivan for being a coward, etc., who tried to lie out of it, but made a poor attempt.[8]

When on the march, when there was no danger, Gen. Hunter used to ask me to ride along with him. Frequently, when we passed near houses, women would come running out, begging for protection, saying that the soldiers were taking the last dust of corn meal she had in the house, and she did not see how they were to live, she and her little children. This would be repeated several times during the day's march.

His invariable answer would be, "Go away! Go away, or I will burn your house!" This day, while we were halting at Salem, a woman came up to the general and said she knew it was the intention of the enemy to attack his troops on the march that day, giving the place. Instead of giving heed to her warning, he gave his stereotyped answer of "Go away! Go away, or I will burn your house!" Sure enough, the enemy did attack our troops at the place indicated and took some of our artillery.

Gen. Hunter wanted to consolidate his artillery and have it all march together. I objected to mine being separated from my division, and so saved it, but they captured and destroyed pretty near all the rest. Some of my men were killed by the explosions of some shells from a burning caisson that the enemy could not haul off and had set on fire.

Our cavalry on this trip had been but little or no service. I have omitted to mention that instead of taking the shortest line of retreat as agreed upon when we left Buffalo Gap, for some unaccountable reason we had gone fifteen miles out of our way. There was a place ahead known as Scott's Cross Roads, where the two roads joined, and it was there we expected the enemy to intercept our retreat.

Gen. Averell had a lot of bummers, whom he called scouts and spies, who were thoroughly unreliable and worthless. They brought information that the enemy was occupying the Cross Roads. We held a council of war, and decided if such was the case to strike south and follow the Virginia and Tennessee Railroad

[8] Jeremiah Cutler Sullivan was in command of the First Division, Infantry, in the Lynchburg Campaign.

down to Knoxville. But upon investigation we found the report to be groundless.

From here we had about one hundred and fifty miles to traverse over a mountainous country, barren of everything in the shape of supplies. Since leaving Staunton, we had to depend on the country for all our supplies, so that our rations were scant all the time. Going down to Lynchburg, I, being in advance, had an opportunity to gather some supplies, but upon my return, being in the rear all the way and having one prolonged fight, I could get nothing.

Gen. Hunter ordered the abandonment of our transportation, but I didn't abandon mine that I had any use for. By this time our supplies had become very short, and from here there was much actual suffering for want of supplies. Notwithstanding the disadvantages my division labored under during the whole campaign, we fared better than any of the rest of the command by being more prudent than the rest. We reached the Kanawha Valley in a sad plight. Men were worn out from fatigue and hunger, all sadly in need of clothing. Many were barefoot.[9]

Instead of the enemy following up, they switched off, and went up the Shenandoah Valley and made that memorable march on Washington that created such consternation in Washington and excitement throughout the North.

Before we were rested, we received orders to proceed to Harper's Ferry. The Ohio River was low, so our progress was slow. We arrived at Harper's Ferry by detail. I, being in advance of my division, was ordered to Hillsborough. On the line of Gen.

[9] The Lynchburg Campaign, as it is officially known, lasted from May 26, 1864, when Union troops under General Hunter left Cedar Creek, to June 30, when the troops reached Charleston, Kanawha Valley.

The Lynchburg battle took place on June 17 and 18, and the retreat covered the period of June 19 to 29. Crook's report merely stated that "The division became a little straightened for provisions, but came out in good shape." *The War of the Rebellion*, Ser. I, Vol. XXXVII, Part I, 93–160.

When Hayes arrived in Kanawha Valley, he wrote, with great relief, to his mother, "We got safely back to this point yesterday [June 29] after being almost two months within the Rebel lines . . . . We have had a severe and hazardous campaign, and have, I think, done a great deal of good.

"While we have suffered a good deal from the want of food and sleep, we have lost a very few men, and are generally in the best of health . . . . General Crook has won the love and confidence of all. General Hunter is not so fortunate." Hayes, *Diary and Letters*, V, 477–78.

Early's retreat from Washington I found the odds and ends of several commands. I arrived near Hillsborough, where the troops were, about midday.

No one knew anything about the enemy, no scouts out about the country. It was sufficient to account for all this by the fact that Gen. Sullivan was in command. For, in addition to his many other shortcomings, he lacked actual physical courage. It afterwards transpired that the enemy had mostly passed there within two or three miles of these troops. The Sixth Corps was following Gen. Early up, and had crossed the Potomac at Edward's Ferry.

The next day we joined the Sixth Corps, Gen. H. G. Wright commanding, and marched to Snicker's Gap.[10] The enemy was across the Shenandoah River, but we could not tell whether they were in force or not. Gen. Wright ordered me to send a force across the river and develop the enemy, which I did, waiting myself with Gen. Wright to watch developments. He occupied a commanding position from where we could overlook the country where the enemy was supposed to be.

The rough country seemed to end in the bluff just under us made by the Shenandoah River. On the opposite side was mostly bottom and rolling country divided into fields, with an occasional clump of timber. My troops had no more than crossed the river when the enemy's strength commenced developing. I desired to withdraw my troops to our side of the river, but he said no, he would order Gen. Ricketts' to cross the river and support me with his division.

Gen. Ricketts was standing with us at this time. He gave Gen. Ricketts the order in my presence. Gen. Ricketts' division was lying just in the rear of my men. He and I rode down together to where the crossing was to be made. By the time we had reached this place, the enemy had shown such strength that Gen. Ricketts declined to go to their support, and allowed many of my men to be sacrificed. I lost some valuable men here, murdered by incompetency or worse. I reported the facts to Gen. Wright, but that was the end of it, while I suffered in the estimation of my men as having made a useless sacrifice.[11]

[10] Crook's command joined the Sixth Corps on July 18. That day he was brevetted major general, U. S. Volunteers, for services in West Virginia.

[11] In his official report Crook admitted that "The greater portion of the

My old division under Col. Duval arrived at Harper's Ferry, and marched together with Gen. Averell's cavalry up the Shenandoah Valley, and had a very handsome victory at a place called Cabletown.

The enemy retreated up the valley, and the Sixth Corps returned to Washington. I moved to Winchester to give my men the much-needed rest, and supply them with clothing. My command now consisted of most of the troops who were on the Lynchburg campaign, together with some hundred-day men whose time had nearly expired.

The enemy had retreated only a short distance up the valley, and when he heard of my being at Winchester, he returned. Gen. Duffie, who was in command of part of my cavalry, was kept scouting in the direction of the enemy. He came in one day and reported the enemy advancing in force, infantry, artillery, and cavalry. Having but little confidence in him, I took an escort and went in person some distance beyond the point where Gen. Duffie reported the enemy, and, finding nothing, returned. The next day he made a similar report.

I had so little confidence in anything he said or did that I placed but little confidence in his report. It was not long, however, before the enemy commenced appearing at our front. We formed in line of battle so as to hold the enemy at bay as long as possible in order that we could send our supplies to the rear.

Before this was accomplished, we had some very sharp fighting with the enemy, and were forced back with some considerable loss. Our cavalry was of little or no assistance. Gen. Averell was accused of getting drunk during the fight. With the exception of some of our wagons being burned by some of our stampeded cavalry, we got away with all our supplies. Dark stopped the pursuit. We fell back to Bunker Hill that night, the enemy not pursuing.[12]

This command had so many odds and ends in it, picked up from

'odds and ends' of dismounted cavalry, etc., that composed a part of my command, fled ingloriously across the river at the first assault of the enemy." The loss was 65 killed, 301 wounded, and 56 missing. *The War of the Rebellion*, Ser. I, Vol. XXXVII, Part I, 287–88.

[12] The command reached Winchester on July 21, and the battle took place on July 24. The command was defeated at Kernstown, fell back to Martinsburg, crossed the Potomac at Williamsport, and arrived at Pleasant Valley.

different places. It contained a large number of the professional bummers who became so numerous at the close of the war. They seemed to have an invisible organization amongst themselves. They rarely ever were in the ranks, but could be seen, from one up to four or five, straggling behind, or on the flanks of the column on the march, or having their campfires off from the organization when in camp.

They do most of the pillaging and other outrageous acts which disgrace the army's fair name. These people never fight, and can by some instinct presage a battle and keep out of it. This morning, long before I knew there would be a fight, these bummers commenced falling back.

The number of these people in an organization are in inverse proportion to its discipline. It was a notorious fact that one Kentucky regiment furnished most every organization out west with some of these men, and I heard that some of them even found their way to the Army of the Potomac.

12. *No time to be hunting up generals*

WE EVENTUALLY FELL BACK to the Monocacy, and shortly afterwards Gen. Sheridan was ordered, or either a War Department created [*sic*], composed of the 6th Corps, the Cavalry Corps from the Army of the Potomac, and all the troops in West Virginia, Maryland, and vicinity. This army was concentrated beyond Harper's Ferry, at Hall Town. In addition to this, the 19th Corps, Gen. W. H. Emory commanding, was added to his command. This was about the first of August.

We then moved forward to the summit, and from there backed and filled, sent out reconnoitering parties until the 19th of September, when we advanced to attack the enemy. They were encamped between two and three miles beyond Opequon Creek. The Cavalry of West Virginia under Gen. Averell was stationed between the enemy and Martinsburg, somewhere near Bunker Hill. The remainder of the cavalry, or rather the Cavalry Corps, was with the main army.

The order of march was as follows: first a division of cavalry under Gen. Wilson, second the 6th, and third the 19th Corps. My command was really the Army of West Virginia, but was called the 8th Corps. I had started in the campaign with about 6,000 men, but had lost some by different reconnaissances up to this time. Our transportation was parked on the east side of Opequon Creek where I was ordered to post my command in order to protect our impedimenta. But I requested to be with Gen. Sheridan and remain on the battlefield with him.[1]

The Cavalry opened the attack. The enemy were posted on a timbered ridge some five hundred yards from the one we were on, separated by a depression with a creek running through it. All of this intervening space was covered with timber, and in some places considerable underbrush. The ridge we were on was mostly open. The road that ran from our wagons up to the battlefield wound around through a wooded ravine until it reached our line of battle. From there it continued on toward the enemy, but I don't know where it went from there. This road ran nearly through the center of our line of battle.

The Cavalry was repulsed, Col. McIntosh losing his leg. The Sixth Corps was formed to the left of the road, and the Nineteenth Corps was to form on the right of the road. The Sixth was prompt, and went into line at once, while the Nineteenth was late in getting up. Gen. Sheridan was furious at the delay, and was anything but complimentary to Gen. Emory for his tardiness, for quite a time elapsed since the repulse of the cavalry until our infantry were ready to make the advance. In fact, I think it was a mistake to have

[1] Gen. Early's threat on Washington forced the Union Army to take adequate countermeasures. Forces were assembled at Harper's Ferry consisting of the Sixth and Nineteenth Corps under Generals Wright and Emory, the two infantry divisions, and a portion of the artillery which had taken part in Hunter's Lynchburg Campaign under General Crook, and Merritt's and J. H. Wilson's cavalry divisions from the Army of the Potomac.

These cavalry divisions, together with Averell's, taken from that of the Lynchburg Campaign, constituted a cavalry corps of three divisions, under Brigadier General Alfred Torbert.

Crook's forces were styled the Army of West Virginia and commonly known as Crook's Corps, although their strength did not justify the titles.

Major General Philip H. Sheridan was assigned to command this new army, called the Army of the Shenandoah. Henry A. DuPont, *The Campaign of 1864 in the Valley of Virginia*, 101–103.

made the attack at all until our infantry were ready to have followed it up.

Finally the infantry advanced to the attack. The enemy's position was a strong one. I understand it was selected by Stonewall Jackson on some previous occasion. On the left of their line were breastworks of stone thrown up. The underbrush our men had to advance through necessarily disorganized their ranks, and attacking the enemy strongly posted on their ridge gave the latter a great advantage. They not only repulsed the Nineteenth and extreme right of the Sixth Corps, but charged them in turn, driving them in some confusion.

When Gen. Sheridan ordered me to bring up my command, not only were all my staff officers dispatched to hurry them up, but he sent some of his own staff officers on the same errand. My command was divided into two divisions. Colonels I. H. Duval and Thoburn were commanding them.

The road from Opequon Creek up to the battlefield was one jam of ambulances, ammunition wagons, etc., so the troops could not march on the road. About one division marched on either side of the road, and met with more or less delay. They met the fugitives from the two corps engaged seeking safety in the rear, spreading the most doleful and alarming reports of our disaster at the front. There seemed to me to be as many fugitives as there were men in my command.

When my men came up, Gen. Sheridan ordered me to go in on the right and rear of the Nineteenth Corps. It seemed that Gen. Rodes' division of the enemy was absent on a raid up toward Bunker Hill that morning when our attack was made, but he was just returning.

I felt morally sure that if the enemy were to renew their assault on the Nineteenth Corps and succeed in driving them back, they would carry me with them. So I left one division, Thoburn's, on the right of the Nineteenth Corps, while I took the other division in person and felt my way around the enemy's left, intending, if possible, to turn his flank.

The country to be passed over was partly wooded, with an occasional open field. I found their left refused, and behind a breastwork of stone. In front of their breastworks was a swamp made by the creek before mentioned. It was impassable for horses. It was reported to me that some of my men were drowned in attempting to cross.

My right overlapped with their left, and at the same time I struck them in the rear. At this juncture I sent for the other division to charge the enemy in front, and at the same time I made a charge with the division I was with. We captured over 1,000 prisoners. Just then our cavalry came up on a charge and gobbled up all the prisoners and afterwards turned them in and was allowed credit for them.

I complained of this to Gen. Sheridan, who asked me to say nothing about it in my report, but that he saw the whole affair, and would give me credit for it. But instead of that he didn't write his report until after the war was over, and then instead of giving me the credit I deserved, he treated the subject something in this wise: that I was placed in a fortunate position where I could turn the enemy's flank, giving the impression that my turning the enemy's flank was part of his plan, whereas so far as I know the idea of turning the enemy's flank never occurred to him, but I took the responsibility on my own shoulders.[2]

In the morning[3] I asked him to give me a division of cavalry, and with my troops I would turn the enemy's right and cut off his retreat up the valley while the remainder attacked the enemy in front. He told me that he had 41,000 men, while I was morally

[2] Sheridan wrote his report while commanding the Military Division of the Gulf, in February, 1866. He stated: "I still would not order Crook in, but placed him directly in rear of the line of battle; as the reports, however, that the enemy were attempting to turn my right kept continually increasing, I was obliged to put him in on that flank instead of on the left as was originally intended.

"He was directed to act as a turning column, to find the left of the enemy's line, strike it in flank or rear, break it up, and that I would order a left half-wheel on the line of battle to support him." *The War of the Rebellion*, Ser. I, Vol. XLIIII, Part I, 47.

H. A. DuPont, commenting on the Winchester battle, remarks on the characteristics of Sheridan and Crook: "There was a radical difference in temperaments. Crook was a notably keen and clear-headed man—genial, patient, slow-speaking, and inclined to reticence, whose equanimity was rarely, if ever, disturbed, even under the most trying circumstances. Sheridan, on the other hand, was naturally eager and impulsive, which characteristics, as we have seen, seem to have fully accounted for his abrupt change of plan at the battle of Winchester on the 19th of September." DuPont, *The Campaign of 1864*, 135.

[3] That is, on the morning of the nineteenth.

certain the enemy had less than 20,000. Just about that time our line was repulsed, as before mentioned, when I was ordered to go in on the right.

My troops had charged so far that my line was all broken up. Every man was fighting on his own hook. The enemy was taking shelter behind some stone fences that here paralleled our front and were at right angles to the line of the Nineteenth and Sixth Corps. Not hearing any firing in this direction, and since the enemy behind those fences were playing havoc with my men, I rode in to where the Nineteenth Corps was.

I found them lying down in line of battle just behind the hill that was previously occupied by the enemy. I explained the situation to such of them as I could, and would get regiments and brigades to make an advance and enfilade the stone fences. I would go in with them, and wouldn't more than leave them to get the remainder to do the same thing when they would flop down again, and wouldn't fire a shot. I saw only one general officer with the corps, and he was a brigadier in charge of a brigade, by the name of Stevenson, I think, from Indiana.

By the time I reached the left of this corps, I met Gen. Emory Upton, who, upon the death of Gen. Russell, was in command of a division. He was wounded in the thigh, and was very much excited. He asked me to prefer charges against Gen. Emory, saying that he was a damned old coward, that he had tried to get him to go in to enfilade those fences, and he said he wouldn't do it without orders from Gen. Sheridan, etc. Upton was nearly crying, he was so mad.

Soon afterwards he came to see me again, and asked me to go and see a Col. Thomas who was commanding a brigade, and see if I could not induce him to fight, saying that he was a damned coward, etc.[4] I went to Thomas, and told him the accusation against him. His face had an ashy hue, and I told him I didn't believe it, but now was the chance for him to disprove this soft impeachment. He said, "Do you want me to go in without my Generals, Gen. Dwight and Gen. Emory?" Whereupon I explained that this was

[4] Colonel Stephen Thomas, later brevetted brigadier general, was awarded the medal of honor on July 25, 1892, "for distinguished conduct in a desperate hand-to-hand encounter at Cedar Creek, Va., Oct. 19, 1864, in which the advance of the enemy was checked."

no time to be hunting up generals. I then left and went back to my command.

Gen. Upton and his division were the only people along the whole line as far as I went who were doing anything, or who were apparently taking any interest in the fight. Soon after I reached my command the last of the enemy had fled, the whole of the enemy retreating in the direction of Winchester.

I had some occasion to go back in the field, when I saw Col. Thomas marching his brigade along in splendid line. He called me to look at his brigade, and "Who said they were cowards?" The enemy must have been at least three miles away, in full retreat.

We went into camp just beyond Winchester for the night. The next day we followed up the enemy, who made a stand at Fisher's Hill, a point where the North and Massanutten Mountains came close together. The enemy could occupy from the foot of North Mountain to the bluff overlooking the Shenandoah River, coming close to the foot of Massanutten Mountain, and his line of battle would not be over two and one-half miles long.

We again formed on a range of hills opposite to his position, and about one-half a mile distant. His position was stronger than ours, as his right flank and his right front was protected by sharp bluffs. Before reaching the foot of North Mountain, the ground he occupied graded off into a small valley or bottom that ran parallel with the mountains. His position was strengthened by earthworks, his batteries occupying the bluffs, and commanding all the ground between the two lines of battle. The Sixth and Nineteenth Corps were formed in line of battle in front of the enemy, while I was held in reserve in the rear of our line, my divisions lying parallel to each other.

While in this position, a fox by some mishap got between the two divisions. The men set up such a yell that poor Reynard was paralyzed with fear and lost all his cunning, jumped around in a circle, and allowed himself to be captured.

Gen. Sheridan's first idea was for me to turn the enemy's right flank, but after discussion saw the folly of such an undertaking, and finally let me go to the right, their left.[5]

[5] Sheridan's report says that he had conceived the plan of attacking the enemy's left the night before.

DuPont remarks "It was fully understood by everyone at Corps Head-

The enemy had a signal position on Massanutten Mountain that overlooked our position, and from where our movements were being watched and reported to the enemy. Gen. Averell with his cavalry was on the right line of our line, and at the foot of North Mountain. His headquarters were on a dirt road that ran along the foot of the mountain through the enemy's lines. I might here mention that the main pike ascended the bluffs near the right of the enemy's lines, running through both lines.

I led the way in person, following my way up a succession of ravines, keeping my eyes on the signal station on top of the mountain, so as to keep out of their sight, making the color bearers trail their flags so they could not be seen. I followed in this way just in front of Averell's headquarters until I reached the timbered slopes of the mountain. As soon as I got under cover of the timber, I halted and brought up my rear division alongside of the first, and in this way marched the two by flank, so that when I faced them I would have two lines of battle parallel to each other.

We had not proceeded far before we ran into some of their pickets, who fled and reported us to their commanding officer. Upon the strength of this report, a battery stationed on a little eminence below in the valley shelled the woods awhile. Eliciting no response, they concluded that the pickets were stampeded. By the time we got pretty well in the rear of their right, we ran into their reserve pickets, who, after a few shots, fled, and reported the whole woods full of Yankees. Then they opened on us again with their batteries.

The slope of the mountain was one mass of rocks, some of them weighing more than fifty tons, covered with a small growth of timber, amounting to underbrush in places. Having reached the desired distance, I faced the command to the front, and then had two lines of battle, one in the rear of the other.

---

quarters . . . that Crook had suggested this movement, and asked permission to move his infantry along the almost precipitous slope of Little North Mountain, so as to turn the enemy's left." DuPont, *The Campaign of 1864,* 134.

Rutherford B. Hayes, in another letter, to his uncle, observed that "At Fisher's Hill the turning of the Rebel left was planned and executed by Crook against the opinions of the other Corps generals . . . . General Sheridan is a whole-souled, brave man, and believes in Crook, his old class and roommate at West Point. Intellectually he is not Crook's equal, so that, as I said, General Crook is the brains of this army." *Diary and Letters,* V, 514.

I gave instructions not to yell until I gave the word, intending to march quietly until within a short distance of the open valley where the enemy's line was before commencing the charge. But their shells and round shot were crashing the trees in our midst so fiercely that when I gave the command to face to the front and move forward, they started to yell. And unless you heard my fellows yell once, you can form no conception of it. It beggars all description.

The enemy fired a few shots afterwards, but soon the yell was enough for them. The most of them never stopped to see the fellows the yell came from, but dug out. By the time we reached the open bottom there weren't any two men of any organization there. The batteries from the bluffs toward the center of the enemy's line, together with some troops near there, were making the ground hot for us. Some of my men were disposed to linger in the edge of the woods. I gathered my arms full of rocks and made it so uncomfortable for this rear that they tarried no longer.

We had to charge across this open bottom and then ascend a wooded hill sloping up to their batteries also. Their infantry had partially rallied behind some stone fences on top of the ridge. Gen. Ricketts' Division of the Sixth Corps was to support me after I made the attack.

As we were crossing the open bottom, his division was marching down in line of battle to our right, and as my troops were temporarily checked on the ridge, Gen. Ricketts made a temporary halt. Remembering his conduct at Snicker's Ferry, I feared he was about to leave us to our fate, but he soon moved on the cheek of the ridge.

When sufficient of my men got up to start them again, the enemy made no further stand until some distance down the pike. After reaching the pike, the balls were skipping down it in a very uncomfortable manner, and so many of my men had not come back yet that I went back to hurry them up.

I saw some fifty men pulling some captured artillery out of the enemy's breastworks. I pitched into them for not being at the front, thinking they were some of my men. They replied that they were pulling them by order of their general, Gen. Ricketts. Just then Gen. Ricketts, who looked as though he was stealing sheep, said he wanted to turn them in as his captures. I told him that my men had been over there some time previous, and that all able-bodied men were needed at the front.[6]

It was now getting late, and other troops went forward, and I stopped further pursuit. After following the enemy some distance up the valley, we returned and went into camp on the north side of Cedar Creek, the Sixth Corps on the right, the Nineteenth Corps in the center, and my command on the extreme left.

My division was over a mile away from any other troops, stationed on some high ground some little distance from Cedar Creek, which at this point made a big bend to our right, running through rough country at the foot of Massanutten Mountain. The distance from the creek in my front and left was too far for me to picket it, so Gen. Sheridan sent cavalry to picket it.

The cavalry of the Potomac was still to the right of the Sixth Corps, while the cavalry of the Army of West Virginia was down the Shenandoah at Luray Valley. I might say here that all the cavalry reported directly to Gen. Sheridan, so that I had nothing to do with anything but my two divisions of infantry. Gen. Averell had been retired, and Col. W. H. Powell had his command.

Somewhere about the middle of October Gen. Sheridan temporarily took the cavalry pickets from my front on Cedar Creek, leaving several fords unpicketed. Gen. Sheridan was suddenly called to Washington, leaving Gen. Wright in command. Soon after Gen. Sheridan left, I called Gen. Wright's attention to the pickets having been taken off, and he promised to replace them.

My command was then reduced by losses during the campaign and by details for guards of different kinds to less than three thousand men, divided into two divisions, one of which was on our extreme left, as before mentioned, while the other, Col. R. B. Hayes commanding, was held as a reserve just back of the left of the Nineteenth Corps.

On the night of the 18th–19th of October, the enemy, who was lying at Fisher's Hill, made a secret march around the foot of Massanutten Mountain, crossed the fords where our cavalry pickets

[6] Crook took position in the timber on September 20. He remained there on the twenty-first, hidden from view. That night he moved again, to the timber near Strasburg, and the next day moved to the timber around Little North Mountain, after which the attack was made.

had been taken off, and formed in line of battle close under my extreme division's left and rear, and, in fact, enveloping it entirely. During the night my Officer of the Day in making his rounds heard noise outside of my pickets, and, thinking it was our cavalry, went out to investigate it. He was captured by the enemy without being able to give the alarm.

The morning was extremely favorable for the enemy's purposes, as there was a mild fog covering the whole country. The enemy, just at the peep of day, and without any warning, made a rush at my little attenuated line, and drove them back, meeting with but little resistance.

My two batteries were posted on the right between this divison and the left of the Nineteenth Corps. My troops resisted sufficiently, however, to enable some of the twelve pieces to escape capture. Almost simultaneously with this attack the enemy came pouring in at the rear of Hayes' division, and the left of the Nineteenth Corps. The fugitives from the extreme left were fleeing to the rear of the Nineteenth and left.

Hayes' division held its own for a short time, but Gen. Wright came up and gave the order for it to retreat under heavy fire, when it broke, and only rallied again in small detachments until it got some distance back.

There was also a provisional brigade still on Hayes' right, which gave way about the same time. The whole army fell back some distance behind where the extreme right of our line was formerly occupied by the Sixth Corps. Here it formed in line of battle, and resisted an attack of the enemy at about ten o'clock.

Our losses were not so great as we had reason to expect. Our losses in artillery were as follows: Sixth Corps: 6 pieces; Nineteenth Corps: 11 pieces; my command: 7 pieces.

Our new line was getting stronger all the time by stragglers joining from the rear. About mid-day Gen. Sheridan came riding up from Winchester, and assumed command. Shortly afterwards the whole line was ordered to advance. From the enemy's account, his men were scattered, pillaging and having a good time over their captures, so that he was in no condition to meet us, besides being numerically so much smaller than we were, for our cavalry was almost as strong as their whole effective force. The enemy was routed, dark saving many of their number from being taken prisoners.

Sitting around the campfires that night, Gen. Sheridan was feeling very good. He said, "Crook, I am going to get much more credit for this than I deserve, for, had I been here in the morning the same thing would have taken place, and had I not returned today, the same thing would have taken place." This saying was full of meat, but it made little impression on me at the time.[7]

Myself and division have never had justice done us in this affair, for we had always been spoken of as the Eighth Corps, giving the impression that we had enough men to constitute a corps. We were assigned to duties that required a corps to perform, and then were not properly supported, and have been held responsible for the surprise that does not belong to us, for had the cavalry pickets been where we had every reason to expect them, the surprise never could have happened, and without the surprise the enemy would never have dared to have gotten so near us with their small force.

This ended the Valley Campaign, which should have ended with the battle of the Opequon one month before, for we had over double the number of men they had. We had nearly 10,000 cavalry, had the advantage in position, and we could have cut off their retreat by occupying the pike running up the valley with part of our force, while we overwhelmed them with the remainder.

---

[7] Twenty-five years later, on December 26, 1889, Crook visited the battlefield again for the first time. His diary for that day indicates that he never forgave Sheridan for what appeared to be deliberate withholding of proper credit and assumption of honor not due him.

"We then took horses a little after sun-up, and went to the Cedar Creek battlefield, some two and a half miles, getting back for dinner. After dinner, we with the same horses rode over the Fisher Hill battleground, a couple of miles up the valley.

"After examining the grounds and the position of the troops after twenty five years which have elapsed and in the light of subsequent events, it renders Gen. Sheridan's claims and his subsequent actions in allowing the general public to remain under the impressions regarding his part in these battles, when he knew they were fiction, all the more contemptible. The adulations heaped on him by a grateful nation for his supposed genius turned his head, which, added to his natural disposition, caused him to bloat his little carcass with debauchery and dissipation, which carried him off prematurely."

13. *The Confederate Army was in its last throes*

THE CAMPAIGN ENDED, I being in command of West Virginia. I went near the center of my department, at Cumberland, Maryland. When I returned to West Virginia in 1864, my sphere of operations gave me control of country that had never been rid of bushwhackers, so I organized to suppress them, employing the same principles which were so efficacious when I was in that country before.

To that end I organized a body of picked men from the different regiments, and selected as their commander a Capt. Blazer, who evinced an adaptability for that kind of work, and became so efficient that he was not long in ridding the district infested with these people. He had made considerable headway against Mosby's men after the theater of operations was transferred to the east, but his force was too small to cope with Mosby. I would have increased the size of his command, but about that time he had an unsuccessful encounter with an overpowering number of Mosby.

General Sheridan organized a similar force for the whole army, after which I was relieved from any further service of that nature. These men of Gen. Sheridan were under a Major Young. Just what they accomplished I don't know, but they would dress at times in Confederate uniforms, and at times in our uniform. Our pickets and outposts were instructed to let them pass and repair uniform.

While I was in Cumberland on the night of 21st of February, 1865, a company of guerrillas, known as Capt. McNeill's company, whose men were from Cumberland and vicinity and had relatives and sympathizers all through that country who kept them posted on everything that transpired within our lines, came to the pickets outside of Cumberland in Confederate uniform and represented themselves as Sheridan's scouts.

By threats they made the ignorant Dutchman who happened to be on picket give them the countersign. Armed with that they passed the sentinels right along, and came up to the hotel where Gen. Kelley and I had our headquarters, and came to our rooms.

Finding ourselves completely at their mercy, there was nothing left for us but to go with them. We were mounted on horses provided for the purpose, and were taken to Richmond. After staying there two weeks a special exchange was made.[1]

General Grant intended giving me command of all the Cavalry of the Potomac at the final struggle. But Gen. Sheridan, having marched from Winchester to join the Army of the Potomac with that portion of it that was up in the valley of the Shenandoah, was given command. I was given command of the Cavalry which remained back with the Army of the Potomac, which was organized into a division of three brigades.[2]

In the latter part of March all the cavalry under command of Gen. Sheridan left the rear of the Army of the Potomac, then lying in their trenches fronting Petersburg, and marched toward Dinwiddie Court House, around to our left, and the enemy's right, with the intention of being on our extreme left when our army assaulted the enemy, as I understood it was our intention to do. I understood also that if the assault was successful, all right, and in case of a repulse, the cavalry was to turn the enemy's right, and raid down to Sherman's army, while the Army of the Potomac was to return to their trenches. The country was to be given to understand that the object of this demonstration was to let out our cavalry.

Soon after our departure for Dinwiddie it commenced pouring down rain, and the roads were almost impassable. The ground seemed mostly a clay on top, with quicksand underneath. A field might look perfectly solid, but after a squadron or two of cavalry passed over it, the horses would break through the top crust of a foot or so thick, into the quicksand, letting the horses in up to their bellies. The more they struggled the deeper they sank, until many had to be abandoned.

On the 29th of March we met the enemy's cavalry near Din-

---

[1] For a detailed account of the capture of Generals Crook and Kelley, see Appendix II, pages 304–306.

[2] By *Special Order No. 78,* Headquarters Army of the Potomac (March 27, 1865), Crook was brevetted brigadier general, U. S. Army, for services in the 1864 campaign in West Virginia, and brevetted major general for his services at Fisher's Hill, Virginia. *The War of the Rebellion,* Ser. I, Vol. LI, Part I, 1207.

widdie Court House. The fighting was very sanguine, particularly in my division, which lost nearly a third of its effective forces. In the evening the enemy advanced on us with a division of infantry. I understood it was Bushrod Johnson's. We could scarcely use our cavalry and artillery, the ground was so heavy. We, however, showed a bold front, and hung on with determination. Fortunately, night was at hand and relieved us of our embarrassment.

During the night we received orders to fall back, but I understood from Gen. Sheridan's headquarters that Gen. Sheridan had made the proposition to Gen. Grant that if he would give him a corps of infantry to act in conjunction with his cavalry, he would break through the enemy's lines. The next morning the Fifth Corps, Gen. Warren commanding, were ordered to report to Gen. Sheridan in light marching orders. Shortly afterwards the battle of Five Forks was fought, but as my division was badly handled at Dinwiddie, I was left behind to guard, so did not participate in that engagement.[3]

The enemy's lines were broken through at this point, where their army gave way, and commenced retreating, first in the direction of Lynchburg and afterwards more directly south. In fact, their line of retreat seemed to vacillate, evidently more or less influenced by our movements.

Our cavalry were untiring. We scarcely rested, but were going day and night. The enemy could not take any new direction, but what he would find some of our cavalry at his front. We all felt that the end of the war was near at hand, and that the Confederate army was in its last throes.

We were emboldened by the fact that the enemy was fleeing for his life, that his spies and superior sources of getting information about our movements were gone. His partisan soldiers, who used to make it unsafe for small bodies of our troops to leave the main army even sometimes inside of our picket lines, were all gone, and our men were free to roam everywhere.

It was evident from the enemy's movements that his sources of information about our movements were gone. He seemed to be moving in the dark. Several times he would change his course from

---

[3] The Battle of Dinwiddie Court House was fought on March 31, and the Battle of Five Forks on April 1, 1865.

the appearance of a few of our cavalry in his front. He seemed to have lost his cunning entirely. My division had several severe engagements with them at Petersburg, Sailor's Creek, Farmville, and Appomattox.

We were harassing him all day at Sailor's Creek. One of our divisions would engage his front and fight him until his rear had passed him, when we would again flank around to his front and engage him again. Our three divisions in this way harassed him all morning,[4] not strong enough to oppose any serious obstacle to his advance.

Our object was to detain him as much as possible. In the afternoon he made a stand, or a portion of his force at least, on a little round knoll. He had thrown up temporary breastworks out of rails and earth, encircling the top. Gen. Custer's division was to my right. We couldn't tell whether the breastworks was occupied or not. I sent one of my brigades to develop the enemy by a charge up to the works.

The charge was handsomely executed, but when within a few yards of the top they received a volley which gave me all the information I desired. The brigade fell back, under cover. Noticing the many empty saddles, I thought my loss very heavy, but afterwards ascertained that many of the men were mounted on mules, and under the excitement of the charge, and the natural perversity of the animal, when he got under full headway, he refused to stop, so the riders slid off the mules' backs and let them go. One rider stuck to his mule, who never stopped until he jumped over their breastworks. The soldier demanded their surrender, and in the confusion he escaped to our troops on the opposite side and reported to Gen. Sheridan.

Gen. Custer then ordered a charge of his whole division. His bands struck up, and the division was ordered to charge with a yell, but not to exceed 300 men broke cover to make the charge. Nothing was accomplished, and they again returned to cover, and remained until the surrender sometime afterwards.

I then dismounted two of my brigades, and sent them to the rear of the enemy's position. I will here mention that some of the Army of the Potomac were operating on the side of the enemy op-

[4] April 6, 1865.

posite us. Shortly after my men got to their rear, the enemy surrendered, Capt. Roberts of my staff bringing in forty-odd prisoners.

As soon as the enemy hoisted the white flag, Gen. Custer's division rushed up the hill and turned in more prisoners and battle flags than any of the cavalry, and probably had less to do with their surrender than any of the rest of us.[5]

We still followed up the rest of the retreating foe. At a small place called Farmville I attacked the enemy's column in flank as they were marching along the road. For some unaccountable reason one of my brigades, Col. Gregg's, became stampeded by some of the enemy's cavalry appearing on their flank. There were less than one hundred of them.

This brigade was advancing in line of battle through some unplanted fields, the ground of which was a little heavy from rains. Since the pursuit commenced, we had to subsist chiefly on the country, so the soldiers had more or less provisions tied to their saddles. Some would have a ham, others chickens, ducks, geese, turkeys, etc. etc. So after the stampede, hams, chickens, geese, etc. could be seen scattered on the fields, fowls with their legs tied, and sticking their heads up, struggling to get loose. The whole presented a most ludicrous spectacle.

Col. Gregg, being a heavy man, and riding a small horse, couldn't keep up with his men, and was captured. The men converged to the road in their flight, so that a little further to the rear the road was jammed with the fugitives going to the rear. I cut in ahead of about a squadron, and faced the fugitives, using my sword over their and the horses' heads. I would seize the reins of some of their horses, and try to re-establish their morale by asking them what they were doing. When I thought I had one man alright, I would turn my attention to another, feeling certain that if I could only stop my squadron, I could drive back the enemy.

But the first I knew, all of my men were past me, and the enemy was right on me. I again cut in ahead of a lot of men, trying by the same process to stop them. This time the enemy was so close that

[5] Custer's report of the battle mentions that his command captured General Ewell and six other general officers. "In addition we captured fifteen pieces of artillery and thirty-one battle flags." *The War of the Rebellion*, Ser. I, Vol. XLVI, Part I, 1132.

Col. S. M. B. Young of the Pennsylvania Cavalry, by my side, had his hat cut off by an enemy's saber.

I thought I was certainly captured this time, as there was a high fence on either flank, but fortunately there was a gap that let me through into a field in which Capt. Lord had a battery which he had just gotten into action. This soon checked the enemy and drove them back and allowed our cavalry to settle down and feel sheepish for their behavior. Most of these men were old veterans, and had served through the war. I was unable to account for their conduct, and what was still more strange was to see men who were fleeing down the pike deliberately discharging their revolvers into their comrades ahead of them.

We marched all the night of the 8th and 9th, arriving in front of Appomattox Court House about daylight. In the morning I received orders to resist the enemy with all my power, so as to detain him, if possible, until our infantry got up. For this purpose Gen. MacKenzie was ordered to report to me.

We held on till I hadn't more than fifty men left with me on the little prominence I was holding, and a section of artillery. We held on till the enemy in force came so close that we could possibly do good no longer, when we fell back. The section of artillery stayed there till the last, and as we were going back there lay a piece of artillery in the ditch. Lord, thinking it was one of his, cried, but it turned out afterwards that it was not his.

We had not proceeded far before we met the Twenty-Fourth Corps of "Darks" marching up to the front. I had heard so much pro and con about the fighting qualities of the Negroes that I sent my staff back to reorganize my command while I went along with this corps to see for myself how these people would fight. They were the first I had seen in any numbers. They looked like so many crows, they were so black. They marched up in splendid order, and although some of them were knocked over, they showed no flinching.

But as soon as General Lee saw that we had infantry in his front, he hoisted the white flag, and that ended the fighting.

When the President disapproved of the stipulations entered into between Gen. Sherman and Johnston, Gen. Sheridan was sent down to Sherman's Army. After proceeding several days' march, the matter was satisfactorily adjusted, and we returned to Petersburg.

It was en route that the news of Mr. Lincoln's massacre was sent us.[6] At Petersburg Gen. Sheridan left us, and in command of the cavalry I marched up to Fairfax Court House, from where I went on leave to Ohio, so was not present at the grand review of the armies in Washington.[7]

I was married on August 22, 1865.[8]

Shortly afterwards I was ordered to Wilmington, North Carolina, to take charge of a district, where I remained until I was mustered out on Jan. 22, 1866. I was appointed Lieutenant-Colonel of the Twenty-Third Regiment of Infantry,[9] while two of my brigade commanders, Colonels Gregg and Smith were made Colonels, and Smith assured me that he was made on my recommendation.

I regret to say that I learned too late that it was not what a person did, but it was what he got the credit of doing that gave him a reputation and at the close of the war gave him position.

[6] This is probably the only time the word "massacre" has been used to refer to President Lincoln's assassination. Crook could not write except in terms of the West.

[7] Crook was relieved from command of the Cavalry Corps by *Special Order No. 336*, Headquarters of the Army, Adjutant General's Office (June 27, 1865). *The War of the Rebellion*, Ser. I, Vol. XLVI, Part III, 1300.

[8] For details of Crook's courtship and marriage see Appendix III, pages 306–307.

[9] He was appointed major, Third Infantry, July 18, and lieutenant-colonel, Twenty-third Infantry, July 28, 1866.

V

PAIUTES TO
APACHES

14. *I got interested after the Indians*

IN NOVEMBER, 1866, I left New York to join my regiment.[1] I arrived in Boise City, on December 11th. On my way out on the steamer I met Lt. Nickerson and his first wife. He was under orders to proceed to Arizona to join one battalion of the 14th Regiment, but as the battalion was not designated, and as one of them was in Idaho, I persuaded Gen. Halleck to send him up with me.[2]

When I arrived at Boise, Indian affairs in that country could not well have been worse. That whole country, including Northern California and Nevada, Eastern Oregon and Idaho, up to Montana, you might say was in a state of siege. Hostile Indians were all over that country, dealing death and destruction everywhere they wished. People were afraid to go outside of their own doors without protection. There was scarcely a day that reports of Indian depredations were not coming in.

The district in which Boise was included was commanded by

[1] Crook sailed from New York on November 5, 1866. In his diary, twenty-four years later, he recalls the date.

Under the Act of Congress of July 28, 1866, Crook had been appointed lieutenant colonel of the Twenty-third Infantry, one of the new regiments. It was not actually formed at the time but was to be activated by adding two companies to one of the battalions of the Fourteenth Infantry, the Second, which had been formed by direction of the President, May 4, 1861. Philip Reade, "Chronicle of the Twenty-Third Regiment of Infantry, U.S.A.," *Journal of the Military Service Institution of the United States*, Vol. 35, No. 132 (November-December, 1904), 419–27; Adjutant General's Office, *General Order No. 92* (November 23, 1866).

[2] Azor H. Nickerson was one of the Volunteer officers who remained in the army after the Civil War. He served on Crook's staff for over ten years and wrote a sketch of his experiences which he called "Major General George Crook and the Indians."

Col. L. H. Marshall.[3] The feeling against him and many of his officers was very bitter. They were accused of all manner of things. One thing was certain: they had not, nor were they, making headway against the hostile Indians. There was much dissipation amongst a good many officers, and there seemed to be a general apathy amongst them, and indifference to the proper discharge of duty.

All kinds of irregularities were charged against them. The transportation was in a very bad state. The pack mules were scarcely able to carry the aparejos.[4] The citizens, too, were in a very excited frame of mind from other causes. Just before my arrival the vigilantes had executed a gang of horse thieves, highwaymen, and murderers, extending through the country above mentioned, including Montana. They had spent some time in organizing and getting information, until all was ready. At a given time some sixty were hung. Amongst them was the Sheriff at Boise.[5]

It seemed that these desperadoes had worked their men in all kinds of capacities and positions throughout this country, so as to allay suspicions and get information. Then too, there were many bad men from the south congregated in that country, refugees, deserters, etc.—all against the government. The Legislature that met there that winter was composed mostly of that element. They were

[3] The District of Boise, in the Department of Columbia, was discontinued per *General Order No. 5*, Division of the Pacific (January 29, 1867). Fort Boise and Camps Lyon, Winthrop, C. F. Smith, and Warner constituted the District of Owyhee, with Brevet Major General George Crook in command. Camps McDermitt and Winfield Scott were also under his direction for the guarding of public roads and for expeditions against the Indians.

In August, 1867, Crook was assigned to command the District of the Lakes, comprising Fort Klamath, Camps Warner and Watson, and the new post in Harney Lake Valley. The troops at Camp Bidwell also remained under his orders.

[4] Aparejos are large packsaddles made of heavy leather and stuffed with straw. Pack-train terminology was largely Spanish, for the art of packing by mule reached its height in the Southwest.

[5] Sheriff Dave Opdyke was hanged on the Overland Stage Road by three employees of the stage company. The hanging was credited to the Boise City Vigilance Committee, because a card or label with the insignia of the committee was attached to the body, but the committee had no part in the act, and none of its members was present. No regrets were expressed, however. William J. McConnell, *Early History of Idaho*, 250.

so obstreperous that the governor had to call on the military to keep them within bounds.[6]

One week after my arrival the Indians committed some depredations near the mouth of the Boise River, some twenty miles from Boise. So I took Capt. Perry's company of the 1st Cavalry and left with one change of underclothes, toothbrush, etc., and went to investigate matters, intending to be gone a week. But I got interestd after the Indians and did not return there again for over two years.

The Indians who had been depredating had gone up the Owyhee River, so I concluded to follow them. Everybody was opposed to it. The weather was inclement, and campaigning was disagreeable. Marshall's scouts, or rather his chief of scouts, Cayuse George, was utterly worthless and demoralized. I had not proceeded far before I caught him in a lie, but, not discouraged by that, we went on until we found the rancheria. We attacked them just after daylight, and killed a good many, demoralizing the others. That ended any more depredations from that band.[7]

After the fight was over, I wanted to make a certain place that evening that we had encamped at on our way up. As we traveled over much of the distance after night, I only got the lay of the land imperfectly. After two days march, when we came near to where I thought we were going to camp, I saw some sheep sign, and thought I would go up on the bluffs overlooking the Owyhee River. So I dismounted, sending my animal to camp with the command.

I went up on the bluffs, which were over one thousand feet above the Owyhee River, mostly terminating in sheer precipices, with side canyons cutting these bluffs at right angles. I had no more than reached the bluffs when a thick fog set in. Shortly afterwards I commenced descending the mountain, but by the time I had reached the trail, night had set in, and that, combined with the fog, made it so dark that I could not see my hand before me, let alone the trail.

[6] The legislative riot is described in McConnell, *Early History of Idaho*, 344–54.
[7] "On December 18, 1866, Bvt. Maj.-Gen. Crook, commanding the District of Boise, with Capt. Perry and forty-five men of Company F, 1st Cavalry, ten Indians and two citizen guides went up the Owyhee River, attacked the Indians, chastising them severely, capturing all their stock. Our loss, Sgt. O'Toole, mortally wounded." Secretary of War, *Annual Report*, 1868, 58.

It now commenced sleeting, and as I had nothing but a thin coat on, I became wet through. While I could see nothing, I had an idea from the direction of the wind and the character of the country I was passing through that I was going in the right direction. I noticed in going up the night before where the small streams running into the river had cut through chalky hills, leaving perpendicular banks, some of which were twenty feet high.

I fell down some of them during this night, and in one place the bank sheltered me from the cold, sleety wind. So I thought I would rest there awhile and warm up. But shortly a big chunk caved in, which reminded me that I might be covered up entirely, and no one would ever be the wiser of my whereabouts. So I pulled out of there, and like the Wandering Jew I moved on.

I had no matches, and everything was so wet that I couldn't start fire with powder. About eleven or twelve o'clock, fearful of passing camp, I sat down on top of a sage brush, crossed my arms, and put my hands on my bosom under my shirt, rubbing them against my warmer skin, and at the same time knocking my knees together. I managed to keep up a fair degree of circulation.

About two or three o'clock in the morning the heavens cleared up, and the moon came out to shine, and I looked down into our camp. I was not long in reaching my blanket. It seemed that when I did not come into camp at dark, Perry had fires built on high points in the vicinity and guns discharged, but I was entirely out of their sight or hearing.

We moved down to the Snake River, from which point I sent to Boise for more supplies and Indian scouts. Upon their receipt I made a scout up the Malheur River. We found a camp not far up the river, but by the misbehavior of the chief of scouts the Indians discovered us, and made their escape.

We followed them up the river until we came to a bottom about one-half of a mile wide, which was cut up with sloughs, sand washed in sharp ridges, etc., all covered with a thick growth of willows. Winding around through this was the river. The Indians who had fled up the river joined others in these willows.

The willows and rose bushes were so thick around the edge that it was impossible to see over ten feet into them, much less get our bodies through them. We tried to take the place by an attack through the brush, but had to abandon it as utterly impracticable, for not only were the bushes impenetrable except by cutting roads through them, but the Indians had such odds against us by being in the brush, and we on the open ground outside. One of our men was shot by an Indian only a few feet distant, but a horse shoe in his shirt pocket saved his life. In all of my experience in campaigns against Indians, this was the only time I could have used artillery to advantage.

Being so near dark, it gave me an excuse to postpone operations. That night we got into a talk with them. They expressed a willingness to make peace, but I had no confidence in them. They had been depredating all over that country, and never had been punished. They were occupying this stronghold that we had gotten the worst of in trying to penetrate, nor were there any prospects of our being able to drive them out of this place.

I didn't like their tone; they were too independent and saucy. The next morning a truce was declared. They came to our camp and sat around. We gave them something to eat, and gradually they began to feel more at their ease. But they were not going to make a peace that was not all in their favor, nor did I feel certain they would not commit some act of treachery on us. I was strongly urged to take the initiative and kill them while in my camp.

After a while our men gradually got to visiting with the Indians, trading with them. After a while sufficient number had sifted into their camp, leaving their guns behind, but had on their pistols, to hold their camp. When the Indians saw this, their whole demeanor changed at once, and they got ready to go with us.

Their stronghold was much more impregnable than I had any idea it could be from its outside appearance. Their camp was between parallel ridges of sharp sand, ridges overgrown with willows of from two to six inches in diameter, furnishing most excellent breastworks. This was only approachable by one trail that wound around amongst similar ridges and sloughs of nearly one half a mile in length, with one continual ambush the whole distance. I thanked my stars that affairs terminated as they did.[8]

I wished to cross over to the Owyhee River, higher up, so as to go to Fort Lyon.[9] To do this it was necessary to cross a high plateau.

[8] January 23, 1867. Secretary of War, *Annual Report*, 1868, 58.
[9] Camp Lyon was established on June 27, 1865, on the north fork of Jordan

We started in the morning from the Malheur. Soon after reaching the high ground, the wind came on to blow. The ground was covered with a light snow, and in a short time the sun was obscured, and so far as we could see we were in a frightful snowstorm. At times we couldn't see fifty yards ahead of us. We had to make a certain point some ten or twelve miles ahead of us, so as to avoid some impassable cañons.

This blinding storm obscured all landmarks, but fortunately our guide's (Archie McIntosh)[10] instincts were reliable, more so than the knowledge of any other guide I have ever seen, and his course did not deviate from this point a foot in the whole distance. The wind blew so hard at times during the day that my weight was insufficient to keep me in the seat, and I would be thrown forward in the pommel of the saddle. The fine snow would sift through my clothes and wet me to the spine in places.

We had to encamp that night on this plateau with no protection from the storm. There was nothing but sagebrush for fuel; had to dig that out of the snow. Our repeated efforts to kindle a fire were unsuccessful until we pitched an "A" tent, the only tent we had, with its back against the wind, then built two wings out from the front of the tent, so as to break the wind from edging. In this way we finally started a fire.

When we awoke the next morning the blizzard was still in full

Creek, northernmost tributary of the Owyhee River. It was erected to serve as a guard against Indian attacks on the stage line, and was abandoned on April 27, 1869, per *General Order No. 7*, Division of the Pacific. James V. Frederick, *Ben Holladay, Stagecoach King*, 232 ff.; *Posts, Camps, and Stations File.*

[10] Archie McIntosh, a half blood, was no cast-off, as were many self-styled guides on the frontier. He had been brought up by the Hudson's Bay Company and knew his business.

Archie, though he drank to excess whenever the opportunity offered, served as guide for Crook throughout the Indian campaign in the Northwest and later accompanied him to Arizona; he proved himself a "wonderful man in any country." When Crook was transferred to the Department of the Platte in 1875, Archie stayed on his ranch at Mesquite Springs, but during the Bannock outbreak of 1879, he offered his services to Crook once more.

His chance came when Crook took command in Arizona for the second time, in 1883, but after a short campaign he was dismissed, the rigors of soldiering in that country proving too much for him. John G. Bourke, *On the Border with Crook*; Bourke, "General Crook in the Indian Country," *Century Magazine*, Vol. XLI, No. 5 (March, 1891), 643–60; *Owyhee Avalanche*, August 3, 1867.

blast. We traveled through it until the afternoon, when we commenced descending on to the Owyhee River. Before we reached the bottom everything was serene and lovely. No snow, and the temperature lovely. I actually saw grasshoppers jumping about this 24th day of January.

We went from here into Camp Lyon, not far from Silver City, Idaho, where Capt. J. C. Hunt, 1st Cavalry, was in command. From appearance and information the normal condition of the officers there was drunkenness. They didn't seem to do much else but get drunk and lie around doing nothing.

From here I took Capt. Hunt's company out with me, sending Capt. Perry with the Indians to Boise. When coming in from the Malheur River, we saw some Indian signs near the Owyhee. So I took Capt. Hunt's company to examine that country. After scouting the country, traveling mostly after night with the command, and keeping the scouts ahead, the scouts reported having seen some Indians near the eastern slope of Stein's Mountain.[11]

We traveled to near where we expected their ranch to be in the evening, and then waited until midnight, when we started so as to arrive at the point by daylight next morning. The scouts in the meantime went ahead, so as to locate the exact spot where the rancheria was. By daylight next morning the company was drawn up in line of battle within a couple of hundred yards of the rancheria, which was on a sagebrush plain, close to some low foothills, evidently oblivious of any danger.

In the meantime I had sent the scouts in the small foothills to pick up any that would try to make their escape in that direction. I gave particular instructions that not a shot was to be fired until we got in amongst the Indians.

I intended remaining in the rear to see that the men did their duty, but just as soon as the charge commenced my horse took the bit between his teeth and became unmanageable, and led the charge. Instead of obeying my instructions, they commenced firing the moment that the charge commenced. The balls whistled by me, and I was in much more danger from the rear than I was from the front.

11 Joe Wasson, reporter for the *Owyhee Avalanche* wrote in his story for September 14, 1867: "I am told by good authority that said mountain was named after Major Enoch Steen—hence the spelling is usually wrong."

My horse ran through the village, and I could not stop him until he reached some distance beyond, most of the men following me.

At once I jumped off my horse, and let him go. Running back, I found some of the Indians coming towards me. Particularly one fellow, stopped, surrounded by soldiers, singing his death song, and letting slip his arrows at his enemies. He must have been shot through and through a half dozen times before he fell.

There was a citizen from Silver City with us. As he and I were going up to the front of a wick-a-up that had a sage brush covering its entrance, he on one side of the brush and I on the other, an Indian lying ready at the entrance shot him through the heart. I kept cautioning him not to be so venturesome, but either he was reckless or else didn't appreciate the danger. The Indian was killed by firing a volley into the wick-a-up.

We killed all the grown bucks except two who were on the outside of our lines when the attack was made. We gathered up the women and children who had not been killed, and took them into Camp Smith.[12] From here the prisoners were taken into Boise.[13] I took the Cavalry company stationed at Smith, in addition to Hunt's, and started for Old Camp Warner, scouting on the way.[14] Several small bands of a few Indians each were cleaned up on the way.

[12] Camp C. F. Smith, named after General Charles Ferguson Smith, was established on White Horse Creek near the Pueblo mines in May, 1866. It was named by *General Order No. 19*, Division of the Pacific (August 3, 1866). As was the case with all the temporary camps established in this region, once the roads had been rendered safe from Indian attacks, it lost its reason for being. It was discontinued on March 15, 1869. *Posts, Camps, and Stations File.*

[13] General Crook, with Company M, First Cavalry, twelve Indians, and four white scouts left Camp Lyon on January 21, 1867, for Owyhee River and Stein's Mountain. They attacked Indians, killing sixty and capturing twenty-seven. Only one buck and two squaws escaped. Loss to the expedition was one citizen killed and one wounded, and three soldiers wounded. Secretary of War, *Annual Report*, 1868, 59.

[14] Camp Warner, named in honor of Lieutenant William Horace Warner of the Topographical Engineers, was first located twenty miles east of Warner Lake and established on July 15, 1866. The first commanding officer was Captain Patrick Collins, Company D, Fourteenth Infantry.

About September 1, 1867, the location was changed to a point about fifteen miles west of the lake and thirty-five miles from the Oregon-California line, for reasons which appear in the text. The new post was occupied until October 2, 1874, when it was abandoned. *Posts, Camps, and Stations File.*

We camped for the night fourteen miles from Warner. Next morning there was a blizzard raging. The guide, Archie McIntosh, showed by his actions that he did not approve of moving. He never advised anything, or expressed any protests in words, and had I known him better or the nature of blizzards better, I should have remained in camp that day. But we started in a storm that obscured everything, sun, landmarks, and even one part of the column from the other.

We had a couple of wagons and a few captives we had picked up after leaving Smith. The snow became deeper and deeper as we progressed. It was drifted in places fifteen or twenty feet deep, offering about as little resistance as so much water. Animals would at times go out of sight in these banks, the wind whirling in all directions, filling our eyes and ears, in fact, every place where it would find a lodgement. As fast as an animal pulled his feet out of the snow, the wind filled it up with shifting snow, so that the two companies passing would leave no trail.

It was almost like traveling in the dark. It was more difficult getting our animals along, either mounted or dismounted, than it was for ourselves. A gush of wind went off with my hat sometime in the afternoon. From there on my hair and whiskers were one mass of sleet and snow.

It was nearly sundown when we reached the post. The wind abated a little, and our animals commenced making a trail. I had turned my horse loose, and I was afoot. I never in my life was so nearly exhausted. It was not so much the fatigue as it was the incessant blowing of the wind, which seemed to blow one's vitality out of him.

I was near the head of the column. When I sat down to rest afterwhile, a mule came along, saddled, with no one on his back, which was nearly on a level with the surface of the snow, the trail was so deep, I dropped into the saddle, where I was carried in safety.

The snow was on a level with the tops of the houses; the haystacks in the bottom were covered up entirely. This was another remarkable instance of Archie's instinct, for he had never been at the post but once before, and was drunk at that. The next day the storm calmed down, so we sent out for the wagons we were compelled to abandon the day before.[15]

A couple of days afterwards I moved down on Warner Lake, so I could operate against the Indians, as that country was comparatively free from snow, and blizzards did not prevail. I sent Archie with the scouts to the southern end of the lake, and to scout over to Goose Lake and on the west of Warner's Lake.

This lake was some seventy miles long and fifteen miles wide at the widest places, but opposite to where I was encamped it narrowed down to about three or four hundred yards in width. Here I commenced building a stone causeway across this narrow neck. At the edges the water was shallow, but in the center there were deep holes, with patches of a species of cane growing in the center on apparently firm ground. But after the weight of the rock remained on it for some time, it suddenly disappeared, rock and all. It seemed this ground was simply floating. After rocks enough were thrown in, the holes were filled up, but not in time to bring over Archie's party dry shod. This causeway was afterwards made wide enough for wagons to pass, which made a great saving in distance, besides being a great convenience.

Archie overstayed the time allotted him several days, until I became right uneasy about his safety. They reached the opposite side of the lake about ten o'clock at night. We had a rough time getting them across, for the ice was not strong enough to bear their weight, and the causeway was not sufficiently advanced to assist much. He made some cock and bull report, but I was satisfied he was drunk the greater part of the time, and the hostiles he saw and slayed were mostly in his mind.

15. *Our beards were one mass of ice*

SHORTLY AFTER THIS I made a scout with both companies to the "Dunder and Blixen" country. While we were encamped on a

[15] On February 22, General Crook with Companies H and M, First Cavalry, left Camp C. F. Smith on a scout around Pueblo Mountain, killing two

creek of that name, the Indians stampeded and got away with most of our stock, so we had to go back to Warner Lake by using what animals we had left to pack us in. By making two loads we got back all right. As this left us powerless to operate against the Indians until we could have our stock replenished, we remained in camp on the lake in preference to going back to the post.

While here I had a good opportunity to explore the lake. I had a canoe dug out of a pine log, and with that went all about the lake. It was mostly overgrown with tule, or bullrushes. In low water, except in only a few places, the water was not more than from four to six feet deep, shading off into water only a few inches deep at the edges.

In the fall and spring swan would congregate in large numbers, remaining in the fall until all the water was frozen up, when they would go farther south. When the ice commenced freezing, the ice would crack like the discharge of artillery. In freezing, there would be air holes that would not freeze over until the very last, and in these the swan would collect in great numbers, and if you would conceal yourself, you could get several shots before they would fly, doubtless under the impression that the reports of the gun was the ice cracking.

Geese and ducks left much earlier than the swan. In the spring they would be the first waterfowl to make their appearance on the way north. Then would come the geese and ducks. A few of the geese and ducks would breed there during the spring and summer. The canvas-back would congregate there by the acres while waiting for their breeding grounds up in the British possessions to open. The cormorants and coots, however, bred there. One day I got sixty-seven dozen eggs of these birds. The coot eggs were good eating, being about the size and color of a guinea fowl egg, but the white of the cormorant egg was bitter and strong when cooked, and were not healthy.

Old Camp Warner was situated on a high, bleak mesa, which was inaccessible at times in the winter. So it was moved to the opposite side of the lake, in a nice body of timber that was accessible

---

warriors and capturing their women and children. Owing to the difficulties of marching through the snow, no further results were obtained. Secretary of War, *Annual Report*, 1868, 59.

at all seasons of the year. That spring mules and horses were sent from California, so that scouting was resumed. Many side scouts were made, with numbers of small parties of Indians being killed and captured.

I made a scout from Camp McDermitt[1] in the Quinn River country, but beyond my hard work, nothing was accomplished. In returning to Old Warner, I found a band of Indians on a little lake, almost in sight of Warner. (It had not been transferred yet.) These Indians had evidently been getting ammunition somewhere. We killed a lot of them.

Later, when the new post was being built, I started on an expedition scout to the country between about Lake Klamath River, and Goose Lake. We found nothing until south and west of a marsh near the forks of Pit River. Indians were found occupying, or rather ran into some rocks. In prospecting these rocks, we had some men killed and wounded.

This was late in the evening, so the next morning (they had their horses in these rocks, also) I concluded to charge them in their stronghold, the nature of which was something like this: There was a high palisade bluffs running about north and south, and a smaller hill about one quarter of a mile east of these bluffs, running parallel with them. At some time in the past a mass of these palisades rocks had tumbled down and filled the depression between the two, on a level with the lower area. This mass of tumbledown rocks was thrown together loosely, one on top of another, leaving large rooms and caverns scattered around through this mass, with egress and ingress through the openings between the rocks, some of which would weigh hundreds of tons.

On top of this mass, and about fifty yards from the top of the lower hill, and flush with it, was a natural fortification, large

[1] Camp McDermit, Nevada, was established in the summer of 1865 by the Second Volunteer Cavalry of California as Quinn River Camp Number 33. The name was changed to Camp McDermit in August, 1865, after Colonel Charles McDermit, commander of the Nevada Military District, who was killed near it by Indians on August 7, 1865.

The post was situated on the right bank of the east branch of Quinn River and was erected from 1866 to 1867. In 1889 the post was turned over to the Interior Department for an Indian reservation, which now has as headquarters buildings the reconstructed buildings of the old fort. *Posts, Camps, and Stations File;* Writers' Program, Nevada, *Nevada, a Guide to the Silver State,* 213.

enough to hold several people, with a hole in its bottom large enough for their passage to and from the caverns below. Between it and the top of the hill was a deep cavern that had to be crossed before ascending the elevation where the fort was situated. In making the charge, one man was killed, and a couple were wounded. Lt. Madigan (a braver officer never lived) was killed just before a Mr. Joseph Wasson, a reporter for the *Owyhee Avalanche*, was one of the first in the fort.[2]

After we had got possession of the fort, we had drawn the "White Elephant" prize, for the Indians were deep down in the rocks, where all was darkness, and we could see nothing, whereas they, being in the dark and we in the light, they could see us. We kept up a fusilade down in the rocks in the hopes that we might hit some of them accidentally, and, assuming the air of conquerors, held the fort all day, carefully avoiding the cracks and open spaces. That night we watched around the outside, in hopes of killing some, but the next morning they were gone, much to my relief.

I knew that several had been killed or wounded, and suspected that some must still be in the rocks, so I cautioned everybody about exposing themselves in the rocks, but one of the soldiers was too venturesome and was killed by a wounded Indian. His body dropped down amongst the rocks, which we had much trouble in recovering. I never wanted dynamite so bad as I did when we first took the fort and heard the diabolical and defiant yells from down in the rocks.

We gathered up our wounded, rigging litters to carry them on, also taking our dead with us, until we reached the main Pit River, where we buried the dead. Then we tied our horses to a picket line over the graves, so as to obliterate all sign, which we thought at the time we had successfully accomplished. Afterwards a party consisting of an officer and a detachment of men were sent to disinter

2 Joseph Wasson was reporter and part-owner of the *Owyhee Avalanche*, Silver City, Idaho, in partnership with his brother, John. His stories dealing with the various expeditions which he accompanied indicate a remarkable education coupled with a sense of humor. His attitude toward Indians was typically frontier and expressed through a version of Pope:

> Lo! the poor Indian, whose untutored mind
> Sees God (damn) in everything,
> And hears Him (when three sheets) in the wind!

the bodies, but could find no trace of them, their belief being that the Indians had dug them up and disposed of them.[3]

Soon after my return to the post near Warner, I went to Camp Harney[4] to meet Mrs. Crook, who had come out from the East under Gen. Thomas' care a month or so previously, and had been waiting my return from the field in San Francisco and Portland. It was just one year to the day from the time I separated from her in Baltimore until she joined me at Harney.[5]

Three families of us, Capts. Gillis, Pollock, and myself, Paymaster Johnston, his clerk, Mr. Day, and Lt. Dodge traveled over to Warner together. Warner was only partly finished. Mrs. Crook and I lived through the winter in a log hut, with the cracks plastered with mud, no windows, and a tent fly for a covering. Our only light by day was through the roof.

The garrison became short of supplies before the winter ended, the snow being too deep for wagon communication. The cattle became so poor that it was almost impossible to eat their meat. The snow covered the whole country, and drifted in places about the post ten or fifteen feet deep, and the thermometer was below zero a great portion of the time. I supplemented my larder by killing the large jack rabbit that turned white in the winter.

In the spring the garrison commenced getting scurvy from

[3] This fight became known as the Battle of Infernal Caverns. The ground was volcanic in origin, and the "bluffs" were the rim of an old crater. The opposing forces consisted of Company D, Twenty-third Infantry, strength forty enlisted men and one officer, Company H, First Cavalry, strength sixty-eight enlisted men and one officer, about fifteen Warm Springs Indian scouts under Archie McIntosh, versus about seventy-five Paiutes and thirty Pit River Indians, plus a few Modocs, all led by chief Si-e-ta.

The casualties suffered by the troops were seven killed and ten wounded, plus one citizen wounded. Bancroft claims that Crook bought this dear victory to prove that he was doing something. Bancroft, *History of Oregon*, II, 538–44; William R. Parnell, "Operations against Hostile Indians with General Crook, 1867–1868," *The United Service*, n.s., Vol. I, Nos. 5 and 6 (May and June, 1889), 485–91; *Owyhee Avalanche*, November 2, 1867.

[4] Camp Harney, Oregon, was established August 16, 1867, as Camp Steele, the name being changed to Camp Harney on September 14, 1867. It was named after the lakes in the vicinity, which, in turn, were named after General William S. Harney. It was situated at the mouth of Rattlesnake Cañon, opening into Harney Lake Valley, about seventy-five miles south of Cañon City. The camp was abandoned on June 14, 1880, having been added to the Malheur Indian reservation in 1877. *Posts, Camps, and Stations File.*

[5] Mrs. Crook arrived at Harney about the twentieth of October.

want of proper anti-scorbutics. We discovered a wild onion that grew in abundance in the vicinity, which relieved us from the disagreeable consequences which would have followed without them.

I made several scouts during the winter. One in particular in the "Dunder and Blixen" country.[6] Our scouts discovered a small camp of Indians on the creek just bordering on the low, marshy ground that formed the lower part of the valley. It was bitter cold. The thermometer must have been several degrees below zero. Some of the sloughs and creeks were frozen so hard that we had no difficulty in crossing on the ice.

When we got near the rancheria, the growth of willow brush made it difficult to tell just where the Indians were, as the country was flat, and all looked alike, and was new to us. I was next to the guide, and the first thing we knew his horse ran into the door of a wick-a-up. Their dogs gave the alarm, and the Indians commenced scurrying at once through the brush, which was quite thick off the trail. We at once dismounted, and commenced firing at what we could see, but soon discovered that immediately in rear of the rancheria was a deep, muddy creek which from some cause or other was not frozen over, across which they had made their escape.

We had an Indian boy with us, who, while prowling like the rest of us around through the brush after all supposed the Indians had fled, was shot at by an Indian lying on the ground. The bullet passed diagonally across his body, between his skin and shirt. I never could understand how this occurred, for certainly others of the party had passed over the same ground before, and I don't see how he could have recognized the boy in the dark.

We could not cross this slough or creek in time to have caught any of them. We did not attempt it. But having noticed smoke several miles farther down the valley the previous evening and thinking these people would give the alarm, we at once started for the other village, so as to be there by daylight the next morning, so that, in case they hadn't been alarmed, we could attack them by surprise.

We reached near the place sometime before daylight, so we

[6] The creek and the country are elsewhere referred to as "Donner and Blitzen," i.e., Thunder and Lightning. It is supposed to have been named in 1864 by some of George Curry's men during a severe thunderstorm. Lewis A. McArthur, *Oregon Geographical Names*, 170.

had to pass the time as best we could. We dismounted and scraped the loose snow off the ground sufficiently that each person could stamp his feet on the bare ground. By personal exertion in this way, and also by pounding our bodies with our arms, we managed to keep from freezing, as we dared not make fires. Our beards were one mass of ice.

When daylight did appear, we found a slough between us and the Indians, which was only partly frozen over. We managed to get across in time to get some few of them, but the remainder made their escape. Sometime in the afternoon there came up what is known as a chinook wind, which blew a little south of west. The snow at once commenced melting, so that the next morning we had to pack up and leave the country for fear of being waterbound in that country.[7]

The water was running in every direction. A couple of feet of water was running on top of the ice. The snow had disappeared from the southern slopes of the hills. The flat country bordering on Warner's Lake was covered with water. Fortunately the ground was still frozen, or we would have had a serious time getting over the low alkali flats ahead of us.

In the spring we were in the habit of going to the lake for a day or so to hunt. Capt. Nickerson and I had encamped on the lake, hunting. At night came up a fearful rain and snow storm. The night was inky black. Our tent was pitched close to the wagon. The teamster and another man slept within a few feet of our animals, which were tied to the tongue of the wagon. In the morning a pony ridden by the man was missed. After searching for an hour or so, an Indian track was discovered. Presently the track of the pony led in the direction of the stone causeway before mentioned.

Capt. Nickerson and I at once mounted our horses and took the shortest route to this crossing of the lake, where we found the pony, but no Indians. The water over the causeway was sometimes

---

[7] "March 19, 1868. I was in command of the District of the Lakes; all available mounted troops were ordered to rendezvous at the north end of Warner Lake, but owing to the non-arrival of supplies, were unable to reach there as soon as expected. On the 14th I reached Donner and Blitzen valley, near Steen's mountain; I found a band of Indians up a large cañon; killed and wounded several, but how many could not, from the nature of the ground, be ascertained. Supplies being exhausted, returned to camp the 26th." Secretary of War, *Annual Report*, 1868, 83.

three feet deep in places, with a strong current. Either the pony had gotten away from the Indian, or else he could not get it across the lake. The strange thing of his taking the pony was that on the opposite of the wagon tongue from where the man was sleeping were some mules tied, and how the pony could be distinguished by the Indian in the dark is more than I have ever been able to satisfy myself about. It was not possible, owing to the lay of the country, for him to have gotten his information before dark.

In May I was temporarily assigned to the command of the Department of the Columbia, so I proceeded to Portland, Oregon, via San Francisco, to assume command of the department, and acquaint myself with my new duties.[8] After staying a few days in Portland, I returned to Warner via The Dalles and Old Camp Watson.[9]

Soon after my return, some white people were killed by Indians below Surprise Valley. Being satisfied that my old friends, the Pit River Indians, had a hand in it, I started down in their country with two companies of cavalry. I proceeded to the vicinity of Big Valley on lower Pit River. I sent for these Indians.

They came with rather a reluctant air. They were informed that they would have to bring their own provisions. When they came, their provisions consisted chiefly of young ducks in various stages of putrefaction and smelt so that I would not allow them to camp on our side of the river. After skirmishing for position for some time, I asked them if they did not remember me eleven years ago, when I was operating against them. Yes, they said, they remembered how they had pounded me, etc. I told them if they didn't stop lying, I would give them another opportunity of pounding me right then and there, whereupon they changed their tactics.

I then accused them directly with the murder of the white men

[8] U. S. Army, Military Division of the Pacific, *General Order No. 10* (April 1, 1868).

[9] Camp Watson was established in 1863 by the Oregon Volunteers of the Cañon City road expedition, and named after Lieutenant Steven Watson of the First Oregon Cavalry. The post was on the middle fork of John Day River, on the road between The Dalles and Cañon City.

The First Oregon Cavalry occupied the post until 1866, when it was relieved by Company I, First United States Cavalry. It was discontinued on March 15, 1869, per *General Order No. 7*, Military Division of the Pacific. *Posts, Camps and Stations File;* Writers' Program, *Oregon, End of the Trail,* 447.

below Surprise Valley, telling them that I knew all about it. Not knowing how much I did know, they confessed the whole thing. I told them that if they did not deliver up the murderers I would make war on their whole tribe, but that I didn't care for them just then.[10]

Soon after our return to Warner, I sent Capt. Munson from Surprise Valley to old Fort Crook. Sure enough, the murderers were turned over to him, who turned them over to the nearest civil authorities.

Soon after my return to Warner, word came from Camp Harney that the Indians had expressed an anxiety to make peace. I at once repaired to Harney and concluded a peace. I had much difficulty in conciliating the white men who came into Harney, as they had no faith in the Indians' promises. Many were feeling ill over their wrongs at the hands of the Indians. Some had lost friends, relatives, and stock at the hands of the Indians, and were necessarily bitter, and had sworn vengeance against all Indians. But when I explained it was to all's interest to have peace so the citizens could develop the country, etc., that I had not [made] peace out of friendship for the Indians, they finally agreed not to throw any obstacles in the way by committing any unlawful acts.[11]

In September quiet reigned in all the upper country, when I moved to Portland, and from thence commanded the department until relieved by General Canby in 1870.[12] Nothing of note occurred during these two years.

16. *Arizona had a bad reputation*

SOON AFTER being relieved from command, I was assigned as a mem-

[10] The chronology of this and the following event, the making of peace, is inverted. Crook went on the expedition against the Pit River Indians after concluding the peace during the first days of July, 1868.

[11] For Nickerson's description of the surrender, see Appendix IV, pages 308–310.

[12] Edward R. S. Canby, graduate of the Military Academy in 1839 and brigadier general, U. S. Army, as of July 28, 1866, commanded the Department of the Columbia from August, 1870, to January, 1873. He was murdered

ber of a retiring and "Benzine Board"[1] in San Francisco, on which duty I remained until I was relieved by assignment to the command of the Department of Arizona. In regard to the command of the Department of Arizona, Gen. George H. Thomas, while I was still in command, asked me if I would like to take the command of Arizona. I told him that I was tired of the Indian work, that it only entailed hard work without any corresponding benefits. Besides, the climate of Arizona had such a bad reputation that I feared for my health. He then remarked, very well, then, so far as he could control, I should remain in command of the Department of the Columbia.

After the General's death, Gen. Schofield came in command, and he made the same proposition, which I met as before. Shortly afterwards, the Governor of Arizona, A. P. K. Safford, interviewed me on the same subject in San Francisco. After my telling the substance of what I had said to the others, he assured me that he would not urge the matter in Washington, whither he was going. I afterwards learned from himself that he had got the California delegation to see Grant, who was then the President, and have him assign me over the heads of the Secretary of War and General Sherman, who both opposed my assignment over the heads of so many who ranked me, as I was then only a Lieutenant-Colonel.

The worst feature of my assignment was that I was furnished at the same time with a letter from the Adjutant General stating that my detail was only temporary, and that in the fall a new deal would be made.[2]

I at once proceeded to Portland and disposed of my effects, and

---

on April 11, 1873, by Modoc Indians while holding a conference with them in the vicinity of the lava beds, Oregon.

1 The reduced Army Appropriations Bill of 1869 made immediate reduction of personnel necessary. The field officers to be retained were chosen in Washington, and the junior officers in the various departments.

The boards which selected the men to be released and retained were known as "Benzine Boards," from their tendency to clean matters up. William A. Ganoe, *The History of the United States Army*, 324-25.

2 In May, 1871, the Adjutant General wrote Secretary of War Belknap: "The President directs me to inform you of his desire that Lieutenant-Colonel George Crook be assigned on his Brevet Rank to relieve Colonel Stoneman in command of the Department of Arizona until the new arrangement next fall." National Archives, Adjutant General's Office, *Letterbook No. 54*.

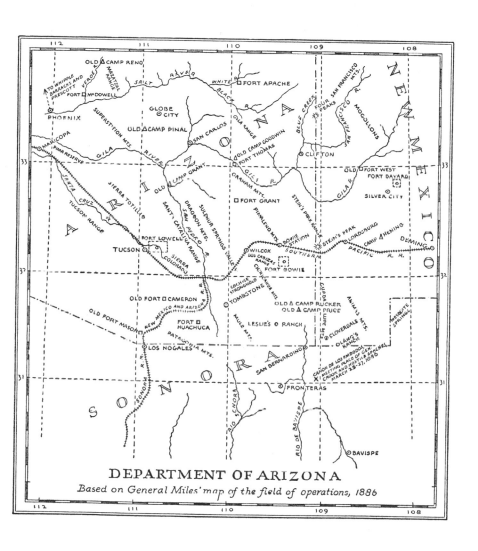

DEPARTMENT OF ARIZONA
Based on General Miles' map of the field of operations, 1886

returned to San Francisco, leaving the latter place for Arizona on the third of June, with Capt. Nickerson, Archie, and Peisen.[3] Archie was drunk and had to be taken aboard the ship under guard.

The steamer stopped at Wilmington for several hours. I assumed command and left Capt. Nickerson to do the routine work in my name. I left on the same steamer with Archie and Peisen for San Diego.

While at Wilmington, I was invited to dinner at the Stoneman's (when he was relieved from command). I had to accept out of politeness, but never passed through such an ordeal. Mrs. Stoneman, while trying to be polite, could not help showing in every action that she would like to tear me to pieces, and there I had to sit and sit, and if she only knew how I hated to go to Arizona, she might feel differently. This assignment had made me the innocent cause of a great deal of heartburning and jealousy.

From San Diego we took a stage for Yuma, a distance of about 200 miles. San Diego had just had a boom, and the principal owner, Dr. Horton,[4] was very sanguine about San Diego's rivaling San Francisco. The spirits had told him to locate there and were still keeping up his enthusiasm, but I have since learned that he was entirely bankrupt.

The first hundred miles from San Diego was over a hilly, mountainous country. We then dropped down into the Colorado desert, and from there to Yuma it was like being in an oven. Even at midnight the heat was so intense that rest or sleep was impossible. This desert was one vast expanse of shifting sand, with some mesquite

[3] Andrew Peisen acted as General Crook's "striker," or personal servant, from this time to the end of Crook's life. Peisen, who was usually known as "Peisy," was born about 1840 in Niebuel, Schleswig-Holstein. His enlistment papers describe him as having hazel eyes, light complexion, and being about five feet, nine inches tall. By 1886 he was married and had two children. His eighth, and final enlistment, was as a general service messenger in the Department of the Missouri, Chicago, May 7, 1888.

[4] A. E. Horton owned the "Horton House," among other properties in San Diego. The Texas and Pacific Railway had just been completed to San Diego, and Horton expected a lot of business.

His hotel advertisement set the tone for all future puffs for California: "This first-class house contains one hundred rooms; several of them arranged in suites for families, all furnished in best style, lighted with gas, supplied with fresh, soft water, half of them warmed by steam heaters, and every one made wholesome and cheerful by the loveliest sunshine some part of the day." *San Diego, the California Terminus of the Texas and Pacific Railway,* 35.

bushes and desert willows around. The sand would collect in dunes of all heights, up to twenty or thirty feet. No grass of any kind.

Archie, previous to leaving San Francisco, had traded off his suit of clothes which had been furnished him from division head-quarters for an inferior suit, and with the difference purchased whisky with which to get drunk on. At Yuma the same process was gone through again, so Archie was stupid drunk in the morning when we were ready to start, and his last suit of clothes was an object to behold. He looked as though he had dropped out of a comic almanac.

From here to Tucson we went in an ambulance, so Archie was bundled in to sober up on the way. The heat on our trip up the Gila River was quite as bad as it had been over the desert, and the dust and flies added made it almost unbearable. When we arrived at Tucson, but little relief was had, as the thermometer showed that for three weeks at some time of the day it had been up to 103 in the shade, and at several times it had been up to 116. The worst feature was that the nights were so hot that it was impossible to sleep, and we would get up in the morning almost as tired as when we went to bed.

I stayed here until the 11th of September, organizing for op-erations against the Apaches. From want of something better, and from the recommendations of the governor and other prominent men, who said that the Mexicans were the solution of the "Apache Problem," that they knew the country, the habits and mode of Indian warfare, that with a little pinole and dried beef they could travel all over the country without pack mules to carry their pro-visions, that with ten days' rations on their backs they could march over the roughest country at the rate of from thirty to fifty miles per day, that they could go inside an Apache and turn him wrong side out in no time at all, I hired fifty of their people for scouts. I had some Mexicans in Tucson preparing the dried beef and pinole for a week or so before I was to start.

On the eleventh day of July, 1871, I left Tucson for Fort Bowie[5]

---

[5] Fort Bowie was located in Apache Pass, Chiricahua Mountains, on the road from Tucson to Mesilla passes. The establishment of a military post at this site dates from July 28, 1862, when the "California Column" under Brigadier General James H. Carleton, on its way to Santa Fé, passed that way, and detached a company to guard the spring at that point.

Major T. A. Coult, Fifth California Volunteers, was assigned to command with five companies of cavalry and the fifty "Destroying Angels." We reached Bowie on the 14th, saw no Indians on the way, and no signs of any. We left Bowie after dusk, so as to conceal our movements, and the first night camped on the edge of Sulphur Springs Valley in an arroyo that ran down southeast of Dos Cabezas.

In the morning, just at daylight, some of our packers in search of water lower down the ravine came on some stock that had been brought in there during the night, across the valley, from Mexico. The Indians, seeing our men first, made their escape. Having thus been discovered, we continued our march next day. We saw a couple of Indians, but no harm was done, they making their escape in the Dos Cabezas Mountains.

From here we marched to the foot of Graham's Mountain. A scouting sent to the top of that mountain discovered a small party of Indians on its summit, but they made their escape on the north side of the mountain, over almost a precipice, unhurt.

Discovering a dust in Sulphur Springs Valley, which I was satisfied was being made by a party of Indians, I sent Capt. Moore to a spring, I think named Cottonwood, situated in a low range leading from the Dos Cabezas range to Graham Mountain, while I stationed the remainder at other points they would likely come to on our side of the valley.

They came to the spring before mentioned some time during the night, but instead of Capt. Moore's going directly to the spring, he went out on the plain, ostensibly to cut the Indians' trail, which brought him in plain sight of the Indians, who made their escape as a matter of course. We thus lost one of the prettiest chances of giving the enemy a severe blow, for it turned out to be a party of some sixty bucks returning from Mexico, where they had been on a raid.

I was then satisfied that Capt. Moore lacked one of the most

---

of the post on July 27, 1862. Temporary huts were erected, and the post was called Fort Bowie in honor of George F. Bowie, colonel of that regiment, then commanding the District of Southern California.

On May 3, 1866, the Volunteer garrisons were relieved by Company E, Fourteenth U. S. Infantry, and from that date occupation of the post was continuous to 1894, when troops were withdrawn and the post abandoned. In 1894 the post was turned over to the Secretary of the Interior. *Posts, Camps, and Stations File.*

essential qualities of a soldier, and my impressions were fully corroborated in 1876 when he was tried for misbehavior before the enemy in an engagement with a band of Sioux and Cheyennes.

In moving from this point towards the San Carlos River, I encamped on the stream where Fort Grant[6] is now situated. I was particularly struck with the pure and soft water of the stream, and so, over one year afterwards, when it became necessary to break up Old Grant on account of its unhealthiness, I ordered it removed to this place.

From this point we scouted the mountains on either side of Aravaipa Cañon, but finding nothing, we continued our scouting over to the Gila and up the San Carlos River to near the source of the western branch of it, but were still unsuccessful. Now being near Fort Apache,[7] I became uneasy for fear I might mistake some of the friendly Indians of the latter place, I having been informed that there were some there. It was difficult to realize that there could be any of the Apache tribe who were friendly to anybody.

We continued our march until we struck the Salt River just below the junction of the two rivers, the White and Black forks. Being afraid to attack any Indians for fear of making a mistake, I marched directly to the post of Fort Apache. Here I refit, leaving my Mexican outfit, pinole and all, to be discharged.

I had many long talks with the Coyoteros, White Mountains, and finally got them to join in my plans for subduing the hostiles, which was for them to enlist as scouts and act in conjunction with

[6] Old Camp Grant, situated at the confluence of Aravaipa and San Pedro rivers, was established in 1856 as Camp Breckinridge. The camp was abandoned in 1861, but re-established by the California Column in 1862 and named Fort Stanford in honor of the Governor of California. It was renamed Fort Grant in 1866. That year a flood carried away twenty of the twenty-four buildings on the post. Fort Grant was transferred to its new location in 1873. Control of the post was relinquished by the War Department on July 22, 1884, and control of New Camp Grant was relinquished August 10, 1911. *Posts, Camps, and Stations File.*

[7] Fort Apache, on the south bank of the east fork of White Mountain River, was selected as a camp site by Major John Green, commanding officer of Camp Goodwin. Camp Goodwin was broken up because of the high incidence of malaria and Apache established as a temporary camp in 1870. In 1873 it was made a permanent station, successively named Camp Ord, Mogollon, Thomas, and finally Apache. The post was abandoned in 1924 and turned over to the Indian service for school purposes. *Posts, Camps, and Stations File.*

our troops. Old One-eyed McGill and Pedro were the principal Indians, or chiefs.

I organized a company of scouts, and left Capt. Guy V. Henry, 3rd Regiment of Cavalry, to command the first expedition so organized, while I went on to Camp Verde[8] to organize similar expeditions.

We left for Verde about the end of August, without a guide, being assured that there was a plain trail all the way, which I soon found out to be pretty much a delusion. Our route lay along the summit of the Mogollon Mountains. The trail, at best dim, soon ran out, and the summit was in places very broad and in places cut up by ridges and cross cañons. Not being able at times to tell the main summit from some of the minor ones that ran off to the east, principally, we experienced much difficulty in finding our way.

Our chief trouble, however, was in finding water after traveling all one day in the hot sun. It was true that the mountain was timbered. It began to look as if, though, we would have to camp without water. The men and animals were nearly famished with thirst, when a dark thunder cloud came up, and we at once went into camp, and spread all the canvas we had.

In a short time the rain came down in torrents, and shortly we had all the water we wanted, both for man and beast. The thunder and lightning was terrific. Trees were crashed to splinters not far from us. Judging from appearances, this country was subject to such storms very frequently, as in places there were acres where most of the trees had been struck by lightning at some time or other. I saw where some trees over 150 feet high had been smashed into fine splinters clear to the ground, while many others were more or less demolished from the same cause.

The next night we struck a large and well-defined trail leading

8 Camp Verde was about forty miles east of Prescott. Originally established by the Arizona Volunteers in 1861 as an outpost of Fort Whipple, the camp was first occupied by Regulars in 1866 and was then known as Camp Lincoln. The name was changed to Verde in 1868 to avoid confusion in the mails, there being another Camp Lincoln in Dakota.

The original site of Verde proved to be unhealthy, and in 1871 a new site, on a mesa about one mile south of the old post, was selected. Little work was done on the new post until 1873. In 1879 the post was designated as Fort Verde. The property was relinquished to the Interior Department in 1884. *Posts, Camps, and Stations File.*

to the north. After following it for a short distance we came upon a nice spring of delicious water in a little bottom covered with grass. This is now called General's Spring.[9] Although this trail was not going in the direction of Verde, I thought it might lead to some trail that would take us there, so the next morning we pulled out on this trail.

We followed it until we crossed a very deep cañon, and as it bore off still farther from the direction I wanted to go, and the country ahead was apparently comparatively a level plateau country, I turned off more to the southwest. Fortunately, just before dusk we came to a tank which furnished us with all the water we wanted.

The next morning we pulled out bright and early. We traveled all day by the compass over a country covered with pine and juniper, with patches of oak in places. We traveled till about dark, when we struck the Stoneman road leading from the Little Colorado to the Verde. After traveling until ten o'clock at night we struck the Beaverhead, where we found water standing in holes. Capt. Brent came near dying when he reached camp. Nothing but his pluck saved him. He was very delicate, arising from pulmonary troubles.

The next day we traveled down the Verde River to a point some four miles above the post, where we went into camp. I had directed that my mail be sent to the post. When I received my mail, I discovered from the newspapers that a Mr. Vincent Colyer had been sent out by the "Indian Ring" to interfere with my operations, and that he was coming to Apache from New Mexico, and was going to make peace with the Apaches by the grace of God, and was going to travel in the Territory for that purpose.[10]

I had no faith in the success of his enterprise, but I was afraid

---

[9] The spring was named after General Crook. The trail which Crook followed over the Mogollons became known as "Crook's Trail." In 1874 two companies of soldiers and several women formed a wagon train which was the first to traverse the trail. The going was very rough, no real road ever having been prepared. Summerhayes, *Vanished Arizona*, Chap. IX.

[10] The Permanent Board of Peace Commissioners sent Vincent Colyer, Quaker and friend of the Indian, to Mexico and Arizona. Congress had appropriated $70,000 to "collect the Apache Indians of Arizona and New Mexico on reservations, furnish them with subsistence and other necessary articles, and to promote peace and civilization among them."

if I continued my operations and he was to fail, I would be charged with interference. So I at once countermanded all my orders looking to active operations against the hostiles, and directed all persons under my control to furnish Mr. Colyer all assistance within their power in the carrying out of his peace policy.

From Apache Mr. Colyer went down to Old Camp Grant on the San Pedro. He harangued the Indians on his way, making peace as he went, and the Indians just immediately behind him left a trail of blood behind them from the murdered citizens. One Indian, Eskimi-yan,[11] told Colyer that he was convinced that he, Colyer, could not come of mortal parents, for no man so good as he was could be so born. The discernment on the part of old "Skimmy" tickled Colyer's vanity to such an extent that he preached two sermons of which that was the text.

When he reached Prescott, he was feeling highly elated over his success and expressed himself as being particularly pleased and gratified at my course, saying that my coinciding with his view would make one host of friends east of the mountains, etc. I disabused his mind of this impression by informing him that I had no confidence in his peace policy, but as he came out to Arizona clothed with powers from my superiors in authority to carry out his peace policy, and as I was directed by this authority to give him all the assistance at my command, I proposed to do so conscientiously, so that in case his policy was a failure, none of it could be laid at my door.

By this time news of the outrages committed by the Indians he had made peace with began to come in thick and fast. Many of these outrages were so flagrant that pretty much all the newspapers on the Pacific Coast took up the cry against a policy that kept life and property unsafe within the reach of these Indians, and paralyzed all business within the territory so ravaged.

By the time Colyer reached San Francisco, his confidence was considerably shaken, and by the time he reached Washington his head was chopped off.

[11] After several changes of heart, Eskimi-yan ["Eskiminzin," according to Bourke] became a good Indian, settling on a plot of ground near the San Carlos agency. He prospered until Crook left Arizona for the second time, when the land he had improved was taken from him and given to settlers. He died shortly after. Britton Davis, *The Truth about Geronimo*, 61–64.

Then I was given permission to commence operations against the hostiles, but just as I commenced another embroglio was placed on me. So I suspended again when Gen. O. O. Howard was sent out, clothed with even greater powers than those given Mr. Colyer.[12] He intimated at Yuma that he had authority to supersede me in command in case he saw fit, but for some cause better known to himself, he did not take advantage of the power granted him, but seemed anxious to have persons under my command espouse his views as contrary to mine. It was reported to me that he had held out inducements to some of duty East.

He had with him a Rev. Mr. E. P. Smith, afterwards Commissioner of Indian Affairs, who was a bright man, and who tried to restrain many of Howard's weaknesses, but, after remaining a short time, returned to Washington. He also had an aide-de-camp by the name of Wilkinson, whose stock in trade was religion, who acted as capper for the General. General Howard was fond of public speaking. His themes generally were "How He was Converted" and "The Battle of Gettysburg."

At McDowell, on his way to Prescott, he told the commanding officer that he had been requested to deliver a speech to the soldiers. The C.O., not being an admirer of his, and at the same time pressing him on the point as to who had asked him, he finally had to acknowledge that it was Capt. Wilkinson.

Soon after his arrival at Prescott, General Howard expressed his wish for a general council with the Indians. So word was sent to Old Camp Grant that on such a day all the Indians were to meet for a council. Our party rode on horseback from Prescott to McDowell.

I was very much amused at the General's opinion of himself. He told me that he thought the Creator had placed him on earth to be the Moses to the Negro. Having accomplished that mission, he felt satisfied his next mission was with the Indian. This struck me as particularly funny, as the "Freedmen's Bureau Denouement"[13] was still on the mouths of everybody, and things certainly

[12] Oliver O. Howard graduated from the Military Academy in 1854. He reached the rank of major general in 1886, though many persons thought the vacancy should have been filled by Crook. His memoirs reveal interesting variations between Crook's point of view and Howard's, especially on the question of Indians.

[13] Referring to the rather inglorious demise of the War Department

looked very bad for those connected with it, especially for General Howard. I was at loss to make out whether it was his vanity or his cheek that enabled him to hold up his head in this lofty manner.

Camp Grant was situated on a little plateau. Underneath and about fifty feet below ran the San Pedro River, a stream about ten or fifteen feet wide. On the banks of this stream, and under the shade of some large cottonwood trees, General Howard and I spread our blankets.

At this post was a Lt. Royal E. Whitman,[14] who had deserted his colors and gone over to the "Indian Ring" bag and baggage, and had behaved himself in such a manner that I had preferred charges against him. He was then under arrest, awaiting trial. There was more or less feeling against me amongst the officers at this post. One of the first things General Howard did after his arrival was to parade up and down the garrison, arm in arm with Whitman.

The council was to be held on the opposite side of the stream where we had spread our blankets. The Indians had assembled in quite large numbers, and a more saucy, impudent lot of cut-throats I had never before seen. Many of them were armed with lances and guns. They would walk through our camp in that defiant, impudent manner, as much as to say, "I would like to kill you just for the fun of it, just to see you kick." When they would want to cross the stream they would take off one moccasin and hop across on that leg, and when they reached the opposite bank, would sit down and replace that moccasin.

Not long before they had deliberately murdered a citizen at this post in the most wanton manner. The murder had been condoned by the Indian Ring, and as a consequence the villain was a hero amongst his people. I must confess I was afraid of them, and kept close to camp for fear some of them would want to be a hero at my expense. Several citizens from Tucson and elsewhere had also assembled to witness the council.

Bureau of Refugees, Freedmen, and Abandoned Lands, which had been headed by General Howard.

[14] Whitman was a drunkard and had been court-martialed only a few months before. Though found guilty, he was set free by General Crook because of a technicality. He retired in 1879.

General Howard opened the council by stating the object of the council, and informing the Indians that he had commanded 30,000 men during the war, and if they did not behave themselves and do what he told them, he would come sweeping through their country and exterminate them all.

Eskimmi-yan was the "head center" of the cut-throats there assembled, and looked at General Howard in a half-quizzical, half-contemptuous and defiant manner, as much as to say, "Go to hell!" When it came Skimmy's time to talk, he evaded all the points at issue, but told General Howard that he, Skimmy, had heard all his life of a man who was so pure that the Great Spirit had kept him on an island in order that he could not witness the frailties of mortals, and that he was satisfied that Howard was that man. He said he wanted the children.

To digress a little. This council was held in the first part of April, 1872. Some time in March the year previous a party of citizens from Tucson, provoked by the brutal outrages of the Indians, and not getting any redress from the government, also believing that the government was feeding and protecting the very Indians who were committing the depredations, marched clandestinely to the vicinity of Grant and murdered a lot of Indians who were there under the protection of the government.[15]

The bucks being mostly absent, they killed mostly women and children, and a good many children were carried off into Tucson and vicinity. These children had been taken into many of the families, and in the year that had elapsed became more or less identified with their new associates, and had correspondingly become weaned from their people, in fact, dreaded going back to the Indians almost as much as white children. Most of the people who had them had been much attached to them, and were very loath to give them up.

General Howard had induced some of the people to bring the children with them to the council under the promise, so the people claimed, that if the children had no parents living, he would not turn them over to the Indians. When he asked Skimmy if these children's parents were still living, he said, "Of course not, they were killed by the citizens," but the Indians wanted the children all

[15] This affair is known as the "Camp Grant Massacre."

the same. General Howard tried to talk him out of it, but Skimmy remained firm. So Howard decided to turn over the children.

One little girl in particular, nicely dressed, clean, tidy, and nice looking was brought in to be turned over to the Indians. She shrieked, fought, and showed as much horror at being taken by the Indians as any white child would. There were many there with wet eyes. One old, gray-haired man ran out of the council crying, declaring he could not stand that.

Judge McCaffrey, the U. S. District Attorney at Tucson, got up in the presence of all and denounced Howard as being a liar and a brute, that he had deceived the people into bringing the children under false pretenses, etc. General Howard tried to deny the soft impeachment, but McCaffrey and the others would not permit him to do so. He was very angry, and said he would have McCaffrey removed from his position, etc. McCaffrey retorted that the fear of losing his position was not going to shut his mouth against such an outrage against decency and humanity.

Finally the council drew to a close with Skimmy giving General Howard a stone, saying that when that stone melted, he would break his word, and not before. The rascal had gone through this same operation so many times with other persons that he had it pat. He hadn't promised anything, and didn't intend keeping this promise if he had. When we left, he was very profuse in his demonstrations of friendship and good will towards General Howard, but he scarcely noticed me, didn't even offer to shake hands with me.[16]

After General Howard and I returned to our camp, he was very indignant that McCaffrey had spoken to him, which gave me an opportunity to make a few remarks myself. I said: "General How-

[16] General Howard, describing the events of the day, says that the children were remanded into the care of a "good Catholic woman" until the case had been decided by the President himself.

He describes the close of the conference differently, also: "Thereupon a wonderful scene followed. The Indians of different tribes doubly embraced each other—Apache and Pima, Papago and Mohave—and even the Mexicans participated in the joy that became universal. I said to myself, 'Surely, the Lord is with us.'

"In due time our differences were laid before President Grant, and I need hardly say that he sustained me in my decision, and that the children were returned to their relatives." Oliver O. Howard, *My Life and Experiences among Our Hostile Indians*, 162.

ard, many of these people have lost their friends, relatives, and property by these Indians. They carry their lives constantly in their hands, not knowing what moment is to be their last. Now, if, instead of affording relief, you not only fail to give it to them but outrage their feelings besides, you must not expect your position to shield you from hearing plain words. These people have suffered too much to have any false ideas of sentiment. Besides, you have come here under the garb of religion, and have been prostituting my command by holding out inducements of eastern stations if certain officers would do so and so. Then, too, when I had Lt. Whitman under guard for gross misbehavior, you walked publicly, arm in arm with him, thereby showing that you espoused his cause as against myself."

He tried to deny and explain, etc., but I held him up to the facts. He in his report mentioned that from something I had said to him he could not go to sleep until he found relief in prayer at about three o'clock in the morning.[17]

17. *The copper cartridge has done the business*

THE INDIANS still kept up their deeds of murder and rapine until about September, when I was again allowed to commence hostile operations against these wretches. In the fall of 1871 Lt. Wheeler's exploring expedition from Nevada to Arizona terminated at Whipple Barracks.[1] The stage that carried several of his party to Cali-

[17] Secretary of the Interior, *Annual Report*, 1872, I, 533–59.

[1] Fort Whipple was first located near Postle's Ranch, twenty-four miles northeast of Prescott, established in December, 1863. The location was changed to the left bank of Granite Creek, one mile northeast of Prescott, May 18, 1864. It was named after Major General A. W. Whipple.

The post was first garrisoned on September 14, 1864, and became the headquarters of the District of Arizona. In 1879 the two parts of the post, Fort Whipple and Prescott Barracks, were combined into Whipple Barracks. The post was discontinued in 1898 and then regarrisoned in 1902. In 1922 the reservation was transferred to the Secretary of the Treasury for use in the Public Health Service. *Posts, Camps, and Stations File*.

fornia was passing from Wickenburg to Ehrenburg, and was attacked by Indians, and several of the party were killed, amongst whom was a Mr. Loring from Boston.

Not long afterwards, money in large denominations was brought to the agency on the Colorado River. Also some other evidences appeared of the killing having been done by the Apache Mohaves. It was ascertained from some confidential Indians who the guilty parties were, and that these Indians were at the agency at Date Creek. My plan was to open the campaign by capturing the guilty parties.

On the eighth day of September, 1872, in attempting to make the arrest, some of the Indians were killed, and some of our party narrowly escaped being shot.[2] Some of the parties were captured and killed, which stopped all further depredations in that section of the country, as the Indians discovered they could no longer murder white men under the cover of peaceable Indians on the reservation.

Shortly after this, Colonel Mason, 5th Cavalry, stationed at Old Camp Hualpai,[3] attacked some hostiles at Muchos Cañon on the breaks of the Santa María, killing a good many and demoralizing the balance, so that hostilities ceased in that section of the country.[4]

About the first of November I sent Capt. Brown, 5th Cavalry, to Fort Apache to virtually assume charge of the Indians there, not to interfere with the prerogatives of the agent so far as finding

[2] The incident at Date Creek was the attempted murder of Crook by discontented Apache-Yumas. Crook's life was saved by his aide-de-camp, Lieutenant Ross, who deflected the rifle of the Indian who shot at the General. The story, first related by Bourke, has been improved on by every writer since. Bourke, *On the Border with Crook*, 167–71.

[3] Camp Hualpai was located forty miles northeast of Prescott. It was established in 1869 as Camp Toll Gate, the name being changed to Hualpai per order of October 4, 1870. The post was abandoned on July 31, 1873. *Posts, Camps, and Stations File.*

[4] "I commenced operations against the hostile Apaches with an expedition consisting of troops of the Fifth Cavalry and a detachment of Hualpai Indians under command of Captain J. W. Mason, 5th Cavalry. By means of spies I had carefully located the rancherias to be attacked, and had strong reason to hope that the entire band would be killed or captured. The fight took place on the morning of September 25th in the Santa María mountains, and although the entire band was not destroyed, it was otherwise a complete success." National Archives, Department of Arizona, *Annual Report of Lt. Col. George Crook, Brevet Major-General, Commanding, for Fiscal Year 1872–1873.*

them was concerned, but the military was to see to their control, and make a daily count of the Indians. When he had started the thing all right there, he was to go down to Grant, and inaugurate the same thing, and I would follow soon after him.

When I arrived at Apache a few days after Brown had stirred up the animals, I found the Indian people there very indignant at me, and hinting around that I would soon have my comb cut for transcending my authority, that I had been reported to the Secretary of the Interior, Mr. Delano, for outraging their service by unwarranted assumptions, and that they were daily expecting a reply. I had to leave for Grant before the document arrived, which I expected would be all they were claiming for it, as they seemed hostile to me in Washington.

In anticipation, however, I had made up my mind to disobey any order I might receive looking to an interference of the plan which I had adopted, feeling sure if I was successful my disobedience of orders would be forgiven. I felt sure of success, for all the time I had been prevented from operating against these Indians I had been hard at work organizing, and getting a good knowledge of my scouts, which I saw was to be my main dependence. Also, I had been stopped twice from assuming the offensive, and felt if I was again stopped, I would lose my head anyway.

So, before leaving Apache for Grant I organized the troops there into commands composed of white troops and Indian scouts with a pack train for each, so they could act independently of each other. While they were sufficiently large to prevent disaster, they were small enough to slip around out of sight of the hostiles. I also instructed the commanding officer to obey no orders, even from the President of the United States, until I first saw it, fully intending to disobey it, as above stated.

Almost the first person I saw at Grant was Es-kim-in-yan, who was delighted to see me, saying that he had heard of me for a long time. What a great soldier? Was I that courageous in battle and considerate to the fallen?, etc. There are very few white men who are equal to the delicate touch he gave the taffy brush. It was but a very short time until I had Skimmy in irons for some of his rascalities.

I had collected all the available troops in the southern part of the Territory, and now organized them into commands similar to those I had organized at Apache.[5] I have omitted to mention that before leaving Whipple Barracks, I had organized three commands similar to those at Apache to operate in the counties north and south of Camp Verde. I started these commands out from Apache, Grant, and McDowell.[6] When they would start out from Apache, after giving them detailed instructions what to do, I would go to Grant, and from there to McDowell by ambulance, and be at these points when these commands arrived, and, giving fresh instructions, I would go again to Apache.

This operation was repeated until all the Indians within reach of these commands were so severely punished that they virtually left that section of the country.[7] Then I moved all these commands to where New Grant was being constructed, intending to iron all the wrinkles out of Cochise's band of Indians who were then in the Dragoon Mountains. I already had my spies in his camp and intended moving on him with my whole force after night, and surrounding him by daylight in the morning and give them such a clearing out that it would end him for all time to come, as his band was recognized as the worst of all the Apaches. Then, too, he

[5] "Major George M. Randall, 23rd Infantry, managed affairs at Camp Apache, having under him as chief of scouts, Mr. C. E. Cooley. Maj. George F. Price, 5th Cavalry, commanded from Date Creek; Maj. Alexander McGregor, 1st Cavalry, had the superintendence of the troops to move out from Fort Whipple; Col. Julius W. Mason, 5th Cavalry, of those to work down from Camp Hualpai, while those of the post of Camp McDowell were commanded by James Burns, 5th Cavalry. Col. C. C. Carr, 1st Cavalry, led those from Verde." Bourke, *On the Border with Crook*, 182.

[6] Camp McDowell was located on the west bank of the Río Verde, about eight miles above its junction with Salt River. The post was established in 1865 by five companies of California Volunteers as a point from which to operate against or treat with the Indians in the neighborhood. It was intended to become one of the most solidly built posts in the Territory, but the rains came and washed it out. It was named after General Irvin McDowell. The post was abandoned on April 10, 1890. *Posts, Camps, and Stations File*.

[7] Crook's ambition had been to make the Apache campaign short, sharp, and decisive. On December 27, 1872, Captain Brown's command gained the important victory at the so-called Battle of the Caves, in which an entire band of Apaches were killed or captured. From that time to April, 1873, the various commands scoured the country, and gained one success after another, aided by allies from the Apaches themselves. Most of the approaches to Indian strongholds were made at night, under difficult circumstances. As Crook said, "The examples of personal exertion and daring among the officers and men, if all told, would fill a volume." National Archives, Department of Arizona, *Annual Report*, 1872–73.

claimed both countries as belonging to him, and when pursued by the troops of one country, he would flee across the line into the other country, and pursuit would have to stop, and there was no treaty then allowing the intercrossing of troops.

Just then General Howard made a treaty of peace with Cochise, giving him a reservation on the border, including all that rough country comprising the Dragoon and Huachuca Mountain ranges. I never could get to see the treaty stipulations, although I made official applications for them, but the Indians understood that they could raid as much as they pleased in Mexico, provided they let us alone.[8]

This treaty stopped all operations against them by me. It had a bad effect on my Indians, as they thought I was afraid of Cochise, because I left him unmolested. They said there was no justice or sense in not subjugating him, as he was the worst in the whole business.

From New Grant I started most of my force to scout up through the Tonto Basin territory to Camp Verde, while I went by ambulance via Tucson to Whipple to Verde, so as to meet them when they got through. They encountered no Indians until the exceedingly rough country where the two forks joined.

Capt. Randall's command ran on some fresh sign of Indians there, and was very discreet in his movements, moving after night, and watching during the daytime. But some of his pack mules got away and fell into the hands of the hostiles. They at once commenced sending up signal smokes, but evidently failed to locate us, our people understanding their signals, and consequently lay very low. One of our scouts, while prowling around and watching, caught a squaw, brought her into camp, and by intimidation made her tell where her people were, and took her along as a guide.

Our soldiers, before starting out, wrapped their feet and knees with gunny sacks, so as to make as little noise as possible. Soon after dark the command started for the camp of the hostiles under the guidance of the squaw. Their route lay down the banks of the river Verde for a ways, and then it took up an incline of broken lava that had become detached from a high palisade of the same

[8] The relations between General Howard and Cochise are treated in Howard's book, *My Life*, Chapters XII and XIV.

material. The angle of this incline was about 45 degrees. That, together with the loose rocks, made the ascent very laborious and difficult, as great precaution had to be observed, so as not to make any noise.

After traveling this way for quite a while, they came to the foot of the palisades. Here they met with a circular mountain running up into a column, with but one mode of ingress. This was caused by a piece of this palisades fallen down, leaving a notch by which, with great difficulty, our people could get up. On top of this notch was lying a huge rock, so our people had to crawl on their stomachs.

The summit was reached just before daylight, and they found the general surface comparatively smooth. The lava was thrown up in irregular masses while cooling, leaving large fissures running to all directions, with this grown up more or less with brush. They crawled up close to the Indians.

Just at the dawn of day our people fired a volley into their camp and charged with a yell. So secure did they feel in this almost impregnable position that they lost all presence of mind, even running past their holes in the rocks. Some of them jumped off the precipice and were mashed into a shapeless mass. All of the men were killed; most of the women and children were taken prisoners. This is called Turret Mountain from its shape.

From the time of our troops leaving Grant, they had heard nothing from the outside world. Some of the prisoners captured told Randall that these Indians had made a raid on the Hassayampa and had killed three white men, at the same time showing some of the effects that had been taken from these white men. The circumstantial evidence was so strong that it left no doubt in my mind that this was the identical band who had killed the three men on the Hassayampa a short time before, cruelly torturing one of them, a young man by the name of Taylor, by sticking his body full of splinters and setting fire to them. When his body was found the prints of his body were still fresh in the sands where he had writhed in his agony. So retributive justice had soon overtaken these brutes.

A singular thing happened on this trip. It was at the time Epizootic was raging in the East, and the disease was traveling west. It hadn't reached Arizona yet, but when the troops were on the way up from Grant, a horse came into Verde from New Mexico with the disease, and about the same time the horses with the expedition were taken with the disease. They were certainly one hundred miles in a straight line from the Verde, and they had come in contact with no outside animals since they started from Grant.

This Tonto Basin country, over which the hostiles roamed and lived, really comprised the territory from the Little Colorado to the western slopes of the Mogollon Range of mountains, from Camp Verde to New Camp Grant, comprising an area of over two hundred miles square, containing some of the roughest country in the United States and known only to the Indians. From this immense stronghold they used to make their forays on the sparsely settled districts and the highways, and when followed would retreat to this country, and when a favorable opportunity offered would ambush their pursuers, and not infrequently kill the whole party. Thus, such a reign of terror existed in that region that troops, even, rarely went into it, which emboldened the Indians into committing the most fiendish acts of cruelty.

All the other Indians having sued for peace, and the Indians occupying this rough country having been so severely chastised, I had some of the prisoners sent out to communicate with the hostiles, holding out the "olive branch," offering them peace on certain conditions, which were that they should all move in on the different reservations and abstain from all depredations from that time forward. They promptly responded to my proposition, and all within reach came in at once.

So, on the seventh day of April, 1873, the last of the Apaches surrendered, with the exception of the Chiricahuas under Cochise, whom General Howard had taken under his wing. Had it not been for their barbarities, one would have been moved to pity by their appearance. They were emaciated, clothes torn in tatters, some of their legs were not thicker than my arm. Some of them looked as if though they had dropped out of a comic almanac.

Old Cha-lipun told me, "You see, we're are nearly dead from want of food and exposure—the copper cartridge has done the business for us. I am glad of the opportunity to surrender, but I do it not because I love you, but because I am afraid of General."

Old Deltchay,[9] surnamed The Liar, said he had one hundred and twenty-five warriors last fall, and if anybody had told him he couldn't whip the world, he would have laughed at them, but now he had only twenty left. He said they used to have no difficulty in eluding the troops, but now the very rocks had gotten soft, they couldn't put their foot anywhere without leaving an impression by which we could follow, that they could get no sleep at nights, for should a coyote or a fox start a rock rolling during the night, they would get up and dig out, thinking it was we who were after them.

This Deltchay had the worst reputation amongst all the Indians for villainry and devilment. He vied with Eskimmi-yan in making treaties and solemnizing them with the stone performance, and probably before the next morning would kill someone and skip out with a lot of stock, etc.

The Indians were placed on the reservation under the most solemn promise to remain there and behave themselves.

I returned to Prescott. In about a month a dispatch was sent me by courier (there was no telegraph then) that the Indians had the night before flew [sic] to the mountains like a flock of quail, and had lit running. I sent word back at once to signal them by smoke to stop, and I at once proceeded to Verde. They all came back, looking as though they had been stealing sheep. Cha-lipun was very much ashamed of himself, and promised if I would forgive him this time he would remain true for the rest of his life, which promise he has kept inviolable ever since. I have never been able to learn the true cause of this hegira.[10]

Later Deltchay found he was of but little consequence on the reservation, compared to what it was when he was out in the moun-

[9] Delt-che, "The Red Ant," according to Bourke.

[10] "On the 14th ult. the Tontos left en masse in the night, being frightened by false reports into the expectation of a treacherous attack by the troops, but on learning through messengers sent to them from Camp Verde of their gross mistake, they showed not only willingness but great anxiety to come back, and all have now returned with the exception of small parties with whom the chiefs have been unable to communicate, and who will doubtless come in as soon as they learn the condition of affairs." National Archives, Report by Second Lieutenant W. S. Schuyler to Assistant Adjutant General, Department of Arizona, on the Condition of Affairs on the Río Verde, September 1, 1873.

tains, "holding high council." The restraint on the reservation was irksome to his wild spirit, which was unused to any curbing. One day, without warning, he surrounded the white men at the agency. Lt. W. S. Schuyler[11] was in charge, with only the agency employees. Deltchay would certainly have assassinated them all but for the interposition of the scouts, who compelled them to desist.

That night Deltchay, with his whole outfit, some forty in number, left the reservation, went into the Verde River, and traveled down it for over twenty miles, so as to leave no sign, until they came to a rocky point on which they could escape into the mountains without our being able to follow them. There were places on this river that must have been from ten to fifteen feet deep. Parties were at once sent out to force them back on the reservation, or destroy them. They had some skirmishing, but couldn't kill Deltchay.

Not long afterwards the Indians at the San Carlos agency broke out and went into the San Pedro Valley and brutally murdered some families living there. They also killed some other people. The troops started out after them at once, had a couple of fights with them, killing a good many of their number. Some of them returned to the reservation and surrendered.

I arrived there at this time. I refused to accept their surrender, but told them I could not harm them, as they had thrown themselves on my mercy, but I would drive them all back into the mountains, where I could kill them all, that they had lied to me once, and I didn't know but what they were lying to me now. They begged to be allowed to remain, making all kinds of promises for the future. I finally compromised by letting them stay, provided they would bring in the heads of certain of the chiefs who were ringleaders, which they agreed to.

A couple of mornings afterwards they brought in seven heads of the proscribed. The same edict was sent out to the Tontos, which was also responded to with alacrity. Deltchay had two heads. When I visited the Verde reservation, they would convince

[11] Walter S. Schuyler graduated from the Military Academy in 1870. He was in Arizona from 1872 to 1875, and aide-de-camp to Crook in 1876–77. For some reason, Crook always addressed him as "Scuyler," omitting the "h." Schuyler was a friend of the General all his life and obtained the majority of the Crook papers. He died in 1932.

me that they had brought in his head; and when I went to San Carlos, they would convince me that they had brought in his head. Being satisfied that both parties were earnest in their beliefs, and the bringing in of an extra head was not amiss, I paid both parties.[12]

This about quieted them, but small parties would still sift out in the mountains, and I knew if I were to permit a party, even if small, to remain out it would get accession to those on the reserve, who, in turn, would become dissatisfied, and it would not be long before they would be pretty much all out in the mountains again. So frequent expeditions were sent out, and destroyed several parties.

One of these parties murdered a man near the Hassayampa, near Wickenburg. The news was telegraphed to me. I sent a scouting party from the Verde. A week or more had elapsed since the occurrence before the expedition reached the scene of the murder. The scouts took the trail of the Indians, followed them a long distance, came up to the Indian camp, and had a fight in which one scout was killed and several wounded. The command returned to Verde more than a month afterwards. Another expedition went out to the scene of the fight, took a single track, followed it for over fifty miles, came up on the Indian camp, and killed the whole party, regardless of age or sex.[13]

[12] The successful campaign was commended in a *General Order* of the Pacific Division, dated April 28, 1873: "To Brevet Major-General George Crook, commanding the Department of Arizona, and to his gallant troops, for the extraordinary services they have rendered in the late campaigns against the Apache Indians, the Division Commander extends his thanks and congratulations upon their brilliant success. They have merited the gratitude of the nation."

[13] In July, 1873, Crook issued *General Order No. 24*, which enumerated the successes of his troops:

"First: Captain George M. Randall, 23rd Infantry, surrounded and captured the remains of Deltchay's band with that notorious chief himself, in the Sierre Madre Mountains on the 22nd of April.

"Second: The operations of the troops under Captain Thomas McGregor, 1st Cavalry, in the Santa María Mountains, resulted in the surrender of Tomaspie's entire band of Apache Mohaves, on the 12th ultimo.

"Third: The operations of First Lieutenant J. B. Babcock, Fifth Cavalry, in Tonto Basin, and his brilliant action on the 16th ultimo, resulted in the surrender of two bands of Tonto Apaches under Na-ta-to-tel and Naqui-naquis.

"Fourth: Reports have just been received of the operations of Captain James Burns, 5th Cavalry, in Castle Dome and Santa María Mountains, resulting in the unconditional surrender of over two hundred Apache Mohaves,

The rough country between the top of the Mogollon Mountains and the Little Colorado was the last place the Indians held out. That country is cut up with deep cañons that can only be crossed in a few places only known to the Indians. This country was furnished with so many almost inaccessible places to hide in that it was with much difficulty they were finally dislodged, but not until after some of those small parties were entirely destroyed.[14]

These people had opened up a traffic with the Moqui Indians, where they were supplied with ammunition. Capt. Bourke[15] and I made a trip to the Moqui villages in October, 1874, to investigate the matter. I became satisfied that they had such a traffic, but the fright we gave them put an end to it.

In the spring of 1874 the Indians on the Verde reservation were removed to the San Carlos in the interest of some persons at Tucson, who were on the inside of the "Ring." The Indians at Apache and Verde had been placed at work. The Indians at Apache had, with a few grubbing hoes condemned by the Quartermaster Department and fixed by the post blacksmith, and with sticks hardened in the fire, raised in 1873 some 500,000 pounds of corn and 30,000 pounds of beans. They had become more or less interested, when the Interior Department commenced agitating the subject of their removal to the San Carlos, although General How-

believed to be the last remnants of all the straggling renegades in Northern Arizona."

[14] Crook was promoted, as the result of his success in Arizona, to brigadier general on October 29, 1873. The news was sent as one of the first telegrams to go over the newly completed line from Yuma to Prescott. R. R. Haines, superintendent of construction, sent the first message informing him of the completion of the line and congratulating him on the promotion.

[15] John G. Bourke graduated from the Military Academy in 1869. He served as aide-de-camp to the General from 1872 to 1883, and probably knew him as well as anyone. Bourke was a remarkable man in any business, and in the army he distinguished himself by collecting and noting information about the Indians wherever he was stationed. The results were produced in several scholarly works on the Southwestern Indians. He also wrote the only two books dealing with General Crook, *An Apache Campaign* and *On the Border with Crook*.

Part of Bourke's copious diary, on file in the library at West Point, has been published under the editorship of Lansing B. Bloom in the *New Mexico Historical Review*. In it Bourke mentions his trip to the Moquis with General Crook.

ard had connected the two reservations into one, known as the White Mountain reservation.

These Indians at Apache were a mountain Indian, and the heat and dust of San Carlos agency was quite equal at times to that of Yuma, besides being malarious. There was plenty of arable land in the mountains about Apache and on the reservation set aside for these Indians. Their removal was one of those cruel things that greed has so often inflicted on the Indian. When the Indian appeals to arms, his only redress, the whole country cries out against the Indian.

They finally succeeded in removing all these Indians except Diablo's band, who said they would rather be killed than go down to the San Carlos to sure death. For fear of an outbreak and an exposure of their infamous schemes, they allowed this one band to remain, provided they would become self-sustaining.

One of General Howard's last acts was to take old Eskimi-yan, with a few other choice spirits, to Washington, saying that "Eski-mi-yan was an Indian who knew no guile."

I had a band of horses driven down from California, and took the scouts' pay due them, and bought horses for them, so as to get them owners of something, so as to anchor them to some fixed locality. These Indians were essentially foot Indians. Being always in a state of war, they were compelled to live in such rough country that horses could not live. They would steal horses, take them into this country, ride them until their feet would give out, when they would kill them and eat them.

As soon as the Indians became settled on the different reservations, gave up the warpath, and became harmless, the Indian agents, who had sought cover before, now came out as brave as sheep, and took charge of the agencies, and commenced their game of plundering. Then there was a Superintendent of Indian Affairs for Arizona by the name of Dr. Bendell, a little General from Albany or Troy, New York.[16] He obtained permission to establish his residence at Whipple Barracks, and built the house now occupied by the telegraph offices. It was generally understood that during his

[16] Herman Bendell resigned from the superintendency on March 26, 1873, shortly before that office was discontinued. He returned to Albany, New York, where he resumed the practice of medicine. He died on November 14, 1932. There is no evidence to support Crook's charge against him.

short stay in Arizona he carried off some $50,000 for his share of the spoils.

As soon as it became safe, he sent an agent to take charge of the Hualpais, then at Beale's Spring.[17] The Indians soon commenced complaining of not getting sufficient to eat. The commanding officer of the troops stationed there at first paid no attention to their complaints, but the Indians got so obstreperous that an outbreak was feared. So Captain Byrne, to be certain the Indians had cause for their complaints, stationed himself with witnesses where they could see the issues made them, and had the Indians bring to him what had been issued to them. He had these articles weighed; and, for instance, an Indian family that was entitled to ninety-five pounds of beef only received fifteen.

Captain Byrne took charge of the issues, which, as might have been expected, raised a big breeze. The Superintendent made a complaint against this "usurpation of the prerogatives of the Interior Department, high-handed acts on the part of the military," etc. Charges reflecting on Captain Byrne were made by the acting agent and Superintendent Bendell. It was suggested to Captain Byrne that he ask for a court of inquiry.

The court was ordered, and upon investigation it came out in evidence that the Indian agent had sent wagon loads of Indian food to the mines, and sold them. And amongst many other little dodges practiced by these Christian gentlemen was to change the pea on the scales, so that a beef that would weigh three hundred pounds was made to weigh 1,300.[18]

Although this exposition had no effect on these people's dealing

[17] Camp Beale, a few miles northwest of Kingman, was named for Lieutenant Edward F. Beale of "Camel Corps" fame, who was a naval lieutenant in the Mexican War and resigned his commission to become an explorer in the West. It was established on May 25, 1871, and abandoned on April 6, 1874. The Indian agency was established in January, 1873. *Posts, Camps, and Stations File.*

[18] On July 29, 1873, the court of inquiry assembled at Camp Beale's Springs "to investigate the facts and circumstances connected with [Captain Thomas Byrne's] administration of affairs at his post, with relation to the tribe of Indians who make that post their rendezvous."

Surgeon E. I. Bailey was president of the court, which found that Byrne's actions had been proper, that he had not exceeded his authority, and that his action in watching the issues to the Indians was both necessary and eminently proper. Department of Arizona, *Special Orders Nos. 63 and 68,* 1873.

with the Indians, the proceedings of this court were placed on file in the Interior Department in Washington, and was a thorn in the side of that thievish department.

VI

VICTORY IN
DEFEAT

18. *The hostiles were apparently everywhere*

IN THE SPRING OF 1875 I was relieved from the command of the
Department of Arizona and was ordered to the command of the
Department of the Platte. On the eleventh day of March I took
my departure for San Francisco by ambulance up the Mohave
River to Los Angeles, and from there by stage and cars to San
Francisco. I was given a banquet at the Lick House.

When we arrived in Salt Lake, long sections of the Union Pacific were washed out ahead of us on the Sweetwater and Green
rivers, so we were detained there two weeks, and were treated
royally. A ball or some other kind of entertainment was given us
most every night. I was given a reception upon my arrival in
Omaha.

Made a trip to Red Cloud agency in May, on our return, and
took the route to Sidney. In crossing the river, we had much diffi
culty, as the water was high, and we had to cross our plunder in
a flatboat by poles and oars. In attempting to swim the horses of
the escort across, they stampeded, and scattered for miles over the
country. Some were never recovered. On June 3 attended General Sheridan's wedding, which was rather a quiet affair.[1]

[1] General Sheridan married Irene Rucker, daughter of General C. H.
Rucker, then quartermaster general of the Division of the Missouri, stationed
in Chicago.
The wedding was held at the home of the bride's father, and the informal
reception that followed featured ice cream and other dainties served in the
Rucker's backyard. Crook was there with his wife. Among the guests were
Generals Sherman, Terry, Perry, Pope, Ord, Augur, Van Vliet, and Whipple.
Crook would probably have enjoyed fishing in Lake Michigan more than the
reception. *Army and Navy Journal*, Vol. XII, No. 44 (June 12, 1875), 701.

The discovery of gold in the Black Hills was attracting much attention amongst the people of the country. Many expeditions were being fitted out with the view of going into that country. As it was on the Sioux reservation, the authorities in Washington were anxious to prevent this violation of the treaty stipulations. Several parties were prevented from going in. General Sheridan, in command of the Division of the Missouri, issued an order directing the troops to arrest any such persons attempting to go into the Black Hills and to destroy all their transportation, guns, and property generally. But notwithstanding all these precautions, many had sifted in.

I was ordered to proceed to that country and eject these people. About the middle of July I started for the Black Hills from Cheyenne, via Fort Laramie[2] in ambulances. Our party consisted of Major Stanton and his clerk, Gen. J. E. Smith and son, George Wilson, and myself. Col. R. I. Dodge was already in that country with an expedition exploring the country, or rather he was escorting some persons, supposed to be scientific, who represented the Interior Department, who were examining the country for the purpose of determining whether the precious metals really existed in paying quantities or not.[3]

I found a good many sovereign citizens scattered about the

[2] Fort Laramie was established in June, 1834, by William Sublette and Robert Campbell, fur traders. The first log building was named Fort William after Sublette.

The fort became a trade center for a large area, being at the junction of the Laramie and North Platte rivers. In 1836 the fort was purchased by the American Fur Company, who replaced the log stockade with adobe walls in 1841, and named the place Fort John. The name did not last, and the post became known as Fort Laramie.

The tide of emigrants, augmented by the gold seekers in 1849, demanded protection from the Indians, and on June 26, 1849, the United States government purchased the fort for $4,000 and converted it into a military post. It became the great way station on the main road to the Far West.

The Grattan and Harney massacres near the fort foreshadowed the Indian war that followed. Fort Laramie became the headquarters for military campaigns. When the Indians were finally subdued and placed on reservations, the usefulness of the fort was ended. It was abandoned on April 20, 1890. James T. Adams, *Dictionary of American History*, III, 245.

[3] Dodge, escorting the Jenney Expedition, represented the Indians as being anxious to give the Hills to the whites as a piece of useless territory and blamed "squaw men" for stirring up trouble. Richard I. Dodge, *The Black Hills*, 137–38.

*From a photograph by Mr. Fly and his
assistant, Chase, Tombstone
Courtesy General Charles D. Roberts*

General Crook and the hostile Apaches meet to discuss surrender
terms on March 25, 1886. This photograph was used as the model
for the plaque on the monument over Crook's grave in
Arlington Cemetery

Seated, left to right: Lt. W. E. Shipp, Lt. S. L. Faison, Capt. C. S. Roberts,
Nachez (behind Roberts), Geronimo, Cayetano (behind Geronimo), Nana,
Conception (behind Nana), Noche, Lt. M. R. Maus, José María, Antonio
Besias, José Montoyo (interpreters), Capt. J. G. Bourke, General Crook,
Charley Roberts. In rear: Tommy Blair, pack-train cook (holding up the
mule), Josanie, Chihuahua, H. W. Daly, packmaster (behind José María),
unidentified Indians, Mayor Strauss of Tombstone (behind Charley Roberts).

Courtesy National Archives

Apache prisoners at Fort Bowie after their final surrender to Lieutenant Gatewood. The squaw at the extreme left, shielding her face, is a "cut-nose" squaw. The officer in the background is Lieutenant Matthew Markland, who later married Mrs. Crook's sister, Fanny.

Hills, prospecting, while others had commenced mining. There was more or less feeling amongst them with what they regarded as an interference with the rights of a sovereign citizen of "these here United States" to go where he pleased and do as he pleased. I circulated around amongst them, got them to come and have a talk, when I explained the whole affair to them, that I was merely executing an unpleasant duty and that I had no feeling in the matter, and advised them to go peaceably.

I issued a proclamation warning them to leave the country. I had suggested that as the claims which they had taken up were invalid and would not hold in case the land was thrown up to settlement without a relocation, I advised them to agree amongst themselves to respect each other's claims when it became lawful for them to go into this country. Most of them left, but a few dodged the troops that I left under the command of Capt. Pollock, 9th Infantry.

The Black Hills was then a most interesting and beautiful country. It was like an oasis in the desert, for here was a broken piece of country covered with a beautiful growth of timber, filled with game of all kinds, surrounded as far as the eye could see with bare, uninteresting plains.

Nothing of importance occurred until the beginning of 1876, when I received instructions to compel the Sioux and Cheyenne Indians, who were off their reservation, to go on it. They were consequently notified that they must either go on the reservation by such a time, or else the troops would attack them wherever found. I might say that these Indians were continually committing depredations on the surrounding country, were insolent, and claimed the whole of Wyoming and part of the adjacent territories, and declined to be restrained in their freedom in the slightest particular.

Sometime during the fall a commission comprised of Senator Allison and other members of Congress assembled at Red Cloud agency to treat with these Indians for the Black Hills country.[4]

---

[4] "In the summer of 1876 the government sent a commission, of which Senator William B. Allison, of Iowa, was chairman, and the late Maj-Gen. Alfred H. Terry a member, to negotiate with the Sioux for the cession of the Black Hills, but neither the Sioux nor Cheyennes were in the humor to negotiate. There appeared to be a very large element among the Indians which

These refractory Indians were present in force while the commission was in session, guarded by a company of cavalry. All of a sudden every white man found himself surrounded by these Indians, stripped to the buff, painted, ready for action. Each white man was covered with one or more of the guns of these imps, who looked as if they would want no better fun than to kill everybody there, just to see them kick.

But for the coolness and address of Spotted Tail our people would have met with disaster. But old Spot, who was decked out in all his toggery, arose and surveyed the whole scene with perfect "sang froid," said that he was as good a man as any of them, and if they wanted to fight, he was ready for them, and in this way bluffed them off.

Old Red Cloud, who had been looking for some small hole to creep into, when he saw the effect of Spot's stand had produced on the hostiles, took courage and assumed the offensive with his mouth. The Commission were the gladdest people to get away from that part of the country that had ever visited there. They didn't recover their courage until they got the Missouri River between them.

In the early part of 1876 I left Cheyenne City with five companies of cavalry to make a campaign in the Powder River coun-

---

would sooner have war than peace; all sorts of failures to observe previous agreements were brought up, and the advocates of peace were outnumbered.

"One day it looked very much as if a general melee was about to be precipitated. The hostile element, led by Little Big Man, shrieked for war, and Little Big Man himself was haranguing his followers that it was as good a moment as any to begin shooting. The courage and coolness of two excellent officers, Egan and Crawford, the former of the Second, the latter of the Third Cavalry, kept the savages from getting too near the Commissioners. Their commands formed a line, and with carbines at an 'advance' remained perfectly motionless, ready to charge in upon the Indians should the latter begin an attack." Bourke, *On the Border with Crook*, 243.

5 "On the first of March, 1876, after a heavy fall of snow the previous night, and in the face of a cold wind, but with the sun shining brightly down upon us, we left Fetterman for the Powder River and Big Horn. . . . We had ten full companies of cavalry equally divided between the Second and Third Regiments, and two companies of the Fourth Infantry. The troops were under the immediate command of Col. Joseph J. Reynolds." Bourke, *On the Border with Crook*, 254.

try.[5] We had beautiful weather, and traveled with wagon trains and pack mules as far as Crazy Woman, where we left the wagons and started out in the afternoon of a beautiful sunshiny day. We traveled all night, and reached a fork of Clear Creek about daylight the next morning.

I turned in my blankets for a little sleep. The sun was just rising, and shone in my eyes. Everything bid fair for a beautiful day, but in a few moments the snow was coming from all quarters, accompanied with severe gusts of wind. The thermometer sank rapidly, until we were having a regular blizzard. The snow and wind were so blinding that everything beyond a few yards from us was obscured from view. We lay here all day and night.

The next morning there was no abatement of the storm, but we had only so many days' rations, and we would probably have a long distance to accomplish before returning to the wagon train, so we pulled out and marched that day until nearly night. The thermometer for the next few days wouldn't register, as the mercury was congealed.

We struck the Tongue River, and after traveling down that to within less than one hundred miles from its mouth and finding no Indian sign, we struck over towards Powder River. Before reaching the latter river, however, we saw two pony tracks, which convinced us that we were discovered. So I sent three of the troops under Gen. J. J. Reynolds to take their backtracks, to find the village, while I would, with the other troops, stay and protect the impedimenta, supposing they would in all likelihood make an attack upon us. Our pack mules' shoes were so smooth I was afraid to take them into the rough country the village was likely to be in.

The three troops left in the afternoon, and came on the village about daylight the next morning, situated on Powder River, close under some bluffs. They made the attack as soon as they could get down the bluffs, as their village was seen from the top of the bluffs under which it was situated.

The troops took the village without any trouble, including all their plunder, with a large number of ponies, but owing to our troops' failing to occupy the bluffs, the Indians soon took position on them, and drove our people out of the village. Our troops left so precipitously that our wounded men were left to fall into the hands of the Indians.[6] A rapid retreat was at once commenced, and continued until next morning, allowing many of the captured ponies to be retaken by the Indians.

I overtook them with the impedimenta the next afternoon while in camp on Powder River. Before reaching their camp, we met a party of Indians driving back some ponies. We gave chase, making them drop all their ponies, and wounded one Indian who made his escape in the rocks. Serious complaint was made against Captain Reynolds and Captain Moore for mismanagement and misbehavior in the presence of the enemy.

The next day all the ponies remaining in our hands were killed as being of no use to us and to prevent the possibility of their falling into the hands of the Indians. The second night, while in camp on Powder River in a blizzard, our camp was fired into by a raiding party of Indians returning from the settlements about Fetterman[7] and Laramie.

Our wagon train had moved back to the crossing on Powder River. The weather still remained cold. Our march back to Fetterman was comparatively pleasant. There was little or no wind, but from there to Cheyenne we had a regular blizzard. The thermometer was below zero, and the light snow was driven in great violence by the wind, which was whirling from all quarters, so at times it was almost impossible to get our breath.

Upon my return I preferred charges against Col. Reynolds and Captains Noyes and Moore for misbehavior before the enemy.[8]

[6] Bourke says that the dead, at least, were left to the Indians, and that it was "whispered" that one wounded man had been left. Considering the importance attached to bodies by the Indians, the abandonment of the dead was sufficient cause for dissatisfaction.

[7] Fort Fetterman was situated on the south side of North Platte River near the mouth of La Prele Creek. The post was established on July 19, 1867, and named after Lieutenant Colonel William J. Fetterman, who was killed in the so-called Fetterman massacre near Fort Phil Kearney, December 21, 1866. Control of the land was relinquished by the War Department on July 22, 1884. *Posts, Camps, and Stations File.*

[8] After a long trial, full of animosity and countercharges, Colonel J. J. Reynolds was found guilty and sentenced to be suspended from rank and command for the period of one year.

Captain Alexander Moore was found guilty of neglect of duty, and sentenced to be suspended from command for six months, and to be confined to the limits of his post for the same period. Lieutenant Henry E. Noyes was found guilty of conduct to the prejudice of good order and military discipline,

After this affair the Indians became more defiant than ever. Many more left the different reservations openly to join those who were known to be hostile and who were openly defying the authorities who dared them to do this. All the available men in the Departments of the Platte and Dakota were placed in readiness to take the field. Those in Dakota were to be commanded by General Terry in person, while those in the Department of the Platte were to be commanded by myself in person.

The latter part of May, 1876, found my command crossing the Platte River at Fetterman by ferry boats. The river being very high, this task was accomplished with much difficulty. On the second of June, while passing over the high ground between the Dry Fork of the Cheyenne and the Dry Fork of the Powder River, we marched in a cold and disagreeable snowstorm which lasted about all day. The snow was accompanied by a high wind, which was particularly uncomfortable. From here our march lay over about the same course as the route of the previous winter, except from Crazy Woman we marched down to the junction of Prairie Dog Creek with Tongue River. These streams were very high.

We could see enough evidences that the hostiles were watching us, so one day as a little bravado, a hundred or so of them appeared on the bluffs opposite us and fired some shots, but did no damage except shooting one or two horses. Seeing that we were constantly watched and that it was impossible to surprise them from here, I fell back to the foot of the Big Horn Mountains, on Willow Creek. We had some Shoshone and Crow scouts.[9]

and sentenced to be reprimanded by the department commander. Bureau of Military Justice. *Record Book No. 38;* Department of the Platte, *General Court-martial Order No. 29* (May 2, 1876).

[9] A small party of eighty-six Shoshones joined Crook's column on June 14 and fought bravely in the Battle of the Rosebud. Dick Washakie, son of the old chief, stated in an interview years afterwards: "General Crook expressed to my father his indebtedness for the services that the warriors rendered the United States troops. General Crook highly approved what Chief Washakie, my father, and his Indians had done for him on this occasion, and it was through the recommendation of General Crook that my father received a pension from the government for the services rendered at this particular instance."

Young Chief Washakie also recalled that General Crook had blond whiskers which naturally parted at the chin. These two parts of his whiskers were usually in braids, and drawn to the right and left.

Crook was obliged to ask for Shoshone and Ute Indian allies because his

On the fifteenth of June we concentrated all our impedimenta except the pack trains, which we took with us, so as to require the minimum guard, and with all our available forces started on forced marches toward the Rosebud, where we had reason to believe the hostiles were in force. On the morning of the sixteenth we saw fresh Indian signs, but were unable to make out whether they had discovered us or not.

On the morning of the seventeenth, after marching for a few miles, some of our scouts came in, said they had discovered some hostiles not far in advance, and asked me to halt while they went ahead to reconnoiter. So we halted and dismounted, and the cavalry took the bridles out of their horses' mouths. They had not been long in this position before the scouts came back as fast as their ponies could carry they [them], followed closely by the hostiles, both yelling at the tops of their lungs, giving the war whoop that caused the hair to raise on end.

In a short time the hostiles were apparently everywhere. I ran up on a bluff, not far from where we halted, to take in the situation, intending to make my dispositions after learning the exact situation. Some of the infantry went up with me and took possession of this bluff, which commanded our camp which was now the place on the creek where we had halted.

When I returned to camp, Capt. Nickerson had scattered the cavalry, sending two companies on a high hill on the opposite side of the creek, and about a half mile distant, while he sent the remainder, under Major Royall, to my left, which were just passing out of sight as I came into camp. The Indians pressed Major Royall so closely that he took up a position on the edge of some bluffs for self-defense.

My intention was to charge the Indians in my front, as there was a comparatively level mesa in front of the infantry. For this purpose I sent orders for Major Royall's command to join me with the least possible delay. With my repeated urging for him to join me, it was over two hours before he finally accomplished the movement. It was there where most of our loss occurred. Capt. Guy V.

---

attempts to enlist Sioux and Cheyenne help had been opposed by the Sioux chiefs and Interior Department representatives on the reservation. Grace R. Hebard, *Washakie*, 200–201.

Henry was very dangerously wounded. By the time this junction was formed, the Indians had withdrawn from my front. Only a few could be seen skulking around in the hills.

Then it became my intention to follow the Indians in the direction of their retreat. To this end I sent Captain Mills with his squadron up a cañon in the proposed direction. I noticed some Indians who were just above where he passed, and who could have inflicted much damage on his troops without any danger to themselves. Instead of doing this, they sneaked off the hill, keeping in advance of the troops, which showed to me plainly that we were doing just what they wanted us to do. So I recalled the squadron.

In a short time no Indians were in sight. We lost over a dozen men killed and a good many wounded. About the same number of the enemy's dead were picked up, and doubtless others were carried off by them. We buried our dead, and prepared to transport our wounded back to our camp. We camped there for the night.[10]

The next morning we took up our line of march, but were not molested on our march.

[*Here ends the Autobiography*]

The Battle of the Rosebud, fought on the anniversary of Bunker Hill, was the only major defeat General Crook suffered at the hands of Indians. Added to the lack of any spectacular success in the Yellowstone Expedition up to this time, it rankled deeply. In his official report the General did not admit defeat, saying: "My troops beat these Indians on a field of their own choosing, and drove them in utter rout from it, as far as the proper care of my wounded and prudence would justify. Subsequent events proved beyond dispute what would have been the fate of the command had the pursuit been continued beyond what judgment dictated."[11]

Nevertheless, the Rosebud was a defeat, strategical, if not tactical. It prevented immediate junction with Terry's command, an

[10] The Battle of the Rosebud, June 17, 1876, was fought by Troops A, B, D, E, and I, Second Cavalry; A, B, C, D, E, F, G, I, L, and M, Third Cavalry; Companies D and F, Fourth Infantry; and C, G, and H, Ninth Infantry. The Second Cavalry was commanded by Captain Noyes, the Third by Guy V. Henry, Anson Mills, and Fred Van Vliet. Major Alexander Chambers commanded the infantry.

[11] Secretary of War, *Annual Report, 1876*, 500.

event which would most likely have written a different beginning, and doubtless a successful end, to the fight on the Little Big Horn. The defeat rankled in Crook's memory all his life, and he steadfastly insisted that had the battle progressed according to his orders, it would have ended in real triumph.

In 1886 Colonel Royall was quoted by two Omaha papers as intimating that Crook had made a bad fight at the Rosebud. The General confronted Royall, charging that: "For ten years I have suffered silently the obloquy of having made a bad fight at the Rosebud, when the fault was in yourself and Nickerson. There was a good chance to make a charge, but it couldn't be done because of the condition of the cavalry. I sent word for you to come in, and waited two hours, nearer three, before you obeyed. I sent Nickerson three times at least. Couriers passed constantly between the points where we were respectively. I had the choice of assuming the responsibility myself for the failure of my plans, or of court-martialing you and Nickerson. I chose to bear the responsibility myself. The failure of my plan was due to your conduct."[12]

Colonel Royall denied that he had received more than one order to return and said that he had obeyed as soon as possible. Colonel Henry, also present at the interview, substantiated his statement. Nickerson, who described the fight in his *Major-General George Crook and the Indians*, says nothing of being sent to Royall. After the Reynolds–Noyes–Moore affair, it seems hardly likely that Crook would have spared a court-martial had he believed there was sufficient evidence for it.

The Rosebud was lost not because of poor tactics or negligence on the part of any of the participants, but because of overwhelming superiority of manpower and firepower on the side of the Indians. They outnumbered the soldiers three to one and were armed with the latest model repeating rifles. For one of the few times in the history of Indian warfare the whites were confronted with a really superior force, which, though composed of "savages," used a system of tactics, dividing the troops and attempting to destroy them in sections. This same condition obtained once more, eight days later.

[12] Diary of Lyman Walter Vere Kennon, on file in Army War College Library.

Early on the morning of June 18, the command moved slowly up the west bank of the Rosebud toward the wagon train which had been left behind under Major Furey on the south fork of the Tongue. The night had been occupied with burial of the dead. Travois were constructed for transportation of the wounded.

Colonel Henry, who had been shot through the face, losing one eye and with the other closed at least temporarily, was one of the wounded. "The mule that was dragging him over an exceedingly rough mountain suddenly shied, bringing one of the poles of the travois over a large boulder, and pitching him headlong down among the rocks some twenty feet below. When picked up, the wounded officer could not speak at all, but after the dirt had been wiped off, and some water had cleared his throat, he was asked the somewhat absurd question of how he felt. 'Bully,' was his somewhat unexpected reply. 'Never felt better in my life. Everybody is so kind,' he continued, and in this might possibly from his tone have included the sad-eyed mule which stood innocently winking and blinking nearby."[13]

By the nineteenth the command reached the wagon train, proceeded to lick its wounds, and consider what was next to be done. Lieutenant Schuyler arrived with dispatches from the East urging Crook to strike again. But now the General was determined to move cautiously and wait for reinforcements and supplies before continuing the expedition.

The surrounding country was alive with Indians, harassing the command in every possible manner. They burned the grass, shot at every stray detail, attempted to stampede the horses and mules, fired into camp at long range, and effectively prevented the command of the Yellowstone Expedition from establishing communication—a factor which proved vital. For more than a month Crook's column remained in the same general location, waiting for the proper moment to move.

Scouts and reconnaissances were sent out from time to time to locate the other columns and find the main body of Indians. On June 25, Anson Mills reported a great column of smoke in the northwest. Later it was supposed that this was evidence of the

[13] Azor H. Nickerson, *Major-General George Crook and the Indians* [MS].

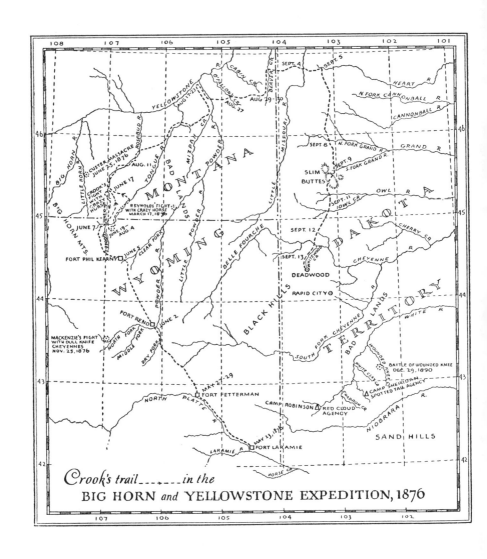

Crook's trail ------ *in the*
BIG HORN *and* YELLOWSTONE EXPEDITION, 1876

battle which the Seventh Cavalry fought and lost on that day. Rumors of the massacre began to trickle into camp, and the Indians reported a large number of "pony soldiers" killed.

General Crook, with a party of officers and men—including Bourke, Schuyler, and the Chicago reporter, Finerty—went to the Big Horn Mountains on July 1 for a hunt and scout to see whether any trace of Terry or Gibbon could be found. On July 4 the party returned, unsuccessful except for a good hunt and an interesting mountain climb.

On the following day Crook determined to detail Lieutenant Sibley with a few men, including the two best scouts in the command, Frank Gruard and Baptiste Pourière,[14] to scout the lay of the land. The scout left on the sixth and was attacked by Indians the next day, forced to abandon their horses and return afoot, hiding from the hostiles the entire distance. The command was still hemmed in.

Finally, on the tenth, Louis Richaud and Ben Arnold arrived with official news of the Custer disaster.[15] This was definite information, but did nothing to improve Crook's position. However, the arrival on the following day of 213 Shoshones under Chief Washakie[16] was a welcome sign of beginning reinforcement.

Three tattered soldiers, Evans, Stuart, and Bell, of the Seventh

[14] Frank Gruard's antecedents are a matter of some doubt. He was variously described as a mulatto, a half blood, and a native of the Sandwich Islands. He knew the Sioux language perfectly and was dark enough to pass for a native. He was nicknamed "The Grabber," and lived for some years with Crazy Horse's family.

Baptiste Pourière, whose name was spelled in various ways, was commonly known as "Big Bat" to distinguish him from Baptiste Garnier, known as "Little Bat," who was also a guide. Big Bat appears as a guide in many frontier tales. He was still living at the Pine Ridge agency in 1921. Mari Sandoz, *Crazy Horse*, 426; James H. Cook, *Fifty Years on the Old Frontier*, 192–97.

[15] Ben Arnold, telling his story, says nothing about Richaud. His description of the campaign, especially the life of a professional courier is very enlightening. The rewards for such service were great, but no more than the risks. Arnold censures Crook severely for his inactivity following the Battle of the Rosebud. Lewis F. Crawford, *Rekindling Campfires*, 246–62.

[16] Bourke observed that Chief Washakie bore a distinct resemblance to Henry Ward Beecher, while Finerty saw the image of the Reverend Robert Collyer. Chief Washakie advised the General to wait for reinforcements before making another attack, saying, "They are three to your one." Bourke, *On the Border with Crook*, 341.

Infantry, arrived on July 12. Each had a message from Terry to Crook sewed in his clothing, first-hand information concerning the fate of the Seventh Cavalry. The next day Colonel Chambers, with seven infantry companies and the wagon train, arrived from Fort Fetterman. With information, reinforcements, and supplies, Crook was ready to move.

Sheridan, however, had advised that nothing be done until the arrival of General Wesley Merritt and his command. Unfortunately for Crook's peace of mind, Merritt was busy fighting some 800 Cheyennes who had suddenly left Red Cloud agency to join the hostiles in the field. This fight, known as the Battle of War Bonnet Creek, drove the Indians back to the agency and established a landmark in the reputation of "Buffalo Bill" Cody, Merritt's chief scout.

While waiting for Merritt, Crook sent his Indians to discover more of the whereabouts and disposition of the Sioux and Cheyennes, their armament and numbers. The scouts reported the Indians moving northeast, toward Powder River. Meanwhile, another group of Shoshones and Utes joined the command.

Finally, on August 3, fifty-six days after the Rosebud fight, Merritt arrived with ten companies of the Fifth Cavalry and seventy-six recruits. Among Merritt's officers was the prolific source of army fiction, Lieutenant Charles King, who later exploited his adventures in *Campaigning with Crook*. The combined command now numbered about 2,000 men and 160 wagons.

Such a large and relatively immobile command was not Crook's style. He knew that the Indians would never be overtaken when wagons set the pace, and therefore ordered all impedimenta left behind with the wagon train. Each soldier was to strip himself of all except the most necessary items—tin cup, frying pan, coffee pot, tin platter, spoon, carving knife, and bags for sugar, coffee, bacon, and bread. Extra rations and ammunition were carried by pack mule.

Lightly equipped, Crook hoped to be able to overtake the Indians and deal them a decisive blow. It was to be a nutcracker operation: the hostiles between Terry and Crook. The General hoped that the Custer fight had given the Indians a feeling of security and power, and that they would make a stand. If they did, they would be destroyed.[17]

19. *I saw men cry like children*

THE SOUTHERN COLUMN of the Yellowstone Expedition now commenced its fifty-two-day "horse-meat march," which, with the exception of a single battle, failed to reach the Indians and only indirectly brought about the distintegration of the hostile host. The march failed in its immediate purpose of squeezing the Indians between the two columns, for Terry and Crook met without further opposition. The Indians had separated, one column moving toward the Black Hills and the other heading for Canada.

The saga of the march of Crook's column has been told in detail by three eyewitnesses, Bourke, Finerty, and King. Lieutenant Walter S. Schuyler, who was attached to Headquarters as aide to the General, also endured the march, and wrote a letter to his father on November 1, 1876, from Fort Laramie, in which he described his experiences:

"Dear Father,

"I want to give you some idea of our operations of the past summer, and think that a concise description of the most important incidents will be more interesting than a daily journal.

"We marched from Goose Creek on the morning of August 5th. Our wagon train with all our baggage was ordered to encamp at the forks of the creek to await our return, or orders to meet us at some designated point. Leaving camp in three columns we moved north-east to Prairie Dog Creek, and then to its junction with Tongue River, the scene of the attack on General Crook's camp June 18th, bivouacking on the river some miles below.

"By moderate marches we moved down Tongue River across to Rosebud Creek, and down that stream to within thirty miles of

[17] Letter from Walter S. Schuyler to his mother, dated July 16, 1876, from "Camp on branch of Goose Creek, Wyoming Territory."

the Yellowstone. Here we met General Terry's column moving up from its steamboats.[1] We caused some consternation among them, as their scouts, seeing our dust, mistook us for the Sioux moving to the attack. We camped together that night, and then marched together to where the Indian trail turned south from Powder River.

"One day, as we were moving up a small stream called Four Horn Creek, the command was marching in four columns. Just before going into camp, the Headquarters came up onto a bluff from which we could overlook the whole valley. As the sun came out with unusual brilliancy for a few moments, the aspect was grand.

"The advancing columns of horse and foot with the glistening equipments and the bright colored flags which marked the head of the different regiments, the long train of pack mules in the center, and the squads of Indian scouts with their parti-colored dress scattered over the hills combined to make a picture calculated to excite a soldier's enthusiasm.

"After going into camp, the Ree scouts of General Terry's command favored us with a "pony dance." A few cattle had been driven along for issue, and on this day the last of them were killed. Our Shoshones consequently had a feast. The Rees had been invited, and about sundown we were amused to see them coming across the creek, mounted, in perfect line, and all singing in chorus.

"The line advanced slowly to the center of the Shoshone camp, riding down every obstacle, trampling over blankets, brush huts, saddles, and everything that happened to be in their path. The Shoshones took up the chorus until the Rees had come to a halt, when the latter broke ranks with a whoop, turned their ponies out to graze, and immediately fell to work devouring the meat that had already been roasted on the fires.

"Some time ago, shortly before this war, the Indians at Standing Rock agency treated the commander of the garrison to one of these pony dances. Setting at defiance the feeble force of the two companies of Infantry, they rode over his tents and nearly destroyed his camp.

"From time to time we came across beds of lignite, which are

[1] Generals Terry and Crook met on August 11 and arrived at the Yellowstone on August 17. The size of the combined commands was about 4,000, including the Indian allies.

numerous in this country. Many of them are burning, and in places make traveling dangerous by reason of the liability of the earth to cave in, the fire having left cavities extending far underground. There is a large bed of this lignite near the mouth of Little Powder River which the Indians say has been burning for forty-five years. Occasionally we would be deceived by such fires, seeing the smokes at a distance, and thinking them made by Indians.

"After some pretty disagreeable marching we arrived at the Yellowstone River, camping just north of the mouth of Powder River. The Headquarters, of which I was an adjunct, occupied the only clump of trees in sight. The rest of the command stretched for two miles up the sandy bank of the stream, which here flows through a broad valley, with no bluffs to shelter from the high winds of that region.

"The order of march prohibited any officer or man from carrying baggage except such as could be packed on the saddle. Each one, therefore, had but one blanket, one saddle blanket, one overcoat and one rubber blanket. We at Headquarters fared like the rest, except that someone found on the march an old piece of canvas which we managed to take along.

"In the field one eats only to live, and we had for rations coffee, which each prepared in his cup, sugar, bacon and hardtack. We had in our mess eight individuals, including the General, who can live on a very small amount of food and sleep.

"Well, we went into camp under the trees, that is, each threw his possessions down on the smoothest spot he could find, and turned his horse loose to graze. As we had made a long, hot march of thirteen days without any change of clothing or chance to bathe, the river, muddy as it was, proved very refreshing. One day General Terry, whose command was camped about two miles below, came up to see the General, and found him with several of his staff serenely seated in the water, washing their only set of garments.

"For three days we had pleasant weather, and then came the rain and wind. We first made a sort of tent with our canvas and some brush, and piled ourselves up in that. About midnight the storm increased to a hurricane, and tore our tent away. We slept in several inches of water for the rest of the night—slept—except when the wind would lick our blankets up and make us stir to secure them.

"In the morning we cooked our breakfast as well as we could in the rain, and spent the day in standing around the fire, trying in vain to dry our clothes. Then came the weary night again! Bourke and myself half dried our blankets over the fire, and made our couch as downy as possible by pulling grass and putting it under the rubber blanket which constituted the lower stratum of our formation. We had another rubber over us, and thought that we should be happy, but the top one drained into the lower, and formed a beautifully watertight bowl in which we lay in soak.

"The next night we passed in sitting around the fire in utter gloom and discomfort. Occasionally somebody essayed a joke, but the best were passed over in silence. Under such circumstances no one seems given to hilarity, at least until one gets sufficiently miserable to be desperate and reckless.

"After remaining on the river for seven days we marched up the Powder in the mud and continued the pursuit of the Indians who had gone south.

"Our Shoshone Indians amused us greatly on the Yellowstone by their admiring interest in the steamboats, they never having seen any before. Whenever the supply boat, the *Far West*, approached our camp, they lined the bank, and continued to gaze and wonder until she was out of sight, when they would return to their camp to reopen the discussion of the new sensation.[2]

"From the Powder to Heart River we passed over a very interesting country of diversified character. Near Beaver Creek we made one camp which deserves notice. We were in some sharp bluffs, bivouacking on the slopes and summits to avoid the damp ground. The grass was very thick and fine, and the camp with its surroundings a fair picture. We, the Headquarters, were on the top of a knoll, protected from the wind by a ridge that overlooked us from the east. At our feet was camped the Infantry, in column, and on either flank stretched the Cavalry, some on the ridges, and

[2] The Utes and Shoshones, disgusted with the lack of action and success in the campaign, left Crook's command on August 20. On the twenty-third the two commands separated. Terry went north of the Yellowstone, and Crook followed the broad Sioux trail south and east in the general direction of Sully's trail of 1864.

Geronimo, Chiricahua Apache

Geronimo and his band, with escort, leaving Fort Bowie for Bowie
Station en route to exile in Florida, 1886

some in the little valleys between the latter. Directly in front of us was a gap in the hills through which we could overlook the country that we had passed over during the two preceding days.

"Two days later we reached the 'Little Missouri,' a shallow, muddy stream, but well timbered. We made our camp in a flat, where the stream bent around, so as to enclose a park of circular shape. The camp was extended along the timber, so as to give the horses shelter should the rainy day terminate in a cold night; and after dark the circle of campfires nearly three-fourths of a mile in diameter gave a very pretty effect.

"From this point to Heart River we occasionally saw small parties of Indians, who succeeded, however, in eluding us.

"We left Heart River one morning with the sun dimly glaring at us out of a dismal sky, and started on a march of two hundred miles to the Black Hills, to relieve the settlements which were believed to be the objective point of the Indians. We had only rations enough for two and one-half days, and our party set the example of living on half allowances.[3]

"The first night, after a very long march, we had to encamp on a pond of white, bitter water, where there was not a bit of wood large enough to make a toothpick,—not even sage brush, which is ordinarily so abundant. Take away coffee, and our rations amounted to nothing, for a soldier will give up everything else before that. With the exception of ourselves, the army went supperless to bed. As for us, we clubbed together and gathered grass in considerable quantities, twisted it into little bundles, then digging a little hole in the ground, set our cups around its edge, lit some grass in the midst, and fed the fire with the little bundles until the water boiled. It is simple enough, but takes patient labor.

"In the morning we repeated the operation, and set out at sunrise, everyone confident of getting wood in a short march. We advanced over thirty miles, and camped on a stream of beautiful

[3] On September 6 Crook still had the choice of going toward Fort Lincoln at Bismarck, or to Glendive on the Yellowstone, either place closer than the Black Hills, where he decided to go. Ree scouts were sent to Fort Laramie with messages to Sheridan, asking for supplies.

The next day Lieutenant Bubb, with the pack mules under Tom Moore and an escort of 150 men under Captain Anson Mills, with Frank Gruard as guide, was sent ahead to Deadwood to hurry supplies. These men were equipped with the best horses left to the command.

water, but where even the grass was scant, and again not a sign of fuel. During the afternoon it rained, and so the grass would not burn. The surgeon had a little keg (one gallon) which had been filled with whisky some time before, so that the staves were soaked with alcohol. With this we cooked our supper. Still the army had nothing.

"For breakfast—water and tightened belts. Then came another long march in rain and mud, but that night we had a little wood, enough for cooking, but not enough to dry our blankets.

"Next morning, the advance, going by forced marches for rations, struck the camp of American Horse, and captured the village, sending back for reinforcements. We got up about 10 A.M., and found that there had fallen into our hands one hundred ponies, and 5,000 pounds of dried meat and fruits, and much other plunder.

"This was a godsend, as we had already been obliged to eat some of our horses, the rain having ruined nearly all of our scanty stocks of rations. In the afternoon the Indians were reinforced, and attacked us, hoping to recover their village, but their property was already disposed of, and we had a very pretty fight until dark, the affair being resumed at daylight.

"From this point we lived for two days on the captured meat, and for five days on the ponies. And let me tell you that fat colts are ever so much better eating than beef, though one does not like to see them killed, nor does one like to see the shanks and hoofs left on the haunches. To us who have to depend on them so much, it seems like murder to kill horses.

"I have told you what *I* experienced on this march, but you can gather from that no realization of the suffering of the men, particularly the Infantry. I have seen men become so exhausted that they were actually insane, but there was no way of carrying them except for some mounted officer or man to give them his own horse, which was done constantly. I saw men who were very plucky sit down and cry like children because they could not hold out. When there came a chance to fight, however, everyone was mad enough to fight well.

"I have never seen such a sight as was presented in the captured village, when 2,000 men were scattered through it in orderless confusion, picking up buffalo robes and other articles, and burning the lodges, while at the head of a gulch a hundred yards away a circle of men were held at bay by a handful of Indians in a hole, and off to the south the pickets were engaged.

"Occasionally a bullet would come in among us, but no one appeared to mind it much, though we were horrified for a moment when White, a scout, was heard to wail out, 'My God, I've got it,' and seen to fall, shot through the heart.[4] And again a few minutes later, when, a rush having been made at the Indians by the rapidly increasing forces at the gulch, two soldiers were carried back wounded.

"But there was a rush when we saw the enemy crossing in force, and the sudden return to discipline and order was wonderful. The alarm was given just in time, too, for they came near getting some of our horses. We were attacked on all sides at once, the Indians being very quick in movement, and being much better mounted than ourselves (our horses at this time could travel only with difficulty, being worn out).

"In carrying orders about the field I had a very good view of the whole thing. General Crook's Headquarters were on a knoll in the center of our camp, whence we could overlook the whole field, and the troops were deployed in a skirmish line nearly in a circle.

"We lost some men, both killed and wounded, and one officer had his leg amputated that night.[5] As for myself, my duties did not

[4] This scout was the well-known "Buffalo Chips" White, friend and imitator of "Buffalo Bill" Cody. White had been Cody's shadow since 1871; Finerty says his name was Charles, King refers to him as Jim. The real Buffalo Bill had left the expedition and gone back East to fill theatrical engagements.

[5] Shortly after the fighting commenced at Slim Buttes on September 9, Lieutenant A. H. Von Leuttwitz was struck in the knee by a ball. His leg had to be amputated above the knee, and his army career was over.

On October 3 he wrote to the General from Crook City:

"General, I am sorry to leave the army, and especially to be deprived of the pleasure of serving under such an able and energetic officer as yourself. I have been a soldier since my seventeenth year, having been graduated at the Artillery and Engineer school of Berlin. Now it is all over.

"Your march from Heart River to the Hills showed both your generalship and your duty as a true soldier. Seeing a large Indian trail going south toward your department, you considered it your duty to follow it and protect your wards. You feared neither hardships nor privations, but shared equally with us.

"Nobody can blame you that our campaign was not crowned with complete success. Our forces were too small. The area of country passed over by your command extends from the North Platte to the Yellowstone, and from

happen to lead me into any dangerous places. I was kept pretty busy carrying orders to the battalion commanders, and in watching to see if anything went wrong. The prisoners captured in the afternoon (in the hole I spoke of) were under guard near the pack mules.

"It wasn't a very great fight, but hurt the Indians considerably. In the morning, when we broke camp, they attacked our rear guard, but only wounded three men, whereas we killed four of them. They now acknowledged to have lost ten men killed in the two days action.[6]

"Many of the Cavalrymen were on foot, their horses having died or given out, and all our animals had to be eased as much as possible by the riders dismounting and walking from time to time. Occasionally we would have incidents sufficiently comical to put us all in a good humor. For instance, one day we saw a Cavalry-

the Big Horn to the Little Missouri—an area more than twice the size of France. Eight hundred thousand Prussians could not successfully occupy France in 1870. How could two thousand men be expected to control twice as large a country?" *Army and Navy Journal*, Vol. XIV, No. 13 (November 4, 1876), 198.

[6] The advance command under Anson Mills attacked the Indian camp near Slim Buttes about 3 A.M., September 9. The camp was attacked from two sides after Lieutenant Schwatka had driven most of the Indian ponies out of the village. The Indians were driven out of their tepees and forced to take refuge among the rocks on the other side of the river and in a ravine near the camp.

The Indians had sent to the camp of Crazy Horse a few miles away for reinforcements, which arrived about the same time as Crook's main command, between 11 and 12 A.M. Crook deployed his men in a huge circle and kept the Indians at bay while the cavalry charged and drove the hostiles farther from the captured camp.

Among the effects in the village were found saddles and other equipment, including personal clothing which had belonged to Custer's men of the Seventh Cavalry. There was no doubt that these Indians, despite their good-conduct certificates, signed by Agent Howard of the Spotted Tail agency, had participated in that massacre.

American Horse, Sioux chief, was among those killed. He was shot through the intestines, and died after much suffering, uncomplaining to the end.

The advance party set out for the settlements after the battle, and arrived in Deadwood late the next night. Bourke, *On the Border with Crook*, Chaps. XX–XXI; John F. Finerty, *War Path and Bivouac*, Chaps. XVI–XXI; Charles King, *Campaigning with Crook*, Chaps. V–XVI; Anson Mills, *My Story*, 170–74.

man who, after getting his weak horse along as far as he could, unsaddled him, shot him, cut out the tenderest steak he could find, built a fire, and philosophically sat down to a hearty meal. This finished, he shouldered his carbine and went on, refreshed.

"The infantry made a standing joke of the boast that if we only marched far enough they would eat all the cavalry horses.

"At last, after the most fearful march of all through mud so thick and sticky that whenever one raised a foot he brought up with it about ten pounds of clay, a march prolonged far into the night, during the last portion of which the command got scattered, and some of the wounded were thrown out of the mule litters by the stumbling and jumping of the animals, the Belle Fourche of the Cheyenne River was reached, and rations arrived from Dead-wood City.[7] The cheer that went up when the herd of beef cattle came in sight was magnificent. The wagons with flour and vege-tables arrived soon after, accompanied by delegations from the towns in the Hills who came out to welcome the army that had come through so much hardship to save them from massacre.

"Everyone ate as though he never expected to see another meal, and indeed it was difficult to realize that such would not be the case. Double rations were issued, and the camp for the first time in many days rang with laughter and merriment.

"I myself was spared the last march—by a worse one. Three companies under Major Upham were sent on a fresh trail of In-dians going toward the hills from the camp previous to that on the Belle Fourche. I accompanied this detachment as a volunteer. After marching two days in mud and rain, we arrived with ex-hausted horses on the Belle Fourche about twelve miles below the main camp. Here we found plenty of wood, and made ourselves comfortable for the night. Our men had had nothing to eat for over twenty four hours, while the officers had made the first day's supply of horse meat last up to this night.

"About three o'clock in the morning I was awakened by hear-ing the howling of coyotes. I listened attentively, and concluded

[7] The final terrible march, resulting in the loss of seventy horses, was made on September 12, according to Finerty. The supplies arrived the fol-lowing day. Among the delegates from Deadwood was an enterprising pho-tographer who took pictures on the spot, developing them in his portable darkroom.

that it was not coyotes, but a tolerably good imitation. Suddenly there came the call of the night owl from below the camp. This was repeated twice, and then all was quiet again. I had been taught these signals by my Indians in Arizona, and immediately woke Major Upham and told him that there were Indians about the camp. He gave orders to double the guard over the horses and to be on the alert.

"At daybreak, when camp was awakened, some of the men wanted to go out hunting. Major Upham at first refused to allow them to go, but was at length persuaded by some of the officers to give the desired permission. The men commenced shooting at rabbits around the camp, and a good many shots were fired up and down the river. On leaving camp we discovered quite accidentally that one of our hunters had been killed and scalped about half a mile beyond our picket, the scene having been hidden from their sight by a slight rise in the ground.

"It seems that five Indians had been watching us all night, hoping to get a chance to steal horses. Seeing this man start out, they had waited for him behind the point of a bluff, and killed him and his horse as he rode toward them. They had taken his saddle, arms and scalp, and had put two crossed gashes in his breast, their mark for a brave man. The empty cartridge shells showed that he had fired two shots before he died. We caught sight of the Indians as they went over a hill about three miles on the other side of the river. After burying the soldier where he fell, we moved on, and reached the main command in the afternoon.

"There are three fruits or berries quite common in this country: the wild plum, which is very fine, the small black cherry and the buffalo berry. The latter is very like a red currant, but more acid. All three grow on bushy trees which seldom attain a height greater than ten feet and form a very close thicket of 'chaparral.'

"While we were on short rations we sometimes ran across patches of these berries, and they, being devoured by everyone with great avidity, undoubtedly did much to prevent scurvy. One day the whole staff, including the General, stampeded into a plum patch, going down on our hands and knees to pick up the ripe fruit that the wind had shaken off.

"The men suffered on the trip more than the officers for the reason that they were so very improvident, it being impossible to impress them with the importance of saving their rations. Then, many of them lost their horses, mostly through inattention. In these campaigns a man has to nurse his horse very carefully, attending to his food and water, seeing that he is always put on good grass. It seems impossible to make some men understand this. Sometimes an hour on good grass will save a horse that if left to stand hungry would give out.

"Such is in brief the history of the closing operations of the Big Horn and Yellowstone Expedition, and of the campaign which commenced so disastrously with the destruction of Custer and his command on the Little Big Horn.

"It has been a march through the heart of the enemy's country, almost wholly unexplored by white men, and thoroughly misunderstood by them, a march which has tried men's souls as well as their constitutions, a march which will live in our history as the hardest ever undertaken by our army, and on which the privation and hardship were equalled only by the astonishing health of the command while accomplishing it.

"Our country, and perhaps the world, can afford no school for the officer and soldier equal to this, and those who have gone through it may congratulate themselves that they have had the opportunity. Upon the older men it has been hard, indeed, for out of fifty-two days we had twenty-six days of rain, the exposure to which has caused many to suffer with rheumatism and kindred ails.

"The success of the Expedition, though at first consideration apparently small, has in reality been great, for a new and fine country has been explored, and the Sioux, though having lost but one small village, have been so kept on the move that they have been unable to lay up the stores of meat, etc., which will be indispensable to them this winter.

"It was very unfortunate that our Indian allies became disgusted with the delay at the Yellowstone, and deserted us at that point, as we could have used them to good advantage at 'Slim Buttes.'

"Not only will the knowledge gained of the country be useful in a military sense, but also in the cause of emigration. The southern portion of Montana and the northwestern part of Dakota afford as fine grazing as can be found, and in addition it has been proved that the land is well fitted for agriculture, for on the Little Missouri we fed our horses on corn which had sprung up from the seed dropped by Terry's wagon train in May and had attained the height of four or more feet.

"And this is only a small section of the country, the gates of which have been locked to civilization on the plea that it was the hunting ground of the savage.

Yours very truly,
Walter S. Schuyler"[8]

Lieutenant Schuyler's estimate of the value of the Yellowstone Expedition proved justified. The hostiles, ruthlessly and doggedly pursued by the General, deprived of every opportunity to gather food for the winter, and in constant danger of surprise by the soldiers, had scattered into small bands and were attempting to return to the reservations. As they straggled in, they were disarmed and their horses taken from them.

General Crook wanted to continue the Yellowstone Expedition with the Black Hills as a base. "Our next objective point," he stated, "is Crazy Horse. He should be followed up and struck as soon as possible. There should be no stopping for this or that thing. The Indians cannot stand a continuous campaign. I cannot tell whether we can go on yet. That depends on our getting the things we want. The best time to strike the Indians is in the winter. They cannot remain together in large bodies at that season. The necessities of subsistence compel them to separate, and then is the time to throw a large force on each band, and crush them all in detail."[9]

However, Sheridan decided to disband the Yellowstone Expedition and organize a new one for the winter campaign. Crook was called in to the agency at Robinson to assist in the gathering of the hostiles. His influence and assurance were necessary for the successful conclusion of that phase of the campaign at that end.

On October 24, 1876, the Sioux bands under Red Cloud and Red Leaf were surrounded and disarmed at Camp Robinson, and the purpose of the Yellowstone Expedition had been largely accomplished.

[8] From the Schuyler papers in the Huntington Library.
[9] *Army and Navy Journal*, Vol. XIV, No. 11 (October 21, 1876), 166.

20. *It is a measure of humanity*

ONE VICTORY yet remained to be won. Crazy Horse was still hostile, still refusing to get on the "white man's island." There were other bands out, too. Dull Knife and his Cheyennes preferred their freedom to the reservation. To gather in these hostiles, the Powder River Expedition was organized on November 4. There were to be no mistakes this time. The weaknesses of the late campaign were considered, and some new tricks were put into the bag.

"The system of moving without a wagon train is the only proper one for a campaign of this character," said the General. "A mule train can go anywhere, there is no rear to protect at the cost of largely reducing your fighting force. Our train was not large enough. That will be remedied. We were unable to carry enough provisions to give us time to scout the country when we cut loose from our base. We had to make straight for another base as soon as we left the last, because our rations were not sufficient to allow us to wait on the way and search the country.

"Then, we were almost without guides or scouts. I had no man I could depend on except Frank Gruard, and he could not do all the work. The others were well enough, but they did not know the country, and could not be got to go out any distance. If we had had Indians with us from the Yellowstone here, we should not have had such trouble in crossing the country. I always try to get Indian scouts, because with them scouting is the business of their lives. They learn all the signs of a trail as a child learns the alphabet; it becomes an instinct. With a white man the knowledge is acquired in after life.

"You cannot always be sure an Indian is telling the truth; he may lie to you; so will the white man. But if you make it to the Indian's interest to tell the truth, you get correct information; a white man will lie intentionally, and mislead you unintentionally."[1]

Using Indians to fight Indians was nothing new to the General. The principle had been followed with success against the Apaches,

[1] *Army and Navy Journal*, Vol. XIV, No. 11 (October 21, 1876), 166.

and there was no reason why it should not work with the Sioux and Cheyennes. The moral effect, he believed, would be great, and the "civilizing" effect on the enlisted Indian beneficial. It would, he said, "break up tribal solidarity" and transform the Indians into "docile inhabitants of the reservation."

"As a soldier the Indian wears the uniform, draws pay and rations, and is in all respects on equal footing with the white man. It demonstrates to his simple mind in the most positive manner that we have no prejudice against him on account of his race, and that while he behaves himself he will be treated the same as a white man. Returning to his tribe after this service, he is enabled to see beyond the old superstition that has governed his people, and thinks and decides for himself. It is a measure of humanity, and commends itself to us, as it shortens the war, and saves the lives of both white men and Indians."[2]

Crook spoke in defense of a principle which he firmly upheld, though it was under attack from many quarters as poor military tactics and inhumane, besides. The Yellowstone Expedition had been obliged to recruit from the Ute, Shoshone, and Ree tribes, instead of from the reservation Sioux and Cheyennes, because of opposition from the chiefs and the Indian Bureau. Now, however, these reservations had been placed under the control of the War Department, and Crook seized the opportunity to enlist scouts and warriors.

The Powder River Expedition established its headquarters near Old Fort Reno,[3] Wyoming Territory, and moved out to the attack on November 19. On the twenty-first, Ranald Mackenzie, veteran Indian fighter, with his cavalry and Indian scouts was detached up the North Fork of the Powder, where, four days later, they completely routed the Cheyennes under Dull Knife. The hostiles now

[2] National Archives, Commanding General, Department of the Platte to Adjutant General, Military Division of the Missouri, October 30, 1876.

[3] Fort Reno, Wyoming Territory, was established on August 14, 1865, by troops under the command of General Patrick E. Connor. The post, first named Fort Connor, was renamed Fort Reno in November, 1865, in honor of General Jesse L. Reno.

Built for the protection of the Powder River country against Indians, the post was situated on that river, 225 miles from Cheyenne, 90 miles from Fort Fetterman, and 65 from Fort Phil Kearney. With these other forts, it was abandoned under provisions of the Sioux treaty of 1868, and was immediately burned by the Indians. Grace R. Hebard, *The Bozeman Trail*, II, 122–35.

knew that the campaign was to continue, even through the winter. No rest could be expected except at the agencies. Even their own people had come out to fight them.[4]

There were only two things they could do—fight to the death or surrender and come in to the reservations. They decided to come in.

The arrival of the hostile bands meant a busy spring for the General. "Three Stars," as the Indians called him, smoothed the path for surrender. The bands came in making a brave show; at least their pride was left to them. The chiefs knew of Crook's dealings with the southern and northern tribes and knew that his tongue was straight. When he promised that he would try to get them the reservations they wanted and would see to it that they would not be punished for what had happened in the past, they believed him.[5]

Spotted Tail, Sioux chief, was the talker. Through him Three Stars sent the welcome message to the waiting hostiles. To Crazy Horse, in particular, the news was sent. He was the greatest of the fighting spirits. If he would lead the way and come peacefully to the reservation, a new campaign would be unnecessary.

The peace talkers sent to Crazy Horse were told that the Indians would be given lands in their own country and that the fights of last year would not be remembered. Their guns and horses, however, would be taken away, at least for a time.

Above all things, Crook wanted to bring in the hostiles without another campaign. Sheridan had urged that all fighting in Indian country should be pushed, for it would be necessary to limit the size of the army in July.[6] He wanted another double-winged

---

[4] John G. Bourke, *Mackenzie's Last Fight with the Cheyennes*, 19.

[5] The history of the surrender of the Sioux and the betrayal of Crazy Horse as outlined here is based largely on Mari Sandoz' *Crazy Horse*, which is by all odds the best treatment of the subject, though the literature on it is voluminous and controversial.

[6] "General Sherman writes me to push things in the Indian country as much as possible before the first day of July, as at that date we will be obliged to reduce the army 2,500 men. If you need any absent officers heretofore kept east by favor, now is your time to get them, as he promises to order them out at once." National Archives, Commanding General, Division of the Missouri to Commanding General, Department of the Platte, March 16, 1877. A month later the suggestion was withdrawn after Crook had reported his confidence that the Indians would come in without another fight.

expedition against the hostiles, with Crook at one end and Miles, in camp at Fort Keogh,[7] on the other.[8] But the General was firm. He felt that a peace offer with a promise of a reservation in their own country would bring in the remaining hostiles.

All spring Crook waited. The people back East were clamoring for a fight. Terms to the Indians, they felt, amounted to the same thing as surrender.[9] General Miles, too, felt that Crook was "stealing" his Indians. He wanted them to surrender to him.

One by one the bands came in, and at last Crazy Horse himself began to move toward the reservation. On May 6 he and his entire following surrendered to Three Stars. The war was over.

Now that the Indians were back on the reservations, and disarmed, the government was faced with the problem of their disposal—which meant their removal. It had been decided long before that the Sioux and Cheyennes could not be allowed to keep their hold on the Black Hills country. The discovery of gold meant that the land which had once seemed like a good place for Indians had now become a good place for white men. The results were inevitable.

In August, 1876, long before the Indians had given up, a commission headed by George W. Manypenny treated with the reservation Sioux for cession of the Black Hills country. The treaty was submitted to the chiefs only. Their people had nothing to say.

[7] Fort Keogh was situated on the right bank of the Yellowstone River, two miles above the mouth of the Tongue, in Custer County, Montana. In 1876 a camp was established at that point by General Terry and used as a base of supply and operations.

General Order No. 2, Headquarters Cantonement at the mouth of Tongue River (September 11, 1876), established a military reservation ten miles square, subject to War Department approval. On November 8, 1878, it was officially named Fort Keogh, in honor of Captain Miles Keogh, Seventh Cavalry, who was killed in the Battle of the Little Big Horn. Built in 1877, under the direction of General Miles, the post became the leading fort of the Territory. In 1907 it was occupied by caretakers only, and during World War I it was used as a quartermaster intermediate depot. In 1924 the property was transferred to the Interior Department. *Posts, Camps, and Stations File.*

[8] National Archives, Commanding General, Division of the Missouri to Commanding General, Department of the Platte, March 30, 1877.

[9] "Do the Indians who surrendered at Spotted Tail's agency belong there? And have they been disarmed and dismounted? The papers this morning make it look as if we had surrendered to them." National Archives, Commanding General, Division of the Missouri to Commanding General, Department of the Platte, April 17, 1877.

This itself was in direct violation of previous treaties which had said that the land could not be given away except by agreement of the people.

There were presents, however, coupled with threats, and there were promises of power, so the "friendly" chiefs signed away their land and agreed to move to a new land between the Missouri River and the northern boundary of Nebraska. In return, they were to receive rations, clothing, and other "advantages," while they, in turn, were to allow three roads to be built through the reservation to the Black Hills. The whites were in a hurry.[10]

This agreement had been made before the surrender of Crazy Horse. Yet General Crook had told the Chief that he would try to get his people a place to live in their old land, on the Tongue, near their hunting grounds, where they were at home. The General spent much time between Washington, Chicago, Omaha, and the agencies, trying to make good his promise. He failed. The Sioux were to be sent to the Missouri.

The Cheyennes, meanwhile, had been tricked into choosing the Indian Territory as their new home. The various bands under Standing Elk, Hog, Dull Knife, and Little Wolf were sent to Fort Reno, Indian Territory,[11] on the reservation with their cousins, the Southern Cheyennes. Later they were joined by others of their people who surrendered in the North.

The Indian Department, having decided what should be done, left the doing of it to the War Department. The task of sending the Sioux to their new reservation fell to General Crook. But the General had made a promise to Crazy Horse.

After his surrender, Crazy Horse gradually gained influence over the Sioux, even those who had stayed on the reservation during the fighting the summer before. It was he who had led them to their greatest victories, and now they seemed willing to follow

---

[10] Doane Robinson, *History of the Sioux Indians*, Chap. XLIII.

[11] Fort Reno, Indian Territory (Oklahoma), is on the south bank of the North Fork of the Canadian River, Canadian County. It was established in 1875, just outside the Cheyenne and Arapahoe reservation and named in honor of Jesse L. Reno, as was Old Fort Reno in Wyoming.

In 1907, the post was occupied by caretakers only, but in World War I it was used as a remount depot. *General Order No. 2*, War Department (1938), named the post Reno Quartermaster Depot. *Posts, Camps, and Stations File*.

him when and where he should lead. But the Chief was waiting for Crook to make good his promise of a reservation in the old country. Time passed, and no word came of the keeping of the promise. Crazy Horse became restless.

Spotted Tail and Red Cloud, too, were restless, but for other reasons. It appeared that they, who had done all they could to please the white man, were now being pushed out of the picture by this renegade who had come in so lately. If the General's promise was kept, Crazy Horse would be the important chief.

Reports of trouble began to come from the agency, and Crazy Horse was always mentioned as the troublemaker. Wagging tongues said that he planned to leave as soon as he got hold of ammunition and horses. Promise of a fall buffalo hunt was broken, because the whites feared that Crazy Horse would take the chance to break away.

News came of the flight of the Nez Percés under Chief Joseph. Crazy Horse was called to a council, and asked to bring his warriors to help fight the northern Indians. After much talk, he agreed, but his reply was twisted by Gruard to mean that he would fight until "all the whites were killed."

The soldiers and the jealous chiefs immediately filled the air with talk against Crazy Horse. But there were a few who knew what had happened, and when Crook came to the agency, they told him the story. The General started out to see the Chief, but on the way Woman's Dress hurried up to tell him that Crazy Horse plotted to kill the General if he should come. Crook turned around.

Soldiers and Indian scouts were sent to bring in Crazy Horse, but he, knowing what had happened, left the agency on September 3. He was soon brought back to Camp Robinson, suffering himself to be taken. On September 5, while resisting an attempt to place him in the guard house, Crazy Horse was stabbed to death. He was killed among his own people, and, some say, by his own people. The last obstacle to the removal of the Sioux had passed.

When Crazy Horse was killed, General Crook was on his way to Camp Brown[12] to lead troops in an expedition against the Nez

[12] Camp Brown was a post on the Shoshone Indian reservation in Wind River Valley, Wyoming. It was established on June 28, 1869, as Camp Augur, in honor of Brigadier General C. C. Augur, but changed to Camp Brown,

Percés. A telegram from Sheridan intercepted him and sent him back to Camp Robinson, where the Sioux troubles had reached a climax. By the time he reached the agency, Crazy Horse was dead.

The removal of the Indians now proceeded. A delegation of chiefs visited Washington to talk about the new reservation. Their big point was that they did not want to settle directly on the Missouri. It was, to them, too close to the white man's road, and unhealthful besides. General Crook supported them, objecting to their removal, trying still to keep his promise that they should have a place in their own country. The matter had long been decided, however, and the Indians were told that they would have to move, though not directly to the river.

Crook arrived at the agency on October 11. "I found part of the Indian supplies exhausted, and the remainder would be so at the end of the month. I also found that the transportation being provided by the Indian Department for the removal of the Indians would not possibly reach there in time, therefore prompt action was necessary. With the consent of higher authority I assisted the Indians by scraping together all the available transportation within reach, improvising many broken-down teams of cavalry horses. By much effort, (many of the Indians going on foot), and by their consenting to subsist mostly on beef during the march, I was finally able to get them off. Had I been required to send any additional troops with them, it would have been impossible for the move to have been made in time.

"I respectfully call attention to the fact that one of the promises made by the President was the positive assurance that they would not be required to go directly on the Missouri River."[13]

"Then came the packing up; ponies were saddled, tepee poles balanced on each side, and packs loaded by the squaws. Once in awhile you could see a buck or a brave holding a restive pony till

March 28, 1870, in honor of Captain F. H. Brown, Eighteenth Infantry, killed in the Fetterman massacre, December 21, 1866.

The post was originally intended to protect the Bannocks and Shoshones against the Sioux, Cheyennes, and other hostile tribes. In December, 1878, the post was renamed Washakie, after the old chief of the Shoshones. In 1899 the post was abandoned by United States troops, and control of the property was relinquished in 1909. *Posts, Camps, and Stations File.*

[13] National Archives, Commanding General, Department of the Platte to Commanding General, Division of the Missouri, December 6, 1877.

GENERAL GEORGE CROOK

the poles were put on each side of him, but no more. Their bundles were compactly put up in skin, and the usual framework over the poles where a papoose had to be carried.

"Rations were issued to them for ten days. Such as they could not carry will go in the supply train, all their rations for this purpose being carefully marked, 'Red Cloud,' 'Six Feathers,' etc., in the name of the chief of each band.

"Cattle on the hoof, some 15,000, were drawn along, and, strange to say, the best they have ever been issued. The reason given was, the contractors had not time to find bad ones, as no delay was allowed."[14]

Spotted Tail and his band settled at the old Ponca agency, and Red Cloud near the Missouri, close to the mouth of the Yellow Medicine. Neither band was satisfied with its location, and the following spring Red Cloud moved to the Pine Ridge agency, and Spotted Tail, with his people, to the Rosebud.

The General kept in touch with his Indians through their agents, and through his subordinates at the various posts. He made every effort to see that at least part of his promises were kept. In a letter to Young Man Afraid of His Horse, Little Big Man, White Bird, American Horse, The Man that Fights, Red Shirt, and Spider, chiefs of the Sioux Nation at Pine Ridge, Crook wrote:

"Lt. Clark has sent me the letter which he received from you at Fort Keogh at the mouth of the Tongue River. I am very glad to hear that you are well, and pleased to know that your hearts are good. I have been a friend to you and your people a long time, and have told the white man that you intended to live at peace with everybody. It makes my heart glad to hear from yourselves that this is so, and that I have spoken the truth about you.

"I tried very hard to get your reservation established at the mouth of Tongue River, as you wished, but I was not able to do it, and had much trouble in getting you sent back to the Missouri River to the place you now occupy.

"I will at all times be glad to help you all I can. You know that I am your friend, and friends must help each other. When I needed

14 *Army and Navy Journal*, Vol. XV, No. 14 (November 10, 1877), 218–19.

soldiers to preserve order on the reservation, and bring in the Indians whose hearts were bad, you helped me, and I have not forgotten you. The grievances of which you complain ought to be redressed by the Secretary of the Interior, as I cannot do much to assist you about them.

Your friend,
George Crook"[15]

21. All the tribes tell the same story

CONCLUSION of the Sioux War did not bring peace to the Department of the Platte. To the north the Bannocks were restless. By a treaty concluded in 1868 the Bannock Indians had removed to a reservation, and were promised a fair chance to live as they had in the past—off the country. This meant that they were to hold a reasonable portion of the "camas prairie," where grew the root which was their bread; but the white settlers paid little attention to the treaty and fattened their hogs on camas.

General Crook paid a visit to Fort Hall[1] in April, 1879, and reported the usual grievances. The Indians had not received the promised protection against white incursions, and the rations, clothing, and equipment due them by the treaty terms had not been issued. In June the Bannocks resorted to war, and swept through the Owyhee country into Oregon, killing as they went. Regular soldiers and Volunteers were sent after them, but no de-

---

[15] National Archives, Commanding General, Department of the Platte to Chiefs of the Sioux Nation, December 17, 1879.

[1] A post named Fort Hall was first established by Nathaniel J. Wyeth, fur trader, July 14, 1834. The post was built near the confluence of the Port Neuf and Snake rivers, and named after the oldest member of Wyeth's firm, Henry Hall. In 1836 the fort was sold to the Hudson's Bay Company, and flourished to 1854, when it was broken up.

The fort was an important way station on the Oregon Trail, being the last major stop before reaching the Columbia River. On May 27, 1870, a United States post named Fort Hall was established about twenty-five miles northeast of old Fort Hall, and fifteen miles from the Shoshone-Bannock agency. The post was relinquished to the Interior Department for school purposes on April 26, 1883. *Posts, Camps, and Stations File.*

cisive battles were fought. Gradually the Indians made their way back to the reservation.[2]

Archie McIntosh, Crook's old scout, heard of the outbreak and wrote the General a letter, offering his services to the new war. Archie knew that country from the old days, and wanted to get in the fight under his old friend, even though it meant leaving his ranch near Picket Post, Arizona.[3] He was assured, however, that the situation was not serious enough to require his services.

Crook believed that the Bannocks had reason enough to break out in violence: "In regard to the Bannocks, I was up there last spring, and found them in a desperate condition. I telegraphed, and the agent telegraphed for supplies, but word came that no appropriation had been made. They have never been half supplied.

"The agent has sent them off for half a year to enable them to pick up something to live on, but there is nothing for them in that country. The buffalo is all gone, and an Indian can't catch enough jack rabbits to subsist himself and his family, and then, there aren't enough jack rabbits to catch. What are they to do?

"Starvation is staring them in the face, and if they wait much longer, they will not be able to fight. They understand the situation, and fully appreciate what is before them.

"The encroachments upon the Camas prairies was the cause of the trouble. These prairies are their last source of subsistence. They are covered with water from April till June or July, and there is a sort of root which grows in them, under water, which is very much like a sweet potato. A squaw can gather several bushels a day of them. Then they dig a hole and build a fire in it. After it is thoroughly heated, the roots are put in and baked, and when they are taken out they are very sweet and nice.

"This root is their main source of food supply. I do not wonder, and you will not either that when these Indians see their wives and children starving, and their last source of supplies cut off, they go to war. And then we are sent out to kill them. It is an outrage.

"All the tribes tell the same story. They are surrounded on all sides, the game is destroyed or driven away; they are left to starve,

[2] George F. Brimlow, *The Bannock Indian War of 1878.*
[3] National Archives, No. 2598, Department of the Platte, July 3, 1878.

and there remains but one thing for them to do—fight while they can. Some people think the Indians do not understand these things, but they do, and fully appreciate the circumstances in which they are placed."[4]

The Cheyennes, too, began to understand. Most of them had been sent to Indian Territory in 1877. They had not found it a good place to live. Some gave up the struggle and joined the bands of their southern relatives on the reservations. Others, however, decided to march back north.

The complaints of the Cheyennes were many, and probably justified. They were suffering from malaria, their relatives did not welcome them, and the government had not kept its promises about rations, clothing, and equipment. Most of all, they did not like this new land where there were no buffalo and the ground itself seemed dead.

Dull Knife, Wild Hog, Little Wolf, and other chiefs kept alive the memories of their people about the land in the North which had once been theirs. The Sioux, even though beaten, were still in the North, perhaps not in the best country, but some of them, under Sitting Bull, had even managed to go far enough so that the soldiers could not follow them. Even some of the Cheyennes were still not captured. Perhaps it would be possible to join them.

During the night of September 9, 1878, the Cheyennes started back. Headed by the warriors of the band under Little Wolf, they fled north over 500 miles, through Kansas and into Nebraska. Time after time they beat off attacks by soldiers who were hastily sent after them from posts in every direction.

When the fugitives needed food, they killed cattle; when they needed transportation, they stole horses. If their march was impeded by settlers, they murdered them. It seemed as though the fury of a generation was let loose in a final desperate drive to nowhere.

Troops in the Department of the Platte were busy rounding up stray hostiles in the north of the department, and were not prepared for the storm moving up from the south. All available units were stationed along the Union Pacific Railway, but the Indians

[4] *Army and Navy Journal*, Vol. XV, No. 47 (June 29, 1878), 758.

crossed this danger line without being intercepted. They then split into two bands, one under Little Wolf, mostly warriors, and the rest under Hog and Dull Knife—both bands going into the Sand Hills of Nebraska.

On October 23, during a heavy snowstorm, the Cheyennes under Dull Knife suddenly came face to face with two companies of cavalry under Captain J. B. Johnson. Not being prepared for a fight, the Indians surrendered. Besides, they were now near the country where they wanted to stay and hoped that if they gave themselves up, they would be permitted to remain.

Captain Johnson, also, was taken by surprise. He was unprepared for the capture, and made every effort to keep the Indians quiet. He suggested that they choose where they should be taken, Camp Robinson or Camp Sheridan.[5] For two days the fugitives deliberated, argued, and threatened. Meanwhile, more and more troops arrived, and the scene became tense. When enough forces had been assembled, Captain Johnson ordered the Indians to move toward Camp Robinson. They were searched for weapons and disarmed, at least partially. The captives then proceeded slowly toward the post, arriving on the evening of October 25.[6]

There were 149 Indians in Dull Knife's band—men, women and children. They were quartered in an unused barracks and left to await word concerning their disposal. So far as they were concerned, there was only one answer—they would not go south. "We

[5] Fort Sheridan, Wyoming Territory, was on the east branch of the west fork of Beaver Creek, twelve miles above its mouth. In 1874, when the Spotted Tail agency was removed from its old site, troops accompanying the move established a camp about half a mile from the agency, arriving on September 8, 1874. The site was maintained as Camp Sheridan until Spotted Tail's band went to Pine Ridge in May, 1881, when the site was abandoned. *Posts, Camps, and Stations File.*

Camp Robinson, Nebraska, was established in March, 1874, near the Red Cloud agency, just south of the Great Sioux reservation of 1869. It was named in honor of First Lieutenant Levi H. Robinson, who was killed on Cottonwood Creek near Fort Laramie, February 9, 1874. Now three miles from Crawford, Nebraska, the post is designated as a quartermaster depot. War Department, *Military Reservations, Nebraska,* 10.

[6] Based on the report of a board of officers convened by the commanding general, Department of the Platte "To examine into and report on the facts attending the arrest, confinement, disarmament, escape, and recapture of a number of Cheyenne Indians, recently at and in the vicinity of Fort Robinson, Nebraska."

will not go there to live. That is not a healthful country, and if we should stay there we would all die. We do not wish to go back there, and we will not go," Dull Knife said. "You may kill me here; but you cannot make me go back."[7]

Behind the Cheyennes lay the Indian Territory which they hated, and, more to be feared, a fresh trail of blood for which they were accountable. Their only hope of escaping such an accounting was to hold out for a place in their old land.

For seventy days the captives lived quietly in the barracks at Camp Robinson, while General Crook showered the Indian Bureau with requests and recommendations concerning their disposal. Finally, in midwinter, with temperatures at Camp Robinson ranging from zero to forty below, the Indian Bureau made up its mind. The captives were told that they would have to go back to Indian Territory. The Cheyennes were still unwilling, so their rations were cut off, and water was withheld from them. The commanding officer at the post, Captain Wessels, was determined to starve his captives into submission.

The result of Wessels' decision was an outbreak. On the night of January 10, 1879, after warning their captors of what they intended to do, the Cheyennes escaped from the barracks and fled across the White River to the hills beyond. Their flight was covered by rifle fire from warriors who remained behind, dying so that others might escape. These rifles, with ammunition, had been concealed during the period of imprisonment, though searches had been made and all weapons found had been taken away.

Escape was hopeless. Eleven soldiers were killed and nine wounded in the next few days during attempts to retake the Indians. The Cheyennes suffered sixty-four killed before the remaining seventy-eight gave themselves up. Seven were unaccounted for. "These last seven," reads the report, "are women and children, and are supposed to have died on the bluffs."

"Among these Cheyenne Indians," wrote the General, "were some of the bravest and most efficient of the auxiliaries who had acted under General Mackenzie and myself in the campaign against the hostile Sioux in 1876 and 1877, and I still preserve a grateful

[7] George B. Grinnell, *The Fighting Cheyennes*, 403.

remembrance of their distinguished services, which the government seems to have forgotten."[8]

Little Wolf and his band of warriors were taken on March 25 by Lieutenant Clark in the Department of Dakota. They were sent to Fort Keogh, where they enlisted as scouts.[9]

While the Cheyennes were making their desperate break from the south, the Utes in Colorado were becoming restless. Affairs at the Ute reservation had been growing steadily worse throughout 1878. Situated on the Gunnison River, the reservation was attractive to the whites. Land to them meant land for cattle, farming, or mining. To their eyes and in their minds it appeared unreasonable and stupid that Indians should occupy a great tract of good ground and neither cultivate it, raise cattle on it, or dig in it for gold.

"It is easy to anticipate the result of leaving these Indians in occupation of valuable mineral and agricultural lands in a section of the country into which white emigration is pouring with its usual energy, and which presents attractions wholly irresistable to the white emigrants of this country."[10] An agreement had been reached with the southern Utes whereby they were to be moved to a new reservation in Colorado, but the treaty had not been ratified. The settlers wanted to push the Utes out of Colorado entirely, and the proposed agreement did not remove the White River band.

By September 10, 1879, matters had reached such a stage that the agent at White River, N. C. Meeker, wrote the Governor of Colorado, asking for help. He wanted one hundred soldiers sent to protect the people, who, he said, were in danger of massacre by a Ute uprising.

A week later, the War Department, by request of the Interior Department, agreed to send troops from the nearest military commander to protect the agent and arrest the "ringleaders." General Crook happened to have troops stationed closer to the scene than anyone else, even though the agency was not in his department. Accordingly, on September 21, Major T. T. Thornburgh, with

8 Secretary of War, *Annual Report*, 1879, 77.

9 Military Division of the Missouri, *Record of Engagements with Hostile Indians*, 96.

10 Secretary of War, *Annual Report*, 1878, 79.

three troops of cavalry and one of infantry, left Fort Fred Steele[11] for the agency.

Thornburgh's command reached Fortification Creek, Colorado, on the twenty-fifth, and started on its march to White River. The Utes were very much excited at the approach of troops. They did not believe that there was any reason for the troops except that they were going to be forced to move. This they were determined to resist.

On September 29, a few miles beyond Milk River, Major Thornburgh's command was ambushed, and the Major was killed. At the same time the Utes at the agency massacred the agent and his employees. The soldiers retreated to the wagon train and prepared a defensive position, holding it until October 5, when Colonel Merritt arrived from Fort D. A. Russell,[12] having marched reenforcements 170 miles in a little more than forty-eight hours, over very rough country. The Utes scattered to the mountains.[13]

Before Colonel Merritt could commence pursuit and punishment of the hostiles, orders arrived from Washington halting all operations. The Indian Bureau had its entering wedge, and a commission was sent out to negotiate with the Utes for their removal from the reservation. The White River Utes were forced to move to the Uintah agency in Utah, and their old reservation was thrown open to white settlement.

The commission to the Utes demanded that the hostiles who had massacred Agent Meeker be delivered for punishment. No mention was made of those Indians who had waylaid Major Thorn-

[11] Fort Fred Steele, Wyoming Territory, was established on June 30, 1869, at the point where the Union Pacific crossed the Platte. The post was to protect the overland route from Indian depredations. It was named after Brevet Major General Fred Steele, who had died in January, 1868. The post was discontinued in 1886. *Posts, Camps, and Stations File;* Writers' Program, Wyoming, *Wyoming,* 239-39.

[12] Fort D. A. Russell, Wyoming, was established on September 8, 1867, two miles north of the newly established railroad town of Cheyenne City. It was named in honor of Brigadier General David A. Russell, killed at the battle of Opequan, Virginia, in 1864. While most of the other posts in the area were disbanded, Fort Russell grew and was an important post during World War I. By *General Order No. 20* (1929), it was renamed Fort Francis E. Warren in honor of the first governor of Wyoming. *Posts, Camps, and Stations File.*

[13] John S. Payne, "Incidents of the Recent Campaign against the Utes." *The United Service,* Vol. II, No. 1 (January, 1880), 114-29.

burgh. Crook was quick to mark this omission, reflecting that "The life of an officer or soldier of the Army is as dear to him, perhaps as valuable to his country, as is that of an agent or employee of any other branch of the government, and it will be a bad precedent to establish that one may be taken with impunity, while the other must be accounted for by the delivery to justice of those who destroy it."[14]

General Crook was never known for disinclination to speak his mind when he was sufficiently interested in a subject. His interest in the treatment of Indians, and the disposition of Indian problems in general was well known, appearing as it did in the public reports of his department. When in 1879 the question of Indian administration was given a thorough airing, the General had an opportunity to put on the record his prejudices in the matter.

The Army Appropriation Bill for the fiscal year ending June 30, 1879, carried with it a section authorizing the formation of a committee "to take into consideration the expediency of transferring the Indian Bureau to the War Department." The committee was organized in June, 1879, and proceeded to take evidence.[15]

In October the committee went to Omaha, and General Crook was invited to express his opinions. It was immediately apparent that the General was in favor of such a transfer. His experiences in Arizona and again in the Department of the Platte with dishonest, interfering, or simply ignorant agents, Indian Bureau duplicity, and shifting of responsibility had settled his attitude. Promises which the General had made in good faith had been broken or modified by orders from the Indian Bureau. This, he felt, was a major weakness which a transfer would eliminate.

"The Indian," he testified, "is a child of ignorance, and not all innocence. It requires a certain kind of treatment to deal with and develop him. One requisite in those who would govern him rightly is absolute honesty—a strict keeping of faith toward him. The other requisite is authority to control him, and that the means to enforce that authority be vested in the same individual.

"As it is now you have a divided responsibility. It is like having two captains on the same ship. For this reason, specially, the neces-

---

[14] Secretary of War, *Annual Report*, 1880, 80.
[15] 45 Cong., 3 sess., *Senate Report 693*, 112–21.

sity of unanimity in action, I think there can be no question but the management of the Indians should be placed under the control of the War Department; there is no comparison at all between the advantage that would accrue by putting the matter in the hands of the military and that which comes from allowing it to remain where it is at present."

Granted that the Indians would be under War Department control, what would be his policy toward their proper disposal? Crook gave his answer to that question, too. "There is no reason why the country should sustain or support any portion of its population in idleness. The Indians can be made self-sustaining, and they are willing to become so—all they want is the proper facilities and the proper instruction. Of course, you have got to use a little force.

"I have had twenty-six years' experience with the Indians, and I have been among tribes where I spoke their language. I have known the Indians intimately—known them in their private relations—I think I understand the Indian character pretty well. They talk about breaking up their tribal relations. The Interior Department have frequently issued letters, etc., looking to that. It might as well try to break up a band of sheep. Give these Indians little farms, survey them, let them put fences around them, let them have their own horses, cows, sheep, things that they can call their own, and it will do away with tribal Indians.[16]

"When once an Indian sees that his food is secure, he does not care what the chief or any one else says. . . . The great mistake these people make is that they go to looking after the spiritual welfare of the Indians before securing their physical. Of course, that is a thing to come after awhile."

Crook believed that "ninety-nine-hundredths" of Indian troubles were caused by Indian agents and traders, by their mismanagement: "If you will investigate all the Indian troubles, you will find that there is something wrong of this nature at the bottom of all of them, something relating to the supplies, or else a tardy and broken faith on the part of the general government."

[16] Crook here voiced a sentiment gaining in popularity at the time. The idea was embodied in a law on February 8, 1887, with the passage of the so-called Dawes Act, granting land to Indians on a severalty basis.

The Indian Bureau was not transferred. Carl Schurz, secretary of the interior at the time, was completely opposed to the change. He recognized, however, that there was a large amount of fraud, malfeasance and nepotism within the bureau; and he made honest efforts to have dishonest practices reduced. He had only slight success. The Indian plum was too rich to leave unplucked.

22. *The Department of the Platte was peaceful*

LIFE in the Department of the Platte during the latter part of 1879–80 was comparatively peaceful. Routine business, inspections, selection of sites for new posts, target practice, reviews, assignment of troops, minor Indian scares—the thousand and one details of army frontier routine—occupied the time of the commanding general.

There was a flurry of excitement in 1879 when the Olive trial was held at Hastings, Nebraska. Ira P. Olive was on trial for the murder of Luther Mitchell and Ami Ketchum. The case was one of the more dramatic of the many border incidents involving cattlemen and homesteaders. Ira Olive and his brothers were cattlemen; Mitchell and Ketchum, homesteaders. Their interest in the land clashed in Custer County, Nebraska. One of Ira Olive's brothers, who went about under the alias "Stephens," tried to arrest Mitchell for alleged cattle rustling. He was shot for his pains.

Mitchell and Ketchum first fled for their lives, but then surrendered to the proper authorities. While they were being taken to the scene of the shooting, they were kidnapped and hanged to a tree. Their bullet-riddled and burned bodies were found on the morning of December 11, 1878, in a lonely gulch up the Loup River.

Suspicion immediately rested on Ira Olive, who had offered a large reward for the arrest of Mitchell and Ketchum, and who had been seen near by the night before the crime was committed. Therefore, he and his men were arrested and brought to trial at Hastings.

Feeling ran high between the cattlemen and homesteaders, and when the case was brought to trial on April 2, there was a large and threatening crowd in the town. Rumor was that none other than "Doc" Middleton and his Plum Creek gang was going to raid the town and release the prisoners. Judge Gaslin, who presided over the trial, appealed to the Adjutant General of Nebraska for troops to maintain order.

The Adjutant General telegraphed to Crook, who immediately sent a company of infantry from Omaha to Hastings. The appearance of the soldiers had a "wholesome influence" on the trial, and no violence was reported.

General Crook had acted too hastily, however. Troops could not be used to suppress civil disorders without direct approval of the President. This approval was not granted, although the Governor had duly requested it, and General Crook had also telegraphed for authority to send the troops. The soldiers had to be recalled, but their work was done.[1]

Ira Olive was sentenced to life imprisonment for second degree murder, but a new trial was ordered in Custer County. When the case again came up, no witnesses for the prosecution could be found, and the charges were dropped.[2]

The Nebraska newspapers, which had been following the details of the trial with great interest, would probably have pushed the matter further, but a new sensation had come along, and a new cause was being fought in the editorial columns. It was known as the "Ponca habeas corpus case" and involved General Crook as defendant.[3]

During the spring and summer of 1877, coincident with the removal of the Cheyennes, the Ponca Indians, peacefully living on a reservation in southern Dakota Territory, had been suddenly removed to Indian Territory. Their removal, it was explained, placed them out of reach of their old enemies, the Sioux, who were soon to occupy the old Ponca reservation.

At the time, the removal evoked little or no comment. The country was too much excited about the removal of the Sioux

[1] National Archives, Commanding General, Department of the Platte to Adjutant General, Division of the Missouri, April 14, 1879.

[2] William L. Gaston, *History of Custer County, Nebraska*, 159–76.

[3] Thomas H. Tibbles, *The Ponca Chiefs;* United States *ex rel.* Standing Bear vs. Crook, *25 Federal Cases*, 695.

and the Cheyennes to pay special attention to a small band of peaceful Indians. The Poncas felt it was important. They had shortly before concluded a treaty of peace with the Sioux and did not fear any more danger from that source. They were interested only in staying on their old reservation. They had waged no wars, taken no scalps, committed no depredations, and saw no reason for being sent to Indian Territory.

Chief Standing Bear of the Poncas was especially vocal in his protests. He undertook to organize opposition to the change. He and his brother, Big Snake, were thereupon taken to Fort Randall,[4] where they were given time and opportunity to reconsider their position. Their change of heart was rapid enough, so that they were able to go to the Indian Territory with the last of their people.

The first season in the new land affected the Poncas much as it had the Cheyennes. Little had been done to supply them with adequate shelter, rations, or provisions for self-support. Malaria and other diseases took a heavy toll. Standing Bear lost a daughter, his only son, and other relatives during the first year. By the end of 1878 he had determined to go back to the old agency.

Early in January, 1879, Standing Bear with thirty followers, men, women and children, left the Quapaw agency and started for home. These Indians bothered no one, took no scalps, stole no stock, and bought or begged their food. On March 4 they arrived at the Omaha agency, where the Indians welcomed them. They immediately started farming in an attempt to become self-sustaining.

The peaceful return of this small band of Poncas was not any

[4] Fort Randall, named for Daniel Randall, was situated on the Missouri River, thirty miles above the mouth of the Niobrara. It was selected as a site for a military post by General Harney. On June 26, 1856, eighty-four recruits of the Second Infantry under Lieutenant George H. Paige landed on the spot and laid out the new post. In August of that year two companies of infantry and four of cavalry arrived and formed the first garrison of the post under the command of Colonel Francis Lee.

By the treaty of April 19, 1858, a reservation for the Yankton Sioux was established east and northeast of Fort Randall; and later, to the south, a similar reservation was set up for the Poncas. For almost fifty years the post stood between the two reservations, holding the Indians to their treaty promises, keeping the road open between Ridgeley and Laramie, and serving as supply base for operations against the Indians.

The fort was abandoned by United States troops on July 22, 1884. *Posts, Camps, and Stations File.*

more welcome than the warlike march of the Cheyennes the year before. Soldiers were sent, on orders requested by the Interior Department, to arrest the Poncas and take them back to Omaha, pending their return to Indian Territory, but their return was delayed.

T. H. Tibbles, crusading editor of the *Omaha Herald*, was responsible for the delay. He had heard of the return of the Poncas and of their arrest, and decided to appoint himself a one-man committee to be protector of a friendless and wronged tribe. Thus Omaha, even at this early date, was able to produce a man who sympathized with a cause involving Indians.

Tibbles was experienced in the reform business. He immediately enlisted the support of churchmen and prominent citizens, who petitioned Secretary Schurz for the release of the Indians and asked that they be permitted to remain at the Omaha agency. The Interior Department, Tibbles knew, would never consent to the release of the Poncas, so he obtained the legal assistance of J. L. Webster and M. J. Poppleton, attorneys in Omaha. They served a writ of habeas corpus designed to free the Indians from the custody of the military.

This was something new. Never before had an Indian been a subject of a writ of habeas corpus. The right of the Interior Department, via the military, to hold and dispose of the person of the red man had not been challenged before. There was nothing on the books, and Judge Elmer S. Dundy, who heard the case, cogitated with the eyes of the nation, and especially of T. H. Tibbles, on him.

The trial of *Standing Bear vs. Crook* was a historic event. The General was brought into the case as the commanding officer of the Department of the Platte, which had arrested the Poncas, not as an individual. His sympathies were with the Indians, but there was no chance to evade official obligations in the matter. He stated bluntly that his interest in the case was official, that personally he sided with the Poncas and considered the arrest and attempt to return the Indians to Indian Territory a "disagreeable duty." The Poncas were to him simply another case of injustice to the Indians, a subject with which he was becoming increasingly familiar.

The Ponca habeas corpus case began April 30, 1879, and lasted two days. The argument for the prosecution stated that the Poncas were being held without cause, since Indians who deserted their tribe were no longer subject to government control. The defense held that the Indians were not entitled to a writ of habeas corpus, not being persons or citizens under the law.

Judge Dundy decided in favor of the Poncas. In his decision he commended General Crook for his attitude toward the case.

The verdict prevented the return of the Indians.[5] But this was only the beginning. The Indian reform groups were determined to bring this case before the Supreme Court, where, if upheld, the decision would establish a precedent that might release all Indians from control, provided only that they renounced tribal affiliations. The Indian Bureau was equally determined to prevent continuance of the case. The Poncas under Standing Bear, said the Bureau, were welcome to what was left of their old reservation.

Tibbles, accompanied by Standing Bear and Suzette La Fleche, an Omaha Indian girl popularly known as "Bright Eyes," launched their campaign with a speaking tour designed to enlist sympathy and raise money. Both were forthcoming, but the Ponca case went no further. Despite the eloquence of Bright Eyes, who had been educated in the East, the Interior Department, guided by Secretary Schurz, parried all efforts to have the case carried into higher courts. However, the fight which grew out of this controversy did much to advance the ultimate reforms in Indian administration of a decade or so later.[6]

By this time the majority of the Poncas, who had remained in Indian Territory, had become settled. They no longer wanted to return to their old agency. In 1880 President Hayes appointed a committee of four to investigate the condition of the Poncas. The committee consisted of Generals Crook and Miles, William Stickney of the Board of Indian Commissioners, and Walter Allen of the Boston Indian Citizenship Committee.

In January, 1881, Crook and the others of the committee met

[5] Stanley Clark, "Ponca Publicity," *Mississippi Valley Historical Review,* Vol. XXIX, No. 4 (March, 1943), 495–516.

[6] Loring B. Priest, *Uncle Sam's Stepchildren,* 76–80. Lawrence F. Schmeckebier states that "The United States District Court for Nebraska held that the Indians were entitled to the benefits of the writ, and that there was no authority to place them under arrest. This decision, however, has never been accepted as final by the Indian Service." *The Office of Indian Affairs,* 258.

with the Indian Territory Poncas, and found that although the original removal had been an error and that the Indians still held title to their Dakota reservation, the Poncas in the south wanted to stay where they were. Those in Dakota also wanted to stay where they were. Recommendations were made to give the Indians a year to decide about their reservation and to make appropriations for the support of both groups. Only Allen, the Boston representative, was unconvinced. He firmly believed that the southern Poncas had been bribed to make their decision.[7]

Once the Poncas had decided to remain stationary, Tibbles and Bright Eyes stopped agitating their particular problem and allied their energies with Indian improvement movements in general. They were married in the summer of 1881. General Crook visited them in Boston a few years later, and spoke on the same platform with Bright Eyes, under the sponsorship of the Indian Citizenship Committee.

Between the Ponca trial and the investigating commission, General Crook enjoyed a vacation in the form of an inspection trip through the Department of the Platte. A new reservation had to be located for the White River Utes, and Crook led a reconnaisance to determine the proper site for a road to the new agency and a military post to be called Fort Thornburgh.

Secretary of the Interior Schurz also took a trip west, accompanied by his two daughters, a retinue of secretaries, and more remote relatives. His trip was largely a sightseeing tour, and Yellowstone Park, already then a goal for the hardier class of tourist, was on the schedule. General Crook was detailed to accompany the Secretary on this part of his tour. The Misses Schurz obligingly left the party and returned east, which must have been all to the General's liking.[8]

In his history of Yellowstone Park, General Chittenden records that "In 1880 the Honorable Secretary of the Interior, accompanied by General Crook, with a large number of officers and soldiers,

---

[7] Clark, "Ponca Publicity," *Mississippi Valley Historical Review*, Vol. XXIX, No. 4 (March, 1943), 495–516.

[8] John G. Bourke, *Diary* [MS], Vol. 37, August 10, 1880. Bourke refers to Schurz as "the spindleshanked Mephistopheles at present presiding over the Department of the Interior."

and an immense pack train, entered the Park from the valley of Henry Fork, and made an extended tour."[9]

The "immense pack train," under the leadership of the prince of packmasters, Tom Moore, commenced moving from Deer Creek, Montana, where the party left the Utah and Northern Railway. Under Moore were seventeen pack mules with provisions and equipment. Seven army wagons were loaded also. Fourteen mounted infantrymen under Major Bainbridge served as escort, and two Shoshone guides, Jack Hurley and Mike Fisher, saw to it that no one got lost. Colonel Stanton, Major Roberts, Lieutenant Bourke, and the President's son, Webb Hayes, were also in the party. After the "expedition" entered the park, it was joined by Park Superintendent Philetus W. Norris and Government Forester Harry Yount. Schurz was in good hands.[10]

The purpose of the pack mules and loaded wagons became obvious whenever Bill Foley, the cook, went to work. One of his menus included tomato soup, baked salmon trout, mashed potatoes, prairie chickens, young sage hens (stewed), pork and beans, hot biscuits, fresh butter, pickles, olives, peaches, pears, cheese, whiskey, claret, tea, and coffee. The Secretary furnished champagne.

The Lower Geyser Basin, with Old Faithful, was the first of Yellowstone's marvels to astonish the expedition. The sightseers eagerly collected "Old Faithful Beans," and watched the eruptions with proper awe. Bourke records that "Colonel Stanton, who hasn't said a prayer for a quarter of a century, tried to mumble a paternoster, but he got it so badly mixed up with the Star Spangled Banner that I don't think it did him much good."

Also in the park at the time were John McNulta, former congressman from Illinois, and his wife. Mrs. McNulta served the officers tea and requested that a searching party be sent out for her husband, who had failed to return from a walk the day before. The stray husband returned of his own accord, however, before a search could be started. He had sprained his ankle, and had been obliged to remain out all night not far from camp.

Despite the general prejudice of army men against Schurz,

[9] Hiram M. Chittenden, *The Yellowstone National Park*, 106.

[10] Bourke, *Diary* [MS], Vol. 37, August 11, 1880. The following description of the tour is taken largely from Bourke's diary.

General Crook at Fort Duchesne, Utah, in 1887

Left to right, rear: Lt. L. J. Hearn, Capt. J. A. Haughey, Maj. George B. Dandy, Lt. Daniel Cornman, Col. James F. Randlett, Capt. J. A. Olmsted (seated), Lt. E. F. Ladd, Col. T. H. Stanton, Lt. Willis Wittich, Miss Jewett, Mr. Chase, Lt. M. D. Parker. Front: Maj. Robert H. Hall, Ernie Olmsted, Mrs. Olmsted, Miss Goodrich, Gen. Crook, Lt. L. W. V. Kennon, little girl (unidentified), Mrs. Benham, Capt. Byron Dawson, Dr. R. B. Benham.

Courtesy General Charles D. Roberts

The Sioux Commission of 1889 at Crow Creek Agency

Left to right: John A. Lott, stenographer, Gov. Charles Foster, Wilson, messenger, Maj. William Warner, John Warner, clerk, Gen. Crook, Irvine Miller, secretary, Maj. Cyrus S. Roberts, aide.

Bourke admitted that he was a "congenial companion, a good shot, and an excellent linguist." The party proceeded to Yellowstone Lake, where Webb Hayes had the pleasure of hooking a large salmon trout and flipping it into a hot spring with the same motion.

Yellowstone Falls and the Grand Canyon were the next stop, and from here Schurz left the main party to return to the East. He was accompanied by the main escort, but Crook and some of his friends lingered on to hunt and fish. On August 19 the General and Webb Hayes went out after game. They started up a large grizzly bear, and Crook's rifle missed fire. Both men came running into camp with the story, but the outcome remained a mystery. Crook's only comment was, "The scenery was the most beautiful I ever saw in my life."

General Crook's comparative idleness on the Indian front gave him an opportunity to indulge in that great weakness of men of medium means—a flier in gold mines. Together with General Sheridan, Delos B. Sacket, General King, and other officers and friends, he "ventured" into the Murchie mine, located near Nevada City, California.[11]

The Murchie mine was discovered early in the eighteen fifties by the Murchie brothers. It was situated about one and one-half miles east of Nevada City, and proved to be a tantalizing vein of quartz. The five Murchie brothers had tried to make the mine pay, but were obliged to support themselves with the profits of a mill, established in 1861, which proved a better investment. The mine itself yielded from five to seventeen dollars a ton, oftener the smaller amount. A shaft was sunk on the mine in 1866 "in the expectation that the ore would improve at a greater depth. A small engine was erected, a shaft sunk to the depth of about a hundred feet, and considerable rock was taken out and crushed, which yielded about the same as that nearer the surface. This was not considered sufficient to justify a continuation of operations."[12]

The history of the Murchie from that date to the present is

[11] The story of the Murchie mine is based on a series of letters from General Crook to Lieutenant Schuyler from January 18, 1880, to December 31, 1881, deposited with the Schuyler papers in the Henry E. Huntington Library.

[12] Edwin A. Bean, *History and Directory of Nevada County, California,* 116–17.

largely a repetition of the early story. Shafts were sunk ever deeper, usually with not enough result to pay for the operations.[13]

At the time General Crook and his partners obtained control of the property, the shaft had been sunk to about 300 feet. Early in 1880 Lieutenant Walter S. Schuyler, then aide to the General, was sent out to the Murchie to see what could be done to make it produce. With him went young Oliver Crook, the General's nephew.[14]

Stock in the mine was sold to friends of the promoters. The president of the concern, with officers in San Francisco, was Andrew Snider, Crook's hunting companion, the former sutler at Fort Ter-Waw. Hopes ran high for a time that with Schuyler at the mine it would become a paying proposition. Crook wrote: "Your being at the mine relieves me from a heavy pressure, and the stockholders have great confidence that you will bring it through all right."

By March, 1880, Schuyler reported hopefully, but Crook was still inclined to be cautious. "While working the mine endeavor to give a good impression to outsiders as to the value of the property, and in the meantime get all the statistics of the mine and those of the neighborhood, total yield of the county, both from ledge and placer, and everything that will go to show that our property is one of the best localities in the country, etc. This may all be useful in trying to sell our property in the future."

The quality of the ore was not improving, but there was another solution: Get the ore to yield more gold than it did under the usual process. Delos B. Sacket, in Chicago, had heard about such a process. It was called the "Maynard Process for Extracting Gold and Silver from Refractory Sulphurets." "Professor" Maynard had used his process on some of his mines on the Rapidan River, Virginia, with great success, so he said.

Charles Knap, the "Big Gun Man," had told Sacket about the

[13] *Nevada County Mining Review*, 52. The mine changed hands frequently after Crook severed connections with it and is now part of the property of the Empire-Star Mines, Ltd. The 1,600-foot level had been reached in 1935.

[14] Oliver Crook, now living in California, supplied the author with much interesting information about the Murchie. He says: "General Crook was an easy mark, Colonel Schuyler a would-be mining operator, and both of them, with very high salaries, died broke."

new process, and suggested that he get in on the ground floor. Knap wrote that "In connection with a couple of believing friends (who put up the money) I have purchased three-fourths of the process, the inventor retaining one-fourth. Now, my friend, it strikes me you should get up a party and bind or lease good, rich mines that have proved too refractory to be profitably worked. I will, for the friendship I have you, see that any samples of ore you send here in parcels of not less than 100 pounds are carefully subjected to the process, and a correct report made on them."

Exuberantly, Sacket asked Crook to lease some more mines in Nevada County.

Schuyler felt he was getting into deep water and tried to arrange for a transfer to duty in Arizona, but Sheridan and Crook would not hear of it, and the Lieutenant, his leave extended indefinitely, remained at the mine. Meanwhile, Crook inquired into the Maynard process, and arranged matters "so we will get the benefit of the process if it is a success, and will not lose anything if it is not."[15]

Schuyler struggled against his predicament and formed wild schemes to escape. The General wrote: "I doubt the wisdom of your plans of going to China just at this time, for the Murchie holders here have great confidence in your integrity and judgment, and none more so than General Sheridan. You have not suffered a particle in reputation by your connection with the mine, and should you leave it now, it would leave room for hard things to be said about you."[16]

The new process won out over all fears, and a new assessment was made on the stockholders. The mine samples assayed $30.74 per ton, in New York. Crook was glad to hear some encouraging news, for, as he wrote, "I fear it will not be possible to tune the people up to another assessment here; they were manipulated through the last two assessments in such a way that they have paid the last one with more alacrity than they did the first, but it can't be done again."

In December, 1880, news was good. Schuyler had made a strike

[15] April 10, 1880. Crook added, "General S[heridan] told me that he would see that your leave was extended as long as you wanted it."

[16] April 28, 1880. Schuyler had suggested shortly before that at least $50,000 would be needed to put the Murchie on a paying basis.

at the 400-foot level. Bourke, who was also in on the deal, was "building castles in the air." But the happiness was short-lived. By March, 1881, Schuyler again wrote that fresh sums would be necessary to develop the mine. This was impossible, and the only alternative was to run the mine at minimum expense and attempt to show a profit. All new underground work was suspended. The ore already available was taken out and processed, and the year's operations showed a profit of fifteen thousand dollars, enough to clear off the mine's debts, but not enough for dividends.

The Murchie was finally obliged to close down, and with it went Schuyler's position as Crook's aide. "I think it better, all things considered, that you resign from position as ADC. I write this now in order that you may assign your own reasons for the step. I was in hope of seeing you here, so as to explain, but I leave this morning for Washington on my way West. Please present my kindest regards to your father and mother and the rest of the family."[17]

In 1882 General Crook went to Nevada City to close down the mine himself, and Oliver Crook was sent to Sonora to shut down another mine that had proved worthless. The dreams of the miners were over.

[17] December 31, 1881.

VII
RETURNING TO
ARIZONA

23. *The Apaches had displayed forbearance*

WHEN GENERAL CROOK left the Department of Arizona in 1875, control of the Apaches already gave evidence of weakening. As the General expressed it, "The Indian agents who had sought cover before now came out, brave as sheep, and took charge of the agencies, and commenced their game of plundering."

Disaffection, suspicion, and unrest gradually worked their poison throughout the tribes. The Interior Department did little that was calculated to introduce an era of peace and prosperity among the Apaches. Instead, a policy of removal was carried into effect. The Indians were gradually forced to leave the reservations which had been assured them, and obliged to move to the hot, dry flats of the San Carlos.

The Chiricahua and Warm Springs Apaches, best known for their cunning and military prowess, were summarily removed from the reservation provided for them by General Howard. This reservation had been promised them so long as they kept the peace, but the greed of the white man for reservation land and the remarkably short-term views of the Indian Bureau observed no promises made in the past. The citizens of the Territory, too, seemed to forget quickly what the Apaches could do when aroused.

Not all of the Chiricahuas were removed. General Kautz, commanding the department, stated in his annual report for 1877: "The two agencies, Warm Spring and Chiricahua, contained in 1875, before they were ever broken up, according to the report for that year, 965 and 2,100; total 3,065. The number removed were 325 and 464; total 779. There are, therefore, 2,286 Indians unaccounted for since 1875. It is unnecessary to comment on these discrepancies."[1]

A succession of Indian outbreaks on both sides of the border, in New Mexico, Arizona, and Mexico, accounted for the whereabouts of the missing hostiles. Even those who had been forced to their new reservation were suspected of slipping off in small bands and returning after a successful raid before their capture could be effected or even their identity established. Victorio, Warm Springs chief, was the leader in most of the more extensive raids. He and his followers, both Warm Springs and Chiricahua Apaches, were determined to die rather than remain at San Carlos.

In July, 1879, Victorio made his final exit from the reservation and commenced a series of raids throughout Arizona, New Mexico, and Chihuahua, terrorizing the whole area. In October, 1880, this unreconstructed chief met his death in a battle with the despised Mexican troops. Nana, seventy-three years old, gathered to him the remnants of Victorio's band, and, joined by stray Chiricahuas, raided in the territories for two years, keeping the entire region on edge.[2]

In 1881 the storm broke with cumulated fury. The dissatisfied San Carlos Indians were deeply stirred by the incantations and prophecies of Nock-ay-del-klinne [Nakaidoklini], a White Mountain medicine man. This Indian seer predicted the resurrection of several old warrior chiefs who would lead the tribes once more after the white man had been driven from Apache land.

Dances, dreams, and tiswin whetted the excitement at San Carlos. Colonel E. A. Carr, in command at Fort Apache, was sent to arrest the medicine man. The attempt resulted in a wholesale outbreak and revolt, in which several of the usually loyal Indian police took sides against the troops. The battle centering about the arrest took place on August 30, 1881, and is known as the Battle of Cibicu. One month later, under the leadership of Juh and Nachez, seventy-four Chiricahuas fled the reservation and escaped into Mexico.[3]

The investigation of conditions at the reservation, which fol-

[1] Secretary of War, *Annual Report*, 1877, 144.

[2] Frank C. Lockwood, *The Apache Indians*, 225-26.

[3] Thomas Cruse, *Apache Days and After*, 93-145. Although General Crook always used "Nachez," this Indian's name is usually spelled "Nahche" or "Nahchi."

lowed the outbreak, indicated that there was something other than simple wildness or discontent at the bottom of the outbreaks. Blame evolved directly on the head of the Indian agent. A federal grand jury of Arizona, after taking evidence, reported that "For several years the people of this Territory have been gradually arriving at the conclusion that the management of the Indian reservations in Arizona was a fraud upon the government, that the constantly recurring outbreaks among the Indians and their consequent devastations were due to the criminal neglect or apathy of the Indian agent at San Carlos; but never until the present investigations of the Grand Jury have laid bare the infamy of Agent Tiffany could a proper idea be formed of the fraud and villainy which are constantly practiced in open violation of law and in defiance of public justice."[4] J. C. Tiffany, it appeared, had mulcted the government and, incidentally, his Indian wards, in every possible manner. The Apache outbreaks, it was claimed, were the direct result of his malfeasance.

On April 19, 1882, Loco and his band of Warm Springs Apaches, which had remained on the reservation, were approached by Nachez and Chato and forced to Mexico with the hostiles.[5]

With the Chiricahuas in Mexico and the reservation Apaches in a dangerous state of discontent and unrest, General Crook was recalled to the Department of Arizona. His successful methods of a few years earlier made him the only choice for the job. The Indians well remembered the stern General and knew that his arm was strong and unrelenting; they also knew that his promise was good.

On September 4, 1882, General Crook resumed command of the Department of Arizona. His first move was to see for himself. He rode about his department on his mule, Apache, and talked with the Indians on the reservation. He learned, first hand, of their grievances. He discovered that the Apaches did not trust those who had been placed in charge of them. They had been made fat with lies to the effect that they were going to be disarmed and sent away to Indian Territory, that they were to be attacked by troops on the

---

[4] *Arizona Star*, Tucson, October 24, 1882.

[5] The difficulties of Apache control between 1875 and 1886 are described in all their unsavory detail by Ralph H. Ogle, *Federal Control of the Western Apaches, 1848–1886*, 118–215.

reservation. They had been robbed of their supplies and cheated by almost every one of their agents. Crook's comment claimed that the Apaches "had displayed remarkable forbearance in remaining at peace."[6]

The General explained to the Indians that their troubles were in a large measure brought about by evil white men in the Territory who wanted to get rid of the Indians and seize the reservation land. It was necessary, he explained, to find some means of distinguishing between good and bad Indians, between those who were peaceful and those who wanted to fight. As in the old days, every male Indian able to bear arms was to wear a tag. Roll calls would be held often to make sure that everyone was still on the reservation. In this way all the Apaches who wanted to stay and raise corn would be known, and be safe, while those who wanted to raise scalps would also be known, and hunted.

The rules of the reservation made it necessary for the Indians to live close to the agency, where rations were issued. This arrangement was unsatisfactory, because it was impossible to scatter to the watered, fertile places and raise crops. No one could become self-sustaining under such a rule. The General recognized the trouble, and in November, 1882, met with the Indians in a big council, and told them that they would no longer have to be counted, that they were free to choose any part of their reservation to live on, and that they would be expected to become self-supporting. They would be accountable to Captain Crawford at San Carlos and Lieutenant Gatewood at Apache, who would supervise matters from those points. The making of tiswin would have to stop. Their agent would be working co-operatively with the military. The Indians were expected to govern themselves as much as possible, keep their own police, and hold their own trials. Soldiers would be brought in only when the Indians found it impossible to control themselves.[7]

The results of this system are indicated by the report of Captain Crawford from San Carlos in 1883. The Apaches raised crops, stock, and hay and cut cordwood. During 1883 the Indians on the White Mountain reservation raised over 2,500,000 pounds of corn,

6 Secretary of War, *Annual Report*, 1883, 160.
7 Secretary of War, *Annual Report*, 1883, 160.

180,000 pounds of beans, 135,000 pounds of potatoes, 200,000 pounds of barley, with wheat, pumpkins, watermelons, muskmelons, and cantaloupes in similar proportions. Crawford reported that they would have raised more, except for lack of sufficient seed, and that the Indians were storing seeds for next year's crop.[8]

The first reaction of the Apaches to the new system was hesitation and suspicion. When they discovered that the General meant exactly what he said, they settled down and lived together in comparative peace and quiet. They committed no depredations and kept their own police, with few exceptions. The making of tiswin was at least diminished, and another favorite Apache practice, wife mutilation, also began to die out. From the time of Crook's arrival to March, 1883, there was no depredation committed by Indians, either reservation or renegade, in Arizona.

The General now had his rear effectively covered and commenced preparations for the campaign he knew was coming against the Chiricahuas in Mexico. It was only a matter of time and convenience before they would raid once more across the border. The General wanted to be ready to welcome them. He reorganized the pack trains in his customarily thorough fashion. He had brought with him his old packmaster, Tom Moore, and with his help the trains were brought up to the level of efficiency so vital to Arizona campaigning. The Indian scouts, also, were reorganized. The old ones were discharged when their terms expired, and new ones enlisted. The scouts, too, were old friends—Al Sieber, Sam Bowman, and Archie McIntosh turned up again.

In March, 1883, the Chiricahuas left their hideout in the Sierra Madre and crossed the line into United States territory. One band, under Geronimo, raided through Sonora to get stock. The other, under Chato, crossed the boundary near the Huachuca Mountains into Arizona to get ammunition. Chato's party struck a charcoal camp about twelve miles south of Fort Huachuca[9] on the evening of the twenty-first, and killed four white men. One of the Indians

[8] Secretary of War, *Annual Report*, 1883, 181–82.

[9] Fort Huachuca, Arizona, is located in Cochise County, twelve miles from the Mexican border and about twenty-two miles southwest of Tombstone. The post was established on March 3, 1877, as part of the system of forts to protect the border from Indian raids.

Between 1886, when the Apaches were finally subdued, and 1911, during

was killed. The raiders were in Arizona for six days, traveled about four hundred miles, and killed twenty-six persons. They moved so rapidly that no troops caught sight of them.

On March 27, one of Chato's party, Pe-nal-tishn ["Panayotishn" according to Bourke], known by the soldiers as "Peaches," deserted the renegades and made his way to the San Carlos agency, where he was arrested. Peaches acted as guide to Crook in the campaign which followed to the Sierra Madre.

On March 31, 1883, the General received a telegram which made his pursuit of the Apaches much simpler. "Instructions just received from the General of the Army authorize you under existing order to destroy hostile Apaches to pursue them regardless of the department or national lines, and to proceed to such points as you deem advisable. He adds that General Mackenzie's forces will co-operate to the fullest extent."[10]

Under orders from Crook, troops were congregating at Willcox for the campaign—six companies of the Third and Sixth Regiments of Cavalry, under Major James Biddle and Captain William E. Dougherty, Lieutenant Gatewood at San Carlos was ordered to hurry the enlistment of seventy additional scouts, and join the forces at Willcox.

Meanwhile Crook went by rail to Guaymas and Hermosillo, Sonora and Chihuahua, to meet with Mexican officials, come to some sort of agreement, and arrange for a campaign that would make the best use of the joint forces. The Mexicans, too, were tired of the Apaches. Generals Carbo and Topete, Governor Torres of Sonora, and officials of Chihuahua welcomed the General and promised assistance.

On April 29 Crook reached San Bernardino Springs and made

---

the Madero Revolution in Mexico, the fort was quiet. In 1935 work was begun by W. P. A., modernizing the buildings and equipment of the post.

The name Huachuca is applied to a mountain range near by, and is thought to be an Apache word meaning "thunder." War Department, *Military Reservations, Arizona*, 4; *Army and Navy Register*, Vol. 61, No. 3181 (November 23, 1940), 4.

[10] Secretary of War, *Annual Report*, 1883, 173. An agreement, signed July 29, 1882, was then in effect permitting regular troops of either country to cross the border if in close pursuit of hostile Indians. *U. S. Statutes at Large, XXII*, 934.

the final disposition of his forces for the capture of the renegades. On May 1 he left the Springs with 193 Apache scouts, commanded by Captain Emmet Crawford, and Captain A. R. Chaffee's company of the Sixth Cavalry, forty-two enlisted men and two officers. The General's staff consisted of Captain Bourke and Lieutenant Fiebeger. The expedition took field rations for sixty days, and 150 rounds of ammunition per man. Every pack horse in the department, 350 animals, carried the load.

The command then marched into Old Mexico, toward the Yaqui River, through country which had been terrorized by the Chiricahuas. The land, formerly cultivated, was deserted, for the former inhabitants had never been safe from raids. By May 8 the expedition entered the Sierra Madre, traveling at night, under the direction of Peaches. The trail of the renegades was hot on the twelfth. The expedition was now in the wildest part of the Sierras. The trail was so rough that several pack mules were lost, falling over high precipices from the narrow paths.

The first Apache camp found was deserted. The renegades, fearing surprise, never lingered in one spot. The enemy was now so close that the General ordered the pack train left behind with Chaffee's company, while the Indian scouts under Crawford scoured the wilds on foot, searching for the Apache camp. On the fifteenth the scouts surprised a camp belonging to Bonito and Chato and precipitated a fight, in which the renegades were routed. Five Indians, children, were captured, and nine of the warriors were killed. The camp, with all its equipment, was taken.

The battle had the effect of thoroughly alarming all the Chiricahuas in the mountains. Further surprise and capture became impossible. The renegades, however, were interested in returning to the reservation. They were tired of the life they were leading, tired of being pursued, and tired, most of all, of fighting Mexicans. One of the captives, an older girl, offered to go out to the hostiles and induce them to come in and surrender. Crook permitted her to leave.

On May 17 six squaws came in. The General refused to deal with them, saying that he wanted to talk with the chiefs. The next day Chihuahua, not a chief, but a prominent member of the tribe, came in for a talk. He informed Crook that the Chiricahuas were willing to surrender and return to the reservation. They could not be taken unless they gave themselves up, he said, for they had scattered in the mountains.

From this time on, the renegades gradually drifted in from all directions. All the chiefs gave themselves up—Geronimo, Chato, Bonito, Loco, Nachez (the son of Cochise), and Kan-ti-no, who had always lived in the Sierras. Only Juh was missing. He, with one man and some squaws, had fled south, far up the Yaqui.

Crook treated the incoming Indians with his usual astute diplomacy. He was not really interested in taking them prisoners, he said. They had committed so many crimes, had killed so many people, and depredated so often that he would rather fight it out with them until they were all beaten into the ground and could give trouble no more. He told them, too, that the Mexican troops were moving in on both sides, and that in a few days they would be completely surrounded.

The Chiricahuas were so impressed by Crook's manner that they begged to be taken to the reservation, offering to send out runners into the mountains to gather up any stray hostiles who might not know of the surrender, and have them all report to San Bernardino for the trip to San Carlos. Crook agreed to the proposal and began his march back to Arizona, reaching the supply camp at Silver Springs on June 10. The Chiricahuas were moved by easy stages to San Carlos, in charge of Captain Crawford and his scouts, arriving there on June 24. They numbered 52 men and 273 women and children.[11]

General Crook had performed the incredible feat of subduing the Chiricahuas eight months after he took control of the Department of Arizona. He was now faced with a much longer and more difficult fight over the disposition of the Apaches. When Crook reached the United States border with his captives, he learned that P. P. Wilcox, agent at San Carlos, had telegraphed to Washington protesting against the settlement of the renegades on the reservation. The protest, so the agent reported, had emanated from the

[11] Secretary of War, *Annual Report*, 1883, 173–78. Only about two-thirds of the hostiles came directly to the reservation. The remainder were still in the Sierra Madre, having promised that they would come in after "two moons." The last of the Chiricahuas, under Geronimo, reached the reservation in April, 1884, escorted by Lieutenant Britton Davis. Davis, *The Truth about Geronimo*, 77–101.

reservation Indians, who were afraid of the hostiles, and did not want them as neighbors. They had held a protest meeting on June 14.

Crook referred to this "fire in his rear" with sarcasm and remarked that "when it is understood how easily such documents can be manufactured at Indian agencies, it will cause no surprise." He immediately sent Captain Crawford to San Carlos to investigate the protest. Apparently the white men on and about the reservation had made every effort to convince the Indians that General Crook was making a great mistake in sending the renegades back to the San Carlos. They hinted that the coming of the hostiles would most likely mean greater control by the military, more soldiers, and might even mean that the entire Apache people would be moved away from their homes. Such words stirred up the reservation Indians, and they were easily induced to protest Crook's policy.[12]

The conflict was great enough to call for official action in Washington. Crook was ordered to a conference between the Secretary of the Interior, the Commissioner of Indian Affairs, and the Secretary of War. The entire problem of Apache management and disposition was discussed, particularly their control, police, and general authority. The result of this conference was a memorandum, published July 7, 1883. The memorandum gave the General the measure of control he had so long advocated for the military and offered him the opportunity to exercise his theories of Indian policy:

"In view of the difficulties encountered in making satisfactory disposition of the Apache Indians recently captured by General Crook under existing methods of administration, it is determined by the Secretary of War and the Secretary of the Interior, after consideration, that the Apache Indians recently captured by General Crook, and all such as may be hereafter captured or may surrender themselves to him, shall be kept under the control of the War Department at such points on the San Carlos Reservation as may be determined by the War Department (but not at the agency

---

[12] Secretary of War, *Annual Report*, 1885, 171, 179–80.

without the consent of the Indian agent), to be fed and cared for by the War Department, until further orders.

"For the greater security of the people of Arizona, and to insure peace, the War Department shall be entrusted with the entire police control of all the Indians on the San Carlos Reservation, and charged with the duty of keeping peace on the reservation, and preventing the Indians from leaving it, except with the consent of General Crook, or the officer who may be authorized to act under him.

"The War Department shall protect the Indian agent in the discharge of his duties, which shall include the ordinary duties of the Indian agent, and remain as heretofore, except as to keeping the peace, administering justice, and punishing refractory Indians, all of which shall be done by the War Department, as above stated."[13]

General Crook was now in a position of responsibility for the behavior of all the Indians on the reservation. He had won his point, and the Chiricahuas were settled and encouraged to live peaceably.

No sooner was the memorandum published, however, and the General back in Arizona, when newspapers all over the country, especially in the West, charged that Crook and his entire command had been taken prisoners by the Apaches in the Sierra Madre, and that he had been obliged to offer easy terms to the renegades in exchange for his freedom. These articles were said to have originated in an interview with the Commissioner of Indian Affairs, who said that Crook had admitted as much in the Washington conference.[14] The General recognized the stories as a sign that not all was harmony between the military and civil administrators, no matter what official documents stated.

In his annual report of 1885 General Crook charged that on the day of the Washington conference the Secretary of the Interior had written the Indian agent that the agreement was merely a method of shifting responsibility to the shoulders of the War Department and did not actually represent the views of the Interior

13 Secretary of War, *Annual Report*, 1882, 179.

14 John P. Clum, former Indian agent at San Carlos, who entertained unique ideas about Indian administration, actually maintained the view that Crook had been captured by the Chiricahuas. John P. Clum, "Geronimo," *Arizona Historical Review*, Vol. I, No 3 (October, 1928), 26–35.

Department. By September, 1883, Agent Wilcox complained that the new arrangement deprived him of authority, and recommended that it be terminated. In December the Commissioner of Indian Affairs wrote the Secretary of the Interior that the agreement had been made "with the express understanding that the military officers were to have the supervision and police regulations on the reservation under the *direction* and with the *approval* of the Indian agent." "The italics," Crook added, "are mine."[15]

The General proceeded as planned, and placed Captain Crawford and Lieutenant Gatewood in full charge of the Chiricahuas.

24. *Geronimo was very nervous*

FOR TWO YEARS, to the seventeenth of May, 1885, "not an outrage or depredation of any kind" was committed by the Indians in the Department of Arizona or New Mexico. Captain Crawford reported that the Chiricahuas were satisfactorily settled away from the agency, apparently walking the white man's road. Work among the hostile elements was reasonably successful. Chato and Geronimo had the best farms in the tribe. General Crook was unable to obtain certain advantages for the Apaches, notably farm implements, a mill at Fort Apache, and a system of competition among Indian traders, but progress was made despite these handicaps, and the former renegades "generally behaved in a way to warrant the most hopeful anticipations."

Agent Wilcox, however, still pursued the policy of regaining civil control over the Apaches, and his attempts resulted in constant friction between the Indian Bureau and the military. In November, 1884, discouraged by the problem, Wilcox resigned, and was replaced by C. D. Ford, who promised full co-operation as outlined in the memorandum of July 7.

Ford was as little able as Wilcox to resist pressure from above, exerted to return the Apaches to civil control. He and Captain Crawford, almost from the outset, failed to agree on either the

[15] Secretary of War, *Annual Report*, 1885, 173.

principles or the methods of Indian control. In January, 1885, Ford protested against the digging of an irrigation ditch by Apache-Yumas on the opposite side of the river from the agency. The work had been ordered by the military, or at least approved by Crawford. On January 17, Ford took away the picks and shovels used by the Indians for their work. Crawford protested to Crook, who immediately requested that the action of his officers be sustained. The evasive reply he received indicated that two years of peace had brought about a shift in Washington. The General had asked to be sustained or relieved from responsibility. The answer promised neither.[1]

Lack of co-operation between the agent and the military meant nothing but divided control, and to the Indians it meant an opportunity to break the laws which irked them most, playing one department against the other for support. The Chiricahuas were equal to the best in diplomacy, and any sign of weakness in the control maintained by General Crook was sure to be used to their advantage. Tiswin drunks, wife mutilation, brawls, and general disaffection were sure to follow if that strong hand was removed.

The General realized his position very clearly, and used all the influence he was able to muster to have military control retained without restriction. He was unsuccessful. The new agent revived the post of agency chief of police and appointed an agency head farmer. Both of these men worked in opposition to Crawford's efforts to extend military control in agency affairs. The policeman shielded men wanted by Crawford for disturbing the peace, and the head farmer interfered with work that had been outlined by the officers.

Crawford again protested to Crook, and his complaint was investigated. The findings upheld him in every respect. His experiences had embittered him so greatly, however, that he requested his transfer to his old command in Texas. The request was granted, and Crawford was replaced by Captain Pierce, First Infantry. The agency officials and politicians had done their work well. Two

1 Secretary of War, *Annual Report*, 1885, 172. During the summer of 1884 General Crook made an extended trip to the East, delivering an address to the graduating class of the Military Academy at West Point and speaking at the reunion of the Army of West Virginia at Cumberland. Both addresses were published as pamphlets.

General George Crook, 1875

Courtesy General Charles D. Roberts

Mrs. Mary Crook, from a photograph taken
in Washington, D. C., about 1886

years of peace had made them brave again, and they were determined to regain the ground they had lost.

The threatened outbreak of the Chiricahuas finally occurred in May, 1885. On the night of May 14 a group of malcontents joined in a general tiswin drunk, and early the next morning, in all the glory of their hangover, they gathered in front of Lieutenant Britton Davis' tent, asking him what he proposed to do about it. They claimed that they were not bound by the provisions against tiswin and did not intend to obey it. They also complained about being obliged to desist from the practice of beating their wives, a privilege which they valued highly.

Davis realized that a showdown had come and acted accordingly. This matter was so serious, he told the chiefs, that he would have to consult with the General about it and would act as he decided. This course was taken partly to convince the Apaches that General Crook was still in charge and still strong. All the men formerly associated with Crook had gone—Wilcox, Crawford, and Beaumont. The Indians needed to be convinced that their best friend and strongest foe, General George Crook, was still around and able to take care of them.

Davis then dispatched the famous telegram to Crook, the message which never arrived. In it, with carefully guarded words, he let Crook know that there had been a general uprising, and that the Indians were awaiting his decision in the matter. The telegram had to be sent "through channels," in this case through Captain Pierce at San Carlos, Davis' superior officer. From San Carlos the telegram would be sent to Willcox Station on the Union Pacific, via its lines to Maricopa, and then by military telegraph line to Whipple Barracks.

The message never passed Captain Pierce. As Davis tells the story, Pierce took the telegram to Al Sieber, chief of scouts, who was suffering from a hangover at the time. Sieber dismissed the message as "another tiswin drunk" and let it go at that. The Captain pigeonholed the telegram, leaving Davis waiting. Four months later, after the damage had been done, Davis went to San Carlos and produced the message for General Crook. He claimed that if Crawford, with his long experience in Apache affairs, had been in charge, he would have understood the importance of the telegram, and the entire chain of events which followed would never have been forged. Crook agreed with him.

Two days passed without word from the General. Both Davis and the Indians were waiting. On May 17, about four in the afternoon, word was brought to Davis that a number of the Apaches had left the reservation, presumably on their way to Mexico. He immediately tried to telegraph Captain Pierce, but the lines had been cut, and the break was not found until the next day. It was then too late to make any effective attempt to stop the renegades.[2]

Pursuit set out as soon as possible, but it was obvious that the troops could not hope to catch up, and they returned to Fort Apache to prepare for a long campaign. The Indians, it was later discovered, had traveled nearly 120 miles without rest or food. Troops sent out from Grant, Bowie, San Carlos, Thomas, and Huachuca failed to stop the hostiles. News of the break was sent everywhere, and settlers were warned to be on the lookout for the band.

Information reached Crook on May 28 that the hostiles had taken refuge in the Black Range, New Mexico, and Crook moved his headquarters to Fort Bayard,[3] directing the movement of his troops from that point. None of the scouting parties or pursuing soldiers were able to reach and hold on to the hostiles, and they crossed into Mexico about June 10. When it became evident that the Indians were moving south, Crook again moved, this time to Deming, and began preparations to follow them into Mexico. Captain Crawford was recalled and put in charge of a battalion of scouts. Lieutenant Davis, who had been chasing the renegades with sixty Indian scouts, was ordered to join Crawford, and on June 11

[2] Davis, *The Truth about Geronimo*, 144–50.

[3] Fort Bayard is located in the southwest corner of New Mexico, about eight miles from Pinos Altos. The post was established on August 21, 1866, by provisions of *General Field Order No. 6*, Department of the Missouri, to protect the area from depredations of the Warm Springs Apaches. The trail of the Indians from Arizona to New Mexico passed near the fort.

The post was named in honor of Captain George D. Bayard, Fourth Cavalry, who died on December 14, 1862, of wounds received at Fredericksburg. It was discontinued as a garrisoned post on January 2, 1900, by order of the Secretary of War. The site is now occupied by a general hospital. *Posts, Camps, and Stations File.*

the combined force of ninety-two scouts and Troop A, Sixth Cavalry, followed the Apaches into the Sierra Madre once more.

Lieutenant General Sheridan, who wanted immediate action, authorized Crook to enlist two hundred additional scouts and promised that the Cheyenne pack train would be sent down to participate in the campaign. He also ordered that Crook establish his headquarters on or near the Southern Pacific Railroad. Thereupon Crook went to Fort Bowie and commenced organizing his second expedition.

A group of one hundred Apache scouts from San Carlos, under Lieutenant Charles B. Gatewood, combed the Mogollon and Black ranges to make sure that there were no renegades left in that area, and then reported to Bowie. They were then organized into an expedition under Wirt Davis, one troop of cavalry and one hundred Indian scouts, with a pack train carrying sixty days' rations. Davis' command was to move co-operatively with Crawford's and drive the renegades from the Sierra Madre, or destroy them there. This command moved into Mexico on July 13. To welcome the hostiles in case they should recross the border, Crook placed a troop of cavalry at "every waterhole along the border, from the Patagonia Mountains to the Rio Grande."[4]

On June 23, Crawford's command had struck Chihuahua's camp in the Bavispe Mountains, northeast of Opunto, but the camp could not be surrounded, and the hostiles escaped. Davis, also, struck the renegades in the Sierra Madre, northeast of Nacori, but small damage was inflicted, although the contents of an entire camp were destroyed and a few squaws and children were captured. The pressure on the hostiles in the Sierra Madre was great enough, however, to make them cross the border again in search of provisions and ammunition. This they did through Guadalupe Cañon, about daylight of September 28, within a few miles of a camp of two troops of cavalry and closely followed by both Davis and Crawford.

During this busy period, General Crook began writing his autobiography and also began a diary, the first entry dated August 13, 1885. The events which Crook saw fit to record reflected only obliquely the campaigns which he was directing. The weather, the comings and goings of various people, and details of his personal life occupied the few lines he wrote each night. The General was

---

[4] Secretary of War, *Annual Report*, 1886, 149.

more outspoken in his official report than in his private diary. Yet the volumes help balance the picture of life at an army post. Annual reports emphasize only the actions during the year, and omit the long periods of waiting, planning, and organizing that precede every active period.

"Aug. 13, 1885. Maj. Roberts returned from Whipple Barracks today. Showery today, but little rain at the post. Heavy showers in San Simon Valley."

"Aug. 14. Slight thunder, and cloudy in spots, no rain. Indian scare in Piney Cañon."

"Aug. 15. Two Indian squaws from Mexico and interpreter Robinson left for San Carlos. Telegram appointing Capt. Pierce at San Carlos came. Sky overcast, but no rain. Played cribbage at Col. Beaumont's this night with Col. Beaumont, Lt. Neall, and Capt. Roberts."

"Aug. 17. Lt. Blunt, 10th Infy., arrived on his way to Leavenworth. Frank Leslie brought dispatches from Maj. Wirt Davis from Mexico, giving an account of fight with Geronimo, killing Nanna [Nana], two other bucks, and Geronimo's 12 year-old son, wounding Geronimo. Also that they had killed two Chiricahua bucks on the 28th of July at the time they captured the five horses, saddles and blankets. Slightly cloudy, close, but no rain."

General Crook was living at Fort Bowie with Captain Roberts, his aide. Colonel Beaumont was the commanding officer at the post, and Lieutenant Neall was post adjutant. The report received from Davis was considerably exaggerated, being written at a time when results were not definitely known. Later only one squaw and two boys were admitted killed. Crook was waiting for reports from troops in the field, waiting for some news that the hostiles had either been cornered and were willing to come in, or were headed back toward the border, where he was ready for them.

On September 1 Crook and Roberts went to Benson to see Governor Torres of Sonora and discuss the campaign. There was a circus at Benson which Crook and the Governor, with his party of thirty, attended.

"Sept. 2. Had a very satisfactory talk with Governor Torres, who said that in case the two governments failed to form treaty to admit reciprocal crossing of the border, he would not interfere with the operations of our troops."[5]

General Crook was still building up his force of Indian scouts, and Lieutenant Britton Davis came in from El Paso with a group of Chiricahuas, among them Chato. It was evident by this time that the campaign would not be over quickly and that the commands would have to come in soon to refit. On September 28, Crook received news of Captain Wirt Davis' fight with Geronimo's band on the twenty-second; and the next day:

"Sept. 29. Rained a few drops this morning. This evening blustery. Dispatch from Davis and Crawford that 20 or 25 bucks crossed Guadalupe Cañon yesterday morning, going north, traveling very rapidly."

"Sept. 30. Courier in from Capt. Martin; followed Indians near Cow Creek when it got dark on him. Courier from Capt. Crawford this evening; followed Indians this side of Gaileyville foothills."

"Oct. 1. Sent three Indian scouts to Apache to look after their families. Capt. Smith and Lt. Locket, 4th Cavalry, arrived with their troops last night, took up their march for Clifton. Sent Dailey's train to Clifton. Indians reputed to have run off fifteen head of horses from Sulphur Springs Valley at three A.M. this morning. Later Capt. Woods reports that Indians went into Cochise's stronghold in Dragoon Mountains. Sent messenger out to Capt. Davis. Sprinkled some in the afternoon. A high wind."

"Oct. 2. Went to Deming, N. M."

"Oct. 3. Had long talk with Governor Tritle and Gen. Bradley. Dr. Ainsworth was with the Governor. Saw Capts. Chaffee and Kendall, and several Lts. Dispatch from Capt. Crawford to the effect that hostiles had gone into the Dragoon Mountains, and thought were returning to Sonora."

Crook's meeting with Governor Tritle of Arizona Territory and with General Bradley of the Department of New Mexico

---

[5] The agreement of July 29, 1882, under which U. S. troops had crossed the border during the campaign of 1883, terminated after two years. Local arrangements had to be made in lieu of a formal treaty.

helped to convince him that the campaign would have to be reorganized, especially since the hostiles had succeeded in reaching the mountains and were again heading for Sonora. On September 5, therefore, he sent Frank Leslie to Crawford, telling him to come in to refit. The enlistment terms of many of the scouts were running out, and the pack trains were worn down.

"Oct. 10. Capt. Crawford with his scouts arrived today. Had a talk with scouts. They are pleased at the prospects of going to their families. Lt. Wheeler, 4th Cavalry, arrived today. Head buzzing with quinine."

Captain Davis was sent to San Carlos and Captain Crawford to Apache to enlist one hundred scouts apiece from the reservation Indians for another campaign. Davis had his scouts ready and at Fort Bowie by November 16, and ten days later Crawford arrived from Apache. That same day Crook received a telegram that the hostiles were trying to make peace at Casa Grande. Crook "had a talk" with the new scouts, telling them of his plans for the new campaign, and assuring them that it was to their benefit to fight the renegades. Chato, now a loyal scout, and primed by the General, also talked with the scouts, warming them up to the job ahead.

Captain Davis and his scouts left for New Mexico on November 27, and on the twenty-ninth Crawford with his outfit set out for the Dragoon Mountains to try to intercept the southbound hostiles. The next day, in order to facilitate operations, on order from the Secretary of War, Crook transferred the District of New Mexico to the Department of Arizona. The campaign was to be resumed in full force.

The General now settled down to wait. Hunting, fox trapping, and routine department business occupied his time. From day to day couriers arrived with dispatches from the various commands in the field, reporting on the progress of the expeditions. Crawford spent two weeks chasing a band of raiders under Josanie, and finally gave up the task when the hostiles eluded him, going south. He then went to Mexico to operate in conjunction with Davis.

Christmas Day at Fort Bowie found Crook enjoying dinner with the Roberts family and sipping eggnog at Captain Markland's.

The rest of the army was not so calm. Hardly a day passed but some news went east about the Apache renegades. All of the news was bad. Horses were stolen, citizens were killed, or there was a general Indian scare over a large area. General Sheridan telegraphed Crook on December 29, saying that the President himself was getting disturbed over the progress of events and asked whether some good news might not soon be expected. Crook answered the query by going out and shooting five quail and two deer. No one was going to tell him how to run the Apache campaign, least of all officers from the East who did not understand Indian warfare as it was fought in the Southwest. Sheridan himself, who was experienced in western campaigning, failed to understand the peculiar problems involved in Crook's department and, above all, failed to appreciate the purpose of the Indian scouts.

Captain Crawford and his Apaches, meanwhile, were making progress. On the tenth of January, after a very difficult night march, Crawford's command attacked the main camp of the hostiles about sixty miles below Nacori. The battle did not trap or annihilate the Chiricahua renegades, but did capture their entire stock, camp equipment, food, and supplies. Geronimo, Nachez, and Chihuahua were demoralized to the extent that they asked for a peace talk.[6]

Before Crawford was able to commence negotiations, he was fatally interrupted by a force of Mexican troops which attacked his camp, supposedly in the belief that Crawford's scouts were hostile Apaches. The Mexicans took the scouts by surprise and fired a number of shots before they could be made to understand that they were shooting friendly forces. Crawford then stepped into the open to speak to them. A single shot rang out, and the Captain fell, shot through the brain. Firing recommenced, this time on both sides, and before Lieutenant Marion P. Maus, second in command, could correct the error, the Mexican commander and fifteen of his men were dead. The hostile Apaches, camped on a ridge across a valley, were "interested spectators."[7]

The Mexicans, after discovering their mistake, pleaded innocent of all intent to attack United States troops. However, Lieutenant Maus pointed out in his official report of the affair that it was

---

[6] Secretary of War, *Annual Report*, 1886, 152.
[7] Davis, *The Truth about Geronimo*, 197.

hardly possible for them to have misunderstood the situation, especially because Tom Horn, who was scout for Crawford in the absence of Sieber, spoke Spanish well and had informed the attackers plainly during the interlude of firing, that they were attacking friendly troops.

After the Mexicans drew off, the hostiles, conferring with Lieutenant Maus, agreed only that they would meet for a peace talk in "two moons." They would meet only with General Crook, and they would choose the spot for the council. In Apache warfare, at any rate, "peace now" was very much better than continued warfare in the wilds of the Sierra Madre, and Lieutenant Maus understood this perfectly. He agreed to the proposals of the hostiles and withdrew the command from the field.

General Crook was apparently one of the few interested parties who was not worried about the Apache promise to meet him in "two moons." He was more plagued by telegrams from the East requesting full information about the arrangements. In his usual fashion, the General went his own way, sending few letters, and fewer telegrams, knowing that nothing could be done that had not been done, and preferring to handle matters without interference.

On March 16 Lieutenant Maus informed Crook that communication had been opened up with the Chiricahuas, that four of them had visited his camp, and that the remainder, excepting Mangas, were within twenty miles. Crook began final preparations for the peace talk. Ka-e-ten-a and Alchesay, chiefs, and the Apache scouts left for White's Ranch on March 22. The following day General Crook, with Captain Bourke, Captain Roberts, and Roberts' thirteen-year-old son, Charles, left for the scene of the peace talk, the Cañon de los Embudos, traveling via White's Ranch, Mud Springs, and San Bernardino. On March 25 the first of the talks was held:

"This morning was clear and cold. March across the country to where Lt. Maus camped near the hostiles. Saw Geronimo and Nachez, and while having a talk with them, Chihuahua came in with some stolen stock. Geronimo was very nervous, and tried to make out as good a case for himself as possible, but he got but little consolation. The result of the interview indicated nothing. After the talk I started Ka-e-ten-a and Alchesay to talk them into going away until this thing was forgotten and the excitement was allayed."

"March 26. Had private interview with Geronimo, Nachez, Chihuahua and a couple of others with reference to their leaving this country for the east to remain there until they change their ideas, and the feeling against them here dies out."

"Had last interview with the Indians on the 27th."[8]

"March 28. Left camp early in the morning for San Bernardino. Met Geronimo and Noche and other Chiricahuas coming from the San Bernardino direction quite drunk. We took buck-board at San Bernardino and took lunch at Silver Creek with Capt. Smith. Stopped a moment at Lt. Wheeler's camp at Mud Springs, and stopped for the night at Frank Leslie's ranch."

"March 29. Left Leslie's at six A.M. Wind blew a gale all day. Arrived at Fort Bowie at about 3 P.M. Killed a curlew, the largest I ever saw in Sulphur Springs Valley."

The long and difficult campaign now appeared to be ended. The last of the hostile Chiricahuas had again surrendered, this time on the proposition that they should all, except the superannuated Nana, be sent to exile in the East for two years. Unfortunately, an unscrupulous white trader named Tribollet plied the renegades with liquor and lies on the night of the twenty-ninth. The effect of the combination was to drive Geronimo and Nachez, with twenty men and thirteen women, back to the mountains.

This final break precipitated the termination of General Crook's command in the Department of Arizona. After an exchange of telegrams with General Sheridan, Crook requested to be relieved of his command, and his request was granted.

The surrender, disposition, and flight of the Chiricahua Apaches was the subject of a pamphlet published by General Crook in December, 1886. Here he presented the correspondence relative to the entire campaign against the Apaches from 1882 to 1886.[9] The pamphlet, prepared with the assistance of Captain Roberts, was intended to call attention to the injustices inflicted on the Chiricahua tribe, which had been completely removed from Arizona after

[8] A transcript of the interview is printed in Davis, *The Truth About Geronimo*, 200–212, from *Senate Doc. 88*, 51 Cong., 1 sess.

[9] George Crook, *Resumé of Operations against Apache Indians, 1882 to 1886.*

the renegades had been subjected by Miles. Not only had the hostiles been removed but also the peaceful reservation Indians, including the scouts who had made the capture possible.

Among the documents published by the General was a letter he had written to the Adjutant General in September, 1885, when it was apparent that the hostiles would be difficult to conquer. Crook believed that the Indians could be induced to surrender if certain promises were made. If the hostiles were assured that they would not be turned over to the civil authorities for punishment, but simply treated as prisoners of war, they would be more likely to come in. Any other course of action would encourage the renegades to fight to the bitter end, a fight which might last for years and certainly would involve extraordinary expense.

The Secretary of War agreed that General Crook "be authorized to secure the surrender of the Chiricahuas now at large upon terms of their being held prisoners of war, but it must be understood that any negotiations looking to their surrender must include all hostile Chiricahuas, and that as soon as the surrender is made they at once be sent under suitable guard for confinement at Fort Marion, Florida."

In February, 1886, when the promised council with the hostiles was soon to be held, General Sheridan spoke to the President regarding the disposition of the Apaches and the terms to be granted to them. The President said that the terms as outlined by the Secretary of War were agreeable, but that no promises were to be made to the Chiricahuas "unless it is necessary to secure their surrender."

On these premises, General Crook entered into negotiations with the hostiles. Both sides knew their strengths and weaknesses. Crook knew that if the Indians were pushed too far they would stampede back to the mountains, and years of campaigning would be necessary to eradicate them. The Indians, too, knew they were strong. Since their last fight with Crawford, they had supplied themselves with new equipment and were fully prepared for any fight that might be precipitated. The general tension was highlighted when the hostiles refused to permit any regular soldiers to approach their camp. Only the General, the Indian scouts, and the General's personal party were allowed in the Chiricahua camp.

The General used his personal influence, a very considerable factor, to sway the Apaches toward peace. He sent Ka-e-ten-a, the reformed renegade, and Alchesay, a trusted scout, into the hostile camp to make talk. Chihuahua and Nachez, especially, were urged to give themselves up. When these two chiefs agreed to surrender, the whole band was split into two factions, and the fight was won. Without the aid of the faithful scouts, the General believed, it would not have been possible to approach the Chiricahua camp, let alone parley the hostiles into a peaceful mood.

The terms of surrender were unfortunately not agreeable to the powers in the East. General Sheridan telegraphed Crook on the thirtieth, saying that the President did not agree to the imprisonment of the Apaches in the East for two years with the understanding of their return to the reservation. These were the terms Crook had offered. The President demanded unconditional surrender, sparing only their lives. Here again, and for the last time, the authorities in the East failed to sustain the judgment and acts of the one man who had demonstrated that he was quite capable, if supported, of keeping the peace and controlling the Apaches. The effect of an "unconditional surrender" stipulation would, in Crook's judgment have been to drive the Indians back to the mountains where they would fight to the last man. This he had tried to avoid by offering terms.

It was now too late to change these terms honorably. The General replied to the rebuff by stating, "To inform the Indians that the terms on which they surrendered are disapproved would, in my judgment, not only make it impossible for me to negotiate with them, but result in their scattering to the mountains, and I can't at present see any way to prevent it." Crook continued to let the Indians believe that his terms had been approved. It was, to him, the only way.

A final explosive exchange of compliments between Crook and his superiors followed the exodus of Geronimo and Nachez, who had fled, full of mescal and lies. General Sheridan's first reaction was given in a telegram dated March 31: "It seems strange that Geronimo and party could have escaped without the knowledge of the scouts." This was a severe blow to Crook's pride. The General relied on his scouts as he did on his pack train; both were part of the system which he felt was peculiarly his own. Without his scouts he believed that the Apache campaign could never have been successful. He pointed this out to Sheridan, whose reply simply aggravated matters: "I do not see what you can do now except to concentrate your troops at the best points, and give protection to the people. You have in your department 46 companies of Infantry and 40 companies of Cavalry, and ought to be able to do a great deal with such a force."

Here again General Sheridan revealed how little he understood the difficulties of Indian warfare in the Southwest. Regular soldiers were useless against the Apaches, who knew their country as their own home and were not burdened by supply difficulties or the intricacies of pack trains, who killed and ate their mounts as they rode them to death, and stole fresh transportation en route. Neither infantry nor cavalry could cope with an enemy such as this, no matter what their numbers. The only effective solution was the one which had brought victory in three campaigns—the use of Indian scouts and pack trains.

The General embodied his thoughts in a dignified and bitter reply, returned to Sheridan on the same day:

"It has been my aim throughout present operations to afford the greatest amount of protection to life and property interests, and troops have been stationed accordingly. Troops cannot protect property beyond a radius of one-half mile from their camp. If offensive movements against the Indians are not resumed, they may remain quietly in the mountains for an indefinite time without crossing the line, and yet their very presence there will be a constant menace, and require the troops in this department to be at all times in position to repel sudden raids; and so long as any remain out they will form a nucleus for disaffected Indians from the different agencies in Arizona and New Mexico to join.

"That the operations of the scouts in Mexico have not proved as successful as was hoped is due to the enormous difficulties they have been compelled to encounter from the nature of the Indians they have been hunting, and the character of the country in which they have operated, and of which persons not thoroughly conversant with both can have no conception. I believe that the plan upon which I have conducted operations is the one most likely to prove successful in the end. It may be, however, that I am too much wedded to my own views in the matter, and as I have spent nearly eight years of the hardest work of my life in this department, I respectfully request that I may now be relieved from its command."

The following day, April 2, General Crook received his orders relieving him from command. That day the remaining Chiricahuas came in to Bowie; and Lieutenant Bourke left on the train, accompanying Captain Crawford's remains to Kearney, Nebraska.

General Nelson Miles was detailed to succeed Crook. Miles attempted to operate against the renegades with cavalry alone and found for himself that it was impossible. Nor was his infantry more successful. After a fruitless chase through the mountains of Sonora, Miles was obliged to treat with the hostiles. He was obliged to call on Lieutenant Gatewood to carry on the negotiations. In August, 1886, Gatewood arranged the surrender of the remaining Chiricahuas, except six, and the campaign was ended. All the Chiricahuas in Arizona, loyal scouts most of them, were then arrested and sent to Florida, into exile with the renegades.[10]

General Crook had not told his prisoners anything about the refusal of their terms of surrender. He explained his actions officially by remarking that the news would prevent the return of any of the others, and two of those who had fled with Geronimo had already returned on their own initiative. Actually, the General could not bring himself to tell the Indians that his word was not good, that his promise to them could not be kept. He had always been known to them as a straight talker and would not be known in any other way.

On April 5 Crook noted the arrival of two telegrams from General Sheridan, "the first approving my acts, the second trying to say something without saying it." The first telegram approved his action relative to the transportation of the captives to Florida and his determination not to inform them of the broken agreement. The second telegram indicated the official attitude of the government with regard to the terms of surrender. Geronimo, it was

[10] Davis, *The Truth about Geronimo*, 223–37; Charles B. Gatewood, *Lieutenant Charles B. Gatewood, 6th U. S. Cavalry and the Surrender of Geronimo.*

The capture of Nachez [Nahche] and Geronimo and subsequent exile of the Chiricahuas form the main theme of a later chapter in Crook's life.

claimed, had rendered the terms invalid by running away. This would be the legal basis for holding the Apaches in exile indefinitely. The Indians alone were to bear the blame.

Finally, on April 7, the Chiricahua captives were sent away. Crook went to Bowie Station to see them off. "There was considerable nervousness amongst the men. There were 77 in all of them—15 men, 33 women, and 29 children. It is a big relief to get rid of them."

Four days later Crook relinquished command of the Department of Arizona, and set out for Omaha, returning to the Department of the Platte. With him went his wife, Mrs. Read, his sister-in-law, Peison, the striker, and Lee, his Chinese cook.

VIII
FIGHTING WITH
WORDS

25. *The Indian is a human being*

THE DEPARTMENT OF THE PLATTE was very quiet. No general Indian war threatened, and "depredations" were of a local nature. The reservations were peaceful; none of the chiefs seemed inclined, at the moment, to lead his people on the warpath. Reconnaissances were the most active of departmental duties. The General settled down in Omaha, and began to recall the past. During this period he wrote the largest part of his autobiography, and his diary contains frequent notices to anniversaries of battles. "Nov. 4, 1886. Today 34 years ago I left New York for San Francisco to join my Regiment. Went to see John L. Sullivan's exhibition of the noble art."

General Crook was entering the ranks of the old soldiers and felt inclined to take his rest. Meetings of the Loyal Legion and the Army of West Virginia began to be part of his life. Dinner parties, euchre, and poker with friends in Omaha, and hunting trips each spring and fall with Webb Hayes occupied much of the General's time. But he was not resting on the reputation of battles won. The diplomatic defeat of the Geronimo campaign stung him into action, and the energies which had been directed toward the Chiricahuas were now directed toward their captor. Crook laid the foundations for his long-term fight with Miles for the return of the Apaches from exile with an article in the *Journal of the Military Service Institution of the United States* and by his pamphlet on the recent Apache campaign. The effect of these two items was not immediately apparent, but they bore good fruit in time.

With no Indian fighting on his hands, the General devoted his official energies to the usual peacetime problems of the United

States Army—barracks, quarters, inspections, rifle practice, and drill. The condition of frontier posts claimed special attention and remark in his annual report. Even the army had changed with the rest of the country. The West was rapidly becoming a populated area. The beaver gave way to the buzz saw, and the buffalo to the bullwhacker. Posts, forts, and stations in the West which had at one time seemed perfectly adequate were now considered too small. Quarters which had seemed comfortable when compared with the trials of a winter campaign on the plains were now discovered to be "illy built and unhealthy." "There would seem to be no reason why an officer's quarters, which, while he is in the service, are his only home, should not have the conveniences which are found in ordinary houses occupied by civilians. No quarters should be constructed which are not provided with bathrooms."[1]

Target practice was a fetish of the regular army during the seventies and eighties. Departmental general orders consist largely of reports of target practice from one post or another. The Department of the Platte, commanded by a general who loved good shooting and took pride in the marksmanship of his officers and men, outdid itself on the ranges. Under Captain Guy V. Henry of Rosebud memory, the department made "excellent progress" in the business of shooting at bullseyes. Crook recommended that the best shots in each department be listed in the Army Register.

The General was also interested in a change of the traditional methods of drill and tactics. He suggested, both in his report and in letters from headquarters to his superiors, that the army drill in vogue at the time was not suited to modern tactics or weapons. Close approximation to campaign conditions, especially on the plains, was more to Crook's liking. Drill regulations for the infantry were still written in the East, where the garrison soldiers regarded the frontier as remote. Crook wanted his soldiers fit for combat, not for parade.[2]

In February, 1887, General Crook received a letter from the Boston Indian Citizenship Committee:

[1] Secretary of War, *Annual Report,* 1887, 133.
[2] General Crook's annual reports for 1886, 1887, and 1888 reveal his interest in new tactical principles. He reflected the "army's renaissance," as Ganoe calls it, a period which began about 1880, when the School of Application for Infantry and Cavalry was established at Fort Leavenworth. Ganoe, *The History of the United States Army,* 355–66.

Dear Sir:

The Boston Indian Citizenship Committee, recognizing your valuable services in behalf of justice to the Indians and their advancement in civilization and all the arts of peace, are desirous of testifying to their appreciation of your great work, and at the same time of securing your further aid and co-operation in the line of action they have adopted.

It would afford us great pleasure and satisfaction to welcome you to our city, and to have you present at one or more public meetings which we propose to hold. The Committee will cheerfully defray all expenses incident to your acceptance of this invitation, and earnestly hope that you may be able to accept.

The time to suit your convenience,

> Frederick O. Prince, Chairman
> H. O. Houghton, Treasurer
> Mrs. Stephen H. Bullard
> Alice M. Longfellow
> Ellen A. Goodwin
> James B. Thayer
> J. W. Davis, Vice-chairman
> W. H. Lincoln, Secretary
> Edward I. Thomas
> Edward E. Hale

We cordially unite in the above invitation,

> Oliver Ames
> Hugh O'Brien

The invitation to General Crook was made with considerable assurance that it would be accepted. The General had followed the activities of the various Indian improvement and Indian rights societies with much interest. They were his best method of applying pressure for the liberation of the Apaches. They represented the outlet for opinions concerning Indian management which he could not express in official papers. Some of his communications had been used in pamphlets advocating the enfranchisement of the Indian. The General believed that the opponents to the Indian franchise movement "have had recourse to very threadbare arguments. I wish to say most emphatically that the American Indian is the intellectual peer of most, if not all, the various nationalities we have

269

assimilated to our laws, customs and language. He is fully able to protect himself, if the ballot be given, and the courts of law not closed against him."[3]

General Crook decided to go to Boston and deliver a few speeches, despite a lifelong disinclination to public appearances of that sort. He took with him Lieutenant L. W. V. Kennon, his aide, and the diaries of both cover the trip adequately. The General's notes were concise and to the point.

"Feb. 23. Arrived in Boston at 8:55. Went to the Young Hotel. Met Mr. Kennon's brother at the depot. He came up with us and took breakfast with us. Then went to Mr. Lincoln's office, there met Mrs. Tibbles, where it was arranged to have an informal meeting of the Indian loving people at half past three P.M. Nine present at it. Mrs. Whitney and Bullard, Messrs. Houghton, Thayer, Davis, Dr. Woodworth, Woods and Thomas. We visited the Faneuil Hall, Old South Church, Boston Commons, and other places of note.[4] I have heard of the crookedness of the streets in Boston, but they are so much worse than I had any idea of that I am certain I would get lost within two blocks of my hotel. Stayed all night at Mr. Frank Woods at Dorchester, where Tibbles and his wife are staying. Interviewed by Mr. Roberts of the Post, and Mr. Delaney of the Journal. Snowed during last night."

The next couple of days were spent sightseeing and meeting interested persons from Boston and vicinity. The projected meetings were meanwhile advertised. By the evening of February 26 the General was ill, and the next day was obliged to miss the first of his lectures at Shawmut Church. On the twenty-eighth, however,

[3] George Crook, *Letter from General Crook on Giving the Ballot to Indians.*

[4] Lieutenant Kennon did not approach the historic spots in Boston with proper awe. His diary for the day reads: "The Old South Church was next visited. Mr. Thomas showed us on one side where Warren entered, on the east or rear end where Washington entered, on the south side where Franklin was brought in to be christened. I suggested that these eminent men had come in from these back doors and side doors, but that it was reserved for the General and myself to enter the front door. The only reward for this sally was a somewhat dark glare from Mr. T."

"Spoke at the Old South Church at 3 P.M. to what was said to be a good audience.[5] After speaking, Mr. Houghton took us in his carriage to his home in Cambridge, where we met some of their friends, dined with their family, and afterwards went to a meeting at memorial church, where Rev. Edward Everett Hale presided. Had a fine audience to whom I told something of my Indian experiences. Afterwards went back to Mr. Houghton's house, and from there was sent back to our hotel in a carriage. Cold, but mostly clear with a strong wind."

Crook's message in each appearance was about the same. He reviewed what he knew of the Indian and touched lightly on his campaigns. He laid most weight on Indian uplift. "The Indian is a human being," was the burden of his talk. "One question today on whose settlement depends the honor of the United States is, 'How can we preserve him?' My answer is, 'First, take the government of the Indians out of politics; second, let the laws of the Indians be the same as those of the whites; third, give the Indian the ballot.' But we must not try to drive the Indians too fast in effecting these changes. We must not try to force him to take civilization immediately in its complete form, but under just laws, guaranteeing to Indians equal civil laws, the Indian question, a source of such dishonor to our country and of shame to true patriots, will soon be a thing of the past."[6]

General Crook managed about one speech per day during the rest of his stay in Boston.

"March 1. Went to the foundry at South Boston to see some heavy guns. Capt. Lyle had charge. Took dinner at Young's Hotel with Mr. Davis. Present were Mr. Woods, Capen, and Kennon. Afterwards went to Wintonville and spoke at the Unitarian Church at 4 P.M. Had a good and responsive audience. Tibbles and Bright Eyes spoke. Came back to the city. Had my hair cut."

[5] Kennon records: "The Collector of the Port, Mr. or Hon. Leverett Saltonstall introduced the General in a very wordy, uninteresting address. Mr. Houghton said that this man was very proud of his family. When asked to subscribe for the history of America edited by Winsor he looked in it and refused to buy it, 'I do not see my family name in it.' "

[6] General Crook's address at Memorial Church, Boston *Post*, February 28, 1887.

"March 2. Cloudy and warm this morning. Lt. Kennon came back from Providence. Mr. Tibbles and I went to Bunker Hill monument this morning. Attended the meeting of committee at Mr. Houghton's room at half past two, where the Florida matter was discussed.[7] Left at 4 P.M. for Springfield. Spoke at 8 P.M. at church in Springfield to a large and responsive audience. Were met at the depot by Col. Buffington, president of the Indian Rights Association. Afterwards Lt. Kennon and self stayed all night at his home on the arsenal grounds."

"March 3. Went through the workshops at the arsenal, and saw how the entire Springfield rifle was made by machinery. Returned to Boston in the afternoon. Spoke to a small audience at the Trinity church tonight."

"March 4. Sky overcast this morning. Left at 10 A.M. for Wellesley College. There addressed some seven hundred girl students, a very appreciative audience.[8] Went to Worcester in the afternoon, and addressed a meeting there. Stayed with Mr. Greene, the editor of the Worcester Spy."

"March 5. Came back to Boston this morning. Weather cold but clear. The committee gave us a farewell dinner at Young's hotel. Present were Messrs. Davis, Houghton, Woods, Thomas, Lincoln, Capen, Tibbles, Kennon, and self. Col. Sullivan looked in. This evening had a meeting at Brookline to the poorest house we have yet had. Ladies of the Indian Rights Committee made me a present of stylograph pen and fixings. Lovely day."

The General left for Omaha on March 7, well satisfied with his experience. His reception in Boston and the outlying towns had been good. As one of the Boston newspapers phrased it, "General Crook seems to be almost as popular in Boston as was his namesake, the Black Crook."[9] But the trip tired him, and early in the

[7] The "Florida matter" referred to the exile of the Chiricahuas to Fort Marion, Florida. Pressure was constantly being brought by the Indian Citizenship Committee and the Indian Rights Association for removal of the Apaches to a reservation where they could be self-supporting.

[8] Kennon noted: "They seemed very much interested in the Indian question. There was to be a debate, I believe, on this question, and the girls were after 'points.'"

[9] A clipping in a scrapbook kept by Mrs. Crook gives this item. The "Black Crook" was a popular variety show of the times. General Crook attended the show in Chicago, March 2, 1889.

spring he took a vacation to Wisconsin, fishing. The rest and sport were enough to recuperate any man interested in fish. In one day the General caught 135 bass. "I could have caught more," he wrote, "but got ashamed. The fish were not large, but right size for the pan."

Summer in Omaha was interrupted by an inspection trip through the department, accompanied by the usual side trips for hunting and fishing. Crook's judgment of a post was likely to be swayed by the number and size of deer and antelope in the neighborhood, or the trout in the near-by streams. But the occasional amusements and exercise did not atone for the heat and dust of Omaha. Crook frequently complained of insomnia and attacks of malaria. He was obliged to dose himself with quinine from time to time, and his illness forced him to miss many of the social affairs—most of them quite willingly. Musicals were his particular aversion, and he preferred not to be bored by them. Mary Crook and "the ladies" attended to the social end of the Crook family life, while the General stayed at home and played whist or euchre with fellow officers, or passed the time tanning skins, stuffing trophies, or killing rats.

Late in the summer of 1887 General Crook left Omaha for an extended hunting trip—the annual fall hunt. His wife accompanied him as far as Cheyenne, and the General and his party continued to Fort Bridger, where the mountain streams were crowded with trout. For two weeks the vacationers roamed through southern Wyoming. The life in the open brought Crook back to his accustomed vigor. He slept soundly on the ground and ate the wild food with appetite after a day spent chasing a deer or tracking a bear.

Lieutenant John Bourke described General Crook as a hunting companion thus:

"General Crook takes his cup of coffee, soaks in it a handful of hardtack, retires to a nook, sits down, and gets through his meal in silence. He is remarkably abstemious, rarely drinks coffee or tea, except when on a trip in the mountains, can scarcely ever be prevailed upon to touch whiskey, and then never more than a spoonful—in brief he is the most abstemious man I have ever been associated with.

"We have no books with us this time, but to him the great book of nature lies always open. He knows the course of rivers and the trend of mountains as if by instinct, and can find his way through dark and tangled forests with the certainty of an aborigine. If there be any game near, his keen eye detects its track, his steady foot follows it, and his unerring rifle brings it down. If the stream on which we camp is trout-bearing, his skill as a fisherman will lure the finny tribe where all others fail."[10]

When General Crook returned to Omaha at the end of August, 1887, he was immediately ordered to participate in the last Indian uprisings ever to require his personal attention. The trouble involved a band of Ute Indians, the same tribe which had perpetrated the Meeker-Thornburgh massacre in 1879. These Indians had been removed from their Colorado reservation, and were settled in Utah at the Uintah and Ouray agencies.

But the Indians had not forgotten their old land. Each year they left their new reservation and hunted in Colorado, grazing their cattle on public lands which had once been theirs and which they knew were good. In the fall of 1887 a band of Ute Indians under Chief Colorow was moving through Garfield County, Colorado. On August 9 Game Warden Joseph E. Burgett, with a posse, ran across Colorow's band on the north fork of White River and attempted to arrest some of the Indians on the charge of violating the game laws of Colorado. The Utes, it seemed, were not "getting their meat in due season." The Indians resisted arrest, and shots were fired, three Indians being wounded.

The warden's posse then retired and joined forces with a second posse led by Sheriff James C. Kendall of Garfield County, who was trying to serve civil warrants on two of Colorow's band wanted for horse stealing. To Colorow the serving of a warrant was the same as a declaration of war. More shots were fired, and

---

[10] Bourke, *Diary* [MS], August 6, 1890. General Crook went on fall hunts with Webb Hayes and John Collins every year after 1878, except 1885 and 1886, when the Chiricahuas kept him busy. The hunts were located as follows: 1878—near Fort Steele; 1879—through the Spotted Tail agencies to Rock Creek, Wyoming; 1880—two hunts: first, Fort Bridger to Yellowstone park; and second, near Rock Creek; 1881—Cheyenne to Medicine Bow; 1882—near Fort Washakie; 1883—south of Fort Bridger; 1884—Fort Casper; 1887, 1888, and 1889, Fort Casper. *Daily InterOcean* (Chicago), April 5, 1890.

the posses decided to wait, knowing that if they attacked now, a general Indian uprising might result.

The sheriff appealed to Governor Alva Adams, asking for help. The Governor sent units of the Colorado state militia, and at the same time telegraphed General Crook for the aid of United States troops. Crook refused help on the grounds that he could not interfere in a case which involved serving civil warrants on Indians. The Governor, who had been banking on help from the regulars, now cautioned his militia not to precipitate any fighting, but simply to protect Colorado lives and property. Meanwhile, he again appealed for help.

"If you cannot aid in enforcing civil law against Indians, it certainly must be within your province to compel Indians to return to their reservations when they wander over our state frightening and shooting at our citizens, compelling them to abandon their homes, stock and crops. The experience of eight years ago prevents the entertaining of too much faith in the harmless intentions of these very Indians. Your immediate intervention would induce Indians to return to reservation, and we think you should force them to go at once and return no more."[11]

General Crook knew too much about Indian troubles and the attitude of the Colorado citizens in particular to be upset by general charges of Indian depredations. He pointed out that "troops could not be used to restore Indians to their reservation unless by request of the Interior Department, and by orders from superior authority."

Colorow had meanwhile had a talk with two men from Meeker and agreed to move back to the reservation, asking for fifteen days to gather stock and prepare for the move. The delay was regarded as an attempt to bring reinforcements from the reservation for a general Ute war against Colorado. Sheriff Kendall did not regard himself bound by the truce and started after part of Colorow's band. His posse was joined on August 24 by about one hundred of the Colorado militia under Major Gavin Leslie.

The Indians, numbering about twenty-five warriors and their families, were moving slowly toward the reservation when they

[11] Colorado, Governor, *Reports of Officers and Official Correspondence Relating to the Military Assistance Rendered by the State of Colorado to the Citizens of Garfield and Routt Counties during the Ute Difficulties of 1887*, 22.

were attacked by the militia and posse on the twenty-fifth. The fight resulted in the deaths of three white men, and an undetermined number of Indians. The report of United States troops was that four Indians were killed, two of them girls and one a small boy. The report of General F. M. Reardon of Colorado claimed about fifteen warriors dead and wounded.[12] The Indians abandoned their stock, 300 to 400 horses and 2,500 sheep and goats, and moved back to the Uintah agency. The whites gathered in the abandoned stock, and moved to Rangely.

Governor Adams had appealed to Secretary of the Interior Lamar, asking for help, and was informed that Agent Byrnes of Uintah and General Crook would meet him at Meeker to settle the difficulty. Meanwhile, he suggested that the Colorado militia avoid following or attacking Colorow's band. General Crook received his orders on August 27, and set out immediately for Meeker, via Cheyenne and Rawlins, arriving by stage at Dixon on August 29.

"Aug. 30. Were transferred to a covered wagon which was so filled with baggage that only one of us could sit on the inside, and in a very cramped position, while the others sat outside with the driver. We reached Meeker a little before one o'clock P.M. Just before we got there it rained, and I, sitting on the outside, got a little wet. Meeker consists of but little beyond the cantonement built by the troops in 1880–81, and now inhabited by the citizens. There are probably two or three hundred people in it."

"Aug. 31. Dana Thayer gave me his bed, and had a good sleep in Hugus and Major's store. Took breakfast at Mr. Major's house. Saw the governor of Colorado, Alva Adams, and his staff, Gen. Shafer, West, and Judge Seymour, and Col. Morrison of the militia, and had a conference about the situation. A little after noon Agent Byrnes and Capt. Dawson's troops came in from Duchesne. Had a long talk in the afternoon. The Governor's outfit have been trying all day to get me to relieve them from their dilemma by making me their scape goat. The whole transaction of this affair has been a disgraceful job from beginning to end. Mr. Major gave us a dinner at 5 P.M."

[12] Colorado, Governor, *Reports during the Ute Difficulties*, 61; Secretary of War, *Annual Report*, 1888, 171–72.

"Sept. 1. The weather yesterday and today has been exquisite. The Governor and party still wanted Agent Byrnes and myself to relieve them from their embarrassment, but we still remained firm that the stock or its equivalent should be given to the Utes before we would in any way become responsible for the Utes behaving themselves. The Gov. and most of his party left for Denver, but before leaving they got the promise from the county commissioner to return the Indians' stock to agent on reservation."

"Sept. 2. Left this morning for Rawlins. Just before leaving Meeker a lady, Mrs. Brasker, jumped all over me for not protecting the country, etc., etc., but ended in her trying to apologize. We stayed all night in Dixon."

Thus ended the "Ute War," described by one officer as "one of the grossest outrages that has been perpetrated on a tribe of Indians in modern times."[13]

26. We want the land

IN THE SPRING OF 1880 Major General Alfred H. Terry requested his retirement. General Crook noted the fact in his diary on March 30. The retiring board met in Washington and duly accepted General Terry's request. On April 6, while visiting the Roberts family in Cheyenne, Crook received a telegram from Adjutant General Drum informing him of his appointment as Major General, vice Terry.

General Crook had been the ranking brigadier, but there was some speculation whether Miles or he would get the appointment. Crook's friends had been busy pushing his appointment ever since rumors of Terry's intentions appeared. On March 20 the General's old friend, former President Hayes wrote to the chief justice, "Our friend, General Crook is, I am sure, the man to take the place of General Terry, if the latter retires, as is now expected, early in April. I believe General Crook is the senior Brigadier. His appoint-

[13] Colorado, Governor, *Reports during the Ute Difficulties*, 63.

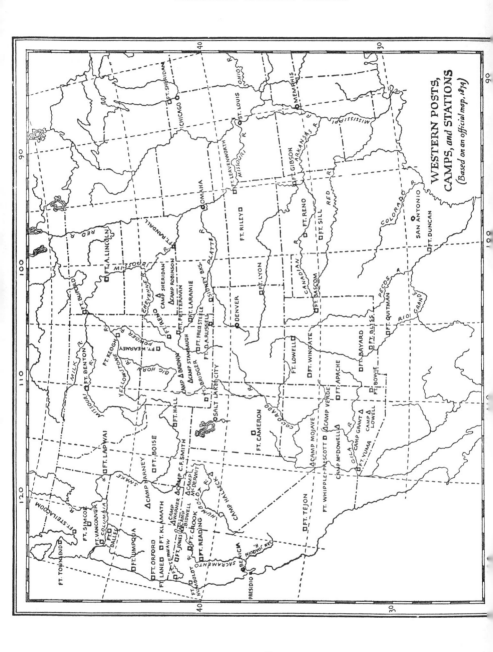

WESTERN POSTS,
CAMPS, and STATIONS
(Based on an official map, 1874)

ment will be especially gratifying to all who take an interest in just and humane treatment of the Indian. His attitude to Mr. Cleveland's administration is not in his way, and he is the most distinguished soldier named for the place."[1]

On May 4 Crook relinquished command of the Department of the Platte and the next day left for Chicago to assume command of the Division of the Missouri, vacated by General Terry. This division comprised the Departments of the Platte, Dakota, Missouri, and Texas, and was by far the largest and most active command in the army, containing 175 companies of infantry, 75 troops of cavalry, and 4 batteries of artillery. Personnel of the division amounted to 13,045, almost half the entire strength of the army.[2]

The promotion and increase in responsibility and power had little effect on Crook's character. Two weeks after his move to Chicago, he sent three turkeys and six chickens to Young Man Afraid of His Horses at Pine Ridge agency.

The move to the Division of the Missouri took the General farther away from the frontier than he had been at any time before or since the Civil War. To him it was a move to the "big city," and his reactions to his surroundings indicated that he felt rather ill at ease, certainly not at home, in his new station. He took long walks and rides through Washington and Jackson parks, went to the zoo, to the races, fished from the government pier, played euchre, poker, and seven-up with his fellow officers, and went to the theater when invited. In every possible way he tried to approximate the amusements of Omaha.

Mary Crook was in Oakland when the promotion was announced and the move to Chicago took place. By the time she and her sister Fanny arrived in Chicago in November, Crook had moved from the Leland Hotel to the Calumet Club. The three then took rooms at the Grand Pacific.

In an effort to make himself more comfortable, the General surrounded himself with as many of his old staff as possible. Lieutenant L. W. V. Kennon, who had been his aide for several years, went with him to Chicago, and the faithful Peison also came along

[1] *Diary and Letters,* IV, 377. A similar letter was sent the same day to Carl Schurz.

[2] Secretary of War, *Annual Report,* 1888, 141.

as general service messenger. Crook then arranged for the transfer of Captain Roberts to his staff.

Headquarters Division of the Missouri, located in the Pullman Building, on the southwest corner of Michigan Avenue and Adams Street, acquired a reputation for informality. In the field, General Crook was famous for his nonissue uniform. He dressed for the climate and for comfort, not concerned with the regulations laid down in the books. His new quarters reflected his casual attitude.

The *Chicago Herald* reporter, who had headquarters as his beat, felt that the new "unmilitary" atmosphere was worth a feature story. "There is precious little red tape around Crook's headquarters, and none whatever of that military exclusiveness which is so often exasperating to the ordinary civilian doing business with the army. The doors are all wide open, and the visitor simply walks in. He doesn't see anybody in uniform. Everybody, from General Crook down is in citizen's dress. No orderly, no messenger, no formality of any kind. If you don't interrupt the General in the midst of a good story, he will be very glad to see you, and tell you so most cordially. Everybody that knows General Crook knows that he is a typical American, and a democrat, and that same spirit of democracy pervades his whole headquarters."[3]

Chicago society welcomed General Crook as the "Conqueror of the Apaches," and displayed him as a trophy for a time, inviting him to theater parties and social affairs for a few months. The novelty wore off, however, and Crook slid back into his social groove. The glimpse he had of the moneyed class impressed him.

"May 9, 1888. Marshall Field, Mr. Doane, and others gave me a banquet at the Calumet Club this evening. A magnificent affair. General Sheridan, ex-Sec. Lincoln, Potter Palmer, Mr. Medill were amongst the guests. There were twenty three in all, and their wealth was estimated at $40,000,000. A nicer set of modest gentlemen it has never been my fortune to meet. I came home with Col. Corbin. It sprinkled a little on the way home. My dinner didn't set well, and consequently I didn't sleep well. This is the anniversary of the battle of Cloyd's Mountain."

[3] *Army and Navy Journal*, Vol. XXVII, No. 24 (February 8, 1890), 461.

The General was never so happy as when old friends of his dropped in on their way through the city. Chicago was "en route" for all east-west travel, and Crook was kept busy greeting old comrades who were on leave, going to Washington on business, or returning to duty in the West. The Division of the Missouri was no longer the bloody battleground of a decade earlier, and the commanding general was able to spend much of his time leisurely.

Crook took advantage of his new station to check on his health. For some years he had been troubled with bleeding from the lungs, and he now consulted a doctor frequently. A physical examination with "an instrument that sketched the beating of the pulse on a piece of smoked paper showed a great difference in the beating of the two mists." Crook's heart was showing the strain of his campaigns. On October 18, 1888, he reported: "Had a bad attack today. Dr. Tully called in Dr. Billings in consultation, who said that I had no organic trouble, but that my lungs were distended and pressed on my heart."

The Division of the Missouri, though not the scene of any major activities at the time, was still potentially the most active division in the army. General Crook had been placed in command because he was recognized as the most capable man in the army for Indian affairs. The Indians were still a problem, even though the major Indian wars were a thing of the past. More accurately, perhaps, the whites were a problem, for it was their constantly increasing pressure which caused unrest, minor outbreaks, and small wars long after the power of the great tribes had been broken.

As the General explained it to the Sioux: "The white men in the East are like birds. They are hatching out their eggs every year, and there is not room enough in the East, and they must go elsewhere; and they come out West, as you have seen them coming for the last few years. And they are still coming, and will come until they overrun all of this country; and you can't prevent it, nor can the President prevent it. Everything is decided in Washington by the majority, and these people come out West and see that the Indians have a big body of land that they are not using, and they say, 'we want the land.' "[4]

It was the cry "we want the land" that had driven the Utes

[4] 51 Cong., 1 sess., *Senate Ex. Doc. 51.*

from Colorado, the Sioux from the Black Hills country, the Apaches from Arizona, and the Bannocks to bloodshed. It was this cry that had been basically responsible for Indian wars ever since the first Europeans had found Indian possession of the land an obstacle to expansion and settlement.

In 1887 Congress believed that it had a solution to the problem of the land. On February 8 the Dawes Act was passed. The Indians were now to be given their land in severalty. The allotment policy found its way into the statute books.

The idea of alloting land to Indians in severalty grew up gradually during the eighteen seventies, when it began to take the form of a movement. It was first recommended by certain commissioners of Indian Affairs, and finally by secretaries of the interior. President Hayes recommended it as early as 1879. The plan was to give each Indian a plot of ground which he would recognize as his own, and for which he would be responsible. The large reservations were to be broken up and divided, communal ownership discouraged, and the Indian was to be forced, by circumstance or otherwise, to walk the white man's road.[5]

Several bills had been introduced in Congress bearing on the subject, but they failed to pass the House of Representatives. Certain tribes, by provision of special laws, were given the privilege of allotment in severalty, the Crows and Omahas in 1882 and the Umatillas in 1885. In 1881 the Utes had been "persuaded" to cede their reservation and accept allotments. In 1886 General Sheridan, in his report, argued in favor of such a division of the land.

General Crook, also, was in favor of forcing the Indians to become property owners. He initiated a similar practice among the Apaches, and believed that once an Indian was given a farm of his own he would become like a white man. "The Apache is becoming a property owner. It is his property, won by his own toil, and he thrills at once with the pride of acquisition, and the anxiety of possession. He is changing both inside and out: exteriorly he is dressed in white man's garb, wholly or in part. Mentally he is counting the

[5] D. S. Otis, "History of the Allotment Policy," *Readjustment of Indian Affairs* (hearings before the Committee on Indian Affairs, House of Representatives, 73 Cong., 2 sess., on H.R. 7902), 428–89.

probable value of his steers and interested in knowing how much of his corn crop the quartermaster may want next month."[6]

Not all the Indians agreed. Some of them, of course, knew that times had changed. "The road our fathers walked on is gone; the game is gone; the white people are all about us. There is no use in any Indian thinking of the old ways; he must now go to work as the white man does. We want titles to our lands, that the land may be secure to our children."[7]

The Five Civilized Tribes, however, had become prosperous under a system of communal ownership. They wanted no change. The Nez Percés, too, objected, saying, "They asked us to divide the land, to divide our mother, upon whose bosom we had been born, upon whose lap we had been reared." The minority report on the Dawes Act pointed out that "it does not make a farmer out of an Indian to give him a quarter section of land." The same, it was said, was true of the white man.[8] The Indian Defense Association, established in 1885, also opposed allotment as likely to be injurious if too hastily adopted.

According to the treaty of 1868, no new treaty could be put into effect without the agreement of three-fourths of the adult male Indians. In 1888, when a commission was sent to the Sioux with a proposed law looking to the division of their reservation, the necessary signatures could not be obtained. The Indians felt that not enough money was offered for the land they were giving up. There were other grievances, besides, which they wanted redressed. A delegation of chiefs went to Washington that winter to present their demands.

A new law proposing division of the Great Sioux reservation was passed on March 2, 1889. It provided that the head of each family should be given 320 acres of land, single persons over 18, and orphans under 18, 160 acres, and other single persons under 18, 80 acres. Double this amount of land was to be granted if the land was suitable only for grazing. The various provisions of the Dawes Act were to apply; namely, that a patent in fee was to be issued to each allotee, the land to be held in trust for twenty-five

[6] George Crook, "The Apache Problem," *Journal of the Military Service Institution of the United States*, Vol. VII, No. 27 (October, 1886), 257–69.

[7] Otis, "History of the Allotment Policy."

[8] Otis, "History of the Allotment Policy."

years, during which time it could not be alienated or encumbered. The idea was to make a white man out of the Indian by changing his attitude toward property.[9]

The land which the Sioux did not take under the allotment principle was to revert to the public domain and be sold to homesteaders. Already land-hungry settlers were crowding the frontier towns. One dollar and twenty-five cents per acre was the price for land sold during the first three years, seventy-five cents the next two years, and fifty cents for the residue. This money was to be held as a fund for the needs of the Indians.

The Sioux delegation had done well in Washington. They had managed to get an increase in the price of their ceded land, a larger allotment per Indian, and a new clause inserted in the law which obliged the government to pay for the horses taken from the Sioux under Red Cloud and Red Leaf in 1876.

A new commission was appointed to explain the new law to the Sioux and offer them the opportunity to "touch the pen." The Sioux Commission of 1889 consisted of Governor Charles Foster of Ohio, chairman, Senator William Warner of Missouri, and General George Crook. The commission left Chicago for the West on May 29, 1889. The General noted in his diary: "The Commission left at 5:30 P.M. on a special car on the Northwestern R.R. Governor Foster, Sen. Warren and myself—Maj. Roberts, Mr. Miller, disbursing officer, Mr. Lott, shorthand and typewriter, Mr. Burrel, Mr. Warner, clerks, and Wilson, colored messenger. Played whist until bedtime. We have fine acommodations aboard the car, a good cook and plenty to eat."

The first agency visited was the Rosebud. The commission put the Indians in a receptive frame of mind by giving them a feast of fifteen beeves. "Afterwards the Indians gave us the 'Omaha Dance,' which consists of a circle being formed, and the dancers stripped all except breech clout, head gear, etc., with their persons painted in the most grotesque and diabolical fashions. There were a dozen or fifteen dancers. They hopped around, in and out, mostly in circles, keeping time to the tom-tom, which in this instance consisted of several Indians sitting in a circle beating on the head of a bass drum.

[9] Schmeckebier, *The Office of Indian Affairs*, 79–80.

"The dancers, after getting tired, would return to their seats, keeping this up to the end. Just before the close, one of their number performed alone, showing how in the past he in an encounter with the Shoshone Indians was wounded and helped off the field by a comrade, etc., which created much old-time excitement amongst the Indian bystanders. But the dance was a mere imitation of what it used to be ten years ago. The whole affair lacked enthusiasm and spirit. Bishop Hare preached, but none of our party attended."

On Monday, June 3, the Indians and commissioners met in council. The chiefs sat forward and did all the talking through their chosen interpreters, Louie Richard, Charles Tackett, and Louie Bordeaux. The largest gathering, on June 7, was attended by 24 chiefs and 700 followers. Governor Foster introduced the bill, and the Indians adjourned to discuss it. The private Indian councils were stormy, and some of the opposition threatened to kill those who signed the bill. General Crook was invited to appear.

"It was about fifteen after two. They had formed a circle by their wagons of about one hundred yards in diameter. The Indian men were squatting and laying on the outer edge. In the center of the circle was a fly tent stretched, with a wagon seat under it for me to sit under. They were very undemonstrative, and inclined to be a little sullen. They showed but little desire to hear me talk, saying they all understood the bill, which was a lie. After explaining the benefits of the legislation to them, they said they would talk over the subject amongst themselves, but didn't want to be pushed, as it took them a long time to work it out amongst themselves. I told them that we could not wait much longer, and that if they did not sign soon we would take it for granted that they were not going to sign, and we wanted to go away, as we had much work elsewhere, that we had no personal interest in their signing, etc. After I left they broke up in a row, which reacted in our favor, as they told Louie Richard not to tell me of it."

Indian objection to the proposed bill was based on three major fears. First, there was the general disinclination of the Indians to part with any land at all. They remembered too well the treaties of the past, how the land which had once been theirs had been taken piece by piece, until there remained only a fraction of the boundless range which had been their life.

285

There was also a general suspicion of any new plan. The chiefs pointed out that other Indians who had their land in severalty were no better off than before; in fact, worse off than the Sioux. The new system meant work, hardships, and a venture into the unknown, and "Indians are, like the rest of mankind, unwilling to vote for present trouble in order to secure an unknown and uncertain benefit."[10]

The influential chiefs were afraid that ownership of land in severalty would mean the end of their power. The Indians might become so independent that they would ignore the chiefs and head men. This point of view carried much weight with the old chiefs— Red Cloud, Iron Nation, and Touch-the-Clouds. There was no answer to their fears, for the new plan was partly designed to break up tribal relations and the power of the warrior chiefs.

The problem of the commission was to get behind the chiefs at each agency and talk to the individual Indians. General Crook was particularly successful at this job, because he knew many of the Sioux personally. Many of the warriors had been scouts under him in the old days. At the Pine Ridge agency, June 9, he wrote thus: "Lovely day. Tuned different Indians up. Got a good many signatures by different younger Indians who were made to see that they must think for themselves, and in this way it is breaking down the opposition of the old, unreconstructed chiefs."

The Pine Ridge agency Sioux proved stubborn. They were determined not to sign. Their opposition was led by American Horse, who, the General admitted, "was too much for the Commission. He was a better speaker than any of us." American Horse raised an objection about the boundary line of the reservation, the north line of the state of Nebraska. This line, he claimed, was different from the one promised in the treaty of 1868. The commissioners could only point to the words of the law, but had nothing else to say. They knew that the Indians had been cheated, but were powerless to change matters, or even promise change.

American Horse was finally convinced that the present bill was better than nothing, and nothing was what the Sioux were likely to get if they did not agree soon. On June 21, "Had a big council this

10 Alice C. Fletcher, quoted in Otis, "History of the Allotment Policy."

afternoon in which American Horse, Bear Nose and a couple of others made speeches in favor of the bill for the first time since we first met the Indians here. American Horse's band commenced signing. I had coached Bear Nose."

The Lower Brule Indians, next on the route, were generally in favor of the bill, wanting only their share of free beeves for a little counciling. In three days the commission obtained the necessary signatures. However, Crow Creek agency, reached July 5, gave a little trouble. The chiefs wanted a trip to Washington in exchange for the signatures of their bands. Crook refused their offer, but "Gov. Foster thought he saw his way out of the difficulty by promising the chiefs they should go to Washington to sign, provided their men all signed here, to which they replied they would do. Kept him waiting until after it was too late for us to go to Chamberlain, and then told him they must be allowed to carry the rolls with them. Foster got his fill of negotiations with Indians."

The Cheyenne agency proved the most difficult of all. Major Randall had been secured by General Crook to be present at the agency to use his influence with what was expected to be a major problem. After much counciling, the Indians appointed twelve chiefs to represent them, and Crook spent all day on July 16 explaining the bill to them, with no success. The next day: "Had a council about noon. Indians commenced filibustering with the evident intention of preventing any conclusion being reached. I stepped in and made a short speech, and said that those who wanted to sign could do so.

"I ordered the signing commenced, when the hostile element crowded in in a boisterous manner with the view to intimidate them from signing. One of them, Black Fox, jumped in the ring with a war club to slug the first one who attempted to sign. I looked around for a club, finding none, and noticing the chairs had a thick wooden bottom, I took a seat near him, where I could see all his movements, intending felling him on his first hostile movement, when he was ousted by the police, and taken off to the guardhouse."

After a few more days of council, Omaha dances and talks, the commission left Cheyenne without the necessary signatures. The rolls were left with Major Randall and the agent, who were expected to get individuals to sign later.[11]

Standing Rock agency was the final stop. Here the Indians were represented by John Grass, who "asked questions that showed he thoroughly understood the subject. His remarks had more sense in them than we have heard from all the Indians since engaged on this duty." Four days later, August 3, "Met the Indians in council about three P.M. After a little talking they commenced signing, John Grass taking the lead. Sitting Bull tried to speak after the signing commenced, but I stopped him. Then he tried twice to stampede the Indians away from signing, but his efforts failed, and he flattened out, his wind bag was punctured, and several of his followers have deserted him."

Finally, on August 7 the commission left for Mandan and Chicago, adjourning August 12. More than the requisite three-fourths of the Indians had signed the bill, and the Great Sioux reservation was to be opened. The Sioux took their land in severalty.

The principle of allotment did not bring happiness or civilization to the Indians. Leasing of land to the whites became a common and disastrous practice. The Indians neither worked the land, nor could they exist on the rentals. Families crowded certain parts of the land to the detriment of others. Laws were soon changed making it possible for the whites to get control of the land patents. "Within thirty-three years more than fifty per cent of the original area of alloted land passed from Indian to white ownership."[12]

When the treaty was signed, however, these weaknesses were not generally foreseen. When American Horse "took the pen," he offered an explanation, "When I am laying on my deathbed, I will have the satisfaction of knowing that I can leave a piece of land to my children, so that they will not have it to say that for my foolishness I deprived them of lands that they might have had."[13]

[11] Besides reasonable persuasion, there were other methods of getting signatures. A letter from Crook to Foster, dated August 27, 1889, reveals that Red Cloud, Little Wound, and Young Man Afraid, all of the Pine Ridge agency, met with Captain Pollock and the agent and were offered two hundred dollars each to feast their bands if they would sign. In 1881 Chief Ouray of the Uncompaghre Utes received several times the value of his farm to help him make up his mind to cede the reservation. 51 Cong., 1 sess., *Senate Ex. Doc. 83.*

[12] Oliver LaFarge (ed.), *The Changing Indian,* 90. The section on land

27. *He, at least, never lied to us*

HAVING SUCCESSFULLY COMPLETED the work of the Sioux Commission, General Crook rested. He, too, "had his fill of negotiations with Indians." Rest to the General meant a session out-of-doors, camping, hunting, and fishing with congenial companions. The projected excursion was neatly combined with a review of troop maneuvers being held by the Department of the Platte under General John R. Brooke at Fort Robinson.

On September 10, 1889, General Crook left Fort Robinson for Casper, the outfitting point for his last big hunt. He and his companions, Webb Hayes and John Collins, went to the head of Cheyenne River and Salt Creek. "Big Bat," assisted by an Indian, went as guide and bear-tracker extraordinary. Lieutenant Wright and several enlisted men formed the escort.

Hunting was good. From September 11 to October 7 the party bagged eighty-six antelope, thirty-eight deer, five bear, five sheep, two wildcats, one skunk, one porcupine, one coyote, one elk, two badger, six sage hens, and four rattlesnakes. Even this large bag represented only the game the party chose to shoot. Many antelope and deer were by-passed while the General and Big Bat were on the trail of more elusive meat.

The hunt was suddenly broken up October 3 when "Pvt. Monahan accidentally killed Pvt. Stephens by shooting the lower part of his face and jaw off. He lived about one-half hour."

The General then returned to Chicago and prepared for another hunt—this time for bigger game. General Miles was the quarry, and he was to be forced to give up the Apache captives.

According to the terms of surrender in 1886, General Crook sent seventy-seven hostile Apaches to Florida. In September and October of the same year General Miles, who succeeded Crook in command of the Department of Arizona, sent eighteen men and

allotment of Allan G. Harper in this symposium gives a graphic account of the fate of the Lower Brules under the new system.
[13] 51 Cong., 1 sess., *Senate Ex. Doc. 51*, 113.

twenty-three women and children into captivity—the result of his long campaign against the handful of Chiricahuas who had fled after their capitulation to Crook.

"In addition General Miles also sent to Florida all the members of their tribe who had remained quietly on the reservation, including the scouts who had done such good service in hunting down the renegades. In short, there were altogether 498 Apaches sent to Florida."[1]

Seventeen of the Chiricahua warriors were confined at Fort Pickens, Florida,[2] removed from their families: a direct violation of the terms of their surrender. Until April, 1887, all the rest of the adults were imprisoned at Fort Marion, St. Augustine, Florida.[3] At that time, largely because of representations made by the Indian Rights Association, led by Herbert Welsh,[4] the families of the Apaches at Fort Pickens were sent to them there. The rest were taken to Mount Vernon Barracks, near Mobile, Alabama.[5] In May,

[1] Cyrus S. Roberts to Johnstone, March 15, 1890. This letter to the editor of the Minneapolis *Pioneer Press* was intended to "manufacture public opinion" in an area where the public was disinclined to concern itself over the fate of the Chiricahuas, loyal or otherwise.

[2] Fort Pickens, Florida, was situated on Santa Rosa Island, Pensacola Harbor. Construction of the fort was begun in 1828, and it was officially named in 1833, in honor of Brigadier General Andrew Pickens. The post was first garrisoned on October 21, 1834. During the Civil War, Pickens was the only defensive work in Pensacola Bay to remain in Federal hands. The post was turned over to the Engineer Department on June 27, 1884. Fort Pickens is still occupied for military purposes. *Posts, Camps, and Stations File.*

[3] Fort Marion, near St. Augustine, Florida, is the oldest masonry defensive work still standing in the United States. Built about 1762 by the Spaniards, the fort was called Castillo de San Marcos. On January 7, 1825, after the purchase of Florida by the United States, it was renamed Fort Marion after Francis Marion, soldier and patriot of the Revolutionary War. It was occupied as a sub-post of St. Francis Barracks, and abandoned September 12, 1900. In 1924 the site was proclaimed as Fort Marion National Monument. *Posts, Camps, and Stations File.*

[4] Herbert Welsh, *The Apache Prisoners in Fort Marion, St. Augustine, Florida*. The story of the Chiricahua surrender and subsequent imprisonment has been the center of bitter dispute ever since. Miles, Crook, Lawton, Gatewood, Leonard Wood, Britton Davis, Parker, Cruse, Clum, and a plethora of lesser lights have spoken their piece and disagreed violently, both in the major events and minor details of the Apache affair. Ralph R. Ogle's *Federal Control of the Western Apaches* brings much evidence together on the subject, and his conclusions are apparently sound.

[5] Mount Vernon Barracks was established as Mount Vernon Arsenal on

1888, those at Fort Pickens were also removed to Mount Vernon Barracks.[6]

Of the Apaches sent to Florida, 120 had died by 1890. This number included 30 Apache children who had died at the Indian school at Carlisle. The statistics of the remnant of the prisoners were no less tragic. "Of the adult males, 79 are living, less than 30 of whom are now strong and able-bodied, the balance being either old men or broken down invalids, due mainly to malaria and other diseases. When it is considered that all the above Indians, including our old scouts, Geronimo's gang, and the women and children are herded together, it is hardly necessary to say anything to make the injustice apparent."[7]

The treatment of the Chiricahua Apaches, particularly General Miles' removal of the faithful scouts, was a constant source of irritation and anger to General Crook. Immediately after the removal he published his pamphlet of correspondence incident to the campaign and surrender of the Apaches. The pamphlet was followed by his article in the *Journal of the Military Service Institution of the United States*,[8] and public speeches in support of his Indian policies.

For two years the War Department attempted to rid itself of the embarrassing burden of the Apache prisoners.[9] Finally, in the fall of 1889, the time seemed ripe. General Crook, accompanying the Sioux delegation to Washington, took a side trip to consult

January 21, 1829, and changed to "Barracks" on July 25, 1873. Fort Stoddard landing on Mobile River was three miles from the post. In December, 1894, the post was abandoned, and in 1895 the land was turned over to the state of Alabama. *Posts, Camps, and Stations File.*

[6] 51 Cong., 1 sess., *Senate Ex. Doc. 35.*

[7] C. S. Roberts to Johnstone, March 15, 1890.

[8] *Resumé of Operations against Apache Indians 1882 to 1886;* "The Apache Problem," *Journal of the Military Service Institution of the United States*, Vol. VII, No. 27 (October, 1886), 257-69.

[9] In his report for 1888, General Schofield, commanding general of the Division of the Atlantic, remarked with some surprise, "Even in the Apache there is a good element of character which is susceptible of development." General O. O. Howard, commanding this division in 1890, recommended that the Apaches be removed to where they could support themselves, preferably to some land in the hill country of North Carolina, Alabama, or Florida. "They cannot live in the lowlands." Secretary of War, *Annual Report,* 1887, 115; 1889, 147.

General Howard, then commanding general of the division of the Atlantic at Governor's Island, to assure himself of Howard's cooperation in the forthcoming drive to relocate the Apaches.

General Howard, supported by the Secretary of War, had already taken positive action and had instructed his son, First Lieutenant Guy Howard of the Twelfth Infantry, to report on the condition of the Apaches in the Division of the Atlantic and make recommendations relative to them. The report, dated December 23, 1889, described the miserable condition of the captives, their high mortality, and their inability to support themselves in their present location and situation. Lieutenant Howard recommended that the Indians be placed on a suitable tract of land under favorable conditions by March 1, 1890. "Another year's delay would be criminal."[10]

General Howard immediately indorsed the report to the Adjutant General, who sent it, with favorable comment through General Schofield to the Secretary of War. On December 28, on order from the Secretary of War, General Crook inspected the country near Bryson, North Carolina, to determine its suitability as an Apache reservation. With the General went Senator Z. B. Vance and Lieut. L. W. V. Kennon. The country, though it was better than Mount Vernon Barracks, was not the place Crook had in mind. He wanted the Apaches removed to a land which more closely approximated conditions as the Chiricahuas had known them before captivity.

After inspecting the North Carolina site, General Crook proceeded to Mount Vernon Barracks for an interview with the Chiricahuas themselves. He wanted to know their grievances and wishes firsthand. On January 2, 1890, Lieutenant Kennon recorded in his diary:

"We reached the little station of Mount Vernon just before 8 A.M. Country poor, sandy and a growth of small pine. A road took us up to the barracks. An ambulance happened to be at the station, and a sergeant, who resented our getting in until he found out that the 'old gentleman' was General Crook.

[10] 51 Cong., 1 sess., *Senate Ex. Doc. 35*, 9–11.

"The approach to the Barracks, with great green trees on either side was very pretty. The post is walled in by a wall from 12 to 16 feet high, without flanking arrangements. It is situated on a knoll, and above the 'backwater' of the Tombigbee.

"We drove direct to the CO's house, rang, and were admitted. No one but the servant was up. Soon Mrs. Kellogg came down, and later the Colonel. There was also a daughter or niece. They were not expecting us. Did not know we were coming, apologized, etc., which was not necessary.

"A young Indian with long, black hair saw the General, and before we had finished breakfast, Chihuahua was outside, waiting. He seemed overjoyed to see the General. Kaetena joined him, and we walked over to the Indian village, which was just outside the gate of the fort. They live in little log cabins which had been built for them. At the gate was a considerable number of Indians waiting for us. Chatto [Chato] came out, and went up to the General, and gave him a greeting that was really tender. He took him by the hand, and with his other made a motion as if to clasp him about the neck. It was as if he would express his joy, but feared to take such a liberty. It was a touching sight.

"The Apaches crowded about the General, shaking hands, and laughing in their delight. The news spread that he was there, and those about us shouted to those in the distance, and from all points they came running in until we had a train of them moving with us.

"We went to the school. A young woman was in charge. Old Geronimo had come up, but the General had not noticed him at all. He was in the school room with a stick with which he threatened the youngsters who misbehaved, and turned to us for some mark of approbation. The children were called upon to recite. A few words of one syllable were written on the blackboard, and they read it off. They were so bashful that they did not look at the board when reading, having learned it by heart.

"Soon the school was dismissed, and we had a council outside. The General asked some of them to tell him about the last escapade in March '86. Geronimo pressed forward to speak, but the General said to Wrattan, 'I don't want to hear anything from Geronimo. He is such a liar that I can't believe a word he says. I don't want to have anything to do with him.' And Geronimo stood back. Then followed the interview which has been published as a congressional document."[11]

General Crook left Mount Vernon Barracks the same day, and returned to Washington to write up his report on the Chiricahuas.[12] This report, written by Kennon, was submitted on January 6. One week later Senator H. L. Dawes, chairman of the Committee on Indian Affairs, introduced Senate Joint Resolution 42, granting authority for the removal of the Apache Indian prisoners to Fort Sill, Indian Territory. The resolution was referred to the Senate Committee on Indian Affairs. On January 20 President Harrison sent his message to the Senate urging removal of the Apaches to Indian Territory and transmitting the reports of General Crook and Lieutenant Howard, favorably recommended by Secretary of War Redfield Proctor. The following day Senator Dawes asked for and obtained immediate action on the resolution.

The resolution, as passed, provided that "the prohibition to the removal of Indians of New Mexico and Arizona to the Indian Territory contained in the Act approved February 17, 1879, be and the same is hereby suspended so far as applicable to the remnant of Apache Indians held as prisoners of war in the eastern states, and it is provided that they may be removed to Fort Sill, Indian Territory, pending a negotiation with the Kiowa, Comanche, and Apache confederated tribes for their permanent location on their land."

[11] 51 Cong., 1 sess., *Senate Ex. Doc. 35*, 5–8. The interview, taken in shorthand by Kennon, is titled, "Notes of an Interview between Maj. Gen. George Crook, U. S. Army, and Chatto, Kae-te-na, Noche and other Chiricahua Apaches." General Crook, through interpreter George Wrattan, tried to discover the truth about the removal of the Chiricahuas by Miles, and to prove that the scouts had brought about the surrender of the hostiles.

[12] General Crook experienced considerable delay en route to Washington because of train trouble. He was obliged to wait in Lynchburg, Virginia, for some time, and went to see Jubal Early. His diary records the meeting on January 4: "While waiting we met Jubal Early, the ex-Confederate Gen. He is much stooped and enfeebled, but as bitter and virulent as an adder. He has no use for the government or the northern people, boasts of his being unreconstructed, and that he won't accept a pardon for his rebellious offenses. He has survived his usefulness, and is living entirely in the past. He has fought his battles over so many times that he has worked himself into the belief that many of the exaggerated, and some ridiculous stories he tells are true. We sat up with him until after 12 M., taking a hot scotch with him the last thing."

On January 23 the resolution was laid before the House and referred to the Committee on Indian Affairs of the House. The battle was now to begin in earnest.

Relocation of the Chiricahuas from Mount Vernon Barracks to Indian Territory involved more than rectifying a departmental error. Such action, indirectly at least, impugned the actions and motives of General Miles, who, in a large measure, had been personally responsible for the imprisonment of the entire Chiricahua tribe. General Miles' opposition to the measure was immediate, insistent, and actively supported by the majority of the western press.

Three major objections were raised to the removal of the Apaches from Alabama to Indian Territory. First, the new country was considered to be unhealthful, "malarious." Second, the location of the new reservation was supposed to be too close to the homeland of the Apaches. Third, and most vital, it was claimed that the incarceration of the Apaches had not involved, and did not now involve, an injustice. The removal, disposition, and continued imprisonment of the Indians was justified—so ran the argument—by the dangerously hostile attitude of the entire tribe at the time. Furthermore, the surrender of the renegades to Miles, it was asserted, had been unconditional, and the Indians had no rights whatever on that score.

General Crook, Lieutenant Kennon, General Howard, Senator Dawes, and the various Indian rights societies answered the objections one by one. Acting on verbal instructions from the Secretary of War, Crook traveled to Fort Reno and Fort Sill, Indian Territory, for an inspection of the country under consideration in Senate Resolution 42. His report to the Adjutant General stated that "the post has in the past been much troubled with malarial diseases, but I am informed for a year or so back they have been much less prevalent. From the examination I was able to make, I could discover no apparent reason why any form of malaria disease should exist.

"In my judgment the country in the vicinity of Fort Sill is well adapted for the location of the Chiricahuas now at Mount Vernon Barracks, Alabama."[13]

The claim that Fort Sill was too close to the old fighting grounds of the Apaches was decried by General Crook's friends as

[13] Crook to Adjutant General, February 20, 1890.

"puerile and absurd." "In the first place, it is 700 miles from San Carlos, and over 400 miles from the Mescallero reservation at Fort Stanton, and this whole distance in an open plain."[14] General Miles and the opponents of the resolution were particularly vulnerable on this point, for Miles in 1886 had at first strongly recommended that the Apaches be removed to Indian Territory. Only the fact that congressional action was necessary for such a move—and such action would have taken a great deal of time—had prevented him from sending the Chiricahuas to Fort Sill in 1886.

Lieutenant Kennon remained in Washington while General Crook returned to Chicago to attend to the business of the Division of the Missouri. There was almost daily correspondence between the two; the General directed the campaign for Senate Resolution 42, and his aide carried out the wishes and instructions of his chief, adding a few touches of his own. On February 21 Lieutenant Kennon testified before the House Committee on Indian Affairs, and the following day gave a story to the Washington *Star* which stated that "At the time of Geronimo's surrender General Miles was anxious that the Indians should be sent to Indian Territory, and strongly recommended it, but now that General Crook wants them sent there he opposes it strenuously. The feeling between these two warriors is such that they cannot agree on any subject."[15]

Geographical objections to the removal of the Apaches to Fort Sill became so palpably untenable that General Miles changed his point of attack. Whereupon General Crook observed, "From here it looks as if M's change of heart about the Indians going to I. T. was 'anything to beat me.' "[16]

The third objection to the removal, involving the attitude of the "loyal" Chiricahuas, largely scouts, and the terms of Geronimo's surrender to Miles, now became the final battleground for the personalities and interests in the case. Roberts, in his letter to Johnstone, hinted that "the details accompanying the removal of the portion of the tribe which remained on the reservation when the renegades left may be investigated, which, I think would hardly stand a rigid inquiry."

General Miles claimed that the Apache scouts had been dis-

[14] C. S. Roberts to Johnstone, March 15, 1890.
[15] *Evening Star* (Washington, D. C.), February 22, 1890.
[16] Crook to Kennon, March 7, 1890.

loyal, that they had supplied arms and ammunition to the renegades, and that when they were sent to Florida, they had been planning a fresh outbreak. The hostility of the "loyal" Apaches, Miles claimed, was the reason he had discharged the scouts when he took command in Arizona.

"In July 1886 I found at Fort Apache over four hundred men, women, and children belonging to the Chiricahua and Warm Springs Indians, and a more turbulent, desperate, disreputable band of human beings I had never seen before, and hope never to see again. When I visited their camp they were having their drunken orgies every night, and it was a perfect pandemonium. One of the most prominent among the Indians was Chatto, who at one time had led what was perhaps the bloodiest raid ever made in that country. The young men were insolent, violent, and restless, and anxious to go on the warpath. I received reliable information that another outbreak was contemplated by the Indians, and was then being arranged amongst them."[17]

General Crook, whose pride in his Indian scouts was well known, responded in a statement to the press: "This is all false. These stories are being circulated for a purpose. Chatto was not only faithful, but it was due entirely to the efforts of his Indian scouts that the hostiles under Nachez and Geronimo surrendered to me in March, 1886.

"It is true that General Miles did discharge the Apache scouts and after operating against thirty-three Indians for over five months without killing or capturing a single one of them, he sent Lt. Gatewood with two of Chatto's scouts, who succeeded in securing the surrender of the renegades upon the promise that they should not be harmed, and should be sent to join their families in Florida.

"It is very improbable that Chatto was planning a fresh outbreak at the time he was sent to Florida, as he and a delegation of chiefs had gone to Washington in June. Nor is it probable that his old scouts would have secured the surrender of the party with Geronimo had they contemplated an outbreak. Instead of Chatto's being sent back to his farm on the reservation with his delegation, they were sent to Florida, where they received the same treatment

---

[17] Nelson A. Miles, *Personal Recollections*, 496–97.

as the hostiles whose surrender had been secured by their efforts."[18]

General Crook's friends in the Senate continued to support him by requesting further documents bearing on the subject of the Chiricahuas. On January 28 Senator George F. Hoar submitted a resolution, which was agreed to, asking that the Secretary of War submit all evidence regarding the seizure of Chato and other Apaches after their visit to Washington in June, 1886. On March 11, Senator Dawes requested all correspondence between Sheridan and Crook relative to the surrender of the Apaches in March, 1886. The former document was submitted on March 17, and the letter on March 20.[19]

Meanwhile, opponents of Senate Resolution 42 offered evidence from the Mexican government designed to prove that the Indian scouts had been unfaithful while serving General Crook. Romero of the Mexican legation wrote to Blaine on February 4: "Mexico cannot regard with indifference the danger of the said Indians returning to their old haunts. . . . It appears to me that the result of the campaign of the United States forces against these Indians rendered it evident that the so-called scouts were nothing more than accomplices of the hostiles." Romero believed that any assurances of peace by the Apaches was simply a stratagem by which they would return to their old haunts and resume killing Mexicans —with rocks, as Geronimo used to boast.[20]

Crook regarded all such statements as "trumped up charges to affect any claim we may ever make for the killing of Capt. Crawford, which they too well knew was a most villainous affair. These Mexicans don't hesitate to give any affidavit which is desired."[21]

As the headline in the *Star* of February 22 expressed it, "The Geronimo Campaign: It is Being Fought Over Again at the Capitol." Interest was widespread, both in and out of the army. Frank P. Bennett, former chief of scouts in New Mexico under Crook, employed as a watchman in the Post Office Department in Washington, wrote the General: "I have listened quietly to the remarks that parties have bin making which ware not true untill I will not keep my mouth shut any longer, and if Gen Miles, Laughton and

---

[18] Military Division of the Missouri, *Letter Book, 1890*, 31–32. No date.
[19] 51 Cong., 1 sess., *Senate Ex. Doc. 83;* 51 Cong., 1 sess., *Senate Ex. Doc. 88.*
[20] 51 Cong., 1 sess., *House Ex. Doc. 299.*
[21] Crook to Kennon, March 5, 1890.

others are bound to fight the fight over then I am going to take a hand myselfe."[22]

Bennett then wrote a letter to the *Star* stating that Gatewood, rather than Miles or Lawton, should be called on to give evidence on the surrender of the hostiles and the behavior of the scouts, who, he believed, were thoroughly reliable. The latter appeared on February 25; and on March 5 Bennett again wrote to Crook: "I received my dismisel from the department today, no reason given or charges prefered. I caled on Cap Bourke this eavning and explained all to him. I served the govt about 15 years and nevere was discharged or a complaint put against me that I know of and cant but feel the little justice shown me for I nevere voted in my life for any party."[23] Crook commented, "There can be but little doubt as to how he lost his position, and it does seem to me that a person must injure his cause in descending to so small a business for revenge."[24]

Despite opposition from most of the Arizona and New Mexico press, and a memorial against Senate Resolution 42 from the Socicty of Arizona Pioneers, General Crook hoped to be able to see the bill out of the committee, favorably reported. On March 15 he wrote Kennon: "Capt. King passed through to Milwaukee a couple of days since. He promised to have some articles written in the Milwaukee papers, and would send you duplicate copies. . . . Stanton wrote to the Salt Lake papers, Roberts to the Pioneer Press, Corbin to write to the Dayton Journal. There will be two or three papers here will have articles on the subject, and when Rosewater of the Bee passes through here I will see him.

"But what is better than all that, Wm. Henry Smith, general manager of the Associated Press, will have the Cincinnati Gazette take hold, also that he would have Governor Butterworth and the press in Washington take hold. He says Boynton enjoys a row, and thinks he would like to pitch into Miles, so you had better get acquainted with him. Smith expects to be here about one week yet. He is a great personal friend of the Hayes.

"I made my report about the Fort Sill country while in Washington; if you want any further description of that country, let

[22] Bennett to Crook, February 23, 1890.
[23] Bennett to Crook, March 5, 1890.
[24] Crook to Kennon, March 9, 1890.

me know. Smith says he will get others interested, and says he got Senator Hoar interested, and that the latter got Senator Dawes to call for the correspondence between General Sheridan and myself, and he was going to the bottom of the business, etc., etc.

"I am feeling much better."[25]

General Crook's health had been poor ever since his return from Fort Sill in February. His diary of February 18, 1890, notes: "I am fairly sick." The next day, "Still feeling fairly under the weather." On March 11 he felt well enough to speak on the Indian question to a small audience at the Chicago Art Institute.

Six days after writing Kennon "I am feeling much better," the General was dead. With him died all hope of a favorable reception to Senate Resolution 42. The Chiricahuas languished at Mount Vernon Barracks until the Act of August 6, 1894, authorized their removal to Fort Sill, a tardy vindication of the General's Policy.

General Crook died the morning of March 21, 1890. General Charles D. Roberts' diary for the day records that "The General was feeling about as usual last night, and went to the theater. This morning he got up as usual, and went into a dressing room, as is his custom, to exercise with dumb-bells. Suddenly Mrs. Crook was aroused by hearing him call to her in a loud voice, 'Mary! Mary! I can't breathe!' and on running to him found him lying on a sofa and gasping for breath. She raised him, but he only said, 'I am choking,' and quietly, without a struggle, expired. He was dead before a doctor could reach him. The cause of his death was heart failure.

"He has not been well for some time, but Dr. McClellan scouted the idea of heart trouble. It probably came in a great measure from his exposure in the Indian campaigns. Papa says that he is sure one of the causes of his death was his great worry over the Indian prisoners at Mt. Vernon, and his desire to have justice shown them. This, and the attack made on him by the Western press, which he felt very keenly, tho' not talking much about it, certainly greatly aggravated his trouble. He is at rest now, and has had justice shown him above, which he very seldom did below."

The General was buried at Oakland, Maryland; and on November 11, 1890 his remains were laid to rest in Arlington Cemetery, where they now lie.

[25] Crook to Kennon, March 15, 1890.

The sudden death of General Crook was a severe blow to Indian management throughout the West. The Indians knew it, and their words and acts testified their debt to Three Stars. Red Cloud, the Siox chief, expressed the thoughts of his people to Father Craft, a Catholic missionary: "General Crook came; he, at least, had never lied to us. His words gave the people hope. He died. Their hope died again. Despair came again." The Indians near Camp Apache "let their hair down, bent their heads forward on their bosoms, and wept and wailed like children."[26]

By December, 1890, Indian troubles reached their final, bloody anticlimax at Wounded Knee, an affair which, in the light of his record, the General would have been able to prevent. Captain Bourke, who was awaiting the publication of his book about the General, commented briefly, "Now that he is dead and we have taken to slaughtering women and sucklings with Hotchkiss guns, the nation feels that it has lost one of its greatest sons."[27]

[26] Bourke, *On the Border with Crook*, 486–87.
[27] John G. Bourke to Charles Scribner, January 8, 1891.

APPENDICES

1. *The Rogue River Wars*

THE SO-CALLED Rogue River Wars occupy a period in California history from about 1850 to 1858. The first explorers in California had found the Indians friendly. As the Pacific Coast became more thickly settled by the whites, Indian troubles increased in number and intensity. Many treaties were made with individual tribes, but none of these agreements was ratified or considered binding.

The Whitman massacre in 1847 highlighted the disaffection among the natives, and the Cayuse war of 1848 resulted, at least in part, from attempts to capture and punish the murderers.

That same year Oregon gained territorial status, and Joseph Lane was made governor and ex-officio Indian agent. Under his guidance the Indians remained peaceful. In 1850 the Territory was supplied with a regular superintendent of Indian affairs and three agents. Thirteen treaties were made, none of which was ratified. The policy regarding Indians began to drift toward segregation on reservations, and when Joel Palmer became agent in 1853 he made serious efforts to carry out the new ideas.

The influx of miners and lawless elements caused friction between natives and whites, and in 1853 the friction broke into flame, the Rogue River War. The Indians were decisively defeated on August 24, 1853, and on September 8 Joseph Lane presided at the Treaty of Table Rock, whereby the Indians agreed to move on reservations and pay for damages inflicted during the war. Delay in the ratification of this and subsequent treaties led to constant trouble in the next two years.

On October 8, 1855, the Indian outbreak again became general, and the natives in the Territory to the north, Washington, also

went on the warpath by a previous agreement. This northern conflict is sometimes referred to as the Yakima War.

The Territories raised volunteer troops, and the Regulars also
went into action. Crook was a participant in this latter phase and
was particularly active in "pacifying" the Pit River Indians.

The effect of this final outbreak was to delay the ratification
of the treaties until 1858, when the Indians were effectively segre-
gated on various reservations. Ethel M. Peterson, *Oregon Indians
and Indian Policy.*

2. *Capture of General Crook and General Kelley*

THE STORY of the capture of Generals Crook and Kelley has never
been told in full. Cyrus S. Roberts, then second lieutenant on
Crook's staff, wrote an account of the event shortly after it occurred and added a few remarks some years later. This account
still survives among the papers preserved by his son, Brigadier
General Charles D. Roberts.

Cyrus Roberts' report, augmented by material from *The War
of the Rebellion* and other sources, is the basis for the story as here
given. Such a daring exploit naturally gave rise to some wild tales
and far-fetched rumors; therefore, it is necessary to reduce the
narrative to the minimum number of facts as known.

On the evening of February 19, 1864, says Roberts, a party of
about seventy men left their rendezvous near Moorefield and
crossed the Potomac about four miles upriver from Cumberland.
These men were members of a guerrilla band known as McNeill's
Rangers, led by John H. McNeill and his son, Jesse. Among their
number was one James Dailey of Cumberland, whose sister, Mary,
later became Mrs. Crook, and may at this time have been engaged
to the General.

It was common knowledge that Cumberland had been for two
years the headquarters of the Department of West Virginia and
that General Crook stayed in the Revere Hotel in Cumberland.
These facts, coupled with information from sympathizers within
the town, settled the determination of the guerrillas to attempt a

capture of the commanding officers of the department and whatever other officers they might be able to seize.

About two o'clock on the morning of the twenty-first the band reached the cavalry pickets about two and one-half miles out of town. Being clothed in Federal uniforms, they were permitted to approach and give the countersign. Instead of the countersign they produced revolvers and captured the pickets.

The infantry pickets closer to town were taken in the same quick fashion, unable to sound an alarm. A party of six to eight men was then detached to proceed to the Revere House, where Crook was staying, while another was sent to Kelley's residence. The guards at the hotel were easily overcome and four men entered the building.

The Negro porter, thinking the men were Union soldiers, led them to the General's room, where the General slept alone. The men entered the room, roused the General, and informed him that he was their prisoner. They told him to dress and come along with them.

Meanwhile, the main party of guerrillas had entered the town after destroying the telegraph lines, and the two generals, accompanied by Captain Thayer Melvin, Kelley's adjutant, were hurried out of town. An officer sleeping in the room across from Crook's heard the noise and got up to investigate, but by the time he determined what had happened, the band was on its way to Staunton.

Pursuit was immediately begun, but the Rangers knew the country too well and eluded all efforts to capture them. The prisoners were finally sent to Richmond, one of the greatest prizes of the war.

On March 10 the three officers, along with several hundred parolees from Libby Prison, were sent north. According to the custom of the day, they were sent home to await word of their official exchange.

Secretary of War Stanton, considerably peeved at the whole affair and irked by some remarks made by Crook after his return, did not want to make an exchange. Grant, however, wanted Crook back in action and arranged for his exchange, ordering him to return to the command of the Department of West Virginia.

Command of this department had, meanwhile, been given to

General Winfield S. Hancock, by order of the President. Hancock, who liked his new assignment, was in no mood to give it up. When Crook reassumed command without any formality, Hancock deemed it a gross breach of discipline, and without further inquiry ordered Crook's arrest and confinement. Crook, however, was simply acting under orders from Grant, and either did not know of the new commander, or assumed that the proper orders had been given.

Grant had decided, in the meantime, to use Crook to command the cavalry of the Potomac and issued orders for the General to report to him for his new assignment. However, because Crook was in danger of arrest by Hancock's order, it became necessary for the President to intervene, sending Hancock copies of Grant's orders, explaining that matters were mixed up, and suggesting that no disciplinary action need be taken.

Hancock then wrote Crook, saying that he took pleasure in believing that Crook had acted without malice, purely in ignorance, without knowledge of the actual situation. By the end of March the tangle was unraveled, with no one's having been arrested. Crook had been given a new assignment, and Hancock was presumably happily in command of the Department of West Virginia.

Hayes, commenting in a letter to his uncle, suggested that Grant had wanted Crook to take command of his old department just for one day to show the public that he was not in disfavor with the War Department. Cyrus S. Roberts, *Account of the Capture of Major-General George Crook and Bvt. Maj. Gen. Kelley; The War of the Rebellion*, Ser. I, Vol. XLIV, Part I; John B. Fay, *Capture of Generals Crook and Kelley by the McNeill Rangers;* Hayes, *Diary and Letters.*

3. *General Crook's Marriage*

ON AUGUST 21, 1865 a marriage license was issued out of the clerk's office of the circuit court of Alleghany County, Maryland, to

Major General George Crook and Mary T. Dailey. The next day the couple was married by the Reverend William L. Heyland.

Crook's courtship was later supposed to be surrounded by considerable romance. The newspaper accounts, printed after the General's death, claimed that Mary Dailey had nursed him back to health after he was severely wounded, ignoring the fact that Crook was wounded only once in the Civil War, in 1862.

Mary Dailey, they said, was "a spirited southern girl, who refused to be gracious to the Yankee officer, although she liked him." Proximity, however, won out, and "the conqueror of Cochise and Geronimo attacked the fair fortress of Mary Dailey's heart until it surrendered."

The truth of the matter is not definitely known. Crook evidently met his wife during his stay in Cumberland in 1865. Headquarters held many social events and "hops," to which the girls of Cumberland were invited, and Crook must have had opportunity to meet and court Mary at these gatherings.

The casual reference which Crook makes to his marriage is not accidental. His wife played a very minor part in his life. The Crooks had no children, and their domestic life was seasonal. After the Civil War, when the General was stationed in the West, his wife spent much of her time at Crook Crest, a sort of family estate near Oakland, Maryland. Crook remained on duty and spent his leisure hunting and fishing, which was more his style than maintaining social ratings in Oakland. His visits to that estate were sporadic, generally made while he was on his way to or from Washington, D. C.

The periods when Mrs. Crook stayed with her husband at army posts were generally marked by social events, hops, and parties—affairs which befitted the wife of the ranking officer on an army post. Crook did not particularly enjoy this type of amusement, and would make the best of the situation by gathering his fellow officers for a game of euchre or poker, leaving the burden of entertainment to Mary.

After the General's death in 1890, Mary took a trip to Europe, telling her experiences in the columns of the *Omaha Bee*. Though her inheritance was small, she was able to live comfortably on a special pension of $2,000 per annum granted by Congress. She died on September 24, 1895.

4. *Nickerson's Account of Indian Surrender*

NICKERSON describes the surrender of the Indians in 1868 in detail.

"When spring came, the Indians sued for permission to surrender and make peace. Crook sent them word to come in at Camp Harney, and in the latter part of the month of June, 1868, we mounted our horses and rode across the country to that post.

"The day following our arrival, the Indians under old We-ah-we-ah, the principal chief in that region, were collected on the Camp Harney parade ground. They were squatted in a huge semicircle, and when Crook and his officers in full uniform approached from the open side of the parade old We-ah-we-ah came toward the center from their side.

"The old rascal came up as smiling, childlike and bland as the proverbial heathen Chinese, and when he and Crook met he held out his dirty, bloodstained paw to shake hands with the General. Imagine his surprise and chagrin when Crook, holding his hand determinedly behind him, and looking him squarely in the eye, refused to shake hands with him.

" 'Tell him,' said Crook, through the interpreter, "that I did not come here to shake hands with him. He has been too bad an Indian, has murdered too many people. I came here to hear what he has to say for himself.'

"Old We-ah-we-ah was very much non-plussed at first, but managed to say that he and his warriors were tired of war, and wanted to make peace.

" 'I am sorry to hear this,' replied the General, 'I was in hopes that you would continue the war, and then, though I were to kill only one of your warriors while you killed a hundred of my men, you would have to wait for those little people (pointing to the Indian children) to grow to fill the place of your braves, while I can get any number of soldiers the next day to fill the place of my hundred men. In this way it would not be very long before we would have you all killed off, and then the government would have no more trouble with you.'

"But We-ah-we-ah insisted that they did not want any more

war, but wanted peace, and had 'thrown away their ropes.' Throwing away their ropes meant a great deal, for by it he intended to emphasize a promise that they would steal no more horses.

"After a little more parley on similar lines the General consented to make peace, though apparently very reluctantly.

"The terms of the agreement were very simple, and easily understood. The Indians were to go back to their old hunting grounds, hunt, fish, dig roots and trap, getting their living as they used to in the old times. If the white people came along or interfered with them in any way they were to come to the military post, the commander of which would be authorized to protect them to the fullest extent of his power.

"If at any time they were unable to secure food without stealing it from settlers, miners or emigrants, then again they were to come to the post, the commander of which would be authorized to give them food, if he could spare it. But of this no positive promise was made. It was to be a privilege, and not a right.

"Underlying these apparently petty details were well-defined methods of treating with Indians that marked all of Crook's dealings with them. The greater number of commissioners sent by the government to the frontier to treat with the Indians would have met old We-ah-we-ah's advances in an effusive manner. According to their ideas Crook should have grasped the old fellow's outstretched hand, patted him on the back, told him what a great warrior he was, and concluded by making no end of promises for the 'Great Father' to perform. Promises, the majority of which must of necessity have proved as great a myth as the Great Father himself.

"Had Crook pursued this method, We-ah-we-ah would have been all puffed up, and really believed himself a great warrior, and that Crook was afraid of him. Then he would have concluded that if he made peace at all, the favor would be of his conferring. The General's treatment took all the conceit out of him, and he was made to feel that the peace was to be a favor to him.

"Then to conclude, the General told We-ah-we-ah that he was going down to Northern California to punish a band of Pit River Indians who had been committing depredations in that locality, and that he should like a few of the Piutes to accompany him, simply to show their sincerity. Other tribes were to send delegations, as it were, and ten or a dozen from We-ah-we-ah's band would be all he would require.

"Immediately ten of the worst, and at the same time the best warriors in the band stepped to the front. We put them in uniform, armed them, mounted them, and the next day they left with us on the last expedition General Crook undertook in that section of the country. Although our new allies were designated as 'wild men,' they proved as loyal and much more useful than any of the other of our numerous 'allies.'

"On our part, Crook made few promises, and none that he could not keep, and the peace then concluded lasted, to my knowledge, for a period of ten years, and when broken, as in 1878 it was, I am not so sure that it was not the fault of the white man. But one thing is certain, it was not caused by the failure to keep any promises made to them by General Crook." Azor H. Nickerson, *Major General George Crook and the Indians* [MS].

BIBLIOGRAPHY

1. *Manuscript Material*

Bourke, John G. Diary. U. S. Military Academy Library, West Point.

Crook, George. Papers. Army War College Library, Washington.

Kautz, August V. Papers. Army War College Library, Washington.

Kennon, Lyman W. V. Diary. Army War College Library, Washington.

Nickerson, Azor H. Major General George Crook and the Indians (n.d.). Army War College Library, Washington.

Roberts, Charles D. Sketch of the Life of Cyrus Swan Roberts. 1944. Army War College Library, Washington.

Schuyler, Walter S. Papers. Huntington Library, San Marino, Calif.

U. S. Army War College. Historical Section, Posts, Camps, and Stations File. Washington.

U. S. Military Division of the Missouri. Adjutant's Letter Book, 1889–90. Charles D. Roberts, Washington.

U. S. National Archives. War Records Office, Annual Returns of the Alterations and Casualties Incident to the Fourth Regiment of Infantry, 1852–61. Washington.

U. S. National Archives. War Records Office, Department of Arizona, Letterbooks, 1872–75; 1883–86.

U. S. National Archives. War Records Office, Department of the Platte, Letterbooks, 1875–90.

U. S. National Archives. War Records Office, Division of the Missouri, Letterbooks, 1875–90.

U. S. Military Academy. Post Order Books; Post Record Books, 1848–52. U. S. Military Academy Library, West Point.

2. *Government Publications*

Colorado. Governor. *Reports of Officers and Official Correspond-ence Relating to the Military Assistance Rendered by the State of Colorado to the Citizens of Garfield and Routt Counties dur-ing the Ute Difficulties of 1887*. Denver, 1888.

Heitman, Francis B. *Historical Register and Dictionary of the United States Army*. Washington, 1903. 2 vol.

Kroeber, Alfred L. *Handbook of the Indians of California*. Wash-ington, 1925. (Smithsonian Institution, Bureau of American Ethnology, Bulletin No. 78.)

Otis, D. S. "History of the Allotment Policy," *Readjustment of Indian Affairs* (hearings before the Committee on Indian Af-fairs, House of Representatives, 73 Cong., 2 sess. on H. R. 7902, Washington, 1934), 428–39.

U. S. Adjutant General's Office. *General Orders, Special Orders, and Circulars, 1852–1890.*

U. S. Adjutant General's Office. *Notes Illustrating the Military Geography of the United States*. Washington, 1881.

U. S. Army. Department of Arizona. *General Orders, General Court-Martial Orders, and Special Orders, 1872–1886.*

U. S. Army. Department of the Platte. *General Orders, General Court-Martial Orders, and Special Orders, 1876–1890.*

U. S. Army. Division of the Pacific. *General Orders, General Court-Martial Orders, Special Orders, and Circulars, 1852–1860.*

U. S. Congress. *House Ex. Doc.*, 33 Cong., 2 sess., *No. 91;* 34 Cong., 3 sess., *No. 76;* 51 Cong., 1 sess., *No. 299.*

U. S. Congress. *Senate Ex. Doc.*, 51 Cong., 1 sess., *No. 35; Nos. 51, 83, 88.*

U. S. Congress. *Senate Reports*, 45 Cong., 3 sess., *No. 693;* 51 Cong., 1 sess., *No. 1422.*

U. S. Inspector General's Department. *Outline Descriptions of the Posts and Stations of Troops in the Geographical Divisions and Departments of the United States*. Washington, 1872.

U. S. Military Academy, West Point. *The Centennial History of the United States Military Academy at West Point, N. Y., 1802–1902*. Washington, 1904.

U. S. Military Academy. West Point, N. Y. *Official Register of the Officers and Cadets, 1848–1852.*

U. S. Secretary of the Interior. *Annual Reports, 1872–1886.*

U. S. Surgeon General's Office. *A Report on the Hygiene of the United States Army, with Descriptions of Military Posts.* Washington, 1875.

U. S. War Dept. *Annual Reports, 1852–1890.*

U. S. War Dept. *Military Reservations.* Washington, 1938–.

U. S. War Dept. *The War of the Rebellion: a Compilation of the Official Records of the Union and Confederate Armies.* Washington, 1880–91. 128 vols.

3. *Newspapers*

Alta California. San Francisco, 1853.

Arizona Star. Tucson, A. T., 1882.

Boston *Post.* Boston, Mass., 1887.

Daily InterOcean. Chicago, 1889–90.

Owyhee Avalanche. Silver City, Idaho Terr., 1867–68.

Washington *Evening Star.* Washington, D. C., 1889–90.

Washington *Chronicle.* Washington, D. C., 1883.

Yreka *Union.* Yreka, Calif., 1857.

4. *Biographies and Personal Memoirs*

Bourke, John G. *An Apache Campaign in the Sierra Madre.* New York, 1886.

Bourke, John G. *Mackenzie's Last Fight with the Cheyennes.* New York Harbor, Governor's Island, 1890.

Bourke, John G. *On the Border with Crook.* New York, 1891.

Cook, James H. *Fifty Years on the Old Frontier.* New Haven, 1923.

Cradford, Lewis F. *Rekindling Campfires, the Exploits of Ben Arnold.* Bismarck, N. D., 1926.

Crook, George. *Address of General George Crook, U. S. Army at the Reunion of the Army of West Virginia at Cumberland, Maryland, September, 1884.* N.p., 1884.

Crook, George. *Address to the Graduates of the United States Military Academy, West Point, New York, Class 1884.* West Point, 1884.

Crook, George. *Letter from George Crook on Giving the Ballot to Indians.* Philadelphia, 1885.

Crook, George. *Resumé of Operations against Apache Indians, 1882 to 1886.* Omaha, 1886.

Cruse, Thomas. *Apache Days and After.* Caldwell, Idaho, 1941.

Davis, Britton. *The Truth about Geronimo.* New Haven, 1929.

Du Pont, Henry A. *The Campaign of 1864 in the Valley of Virginia and the Expedition to Lynchburg.* New York, 1925.

Edgar, John F. *Pioneer Life in Dayton and Vicinity.* Dayton, 1896.

Fay, John B. *Captures of Generals Crook and Kelley by the Mc-Neill Rangers.* Cumberland, Md., 1893.

Finerty, John F. *War Path and Bivouac.* Chicago, 1890.

Gatewood, Charles B. *Lieutenant Charles B. Gatewood, 6th U. S. Cavalry and the Surrender of Geronimo.* Washington, 1939.

Glisan, Rodney. *Journal of Army Life.* San Francisco, 1874.

Hayes, Rutherford B. *Diary and Letters of Rutherford B. Hayes.* Columbus, Ohio, 1922–26. 5 vols.

Howard, Oliver O. *My Life and Experiences among Our Hostile Indians.* Hartford, Conn., 1907.

King, Charles. *Campaigning with Crook.* Milwaukee, 1880.

King, Charles. *Major-General George Crook, United States Army.* Milwaukee, 1890.

Larson, James. *Sergeant Larson, 4th Cavalry.* San Antonio, 1935.

McConnell, William J. *Early History of Idaho.* Caldwell, Idaho, 1913.

Miles, Nelson A. *Personal Recollections and Observations of General Nelson A. Miles.* Chicago, 1896.

Mills, Anson. *My Story.* Washington, 1918.

Semmes, Raphael. *The Cruise of the Alabama and the Sumter.* London, 1864.

Sheridan, Philip H. *Personal Memoirs of P. H. Sheridan.* New York, 1888. 2 vols.

Summerhayes, Martha. *Vanished Arizona.* Salem, Mass., 1911.

Tibbles, Thomas H. *The Ponca Chiefs.* Boston, 1879.

5. *General Works*

Adams, James T. *Dictionary of American History.* New York, 1940. 5 vols.

Bancroft, Hubert H. *History of California*. San Francisco, 1884–88. 7 vols.

Bancroft, Hubert H. *History of Oregon*. San Francisco, 1886–88. 2 vols.

Battles and Leaders of the Civil War. New York, 1887–88. 4 vols.

Bean, Edwin A. *History and Directory of Nevada County, California*. Nevada, Calif., 1867.

Brimlow, George F. *The Bannock Indian War, 1878*. Caldwell, Idaho, 1938.

Chittenden, Hiram M. *The Yellowstone National Park*. Cincinnati, 1895.

Clum, Woodworth. *Apache Agent, the Story of John P. Clum*. Boston, 1936.

Conover, Frank. *The Centennial Portrait and Biographical Record of the City of Dayton and of Montgomery County, Ohio*. Dayton, 1897.

Cullum, George W. *Biographical Register of the Officers and Graduates of the U. S. Military Academy at West Point, N. Y.* Boston, 1891–. 8 vols.

Dodge, Richard I. *The Black Hills*. New York, 1876.

Frederick, James V. *Ben Holladay, the Stagecoach King*. Glendale, Calif., 1940.

Ganoe, William A. *The History of the United States Army*. New York, 1942.

Garber, Max B. *A Modern Military Dictionary*. Washington, 1936.

Gaston, William L. *History of Custer County, Nebraska*. Lincoln, Neb., 1918.

Grinnell, George B. *The Fighting Cheyennes*. New York, 1915.

Hebard, Grace R. *The Bozeman Trail*. Cleveland, 1922. 2 vols.

Hebard, Grace R. *Washakie*. Glendale, Calif., 1930.

Hoopes, Alban W. *Indian Affairs and Their Administration*. Philadelphia, 1932.

Hyde, George E. *Red Cloud's Folk*. Norman, Okla., 1937.

Jackson, Joseph H. *Anybody's Gold*. New York, 1941.

Knauss, William H. *The Story of Camp Chase*. Nashville, 1906.

LaFarge, Oliver, ed. *The Changing Indian*. Norman, Okla., 1943.

Lang, Theodore F. *Loyal West Virginia from 1861 to 1865*. Baltimore, 1895.

Leavitt, Charles. *Genealogy of the Crook Family in America*. Manila, P. I., 1918.

Ledbetter, William G. *Military History of the Oregon Country, 1804–1859*. Eugene, Oregon, 1940.

Leyden, James A. *A Historical Sketch of the Fourth Infantry*. Fort Sheridan, Idaho, 1891.

Lockwood, Frank C. *The Apache Indians*. New York, 1938.

McArthur, Lewis A. *Oregon Geographic Names*. Portland, Ore., 1928.

Memorial Services, Major-General George Crook, Omaha, March 23, 1890. Omaha, 1890.

Military Order of the Loyal Legion of the United States. *In Memoriam, Companion Major General George Crook*. Chicago, 1890.

Nevada County Mining Review. Grass Valley, Calif., 1895.

Ogle, Ralph H. *Federal Control of the Western Apaches, 1848 1886*. Albuquerque, N. M., 1940.

Peterson, Ethel M. *Oregon Indians and Indian Policy*. Salem, Oregon, 1939.

Priest, Loring B. *Uncle Sam's Stepchildren*. New Brunswick, N. J., 1942.

Reid, Whitelaw. *Ohio in the War*. Cincinnati, 1868–72. 2 vols.

Robinson, Doane. *A History of the Dakota or Sioux Indians*. Aberdeen, S. D., 1904.

Rodenbaugh, Theophilus F. *The Army of the United States*. New York, 1896.

Rudd, Augustin G. *Histories of Army Posts*. Washington, 1924.

San Diego, the California Terminus of the Texas and Pacific Railway. San Diego, 1872.

Sandoz, Mari. *Crazy Horse*. New York, 1942.

Sawyer, Charles W. *Our Rifles*. Boston, 1920.

Sawyer, Charles W. *The Revolver*. Boston, 1911.

Schmeckebier, Laurence F. *The Office of Indian Affairs*. Baltimore, 1927.

Shaw, Frederick B. *One Hundred and Forty Years of Service in Peace and War*. Detroit, 1930.

Smith, Edmund B. *Governor's Island*. New York, 1923.

Stout, Peter F. *Nicaragua, Past, Present, and Future*. Philadelphia, 1859.

U. S. Military Academy. West Point, Association of the Graduates. *Annual Reunion, June 12, 1890.* Saginaw, Mich., 1890.
Victor, Frances F. *Early Indian Wars of Oregon.* Salem, Oregon, 1894.
Welsh, Herbert. *The Apache Prisoners in Fort Marion, St. Augustine, Florida.* Philadelphia, 1887.
Williamson, James J. *Mosby's Rangers.* New York, 1909.
Writers' Program, Nevada. *Nevada, a Guide to the Silver State.* Portland, Oregon, 1940.
Writers' Program, Oregon. *Oregon, End of the Trail.* Portland, Oregon, 1940.
Writers' Program, Wyoming. *Wyoming.* New York, 1941.

6. *Periodical Articles*

Abbot, Henry L. "Reminiscences of the Oregon War of 1855." *Journal of the Military Service Institution of the United States.* Vol. XVL, No. 162 (November-December, 1909).
Bloom, Lansing B. "Bourke on the Southwest," *New Mexico Historical Review,* Vol. X, No. 1 (January, 1935).
Bourke, John G. "General Crook in the Indian Country," *The Century Magazine,* Vol. XLI, No. 5 (March, 1891).
Clark, Robert C. "Military History of Oregon, 1849–1859." *Oregon Historical Quarterly,* Vol. XXXVI, No. 1 (March, 1935).
Clark, Stanley. "Ponca Publicity," *Mississippi Valley Historical Review,* Vol. XXIX, No. 4 (March, 1943).
Clum, John P. "Geronimo," *Arizona Historical Review,* Vol. I, No. 3 (October, 1928).
Crook, George. "The Apache Problem," *Journal of the Military Service Institution of the United States,* Vol. VII, No. 27 (October, 1886).
Jordan, Philip D. "George W. Patten, Poet Laureate of the Army," *Military Affairs,* Vol. IV, No. 3 (Fall, 1940).
Keith, Arthur, L. "Notes on Hardwick (Hardidge) Kincheloe, McCarty, McConathy, Crook, Dawson, Lawson and Related Families," *William and Mary College Quarterly Historical Magazine,* Vol. XXII, No. 1 (January, 1914); Vol. XXIII, No. 3 (July, 1914).
Parnell, William R. "Operations against Hostile Indians with Gen-

eral Crook, 1866–1868," *The United Service*, n.s. Vol. I, Nos. 5 and 6 (May–June, 1889).

Payne, John S. "Incidents of the Recent Campaign against the Utes," *The United Service*, Vol. II, No. 1 (January, 1880).

Reade, Philip. "Chronicle of the Twenty-Third Regiment of Infantry, U. S. A." *Journal of the Military Service Institution of the United States*, Vol. XXXV, No. 132 (November–December, 1904).

Robbins, Harvey. "Journal of the Rogue River War." *Oregon Historical Quarterly*, Vol. XXXIV, No. 4 (December, 1933).

Thompson, Henry F. "The Parish Records of Maryland:" *Maryland Historical Magazine*. Vol. II, No. 132 (June, 1907).

Von Leuttwitz, A. II. Letter to General Crook, *Army and Navy Journal*, Vol. XIX, No. 13 (November 4, 1876).

Index

killed by Mexicans, 259–60; body taken to Nebraska, 265

Crazy Horse (Sioux chief): camp on Powder River attacked, 191–92; relations with Crook, 215 ff.; surrenders, 216; influence of, 217 f.; death of, 218–19

Crescent City, California: 55

Crook, George: early life and schooling, xv–xvi; at West Point, xvii–xviii; brevet 2nd. lt., 4th Infantry, 3; trip to California, 3–6; assigned to Company "F," 4th Infantry, 6; goes to Humboldt Bay, 7; suffers from erysipelas, 8; escorts survey under Henry Washington, 11–13; promoted to 2nd lt., 13; at Fort Jones, 14–17; on Klamath expedition, 17–20; on Pacific Railroad survey, 21–30; in command of Company "E," 4th Infantry, 31; suffers from erysipelas, 31–32; joins in Rogue River campaign, 33; promoted to 1st lt., Company "D," 4th Infantry, 34; returns to Fort Jones, 34; on campaign against Pit River Indians, 35–52; wounded, 40; goes to Klamath reservation, 54–55; builds Fort Ter-Waw, 55–56; goes to Fort Simcoe, 57–59; on Yakima expedition, 59–68; returns to Fort Ter-Waw, 68; goes to Rogue River Valley, 77–78; goes overland to New York, 78–80; returns to Ter-Waw, 80–81; at Presidio of San Francisco, 81; goes to New York, 83; appointed captain, 83; obtains leave of absence from Regular Army, 84; appointed colonel, 36th Ohio Volunteer Infantry, 85; trains recruits, 85–86, 88–89; fights bushwhackers, 86–88; commands Third Provisional Brigade, 89 ff., 92 n.; brevetted major, U. S. Army, 90 n.; wounded, 90–91; joins Kanawha Division, 92; at second Bull Run, 92–95; in battle of South Mountain, 95–96; in battle of Antietam, 97–100; brevetted lt. col., U. S. Army, 100 n.; promoted to brig. gen., Volunteers, 101; goes back to West Virginia, 101; goes to Nashville, 101; at Carthage, Tenn., 101–

102; at Hoover's Gap, 102; appointed commanding officer, 2nd Cavalry Division, 103; in Broomtown Valley, 104–105; in command of cavalry corps, 104; in battle of Chickamauga, 105–107; guards Tennessee River, 107–108; in pursuit of Gen. Wheeler, 108–12; chases bushwhackers, 112–13; in command of Kanawha District, West Virginia, 114; consults with Grant, 114; on Lynchburg raid, 114–21; at Snicker's Gap, 122–23; moves to Winchester, 123; retreats to Bunker Hill, 123; in Shenandoah Valley campaign of 1864, 124–34; in command of department of West Virginia, 135; captured, 135–36, 304–306; in command of cavalry, Army of the Potomac, 136; brevetted brig. gen. and maj. gen., U. S. Army, 136 n.; in battle of Dinwiddie Court House, 136–37; in battle of Five Forks, 137; at Sailor's Creek, 138–39; at Appomattox Court House, 140; marriage and married life, 141, 306–307; in charge of District of Wilmington, N. C., 141; appointed lt. col., 23rd Infantry, 141; appointed major, 3rd Infantry, 141 n.; goes to Idaho in charge of District of Boise, 142; operates against Paiute and Snake Indians, 144–58; assigned to command Department of Columbia, 158; council with Pit River Indians, 158–59; member of Retiring Board, 160; transferred to Department of Arizona, 160, 162; organizes campaign in Arizona, 163–67; on Apache campaign of 1872–73; 173–83; promoted to brig. gen., U. S. Army, 183 n.; transferred to Department of the Platte, 187; polices Black Hills, 188–89; on Powder River expedition, Feb., 1876, 190–92; on Yellowstone expedition, 193–212; on Powder River expedition, Nov. 1876, 213–14; negotiates surrender of Indians, 215–16; removes Sioux to Missouri River, 219–21; visits Fort Hall, Idaho, 221; testifies to government committee, 228–29; in-

INDEX

campaign, 121 n.; comment on battle of Fisher's Hill, 130 n.; appoints Ponca investigation commission, 234; urges Crook's promotion, 277–78; remarks concerning Crook's capture, 306
Hayes, Webb: 236 f.; on hunt with Crook, 289
Henry, Guy V.: in Arizona, 166; in battle of Rosebud, 194 ff.; in Department of the Platte, 268
Hood, John B.: 21
Horn, Tom: 260
Horse-meat march: 201–12
Horton, A. E.: 162, 162 n.
Howard, Guy, reports on Apache prisoners: 292
Howard, Oliver O.: among the Apaches, 169–73; treaty with Cochise, 171; and Eskiminzin, 184; on release of Apache prisoners, 292
Humboldt Bay, California: 8 f.
Hunter, David, in Lynchburg campaign: 116 ff.
Hunting and fishing (by Crook): 11, 21, 23 f., 54, 73–77, 267, 272 f., 274 n., 289

Idaho, conditions in 1866: 142–44
Indian administration, Crook's views on: xiv, 69, 228–29, 269 f., 271, 282–83
Indian agents: 184–86
Indian Bureau, proposed transfer of to War Department: 228–29
Indian Citizenship Committee: 235, 268 f.
Indian warfare, Crook's views on: 53–54, 213, 264–65
Indians: see Alagnas, Apaches, Bannocks, Cheyennes, Paiutes, Pit River Indians, Poncas, Shastas, Sioux, Utes, Wiyots, Yakimas
Indians as scouts: 213–14, 297–98
Ingalls, Rufus: 92 f.
Iron Mountain (Sioux chief): 286

Jackson, Thomas J.: 92
Jackson, William L. [Mudwall]: 116
Johnson, John B., captures Cheyennes: 224
John Grass (Sioux chief): 288

Judah, Henry M.: 17 ff., 17 n., 31; on Pit River campaign, 35–38; relations with Crook, 41; at Fort Simcoe, 59
Juh (Apache chief): 242, 248

Ka-e-ten-a (Apache chief): as government scout, 260 f.; at Mt. Vernon Barracks, 293
Kautz, August V.: 6 n.; concerning Crook's early life, xv–xvi; goes to California, 3, 6; in fight with Indians, 27, 29; commanding officer, Department of Arizona, 241–42
Kearney, C. C.: 41
Kearny, Philip: 94
Kelley, Benjamin F., captured by McNeill: 304–306
Kennon, Lyman W. V.: goes with Crook to Boston, 270–72; comes to Chicago, 279; with Crook in North Carolina, 292, represents Crook in Washington, 296 ff.
Ketchum, Ami: 230
King, Charles: on Yellowstone expedition, 200; on release of Apache prisoners, 299
Klamath Indian reservation, California: 55 ff.; 56 n.; uprising at, 56–57
Klamath River Indians: see Alagnas

La Fleche, Suzette [Bright Eyes]: 234 f.
Leslie, Frank: 256, 258
Letcher, John: 117 n.
Lincoln, Abraham: meeting with Crook, 84; "massacre" of, 141
Little Wolf (Cheyenne chief) returns from Indian Territory: 223 ff.
Lockhart, Harry: 34 n., 35
Lockhart, Sam: 35
Loco (Apache chief): 243, 248
Loyal Legion: 267
Lynchburg campaign, 1864: 114–21

McCaffery, James E.: 172
McCook, Alexander McD., in Broomtown Valley: 104 f.
McCook, Robert Latimer, killed by guerrillas: 113 n.
McDowell, Irvin: 95
Mackenzie, Ranald S.: on Powder

323

UNIVERSITY OF OKLAHOMA PRESS : NORMAN